In the Heart of It All

In the Heart of It All

An Unvarnished Account of My Life in Public Service

Richard F. Celeste

The Kent State University Press
KENT, OHIO

© 2022 by The Kent State University Press, Kent, Ohio 44242
All rights reserved

Unless otherwise noted, all photographs are courtesy of the author.

ISBN 978-1-60635-445-2
Manufactured in the United States of America

Cataloging information for this title is available at the Library of Congress.

26 25 24 23 22   5 4 3 2 1

To Jacqueline and to my children,
you keep me going.

Contents

Preface

In eighty years, I have moved my home base from the shores of Lake Erie to the foot of Pikes Peak. But in the eight decades that took me far beyond my early dreams, I have always considered Lakewood, Ohio, home. And I suppose I have carried its influence with me on every step of my life's journey.

That journey has been one richly blessed. My grandmother Bessie Louis liked to say that "it is a mighty long road that has no turns." And I have experienced many turns, some planned and others unexpected, along the way. As I have reflected on and recorded the pulls and tugs toward a life of public service, several themes emerged.

First, people—even, or maybe especially, people we know well—are full of surprises. Early on I developed an enthusiasm for engaging with folks who could be quite different from me—the Latvian family who came to live with us for a year or so as "DPs" (displaced persons), the voice of someone my uncle Wolcott reached on his ham radio (W8BHJ—B-boy-H-henry-J-john), kids at Methodist Youth Conference from all across the country. As curious as I was about others, I was never curious enough. How could I not know what inspired Bessie's love of travel or realize that Carolina, my Italian grandmother, had "healing hands." The pages that follow have only intensified my curiosity.

Second, public service is a calling that unites us all to some degree. But as my family reminded me by word and example, those of us who are especially blessed with talent or resources have a special obligation. No biblical passage was more frequently cited in my youth than "to whom much is given, much is expected."

I suspect that notion has served as a prod for me when, at each pause in my journey, I have considered what might come next. Even now, when someone asks, "What are you going to do when you retire?" I find myself wondering what I might do that would repay the remarkable opportunities I have been given.

Which brings me to the third theme: make room for serendipity in your life. We all are presented with unexpected moments in life. We need to seize them. I had no idea that a chance conversation with the mother of a fellow Yalie as I was leaving a congressional hearing would lead to a vibrant relationship, first with him on our campus, then with his sister at the Peace Corps, and finally with his father in India.

Nor would I have imagined that pursuing the presidency of Case Western Reserve University would lead me to Colorado College. Embracing the unexpected can bring challenges and joy and, yes, sometimes pain. But always growth and usually fresh opportunities to make a difference in lives along the way.

I try in these pages to share as honestly as I can the influences that led me to devote my life to public service—both in and beyond the political arena. I have tried to illuminate some of the dark corners of political life.

But even more I hope that I convey the fun and the fulfillment that come with working to bring people together around a common vision and to build a constituency for change. Today, as much as at any time in our history, we need the energy, the imagination and the enthusiasm of young people engaged in building the constituency for change.

Acknowledgments

I tell the story of the profound influence my parents and grandparents had on me. So did teachers and friends. A career in politics, diplomacy, public service, and higher education is not a one-man-band. I have benefited enormously from the many individuals who inspired me, knocked on doors for me, shaped policy initiatives, fashioned mission statements, and generally did their best to help me pursue ambitious goals.

Some are mentioned in this story. Far too many are not. Without the enthusiasm of both named and unnamed, and their energy and commitment, none of what I have described in this book would have been possible. Come to think of it, each of them might well have a different take on the various events I have described.

I have been encouraged to write a book (not sure whether those doing the encouraging had this result in mind) for a very long time. Dagmar prodded me. Gabriella offered to help. Each of my children nudged me. Finally, Jacqueline and Sam set an example with books of their own.

It took a conversation with Steve Hayward, a young Colorado College professor we had lured from John Carroll University—and a gifted writer—to get me started. With material support from Dennis Gallagher and much more than that from my son Christopher, I began in earnest.

I was an unconventional choice to lead Colorado College. And this book is an unconventional choice for the Kent State University Press. I am grateful, in both cases, to those who took a chance on me.

Finally, this book describes events from my perspective with, I am sure, some gaps in memory and some descriptions shaped in my bias. I have tried to be truthful. But most of all I have tried to convey how blessed I feel for the opportunities to serve that I have been given.

I hope that readers, especially young ones who are eager to shape a neighborhood, or a state or a nation—even the world beyond—will be encouraged to speak out, sit in, and just maybe run and run again.

Chapter 1

In the Beginning

Like my maternal grandmother, Bessie Louis, I keep everything. When I was growing up in Lakewood, on the shores of Lake Erie, Bessie's house on Summit Avenue was just a short bike ride from my parents' on Arthur Avenue. I'd ride over, and the two of us would spend hours together, often sitting under the two fine apple trees in her backyard. We'd share freshly made sugar cookies, and she would show me the things she'd saved. Her father's cutlery from the Civil War, primitive-looking but solidly made. A faded black-and-white photograph of her standing next to her brother in Alaska, the two of them grinning broadly as a lake glints silver in the background. Photos of her trip to Yellowstone.

I have kept everything and added to the collection myself: report cards, campaign buttons, endless photographs, letters written and received.

For most of my life, I have consciously not looked back. Admittedly, it's a kind of contradiction. I keep everything but don't dwell on the past. The experience of writing a book, however, finds me asking questions about days gone by, staring at things I've not looked at for fifty years or more—high school yearbooks, old campaign materials, photographs in which I can recognize some but not all of the people. Where did my story begin?

In an important sense, the story of my life commenced *before* I was born. Long before, in fact, in a small classroom in Monessen, Pennsylvania, the sooty steel town where my father, Frank Celeste, grew up. Most of the pupils in the civics class were immigrants or the children of immigrants. The teacher stood before them, her lesson—who can and cannot be president of the United States. To be president, she informed her pupils, you must be born a US citizen. "For example, Frank Celeste here," she said, mispronouncing the final "e" in order to make it sound more foreign, more Italian, "could *not* be president."

To which my father is said to have quickly replied: "Yes, but my *son* could be."

Two decades later, on November 11, 1937, I was born in Cleveland, Ohio. From the very first, I had a lot to live up to.

Both of my Italian grandparents came from large families: my grandfather had been one of twelve; my grandmother one of thirteen. My grandmother—Carolina Santoro—was born to Ferdinand Santoro and Carmela Greco in Cerisano, Italy, in Calabria. Not long after she married my grandfather, Serafino Celeste, he left to start a new life in the United States. My father was born on March 24, 1907, and arrived at Ellis Island as an infant on December 8, 1907, on a ship called the *Cretic*. My grandfather had already made his way to Monessen by that point, briefly owning and operating a skating rink before going to work in the steel mills.

Though my father was too young to remember the journey from Italy, he would often talk about the way it had changed things for them. It was not just the distances they had traveled or the new opportunities now available—even their names became "American." Francesco became Frank; Serafino, Sam.

Monessen was a tough, unbeautiful place, and they were poor. For a few pennies, my father would fetch fresh eggs from the chicken coops for the women who lived on Morgan Avenue, carrying them upstairs each morning. One of my father's stories described how embarrassed he'd been the day he forgot to deliver one of the eggs and went to school with it still in his pants pocket. When he sat down, it cracked and the yolk went everywhere. He suffered through the rest of the day. There was no point in going home to change; he didn't own a second pair of pants.

Like most of the young men who lived in the steel towns along the Monongahela River, Frank Celeste began working in the steel mills not long after his fifteenth birthday, in 1922. Around the same time, he began to show promise as a student. Admitted first to the College of Wooster and next to the (then) Western Reserve University Law School, academics offered him a way into a different life. My grandparents' house—where my father grew up—was small and narrow, built on the hillside leading down to the river, like all the houses in Monessen. The nearby open-hearth furnaces blazed throughout the night. Flames would light up the night sky, making it for me a magical—and slightly scary—place.

My father, Frank, with his grandmother and me as an infant in 1938

In that home there were two narrow shotgun bedrooms, small living and dining rooms, and a kitchen. Below, in the backyard, a tiny garden made room for a chicken coop and a fig tree. Those, as far as my grandparents were concerned, were the essential signs of their success and of the new life they had built for themselves in America. Just down the street was the little corner store where you could buy milk and butter and other basics. On our visits, we would crowd into the dining room, and I'd watch the adults drinking homemade wine as the roar of the steel mills echoed around us. I would often wonder at how different that house was from the one we lived in on Arthur Avenue in Lakewood or that of Bessie Louis.

We'd visit my father's parents once or twice a year. Dad would come home from work early and announce, "We're going to Monessen."

A great deal of scurrying followed as we threw whatever we needed into suitcases. Then we three kids—me, my younger sister, Pat, and my much younger brother, Ted—would sit in the back of my father's Oldsmobile, with Mom and Dad up front. Before the Ohio Turnpike, this meant a long drive that would, inevitably, involve an appeal to stop at Isaly's, soon to become famous for inventing the Klondike Bar.

As we drove, we'd see the signs: "Stop at Isaly's." One after another, we'd call out from the backseat, "Hey Dad, can we stop?"

Finally, he would pretend to relent, and we would get out of the car for ice cream.

We usually arrived at my grandparents' house unannounced at about nine in the evening. My father never told my grandmother that we were coming because he didn't want her to go to the trouble of getting ready for us. Of course, when we got there, she'd be annoyed and go to all the trouble he wanted to avoid. Nana would become a blur of activity, putting together a meal in an hour—soup, pasta, chicken, pork, salad, and who knows what else. When I was very young, my great-grandmother might join us as well. What I recall about her is that she was missing nearly all of her teeth. She would drink my grandfather's homemade wine but couldn't quite keep it in her mouth. I remember it dribbling down her chin, onto the delicate hair that covered it, as I watched fascinated by the effort she put into drinking her wine.

Once the table was cleared, the cards came out. My grandmother loved to play with us—the Italian game *Scopa*. "Bresta you cards, Dicky," she'd tell me. "*Bresta* you cards."

Then I'd pull the cards up. *Always keep your cards close to your chest.*

An early and important lesson.

The truth: I was always a little intimidated by my Calabrian grandmother—my nana.

My father often described the strict discipline of his childhood. And the relief provided by his extended family. He loved to tell the story about an older nephew of my grandmother who we called Uncle Tony. He was known to the rest of the world as Tony the Greek.

Tony was six or seven years older than my father and had gone to work in the nail mill a few years before dad. Like my father, Tony was an ambitious immigrant who was eager to learn to speak English. He therefore made up his mind to speak as much as possible with the two men who worked on either side of him in the mill. His English, he imagined, would improve measurably as a result. He stuck to the plan for seven or eight months, gradually becoming more fluent with the men. One Sunday afternoon Tony decided to show off his newly acquired English skills at the Italian Club. When he began to speak, however, he didn't get the reaction he was expecting.

"Tony," said one his parents, "what are you doing?"

"I'm speaking English."

They started laughing.

"What's so funny?"

"You think that's English?" came the reply. "That's Greek."

"What is?" he wanted to know.

"You're not speaking English—you're speaking Greek."

The whole time Tony had been learning Greek, the language of his two pals.

From that moment on, he was Tony the Greek. Despite that initial setback, he made it out of the factory to eventually become the first juvenile officer on the Monessen police force. Tony became beloved by folks in the community because he kept many a neighborhood kid out of trouble.

An early confrontation with my father occurred the summer after my freshman year at Yale when Nana happened to be visiting. An argument began at the dinner table. I don't remember what it was about, but I remember being convinced my father was wrong. I told him so, and he disagreed stubbornly. It was infuriating.

This wasn't the first time we'd disagreed. But this exchange was different. I had never been so sure about my position, and my father had never been so resolute in his refusal to admit I was right. Why couldn't he finally acknowledge that his eighteen-year-old son could be right about something? I was a sophomore in college, after all.

I became so frustrated that I stormed out onto the front porch, crying tears of quiet fury.

Suddenly I realized that Nana was on the porch with me. She grabbed me by the arm and poked me in the chest with her free hand. "Dicky," she said, "there's only one kind of smart, and that is when you respect your father."

My grandmother's English was often crude, but on that warm summer night her words were on the mark.

And memorable.

I often described that evening on the campaign trail almost fifteen years later. Because Nana was right. Knowledge is one thing, but wisdom is another, and respect is a sign of wisdom. That lesson would grow increasingly important for me.

When, as governor, I faced the savings and 1oans crisis in 1985, I wanted my father with me. His presence reassured me, yes. But I also wanted him with me as a sign of the respect I had for him.

The other Calabrian lesson Nana had for me that night on the porch had to do with loyalty. Nothing is more binding than blood. Years later, even if my father thought I was totally wrong in closing the savings and loans, he would, like my grandmother, stand up for me. After I closed the S&Ls, Frank Celeste bought sandwiches to share with demonstrators who were outside the state-house protesting my decision, telling them his son was doing his best to protect their deposits.

That was Frank Celeste. There is only one kind of smart.

One of the questions that was often asked about the Celeste family was how we ended up as Methodists. People were curious, for good reason. Frank Celeste had been baptized Catholic, but along the line he had committed what my Nana regarded as the worst thing possible—he had left the church and married a Protestant. Who had ever heard of a Methodist named Celeste?

My father would say his reasons for turning away from Catholicism centered on an afternoon when he and a few other kids were making some extra money by scrubbing the bricks on the side of the parish church in Monessen. This was a perpetual chore because of the soot from the steel mills, and it kept kids busy. They'd scrub away, and every so often the priest would come out to check up on them. During one of those inspections, my father asked a question the priest either couldn't or wouldn't answer. "Frank," the priest told him, "you're too young for this conversation. When you're older, when you understand things, then we'll talk."

My father persisted. He said he understood things well enough already, but the priest refused again.

My father didn't ask a third time. I never learned what the question was (or whether this story may have papered over the real incident.) When Dad left for college, he left the Catholic Church behind. He remained a deeply religious person and became actively involved in the Methodist Church after marrying my mother.

Growing up, much of my own personal development was nurtured by activities at Lakewood Methodist Church. As a boy, I sang in the church choir and attended many events held at the church. I didn't go to beer bashes with class-mates down on the lakefront and was a bit of a goody-goody in high school. I was active in the YMCA, and on Monday mornings I was part of a small group of high school students who would put on a modest nondenominational worship service. Frequently I'd be the one to give a short sermon. My own connection to Methodism and its emphasis on social action would flourish during my college years. But it began with my family and remained so.

I suppose that my father's understanding of himself as someone who had turned away deliberately from the Catholic Church was part of his dismay, years later, when I married Dagmar Braun, a devout Catholic. My decision to marry into the faith that he had rejected must have seemed like open rebellion.

Perhaps to an extent not clear to me then, it was.

It wasn't until I began to study history in college seriously that I became proud of Monessen—and of my Italian American roots. Reading Oscar Handlin's seminal book *The Uprooted* in an American history class was the first time I confronted the prejudice that Italians had to fight, like the Irish before them. I realized this was the world that my father had grown up in. Reading Handlin, I thought: this is my grandfather; this is my father. The toughness of their everyday existence was a source of pride for them, men who shaped molten steel. They welcomed demanding work and brought home a decent paycheck for their families. And they encouraged their kids—kids like my father—to become doctors and lawyers and teachers. Even mayors.

My father never characterized his childhood to me as being either sad or happy, tough or easy. He was his mother's son and kept his cards close to his chest. He certainly never talked much about his humble immigrant beginnings. But the experience of those early days stuck with him. It clearly had required remarkable determination to lift himself beyond Morgan Avenue.

There were many things we never discussed. In fact, the first book I thought about writing would have been titled *Questions I Never Asked My Father*. I imagined questions I hadn't thought to ask him while he was alive. Did he ever regret leaving Monessen? What was his relationship with his longtime secretary? With my mother? Did he have any experience with the Cleveland mob? Did he have any regrets on his life's journey?

Despite his education, despite his effort to cement his place in the American political establishment, my father remained Calabrian—as secretive as he was stubborn. On more than one occasion, a sheriff's deputy would knock on our door, handing my mother a foreclosure notice on some property that she knew almost nothing about.

This might seem strange to those who knew him. To see Frank Celeste in action, filling a room with his presence, the life of the party, one might think he was just as open in his personal life. The opposite was the case. As outgoing and gregarious as he was, as able to immediately and astoundingly recall the names of my college friends after meeting them only once a year earlier, Frank Celeste was a guarded person. I had a wonderful childhood and a great relationship with my father. At the same time, there were certain conversations that we were never going to have.

Among the things my father never talked about was his first—and failed—mayoral candidacy in Lakewood. I knew about it only as a vague memory, a dimly recalled snippet of conversation I was never quite able to dismiss. But that race was not part of the family lore that my brother, sister, and I talked about. My brother, Ted was, in a way, much closer to my father and worked with him more closely in his later campaigns while I was off at college. Yet apparently my father had not discussed it with him either. Figuring that I'd never write my book of questions, I decided to answer at least one. Was there in fact a first, failed bid for mayor of Lakewood?

A few hours digging through archives yielded the answer. In 1939 Frank Celeste had, indeed, run for mayor, challenging incumbent Amos Kauffman. Dad was thirty-two years old, living at 1538 Elmwood Avenue, where I spent my first years. No campaign materials from the race survive—a remarkable fact given my mother's propensity to save everything. But news clippings convey a sense of the campaign and young Frank Celeste.

According to one article, Celeste's campaign literature charged that the Kauffman administration did not believe in "doing things" and was "of that antiquated mold of mind that instinctively closes at hint of improvement." A key theme of the campaign was upgrading city services, particularly hiring more firefighters and garbage collectors. "Lakewood citizens are different," Frank Celeste is quoted as saying, "they paint their homes and improve their lawns ... the administration now in office does not realize the city has to do the same in the major things. Property owners cannot eliminate grade crossings, improve the lakefront or provide recreation centers as individuals. That is the administration's job." Later in the article, the author suggests that a Celeste victory is unlikely: "Because of the Republican complexion of Lakewood and Kauffman's vote-getting in past elections," the author asserted, "his defeat would be classified as an upset."

He was right.

Mayor Kauffman won reelection to his third term by about four thousand votes in an election in which just under ten thousand votes were cast. Kauffman would remain mayor for a total of twenty-four years until 1956—when my father ran again. And was elected.

My father never spoke of that first campaign. *Bresta you cards*, as my Nana counseled.

Frank Celeste must have been a respectable student, if not at the top of his class. What he had was personality—he charmed people, including his teachers, one of whom pointed him out of Monessen toward the College of Wooster, where he met my mother, Margaret Louis.

My father, Frank Celeste, at the mayor's desk in Lakewood City Hall

Born in Cleveland in 1909, "exactly," as she often noted "one hundred years after Abraham Lincoln," my mother was a formidable and focused person. She was a highly gifted professional in her own right who had been trained as a social worker and was a successful volunteer for the YWCA, right up to the final years of her life. She confided in me once that she had really wanted to write, but she never gave herself permission to do it.

One of her more demanding volunteer endeavors was being "Mrs. Santa Claus" for the *Cleveland Press*. She read pleas for warm coats and who knows what else that came into the newspaper during the holidays. She would sit in our living room with a pile of a hundred letters to review, her task being to decide whom they would help and whom they would not. I remember the tears running down her cheeks. She did that for years. I'm not sure why she inflicted those harsh choices on herself, but my mother willingly carried the burden of being Mrs. Santa Claus.

For all my father's love of public service, my mother was at least as involved in the community as he was. Perhaps I never sufficiently acknowledged the example she set, but she was incredibly important—as devoted to bringing her kids up right as my father and every bit as demanding.

She loved to tell us how innocent my father had been when he arrived at Wooster. They met one night on a double date during which they were both supposed to be interested in other people, and, at the end of the evening, he asked her out. The following week Frank came to her "section"—the dorm where she lived—to pick her up, but, when she came downstairs, he told her that her brassiere was showing. Mortified, she ran back upstairs.

It turned out to be the shoulder strap on her slip. "That's how naive Frank was back then," she said.

For one of their first outings, Mom took him to the downtown dry goods store, which sold men's and women's clothing. She introduced him to the proper names of various undergarments. Nana had never talked to him about these matters.

The details of their courtship were never confided to me except for the fact that my father was one of two young men interested in her—Frank in Wooster and Paul in Lakewood. Mom described how Frank would kiss her good-bye as she boarded the train in Wooster and how Paul would kiss her hello when

Left: My mother's favorite picture of me, at age 5. *Right:* My parents, Frank and Peg Celeste, as students at the College of Wooster, March 1927.

she arrived in Cleveland. Eventually Frank got wind that Paul was in the picture and turned up on her doorstep on Summit Avenue one evening when Paul and my mother were sitting in the living room holding hands. Frank was on the front porch insistently ringing the doorbell, wondering why Peggy wouldn't come to the door. My grandmother finally came out and explained that "it wasn't a good time." Mom ended it with Paul not long after that. And married my father.

But she kept one letter and a picture of Paul for the rest of her life.

I am the product of two grandmothers. If my Italian grandmother taught me to respect my father and to be sure I was the only one with a clear view of my cards, Bessie Louis taught me the value of travel and scholarship and instilled in me a respect for public service.

"Dick," she would say, quoting scripture, "remember this admonition: to whom much is given, much is expected."

Bessie was born in Warrensville, Ohio, the youngest daughter—the baby of the family—of Alsom Salisbury and Elizabeth "Betsy" Beckwith. Her father was a carpenter, farmer, and herb doctor, though—like my grandmother Bessie and me—he was a restless spirit, having made a trip west in 1859 on horseback, accompanied by a group of wagons. He made it as far as Pikes Peak, in Colorado, then returned home satisfied that "Ohio was best."

After graduating from high school in Berea, Ohio, Bessie attended Baldwin Wallace College and began teaching on Prospect Road in Middleburg, where she taught as many as forty children in a one-room schoolhouse. In 1893 she traveled alone to Portland, Oregon, to visit her brother Henry, called Hank, before he left for Alaska—packing "an eating basket" to take with her. It was a show of independence that was unheard of for an eighteen-year-old woman. After bicycling through the Northwest, she returned to Chicago, where she studied shorthand as one of John Robert Gregg's first students. For a time after that, she worked at the newly formed Roebuck Company but then married Theodore Andrew Louis, the man who had been courting her for years.

I don't know much about my grandfather's early years. He was born in Baltimore, where he lived until the eighth grade. His mother died when he was nine years old and his father a couple of years later. With his brothers and sisters, he was placed in what was then the German Orphanage in Berea, Ohio, and from there moved to Philadelphia, where he learned the printing trade—eventually contracting lead poisoning from it. He enlisted in the Spanish-American War, serving as a nurse and correspondent in Florida, and returned to Cleveland,

My maternal grandparents, Bessie and Ted Louis, on the back steps of their house on Summit Avenue in Lakewood. (Note Ted's ever-present pipe!)

where he was working as a printer when he met Bessie at the wedding of a mutual friend. Soon after that, he opened his own printing shop, which he—a Shakespeare buff—named the Stratford Press. Like Bessie, my grandfather loved to travel, and the two of them did a great deal of it, visiting Cuba and Canada, as well as Alaska twice, traveling by zeppelin and airplane—which my grandmother thought exotic and exhilarating. My grandfather remains vivid in my memory: tall, quiet, pipe-smoking with a glint of impish humor in his eye.

By all accounts it was a happy marriage, and my mother remembered her childhood as safe and, as she put it in a letter to my children, "filled with parties, trips, gifts and fun." It was, at the same time, touched with tragedy. My grandfather died unexpectedly of a heart attack in early 1941, and some years later Gram lost her son Wolcott. Despite these losses, my grandmother never stopped thinking of herself as richly blessed and instilled in me that same sense of myself as having been similarly blessed.

One occasion when she instilled that sense of responsibility—that I was one of those to whom much had been given and that, therefore, much was expected of me—was her present when I graduated from junior high: a trip to our nation's capita1. Off we went by Greyhound bus to explore Washington. For five days we walked all over town during the hottest month of the summer. Bessie was seventy-eight, and frequently people would stop to ask if she was all right.

"I'm fine," she would reply and delicately wipe the moisture from her brow.

We toured the famous monuments and visited the Smithsonian Museum. All the while she made the point that I was part of this tradition, of the great history of our country. Just as it was part of me, I had a role to play in it.

Whether she would ever vote for me was another question. A lifelong Republican who once shocked me by saying she would rather die than see John Kennedy in the White House, she did in fact change her registration in 1970—at ninety-five years of age—so she could vote for me in my first primary for state representative. Bessie had by that point moved into the Eliza Jennings Home, a retirement home that happened to be in my legislative district. She would go around the Eliza Jennings with my bumper sticker pinned to her walker. And she proved very persuasive. In my first general election, a total of twenty-six people voted in the Eliza Jennings precinct. I received all twenty-six votes.

Bessie Louis had gone to bat for her Democrat grandson.

We remained close until the end of her life. I would often visit her when returning from the legislature on Thursday afternoons. "I had the most exciting experience of my life this week," she told me one Thursday.

"You did?" I said. Remember, this was the woman who had traveled alone from Cleveland to the West Coast to visit her brother, the woman who had seen the Gulf of Mexico from a dirigible. What could possibly occur at this retirement home that would be the most exciting moment of her life?

"On Tuesday," she explained, "I was coming back from lunch and took the elevator up to the second floor. There were two old ladies on the elevator with me." I knew the other women would have had to be significantly *younger* than she was, but she still described them as old ladies. "They were talking to each other," she went on. "And the first lady said to the second, isn't it a shame about Bessie Louis. That got my attention. Because, you know, I'm Bessie Louis."

"I know you are," I said.

"Such a shame," said the second woman, "she passed away so suddenly."

At that point the elevator doors opened, and the two of them got off without a nod in her direction.

"Then," Bessie told me, "I walked down the hallway to my room, the length of the floor. No one said a word to me. Nobody paid any attention to me. I got to my room, and I began to wonder if this was what it's like when you pass away. So I rang for the nurse. I figured that if the nurse came, they'd made a mistake. But if the nurse didn't come, that was it.

"Dick," she told me earnestly, "The next sixty seconds were the most exciting sixty seconds of my life."

"Gram," I said. "When you were on the elevator, why didn't you just reach out and touch one of the women?

"Oh Dick," she said, "I didn't want to scare them to death."

Another Thursday I visited her when she happened to be watching the television footage of our astronaut golfing on the moon. She was glued to the screen, but when there was a break in the coverage I interrupted to say hello.

"Doesn't that frustrate you?" I asked her.

"Yes," she said.

I said, "Me too. We spend all that money sending that guy to the moon, then he's golfing."

"Dick," she said, "that's not what frustrates me."

"It's not?"

"What frustrates me," she said, "is the thought that I'm not going to live long enough to get there myself."

That was Bessie Louis.

She died in 1973, a year before I was first elected to statewide office. She never got to see me in the governor's residence. But her example, and her admonition about there being much expected of those to whom much is given, remained with me throughout my public service.

It remains with me still.

Leafing through the memorabilia, I can see clearly that my mother kept everything: every attendance award I received, every badge I ever earned, every report card, even ones from Grant Elementary in Lakewood. They *are* good reports for the most part, I'm pleased to observe. Mostly As and Bs, only the occasional C. My kindergarten teacher made particular note of the fact that I was never once absent or tardy during the spring semester of 1942. "Dick," the teacher notes, "has made normal progress in all the activities of the Kindergarten. He has shown growth in self-reliance and self-control. He works well and thinks clearly for his age and is doing work in the upper third of his groups. He needs help in singing."

I *still* need help in singing—but who doesn't? My kindergarten teacher—her name is written, printed, strict, angular—was Miss Elizabeth Fithian. She took kindergarten very seriously. When it was time for naps, we took naps. "Dick," I can still hear her say, "stop whispering to Gary."

Gary was Gary Strong, who lived across the street from me on Arthur Avenue. He grew to be tall and good-looking, a natural athlete and a wonderful artist. Gary had a newspaper route delivering the *Cleveland Press,* and I had a route delivering the *Cleveland News.* Gary's older brother had the *Plain Dealer* route, which included the Sunday paper, where you could make real money. At one point it was my ambition to take over that route for the neighborhood, perhaps with Gary. Much of our time was spent comparing the tips we got at Christmas. He usually did better than I did, though neither of us did as well as his older brother. Our sport was baseball, then later tennis, which we taught ourselves on the concrete neighborhood courts.

The world I grew up in was suburban Ohio of the early 1940s. Cleveland was nearby, but we didn't venture there often. It felt far away, a different world existing at the end of the Detroit Avenue streetcar—still running back then.

Lakewood is a small town, and its boundaries were clearly defined in my imagination. Baseball and tennis at Andrews Field, books from the Lakewood Public Library (where I held one of my first paying jobs), miniature golf up on Madison Avenue, matinees at the Detroit and Hilliard Theaters, youth fellowship at the Methodist Church. You could draw the boundaries of the schools I went to, from our doorstep to my grandmothers, to the church, and that was it.

It was an intimate space where we never used a doorbell. Instead, we'd stand on the porch and shout, "Oh, Gaaaaary!" Sometimes Mrs. Strong—Gary's mother—would come to the door and say he's not at home or doing his homework. More often Gary would come out to play.

Then we'd go to Jim Hegenbarth's house.

"OH, JIIIIIIIIMY," we'd shout.

"I have lived most of my life in small towns," writes Ellen Gilchrist, the famous memoirist, "and I'm in the habit of knowing and talking to everyone." Though perhaps Lakewood is a different kind of small town, the experience of growing up there nurtured in me a similar impulse; at the core of my enthusiasm for public office was an interest in and love of people that has never left me. It also planted in me a deep and abiding love of Cleveland and Ohio.

Like Bessie Louis, no matter where my travels took me, I would always return home.

Another figure who exerted a powerful influence in my early life was George Kenneth Cobb—KC—Ellsworth, a dear friend of my father. George had been born in a small town in Minnesota and suffered from muscular dystrophy, though I'm not sure there isn't a more precise diagnosis to be made. He had almost no muscles on his arms and legs and walked always with two canes and a lurching, painful-looking gait. An almost skeletal figure, he gave you the sense that he was somehow shrunken, a man who was five-foot-six in a body that should have been several inches taller. Imagine Stephen Hawking standing up and being able to move around—that's what George looked like.

My father loved to tell us how George's mother paid kids to carry him to school using a wooden door as a kind of stretcher. For my father this provided an instructive example of the high value the Ellsworth family put on education. Despite his physical limitations, George was a brilliant student who excelled at Western Reserve Law School, where he and my father met and became friends. He was a year ahead of my father, and the two made an unlikely pair. As WASPy a person as you could meet, George had a dark, occasionally cynical sense of humor that was unlike my father's. Yet, despite their differences—or perhaps because of them—they were the closest friends,

I first got to know George in the mid-forties, when he was working at the Federal Housing Administration. When he graduated from law school, in the early thirties, he went to Washington, DC, and found a job quickly in the first Roosevelt administration. He was working for Jesse Jones, who ran the Reconstruction Finance Corporation, which played a major role in fighting the Great Depression. My father made a point of visiting George in Washington once or twice a year, and George would do the same, staying with us on Arthur Avenue. I suspect that one of the reasons that my parents built a den in the back of our house with a pull-out sofa bed was so George had a bedroom that didn't require him to go up and down the stairs.

As close as George and my father were, my mother always found him a little disconcerting because of his unsettling sense of humor. Once when he arrived at our house, he was in the process of wrestling his way out of a taxi, and a group of neighborhood kids stopped to watch. He struggled out and began walking up the steps with his awkward, excruciating gait,

"What happened to you?" asked Dukie Haas, a kid who lived across the street.

"My mother put me through a meat grinder," George told him.

Dukie went home screaming.

My mother was mortified.

Another visit of George's occurred right after my father had invested in our first black-and-white television set. The screen was small, not much bigger than the one you'd find on a laptop today, and my parents were showing it off watching *The Ed Sullivan Show*.

"That's pretty nice, Frank," said George, "but it's a bit like looking through a keyhole, isn't it?"

This offended my mother, who believed our investment in a nice RCA television should be treated with more respect. George, of course, was right: watching that television *was* like looking through a keyhole. His cynicism really troubled my mother. She would always tell us, "If you can't say anything nice about someone, don't say anything at all." George was *always* saying nasty things, about *everyone*. He was also a cynic about himself and could make fun at his own expense.

One time, however, my father got him going. "Remember that Labor Day speech you wrote for FDR," he said. "Big success, wasn't it?"

"Sure," said George. "I wrote a Labor Day speech for Franklin Roosevelt, and it became one of his most memorable speeches because in the middle of it he departed from my text. 'Those Republicans don't like anything I do. They criticize me. They criticize Eleanor. Why, they even criticize my little dog, Fala.'"

It became known as Roosevelt's little dog Fala speech.

"I'd felt better if I put that line in the speech," he said, glumly. "But that was FDR."

My father took George with a grain of salt. He understood that George had faced adversity all of his life—and still had a heart of gold. If he hadn't been as physically handicapped, who knew what he might have accomplished?

Having no children of his own, George took a particular interest in how I was doing at school and gave me a dollar for every A I got. But it went beyond that. When, much later, I made the decision to go to Yale, George was tremendously excited and encouraging. If there was any regret on my father's part about my not following in his footsteps to Wooster, George helped assuage it. My father was an American who had grown up in an Italian skin and who aspired to be a successful businessperson and a good public servant. George, by contrast, had four names, George Kenneth Cobb Ellsworth—a WASP whose body was contorted but who became someone very special. George was, in a lot of ways, the yin to my father's yang: he was cynical, my father was naive; he was sour, my father was ebullient; where my father was earnest, George's cynicism would creep in and he'd take my father down a peg or two.

It was fascinating how deeply my father cared for George. My recollection was that whenever George was coming, my father's spirits would pick up and my mother's would droop. The week before I went off to Oxford, I got a card from George saying good luck, along with a check for a hundred dollars. He died soon afterwards.

As is probably the case with most people, when I think back to my childhood, it's my teachers that I remember most. Miss Broderick, my third-grade teacher, was an awful woman who was mean to her students. At the end of the year, a bunch of us were at Dee Waldheger's house on St. Charles Avenue, a few streets over from mine. Dee was the girl my father thought I should marry, a brilliant and pretty girl who would, later, work on my early campaigns. The group of us sat in her kitchen, complaining bitterly because we had just received our report cards and discovered that Miss Broderick had given us all Cs. This, we felt, was completely undeserved. Maybe we weren't brown-nosers like the teacher's pet, Judy Thomas, but we were definitely not C students.

As we were going on about what a terrible teacher she was and how unfair she'd been, Mrs. Waldheger—Dee's mother—was on the phone. What we didn't know was that she was on the phone with Alma Johnson, the principal.

Dee's mom held the phone up, nodding her head, encouraging us. "You see," she said into the receiver, "that's the very thing I'm talking about."

When we returned to school in the fall, Miss Broderick wasn't there. She had disappeared. Evaporated.

An early example of a successful insurgency.

As a boy I was a conscientious student. I had been taught to value scholarship and work hard. At the same time, learning was never a chore for me; I have a good memory and earned good grades from the beginning. In the interest of full disclosure, however, I do note that I got a C in my 1954 wood shop class. From my homeroom teacher! I had to make a darning ball. (Back in the fifties, you mended socks.) Try as I might, I could not get my darning ball to the right dimensions.

It was an early lesson in humility.

I have always loved bringing people together to accomplish a common task. Whether rallying support across a state or across a college campus, my life's work has been to show that people can often accomplish together what they could never do alone—building what I call a constituency for change.

I think that impulse first became evident with the formation of the Panther Organization, which we shortened to TPO. Only insiders knew what it meant.

Founders of the Panther Organization (TPO). *Left to right:* Jim Hegenbarth, me, and Gary Strong

TPO got its start during fourth grade and lasted about two years. It began with a clubhouse that I constructed with my two buddies, Jim Hegenbarth and Gary Strong, against the back of our house using leftover building materials from when my parents added the den. It was basically a lean-to: tiny and damp, cramped and dirty. As a consequence, most of our meetings were conducted in our basement instead of the clubhouse. While it was not an impressive structure, I believe the point the ten-year-old Dick Celeste would want me to make is this: TPO possessed a clubhouse.

As to the origins of the TPO name and the choice of panther, the facts remain somewhat murky. I do recall that sometime during the third grade I became enamored of the panther. Sleek, mysterious, a proven hunter, the sort of animal that could, at a moment's notice, disappear into the darkness, the panther exemplified qualities I admired. Almost certainly the TPO name came out of the conviction that any insignia of the club would include the drawing of a panther—which I was more than ready to provide. Once we had the clubhouse, we had everything, and the Panther Organization was born.

This was my first secret society. There would be others.

Our fifth-grade teacher was Miss Olsen, a young woman with whom the entire membership of TPO was smitten. The particular qualities that inspired such devotion escape me now, but chief among them must have been that she was nice and not at all like the sour Miss Broderick who, although no longer at Grant Elementary, lived on in our memories as a menacing presence. Inspired by her, the membership of TPO decided to raise serious money for the Community Chest.

Since TPO prized its anonymity, the money had to be delivered in an appropriately mysterious way. Jim was our numbers guy, so delivery of our five-dollar contribution fell to him. He discreetly slipped a plain manila envelope onto her desk.

Miss Olsen never figured out where it came from. No one did. Nor did I disclose it to the Federal Bureau of Investigation in any of my background checks or during any of my confirmation hearings.

Now it's out there.

It was also around fourth or fifth grade that I began to talk to Mr. Babbidge. I would speak to him on the phone from the time I was about ten years old. He was a pal of mine, a true though imaginary friend. I would call him and carry on a conversation usually seeking advice on some issue about which my parents were not being very understanding. In response, Mr. Babbidge would usually assure me that I could get through one or another kind of trial. "Your parents are difficult," he'd tell me, "but you have to put up with them. Do what you think is right, but know it is going to work out."

While no one was at the other end of the line, these one-sided conversations served as a way to get things off my chest. What was important was the feeling that I had someone prepared to listen in a way that my mother and father were not.

Mr. Babbidge didn't put any expectations on me, didn't want anything—he was just there for me. I could always pick up the phone and he'd be there.

My guess is that one of the things that I had to deal with was a hidden, lonely, solitary streak that I didn't want to acknowledge and didn't want the rest of the world to know about. I don't remember exactly when I stopped talking to my imaginary advisor—probably just before junior high. I no longer needed to have a conversation with someone who couldn't reply. I moved inward and started having those conversations with myself. I'd give myself a pep talk or talk myself into being patient, and that seemed to be enough. Still, the desire for a solitary place stayed tucked away within me throughout my life.

I have always felt I had to live up to high expectations, even though my parents were not early versions of today's striving helicopter parents. Mom and Dad allowed me to have a private space into which I could retreat. But that separateness did not change the fact that they set high expectations for me. This was clear from the beginning and was reinforced early on by my grandmother Bessie. And by a great many others in the years that followed.

Introversion did not match with the expectations that were everywhere around me, particularly at an early age. I dealt with this pressure by making a space that was mine alone. Sometimes it was a physical space like my bedroom in the attic. But it was also an emotional space, a place where I could tune out and nothing would be asked of me, where I could confide in a friend, free from expectation.

During the beginning of sixth grade my voice began to grow hoarse. I began to sound like I had laryngitis all the time. No pain was involved, but something was clearly wrong. My parents had a friend who was an ear, nose, and throat specialist, and my mother took me to see him. I remember the examination vividly; the doctor looked down my throat, felt the sides of my neck, then stepped back and nodded conclusively. "Yes, well," he said, "there they are."

"There they are?" said my mother.

"They?" I said.

"Growths on your vocal cords," he said. "We've got to get rid of them."

"Get rid of them?" I said. "How?"

"We have to operate." He told us that I'd developed "singer's nodules" as a result of abusing my voice. I was a constant talker and an avid singer (notwithstanding the dismissiveness of my kindergarten teacher), and it had taken a toll.

"Operate?" I looked at my mother. "Isn't there anything else we can do?" I'm not sure what it was exactly, but something about the sound of an operation frightened me. Perhaps it was the thought of a knife cutting callouses off my vocal cords. I recalled getting my tonsils out and not being able to eat solid food and how sore my throat had been. As bad as that had been, I was convinced that this would be worse.

My mother sensed my apprehension. "Isn't there anything else that Dick can do?' she asked the doctor.

"Well," he said. "He could stop talking."

"Stop talking?" I said.

"For at least six weeks," he told us. "If you don't want an operation, you have to stop talking for six weeks."

"That's a long time," said my mother.

"You think you can do it?" asked the doctor.

"If it's that or an operation," I said, "I can stop."

"Not a word," he said.

"It's better than getting something terrible down my throat," I said, but before I could get to the end of the sentence, he held his finger up to his lips. My six weeks of silence had already started.

Driving home with my mother, the seriousness—and the difficulty—of the situation began to dawn on me. Can you just decide to stop talking? Would I be able to do it? I couldn't even ask the question. On the way home I began writing questions to my mother, so she stopped and bought me an erasable pad, the kind that came with a plastic pen, which you erased by lifting the plastic sheet you wrote on. The next day I went to school, and I brought the pad with me. When the teacher asked a question, I would hold up my hand and start writing furiously if I got called. Whoever was sitting next to me would read my answer.

When I went back after six weeks, the doctor told me that I had made a full recovery. He was impressed I had resisted talking for six weeks. "Now," he told me, "you have to lower your voice."

I attended the Speech and Hearing Clinic, where a therapist taught me how to use a deeper register for my voice so I didn't put undue pressure on my vocal cords. "If you do that," he told me, "you will avoid this happening again."

After the doctor pronounced me cured and gave me permission to start talking again, part of me resisted. The interesting thing about the experience of my enforced silence—something that sticks with me even today—is how it made me realize how much of what we think we have to say is superfluous. Apart from social engagement, much of what we say is not essential. I also learned that I could be silent. Sometimes I would use my silence aggressively. If I got upset with people—with family or friends—I could just stop talking. I remember my sister, Pat, complaining. "Mom," she'd say, "Dick isn't talking to me again."

The most memorable moment of my six weeks of silence occurred in Jacqueline Edwards's living room. Jacqueline and I had been carrying on a chaste courtship for a number of weeks, meeting often in the darkness of the Detroit Theater. We would go to Saturday matinees, sit near the back of the theater, and neck. This was a big deal in 1950, the hottest stuff I was capable of imagining at the time. One day in November, around the time of my thirteenth birthday, she invited me to her house. Settling me in the living room, she headed for the kitchen. After a few minutes she came back and turned the radio up. The announcer's voice came on. "This is for Dick Celeste. Happy Birthday from Jacqueline Edwards." And on came the song, now hardly remembered but a hit then, "I'm as corny as Kansas and high as a kite in July . . . I'm in love with a wonderful guy."

It was an unexpectedly sweet moment.

Unfortunately, I could only express myself on an erasable pad. It was hard to be suave holding an erasable pad. Still, I gave it a shot.

High school was the first time I became involved in politics, though, strange as it may seem now, never as a candidate. I became expert at running campaigns— a behind-the-scenes presence. A guy a year ahead of me, running for student council treasurer, enlisted my help. I put a crew of people together—Gary Strong, Ed Freska, a number of others—and we went to work in our basement. We chose a theme, made signs, and posted them around the school. We knew the strategic locations and were successful in growing a team, and our candidate won. Soon we had a reputation for being effective campaign organizers, and other people started enlisting us.

Next, we worked for Eddie Allen, who was running for student council president. The slogan: "Step Ahead with Ed." Another candidate was Jack Christie: "Back Jack" was our slogan. They both won. We always kept it simple. All campaign materials during high school were produced in the Celeste basement, and my parents were always encouraging us. It was original work that produced three student council victories.

Later I would recycle "Step Ahead with Ed" at the 1968 Democratic Convention, trying to draft Ted Kennedy—"Step Ahead with Ted."

But in high school I never ran for office myself. For some reason I didn't think of myself as a candidate, although I was interested in the process. I just enjoyed getting to know my fellow students. I liked to get their stories, and I respected them, no matter who they were. If someone was a C student or not the most glamorous kid in the class, I would still be friends with them.

During high school I also became involved in theater. What appealed to me about theater was the way it allowed me to become someone else. Onstage it is both you yourself and you as someone else. Our drama club, the Barnstormers, allowed me to step outside myself. While I didn't want to be a candidate myself, I could perform in a play. It was easier because, if the audience was judging anything, it was my performance rather than me personally.

Because of my experience in the Barnstormers, I decided to enroll in speech class during my senior year. I figured, how hard could it be? No tests were involved, no final papers, and I was confident that I could get up and recite a speech in front of the class. It would be a breeze.

The class was taught by Wally Smith, who also supervised the Barnstormers. A small man with black-rimmed glasses and close-cropped, black, curly hair, Mr. Smith held class each day in the school's "old auditorium," where he would sit in the back as students delivered their speeches. Each day after four or five, he would gather us together at the front, asking us to talk about what we thought of the various speeches we'd heard. Then he'd give his own notes to each speaker.

The first speech assigned us was one in which we introduced ourselves. About three or four days into the class it was my turn. I figured it would be a piece of cake. I knew Mr. Smith and knew I was poised on stage.

I didn't get far into my speech, however, when he interrupted: "Celeste," he called out from the back of the theater. "Eye contact."

It rattled me, but I kept going.

"Celeste," he shouted, just a couple of sentences in, "where's the logic in that?"

And on it went. He interrupted me every few minutes. When the speeches were over, we all gathered at the front of the auditorium, I could feel the rest of the class was anxious about what would happen next. Something had upset Mr. Smith, and he'd really been tough on me.

When it was my turn to receive his notes, he said simply, "Celeste, you can do better than that." No specifics, no additional comments, simply, "You can do better than that."

It went like that for the rest of the semester. Whatever speech I had been assigned—the speech to persuade, a historical speech, a speech in praise of something—before I got fully into it, Mr. Smith erupted, barking one comment after another from the back of the auditorium. "Posture!" he'd yell out. "Diction!" And always, when it came time to give me his notes, he would simply say, "Celeste, you can do better."

Who are the teachers we remember? What kind of a teacher makes a difference in the life of a child? Most of us have firm ideas about what we should ask of teachers, but what should teachers ask of their students? Wally Smith's repeated comments, his conviction that I could do better, pushed me in the direction of excellence. I can still hear him today, telling me that I can do better.

He was right.

It wasn't until the end of the year—when I spoke at graduation—that I was able to deliver a speech he thought satisfactory. He sat in the front row, and I worried the whole time that he might interrupt me.

I still have a copy of that speech. Looking back at it now, I'm struck by a significant editorial change I had made, apparently at the last minute. Nearing the end of the speech, I ask, "Can we conquer the problem of the United Nations?" In the next paragraph, another question, "Can we conquer the problem of the atom bomb?" Interestingly, however, in both instances I had crossed out the word "problem" and instead written in the world "challenge."

It is a word that I carried with me to Yale. And beyond.

My next exposure to politics came as part of the YMCA Youth in Government program. As a junior in high school, I joined about three hundred students chosen statewide. We arrived in Columbus with bills we had drafted, initiatives we wanted to advance. The event took place over a three-day weekend with a banquet on Saturday night in the Neil House Hotel Ballroom.

Frank Lausche, then in his fifth term as governor, a silver-haired and silver-tongued orator of the old school, spoke. He stood in his bow tie, immaculate white shirt, and rumpled black suit and, with a soaring voice and meticulousness diction, gave the most compelling speech I had ever heard.

Every kid in the room was weeping as he concluded. I do not remember a single thing he said, only that if he had asked us to march on the statehouse, I would have done it. No questions asked.

Lausche went on to serve in the US Senate, and only then did I realize what a conservative Democrat he was, voting for the most part with the Republicans. I saw him perhaps ten years later when he came to India on a congressional delegation. He was an interesting example to me politically. On the one hand, he was ethnic Slovenian, and I—to my father's amazement—celebrated my Italian roots; on the other hand, his positions were antithetical to my own. He was all for the Vietnam War, a kind of super-patriot, and I opposed the war. Yet, despite our deep political differences, there was something appealing about him, something I wanted to emulate. Getting re-elected, perhaps.

In my final months of high school, I was nominated to be senior class president, along with my friend Jim Asbeck. Unlike student council elections, there was no chance to campaign. I lost convincingly.

So much for bright political beginnings.

In the 1950s, upon graduation, our custom was to give yearbook photos to one another, writing brief notes on the back. High school students today would do nothing of the sort. In this era of social media it would be redundant to give anyone an actual photo of oneself. But the symbolism of that old ritual moves me. Like the faces in the photos, the inscriptions are pointed toward the future. "Dick," writes Gary, "You did a tremendous job in the play, keep up the good work in all of your undertakings. Good luck with Sue and all the other girls—let's have a good senior year." Al Baumann—who we called Twoosie because he was Albert Otto Baumann II—writes, "You got stuff that will carry you up and up." Forty years later, Twoosie, now a Lutheran pastor, would preside over my marriage to Jacqueline Lundquist.

And one that I'd forgotten, from Judy Bacon, who I'd taken to senior prom. "Celestial," writes Judy on the back of her tiny photo (I have no idea why she called me that), "People always say that someone you know might someday be President. I think you'd be a terrific one."

A few others offered similar thoughts. They saw something in me. Something I didn't see myself.

I initially applied to Wooster and Williams. Then, just twenty-four hours before the applications deadline, I got a call from a local Yale alum. "Dick," he said, "I'm calling because I'm a Yale grad and I understand that you've visited the campus but haven't applied. I was wondering if there is anything I can share with you that would encourage you."

I told him that when we had visited Yale it had struck me as cold and impersonal. That was true. We had visited in the spring, and it had rained the whole time. To me, the ivy-covered walls looked forbidding.

"Let me offer you this observation," he told me. "You're a very good student. I believe you could get into Yale and do well there. I think you should have more than just two choices. I would encourage you to apply. See what happens."

I don't remember his name, but he convinced me to rethink things. He made the pitch in a very thoughtful way, posing the value of having more choices rather than pushing me in a particular direction. I mailed an application in the next morning.

I was invited to scholarship interviews by Williams and Yale. At that time, scholarships tended to be awarded by the local alumni. They would interview local applicants and then decide how much support you'd receive.

I met the Williams folks first. The Williams alumni club in Cleveland offered one really generous—all-expenses-paid—scholarship. About a dozen of us were interviewed, then told to come back at four in the afternoon when they would announce their decisions. They sat us each down individually. When it was my turn, the interviewer started off by saying how much he wanted me to come. "We can give you a $400 scholarship."

The big scholarship was $1,400. I was disappointed. And I had a Yale interview to come.

"That's very generous," I told him. "Let me think about it."

For a moment he stared at me. "Well," he said, "we're going to need a decision pretty soon."

The next week I was interviewed by Yale alums at the Jones Day law offices. A half dozen men met with me in a much more relaxed atmosphere than my earlier Williams experience.

First question: "Do you swim?"

"No," I told them.

The man nodded. "Well," he said, "that's all right."

I remembered that Lakewood High School had won the state swimming championships; when they saw my application, they must have hoped they were getting a great swimmer. The swimming coach at Yale also coached the Olympic swimming team. They seemed a little disappointed.

But our conversation quickly turned to what Yale had meant to them and what I was looking for in an education.

"Look," said one fellow finally, "at this point we can't say anything about the size of the scholarship, but here's what we typically offer. A third of the amount is a grant, a third is paid by work study on campus, and the rest is a loan. We try to meet your financial need in this way."

At that point I hadn't been admitted to either Yale or Williams, and the feeling that I really should go Wooster—my parents' alma mater—lingered. The next day I went to Columbus for my second YMCA Youth in Government weekend. I stayed at the Neil House with Kent Weeks, an LHS classmate who also had applied to Wooster. When we returned to our room that night, I found a Western Union telegram from my parents tucked under our door. They were thrilled to tell me that I had been admitted to Wooster and offered one of only two full-ride scholarships. The telegram went on to say that they were going to need my decision by the following Friday. I had less than a week to decide. Kent seemed a bit envious and, like the Williams guy, perplexed about my indecision.

Which only got worse.

I still did not know how to choose. I knew my parents would like me to go to Wooster, though Williams was a very good school. Then there was Yale.

Since I had to give Wooster a decision by Friday, I sat down with Wally Smith on Thursday and asked his advice. "I don't even know if I'm going to get into Yale," I confessed, "but I've got to let the people in Wooster know. If I don't take the scholarship, they have to give it to someone else."

Wally thought about it. "Let me ask you this: which place is going to challenge you the most?"

I knew the answer immediately. "Yale," I said. "I don't think there's any question about that."

"Well," he said. "I'd think about going to the place that will challenge you the most. But don't worry," he added, "you're not going to make a wrong decision here."

I went home with this in my mind and didn't say anything to my parents. I sat for a long time alone in our den mulling it over. I finally emerged with tears running down my face and told them I had decided to turn down Wooster's scholarship and wait to hear from Yale.

The following week, at choir one morning, I was summoned to the principal's office. I arrived to find KC Moore, another senior, waiting there as well. "Gentlemen," he told us, "I want to tell you that you've been admitted to Yale."

Yale ended up offering a package worth $1,800—their maximum.

I had made my decision. I hoped it was the right one.

Chapter 2

Yale

My parents dropped me off at Yale in the fall of 1955, making the long drive from Lakewood to New Haven. My first memory, still vivid, was walking into my dorm room and almost tripping over a steamer trunk covered with a dozen stickers from various locations—Nassau, Bali, Saint-Tropez—and a lacrosse stick. I had never seen a lacrosse stick before and had no idea what it was. To what use, I wondered, could such a thing be put? Looking back, the puzzle of the lacrosse stick seems to me a sign of the divide that separated me from most of my classmates. If I had come to Yale because it was the place that would seriously challenge me, it didn't disappoint. I was instantly intimidated.

The lacrosse stick and the well-traveled trunk belonged to my roommate John Lockton Jr., a native of Greenwich, Connecticut. Lockton was the quintessential Yale student: smart, polished, athletic, and very preppy. As confident as he was, he could be surprisingly reticent to talk about himself. Not until the second semester did he mention that his father was treasurer of General Electric. Most other students at Yale would have announced it immediately. As much as I liked John, he was operating on a whole other level than me. He had a clear understanding of the academic expectations at Yale and was bound to do well—in a word, the sort of student you just had to look at to know he was meant to be there.

My other roommate freshman year was Bob Herold, who was a very different type. Bob was a wide-bodied guy from near Palo Alto who, like me, had gone to a public high school. He seemed like a good guy, very smart, but also deeply troubled. He was the first member of his family to go to college, though the bitterness he expressed seemed to go beyond anything that could be associated with that. Midway through the fall semester he confessed to a personal trauma so severe that it was plain he had not resolved it.

In terms of academic ability and social standing, I was somewhere between the two. While my parents weren't a part of the New England aristocracy, they were certainly more solidly middle-class than Bob's working-class parents. More than half of our classmates at the time were privileged kids from expensive prep schools, all of whom had a better handle on Yale's academic expectations than I had. Most important, they were accustomed to writing a five- or six-page essay in response to a single question on a test or exam. Lakewood High School hadn't prepared me for this. Before Yale, I'd never written an essay response to anything; all my tests had been multiple choice.

My first midterm test was in European history, a subject I loved. And it was taught by a professor I admired, "Wild" Bill Emerson. The exam lasted an hour and a half, during which time we were expected to answer three questions. My grade: D. It was a shock. There goes my scholarship, I thought. I'm just not going to make it. I went to see Professor Emerson and ask what I'd done wrong.

"Mr. Celeste," he said (at Yale in the 1950s everyone was "Mr."), "you wrote a terrible exam."

"I'm here because I need to figure out what I can do to improve."

"Let me ask you," he said. "Did you outline your answer before you started writing?"

I admitted I hadn't.

"That's a good place to begin, Mr. Celeste," he said. And that, it seemed, was the end of the conversation. As I walked out of his office, I realized that Emerson wasn't being unsympathetic; he simply set high expectations. I could see how he earned his nickname.

The rigor of Yale was a humbling experience after LHS.

My academic performance improved after our meeting, and I came to like Mr. Emerson a great deal. I eventually earned a B+ in the class—an acceptable grade after my dismal start—and his influence was sufficient to persuade me to major in history

By the end of freshman year, I had fallen in love with the study of history. The element of detective work behind it appealed to me. I remember writing an essay on whether Lincoln had maneuvered to force the Confederates to fire the first shot of the Civil War. I enjoyed trying to answer that to my satisfaction. While not an especially original question, it exemplified the kind of thinking at the core of historical study—the effort to understand the thrust of a particular historical moment.

I also became intrigued by the question of whether a single individual could affect the course of history or whether we are all pulled along by forces beyond one person's control. I came to believe that a single leader—Lincoln, Roosevelt, Churchill—could and did make a difference. They were individuals suited to the moment. How they dealt with that moment, perhaps in ways that were surprising even to them, fascinated me.

I was reminded about the importance of the relationship between the individual and his time when, years later, I was doing research at Oxford into the Berlin Conference of 1884–85. I became interested in Harry Shelton Sanford, who had been appointed ambassador to Belgium during the Civil War and who ran Lincoln's makeshift intelligence service in Europe during that time. I was fascinated to discover that Lincoln had sent Sanford to try to persuade Giuseppe Garibaldi to take command of the Union Army. Sanford pitched Garibaldi, who responded that he would do it only if Lincoln freed the slaves. Lincoln was not yet prepared to take that step. Garibaldi declined.

I was excited to find that correspondence in the early 1960s, unreported at the time, and since widely discussed. I suppose that if I had been an eager PhD student I would have published an article on the Lincoln-Garibaldi exchange. Though I didn't really aspire to be a practicing historian, the perspective afforded by the study of history remained with me. At critical decision points I found myself stepping back and considering the historical context for relevant lessons.

Yale tested me not only academically but also emotionally. I had gone to Yale expecting it to challenge me, not because I wanted to escape Lakewood. My friends and family were back in Ohio, as was my girlfriend, Nancy—to whom I wrote devoted letters almost daily.

I was at a loss socially in the all-male and very preppy environment. I didn't see how I was going to fit in. This was a time when—as my friend and fellow Yalie Daniel Horowitz points out in his excellent history of that era, *On the Cusp: The Yale College Class of 1960 and a World on the Verge of Change*— there were Jewish and Catholic quotas (they probably had me down as one of the Catholics), and a handful of fraternities largely dominated the social scene. I wasn't a big drinker, so I didn't fit in with the fraternity crowd. I was a fish out of water.

I knew my roommate Bob was unhappy, but it was still a sad moment when, at the end of the exams in January, he announced he was leaving. The night before he left campus, we drove across the state line to a New York beer hall where we could all get served what we called "low beer" (it had a reduced alcohol content). I drank too much, smoked a cheap cigar, and was sick as a dog. To this day I have no idea how I got home. It was one of those nights when someone must have been watching over me. It would not be the last time.

Feeling out of place, with my girlfriend hundreds of miles away, I would often occupy myself by wandering the campus. One day I explored the Payne Whitney Gymnasium—the imposing gothic building known on campus as the Cathedral of Sweat. It seemed a magical place, a hive of activity where guys were engaged in every sport imaginable. I walked all the way up to the eighth floor, then started down, looking in on each floor. On the seventh floor I saw fellows rowing a boat with water rushing past them. The boat was fixed, and the coach could mechanically adjust the water to rush more quickly or slowly, forcing the rowers to adjust. I had never seen anything like it.

A few floors further down I happened upon a group of guys lunging back and forth, pressing up against the wall, backing off quickly, and then lunging again. As I was standing there, a small man—perhaps five-foot-three—approached me and asked if I had ever fenced.

"What do you mean?"

He took that as a no and handed me a foil. "Now lunge," he said. I stood there. "Go ahead," he said, "lunge."

"Lunge?"

He demonstrated. Then I did it a couple of times.

"Okay," he said. "Now do it twenty-five times."

So I did. Part of me was wondering why I was even listening to him, but I lunged anyway.

"Come back tomorrow," he said. "We'll do it fifty times."

That's how I joined the fencing team at Yale. I fenced for a couple of years, and, in my senior year, I managed the team. Though I did very little actual competitive fencing, it helped get me through my early years at Yale.

In my isolation, I gravitated toward what was most familiar—namely the gathering of the Methodist Youth Fellowship (MYF) held every Sunday night at a church across the street from campus. Doug Cook, a balding, good-natured man who seemed always on the brink of catching a cold, ran the program. With his encouragement I became an active member.

Eventually Doug asked me to represent Yale in the New England Methodist Movement. I agreed and soon found myself going to Boston for meetings. By the end of my sophomore year, I was president of the New England chapter and a participant in national meetings. My involvement increased during my junior year, and, as a senior, I was elected president of the National Methodist Student Movement (NMSM).

I may have campaigned a little to become president, but I don't recall doing much. Just as Gary Strong and Jim Hegenbarth had been my sidekicks in TPO, I had two friends who were my wingmen, responsible for pulling me up through the ranks. One was David Hagans from Ohio State, and the other was Dave Crocker from DePauw in Indiana. David Hagans went on to be an artistic event planner and theater guy. I was best man at his wedding. Years later, I was one of the first people he told he was getting a divorce because he was gay. And I was at his wedding when he got married a second time, to his partner of thirty-five years. The second Dave—Dave Crocker—married a woman from Wooster, Ohio, named Edna Dix, or Edie. Her family owned a string of Ohio newspapers. Dave went on to get his PhD in philosophy and had a distinguished career at Colorado State University in Fort Collins. The two Daves were the ones who encouraged me. "Come on, Dick," they'd say, and give me a nudge.

I was encouraged by the NMSM staff as well. In particular, Dorothy Nyland from the national staff in Nashville had a long history of mentoring young leaders. I was one of "her boys." She remained in touch with me well past her ninetieth birthday, sending me postcards when I became "her Governor" from the independent-living facility in Columbus where she had retired.

During my teenage years my connection with Methodism had been bound up with the kinds of questions everyone asks themselves when they're fifteen or sixteen: Who am I? What do I stand for? Where am I headed? How do I fit into this world? A faith context gave me a personal grounding. In college that engagement matured and became a way of addressing issues of social justice, an aspect of my intellectual growth that comes across strongly in the articles I wrote at the time for *Concern*. The Methodist Student Movement was an important experience, not just because it made me less lonely; it became the window through which I began to glimpse a wider world, a perspective that would be crucial in coming years when I began my academic work on Africa.

Though I consider myself a religious person, I never ran on a religious platform as a candidate. Despite Tony Calabrese's quip in the 1974 primary—"Celeste, he ain't Italian, he's a Methodist"—I never made my religious affiliation a prominent part of my campaigns.

When Dagmar and I married, we agreed to raise our children in the Catholic faith. Consequently, from the time we got married until our divorce, I had little involvement with the Methodist church. Instead I would go with Dagmar and the children to whatever Catholic church we chose as our home parish at the time. I figured God doesn't get confused about Catholicism and Methodism; maybe we do, but God doesn't. Sometimes on the campaign trail

I would joke that, while I wasn't a Catholic, I had more Catholic children than any of my opponents.

That said, my faith was—and continues to be—an informing presence in my life.

By senior year I had become more involved socially on campus than I realized, something that only dawned on me when I was invited to join a secret society—two, actually. By the time "tap night" rolled around, I had been talking for some time to the members of a so-called underground society known as Spade and Grave. The first person to talk to me was Phil Ritterbush. Now deceased, Phil was a nerdy young man who had been selected a Rhodes Scholar. He sat me down and said that he belonged to Spade and Grave and he thought I would find its members interesting. Phil introduced me to Zack Hall, whom I already knew from the Methodist student movement—Zack went on on to head up the medical school at the University of California at San Francisco—and Victor Kovner, whom I liked enormously and who became a very close friend. These were engaging and respected individuals. So, after some thought, I agreed to join the society.

When tap night arrived, however, I was surprised to find myself asked a second time. This time by Skull and Bones.

Back then tap night was a much-anticipated event at Yale—men in black suits dispersed themselves throughout the campus, each standing poised next to a dormitory door, waiting for eight o'clock. As the bells in Harkness Tower struck eight, they banged on doors, entered, and "tapped" the juniors who had been selected for membership in Skull and Bones or other societies. Which is what happened to me. Eight o'clock arrived, and, the next thing I knew, a fellow charged into my room.

"Celeste?" he said.

I nodded.

"Skull and Bones," he said, touching me—this was the "tap"—on the shoulder. "Do you accept?"

I said, "No."

He looked at me, startled. He stood there, apparently waiting for me to change my mind. I had already made a commitment to Spade and Grave. He went to the window and threw it open. "NOOOOOOOO," he shouted, and hurried out of the room, shaking his head.

The next morning my father called from Cleveland. "What did you do last night?" he asked.

"What do you mean?" I said.

"I just got a call," he told me, "from somebody who said you threw your life away last night."

I didn't know what to say. "Threw my life away?"

"That's what he said," my father told me. "What'd you do?"

I told him. "They tapped me for Skull and Bones."

There was a silence on the other end of the line. "What'd you say?"

I told him I had turned them down.

"What?" he said.

"I told them no," I said.

He let out his breath. "Why?"

"Because I had another commitment," I said, and told him about Spade and Grave.

He understood immediately. It was a lesson he had drilled into me: when you make a commitment, you honor it. That conviction would sometimes cause problems for him. In more than one of his real estate deals that went sour, his partners bailed. But Dad did not, which is why he was on the receiving end of foreclosure notices. Honoring a commitment was one of his cardinal rules. When you made a commitment, you stuck to it, no matter the cost.

Each summer I returned to Lakewood to spend time with friends and family. And, importantly, to earn some money for the next school year. Starting the summer before I headed off to Yale until my senior year, I found myself working at grueling jobs alongside men who were a sharp contrast to my fellow Yalies. For two years I picked up garbage for the City of Lakewood, a summer employment opportunity for a number of kids who had just finished high school. The pay was good, the work was hard, and there was a camaraderie among the young "garbage collectors."

The truck I worked on for two summers began its route at 5:00 A.M. The men I worked with were either Slovak or Polish, men who had immigrated to the United States after the Soviet Union cast its shadow over their countries in the late 1940s. These fellows were hard-working, tough, and determined, proud of their heritage and their families. They initially looked at the kid assigned to their team as a burden, soft and slow at the job. But as we spent time together and as I learned how to manage the variety of challenges—wet garbage that weighed more than one man could manage, places that were notorious for rotting cans, and the like—and match their pace on the job, we grew close. Going out for beer and a shot at the Slovak Civic Club on Fridays after work was a far cry from a table down at Mory's in New Haven.

At the end of my first summer, the guys on my truck gave me a present, a leather briefcase along with the admonition to study hard and not get distracted by girls. I could not bear to tell them that Yale was an all-male place. They might have asked me to return the briefcase.

After two years collecting garbage I moved down in the world, joining a sewer construction company to become a ditch digger. My boss was Joe Kalill, who had started in the ditch himself as an immigrant from Lebanon. Eventually he saved enough money to buy some equipment and start his own firm. Joe could not read or write English; his wife, Ann, was the company's bookkeeper.

I reported for the first day of work on a street named Lark, where I had earlier picked up garbage. That morning Joe had sixteen tons of sand dumped in the street next to the ditch that already had the new sewer pipe laid down. He handed me a shovel, pointed to the sand, and said: "Dickie, put it in the ditch." I wanted to ask him why he hadn't backed the truck up another four feet and dumped the sand in directly. But I realized this was my test—my Wild Bill Emerson of sewer construction. For the next eight hours I shoveled as blisters grew on top of the blisters that appeared on my hands, and I silently cursed my boss. But all the sand was in the ditch.

At the end of the day as I trudged to the bus stop, Joe pulled up in his big, black Cadillac and asked me to get in. I wanted to refuse, but I was so tired I dropped into the seat. As I did, Joe reached over and put something in my sweaty pocket.

"What is this?" I asked.

"Tickets for the Indians game," he said.

"I can't go to a game," I grunted. "I am going home, taking a shower, and going to bed."

Joe laughed and said: "Not tonight, Dicky. Friday night."

For two summers I worked with Joe's crew. His nephews ran the heavy equipment, and I worked alongside the Black guys who handled the ditch. I was paired with a man called Blaise whose uncle, also named Joe, had worked for Kalill for forty years. The two Joes were like brothers. Blaise was one of the strongest men I have ever known, and he'd handle the jackhammer when the shale we were busting seemed more like steel plate. On weekends Blaise sang in his church choir.

More than once during my summers I pondered the dramatic differences between the grown men I worked alongside and the young men who shared my classrooms and dorm. I came to appreciate the spirit of these men who welcomed hard work, took enormous pride in family, and judged me only on whether I carried my share of the job's demands.

Years later my summer experiences would inform my enthusiasm for the diverse character of my constituents across Ohio.

In the fall of 1958—the beginning of my senior year—I was asked by the National Methodist Student Movement to testify on legislation that would end the draft. While based in Nashville, we also maintained a Washington office to pursue our social justice activism there.

Though from the distance of almost fifty years student opposition to the draft seems almost conventional—like a flower-festooned Volkswagen van—it wasn't then. This was 1958; the Korean War had come to an end, and Vietnam not yet had entered our consciousness. The continuation of the draft seemed a carryover from World War II, and therefore unnecessary. That was the substance of my testimony. Mine was the only student voice the committee would hear.

I was excited to be testifying before actual congressmen who were making serious decisions. But the proceeding proved to be anticlimactic. The hearing was in the afternoon; only a few members attended. I found myself speaking to mostly empty chairs.

As I gathered my papers and was walking out, a woman stopped me. I recall her looking a little out of place, dressed deliberately—almost pointedly—plainly. She wore no makeup, no fingernail polish, and her hairstyle looked straight out of a *Life* magazine from the thirties. She looked the part of a typical New England matriarch. "Excuse me," she said, as I made my way out of the hearing room. "May I have a word with you?"

I said of course.

She looked me over carefully. "Allow me to say, I'm really astonished that a student from Yale would testify on this legislation."

"Well," I said, "here I am."

She continued to size me up. Evidently this was not a sufficient explanation, and I went on to explain I was there representing Methodist students and not Yalies.

"Let me introduce myself," she said. "My name is Steb Bowles. You really need to meet my husband."

"Your husband?"

"Chet Bowles," she said. "He's a congressman from Connecticut," she said. "And he's got a vote on this bill."

That was the first I heard of Chester Bowles, a man who would, in the years to come, have a profound impact on my life. But I had no way of knowing that at the time. I replied by saying that I'd be pleased to meet her husband,

"Do you know my son?' she asked. "Sam?'

I said I didn't.

"He's a junior at Yale," she said. "You should really get to know him."

"I'll look him up," I promised.

As I turned to go, she asked me my name one last time. "Dick Celeste," she said, slowly, as if committing it to memory. "I'm going to mention you to my husband."

She was as good as her word.

I kept my part of the promise. When I got back to New Haven, I looked up Sam Bowles. It turned out we had a number of things in common: we were both interested in international affairs and were both decidedly liberal. I was pleased to find a kindred spirit on campus.

At the time I was still figuring out the contours of my own political perspective. I was writing columns for *Concern,* and that helped me express—as much to myself as to anyone who read my articles—my worldview. While I was out of step with the views of most of my fellow Yalies, I didn't consider the positions I took in print and elsewhere as being especially liberal. I saw them simply as expressions of my personal faith and common sense. To a large degree I still feel that way.

Sam Bowles, on the other hand, had a firm grasp of both who he was and what he stood for. He was a brilliant economics student committed to changing the world. He would go on, eventually, after being denied tenure at Harvard, to become part of the so-called radical package of economics professors at the University of Massachusetts. When I met him, he was a junior, excelling academically and active on campus, a founding member of the Yale Russian Chorus, which was preparing for a tour of the Soviet Union. Sam and I quickly became friends, and he introduced me to Ralph Bryant, another economics student. Born into a prominent Quaker family, Bryant had a strong connection to political activism through his faith tradition.

In the spring of my senior year, the three of us were sitting on the grass during an open-air concert, and Sam described how he had been driving home—Chet and Steb lived about thirty miles from campus in Essex, Connecticut—when he observed a billboard that he thought grimly ironic.

"It scared you to death?" said Ralph. "It must have been some billboard."

"What did it say?" I asked.

"It said, 'Sleep well. Your National Guard Is Awake,'" Sam said. "It kept me awake the whole night."

We cracked up. The idea that the National Guard being awake would help anyone sleep seemed ridiculous in the nuclear age. "Most people don't appreciate the irony," said Sam. "They *are* reassured when they see that. As if the National Guard can do anything. What are they going to do in a nuclear war?"

Our laughter led into an extended discussion.

What *would* help people sleep? More important, what would wake them up? As we talked about it, the more Sam's billboard seemed to be pointing us in the direction of a central problem facing our generation. The establishment had it backwards: the issue wasn't to help people sleep—it was to wake them up. But how? Here we were on this celebrated campus, studying with some of the most brilliant minds anywhere, relaxing on the grass, and listening to music. There had to be more.

After the concert, the three of us went to George and Harry's—a now defunct hamburger joint that was then a fixture on campus—and began talking about how we might *challenge* the campus. How might we make our fellow students aware of what was *really* going on in the world? And right there—literally on the back of a napkin—we started sketching out plans. "Why not *call* it *Challenge?*" one of us asked. "Why not devote a semester to the challenges our generation faces?"

It poured out of us after that. The challenge of the Nuclear Age. The challenge of American democracy. The challenge of economic and social injustice. There would be a series of lectures and debates, but there would also be a central event. Artists would perform. Maybe Pablo Casals would come, suggested Ralph, who was himself a gifted cellist. Casals was a peacenik and would understand the urgency of what we wanted to accomplish. It was worth a try, we agreed. Our goal was high-profile speakers who would provoke meaningful discussion among the students, the kind of conversations *everyone* should be having if only they were not asleep.

When we left, we took our napkin scribblings with us, and the idea seemed to pick up steam. We recruited other students, often driving several carloads to the Bowles family home on weekends, where we would sit around singing folk songs and union anthems while planning Challenge.

From the beginning we were loosely organized and had no money. We realized early that if we had women involved, Yale men would be more likely to participate, so we recruited several women who were grad students. There was "Corky" Marcus—she would later marry Ralph—and her classmate Liz

Aaronson. With no formal structure in place, the effort evolved in an organic, spontaneous way. We were creating a movement from scratch. The questions became, what could we get done in the next few months, and what would the following year look like?

We still needed money. Eventually we found our way to one or two alums who donated. But our first big break came when Sam identified a prize—called the Hatch Prize—that was awarded to a Yale senior considered likely to devote his life to building a more peaceful world. It was a thousand dollars. Sam and Ralph approached me to say they believed I could win the prize. They'd nominate me, and, if I won, I'd give the money to Challenge.

"Do you know how much I owe the bookstore?" I said.

Sam and Ralph looked at me. "Okay," said Ralph. "You can pay the bookstore."

It was a good compromise. I won, paid off the bookstore, and gave the rest to Challenge. That was our seed money. We were off and running.

As my senior year began, I was chosen to participate in the newly established Scholar of the House program, which meant that, instead of taking classes, I would research and write a senior thesis in African history. We were twelve students selected on our promise as scholars. Richard Posner—the distinguished jurist and prolific writer—was one; another was Marshall Blonsky, a kid admitted to Yale when he was fifteen who would go on to become a foundational figure in the newly emerging discipline of semiotics. We gathered every other week—I'm not certain I always attended—and one of us would present a portion of what we were working on.

The freedom from classes allowed me to spend most of my time somewhere other than on campus, often in New York for research at the United Nations or Washington, DC, on behalf of the Methodist Student Movement. I had developed a keen interest in Africa, the focus of my senior thesis. Looking back, it seems clear I did not really engage as deeply as I might have with the other scholars, an enormously talented group of people. In retrospect, I frankly lacked their level of intellectual confidence and sophistication.

With the benefit of sixty years hindsight, the senior thesis I wrote at Yale now looks naive. In it, I posited that the development of Africa depended mostly on its ability to function on a pan-African basis, that regional and continent-wide interests would draw these newly independent nations together. I did not foresee the intense struggles these countries would face in sustaining democracy or the extent to which colonial legacies and tribal differences would test the stability of fledgling nations. Growing up in the United States, focused primarily on American history, I didn't have a context for thinking historically about different—sometimes radically different— parts of the world.

There were serious obstacles to African unity that I foresaw and described in the thesis, but I understood those as having to do with the distinctions between countries ruled by different colonial powers rather than more deep- seated and enduring tribal divisions within Africa.

Over the course of the year, I had presented three chapters to my fellow scholars for critical comments and had most of my thesis written. But it was far from complete. In the spring of 1959, I got excited about Challenge, had applied for a Rhodes Scholarship (and was not selected), and won a Carnegie Teaching Fellowship, which meant that I'd be back at Yale the following year to do graduate work and teach.

As the last days of my senior year approached, I figured I'd sort of finesse the thesis. I'd get my diploma, with the understanding that I'd submit my finished thesis by the end of the summer. I hoped Yale wasn't going to be too hard on me since they had already hired me for the next fall. I had a contract with them, after all.

Then, on a Thursday just a few days before the thesis was due, Professor Leonard Kreiger, my thesis advisor, called to say he'd like to read the completed thesis before I handed it in. I had until the following Monday morning to get it to him. I couldn't bring myself to tell him that it was not finished. Scrapping my planned finesse, I told him that I would deliver the thesis as requested.

I had the body of paper written but not the conclusion or the introduc- tion. Certainly not the critical bibliography. But none of it was typed. I ex- plained to three of my close friends that I was in trouble. They offered to help. So Gary Burgard organized a team that included himself, Pete Magee, and Kenny Baer. We needed a place with several typewriters to put the thesis in final form.

I approached Danny Horowitz, a friend who was from New Haven, fig- uring that if anyone knew a place to find a bunch of typewriters, it would be Danny. Sure enough, Danny was able to help. His cousin, Larry Botwinik, had a factory on the edge of town. "We can use the office at Botwinik Broth- ers," he said. Dan recalled this episode decades later in *On the Cusp*, his ex- cellent account of Yale during that time.

At the factory office each of my pals began typing finished chapters as I struggled to decipher and place footnotes. We worked Friday afternoon, then through Friday night. By Saturday morning I was getting drowsy. Pete Magee gave me a pill. "It's Dexamyl," he told me. "It'll give you a boost of energy."

I soon became jumpy as hell. I couldn't keep my pen on the paper. The pill turned out to be uncut Dexedrine. Well, I sure didn't sleep, but I also couldn't write. With my pals typing away, I asked Liz Aaronsohn, my Challenge friend, for a hand. I told her I would dictate my conclusion to her. "Please write it down," I said.

"Why don't you write it down yourself?" she said.

"Because I can't hold a pen," I said, and held out my shaking hands for her to see.

So Liz copied my words down, triple-spaced, and handed back the five or six pages to revise, which I did—over and over—until my revisions were completely unintelligible. "Wait a minute," she said. "This isn't going to work. You're going to have to *tell* me what the revisions are." So together we produced the conclusion of my thesis.

Later Saturday evening there was a knock at the Botwinik door. The police had spotted lights on in the office and come to investigate. I hid in the john, worried that I was so jumpy they would assume that something was wrong with me. Gary and the others explained that they were helping a fellow student finish a thesis. The police called Danny and departed, satisfied we weren't burglars.

The last effort was to tie up several incomplete footnotes. I had collected my references in a shoebox, written the bibliographic details on scrap paper, the backs of matchbooks, even napkins. My team had been working to insert them properly. Two incomplete references, which I had not properly recorded, had stymied them. One was an article entitled "A New Constitution for Kenya," which I proceeded to attribute to L. Botwinik. The other—I don't remember the article now—but the author was cited as Kenneth Gary Magee. Each of my coconspirators, members of the team and our landlord, were memorialized in my thesis.

The thesis was complete and submitted as promised at 8:15 on Monday morning.

The readers gave the thesis good marks. Then—as part of the Scholar of the House program—I had to defend it in front of the three faculty members who had read it. Once we had talked about the thesis, they were going to question me more broadly about diplomacy and international relations—the field I was in. About halfway through our session, one of the professors asked me what I thought of the L. Botwinik citation.

My heart sank.

"Let me ask you a question," he said. "Do you think that analysis is really solid?" He was asking me about the article itself; not the author. Relieved, I told him why I agreed with Botwinik's observation.

Incidentally, later in this oral exam, I flubbed a question about India badly. As it happened, I would have a chance to learn a lot more about India in the years that followed.

I had my first grown-up sexual experience during my senior year. I was visiting my roommate, who lived in Boston, and he asked me if I would be willing to take his cousin for a double date. When I asked him what she was like, he said, hesitantly, "nice."

She turned out to be lovely. One of my favorite artists is Modigliani, and Nancy looked like she had stepped out of one of his paintings: tall, slender, with beautiful dark hair. When we were introduced, I learned that she was enrolled in the Boston Museum School's jewelry program.

We hit it off immediately. She drove an MGB and was not shy about her sensuality. During that first weekend, we spent a great deal of time together. As I departed, she urged me to look her up whenever I was back in Boston. So I did, and we saw each other a couple of times, always finding a good time together.

On one visit she asked me to stay at her home. Her family lived in a lovely old New England home that had two stairways—the main stairway for everyone to use and a low-ceilinged back staircase that had been designed for servants.

When I arrived, I met Nancy's parents, and she showed me to the downstairs guest bedroom. We kissed lightly, and, as I was putting my bag down, she said that she wanted me to come upstairs that night.

That night I crept up the back stairs as slowly and silently as I could. I knew that the stairs were going to squeak—it was an old house—but, as I climbed, the squeaking seemed impossibly loud. I imagined myself encountering her father on the stairs and having to concoct some story about not remembering where the toilet was. In my anticipation I had forgotten the low ceiling. Coming around the curve in the narrow staircase, I whacked my head on the door frame, nearly knocking myself out. I arrived at her room dazed as well as nervous.

Then Nancy gently educated me.

———

The year after graduation, I returned to New Haven as a teaching fellow. Challenge had become a reality. Ralph actually received a letter from Pablo Casals to read at our fall colloquium. We had divided the year into the "challenge of the nuclear age" in the fall and the "challenge of American democracy" in the spring. Our kickoff event during the first week of classes featured Norman Thomas, who had run as a Socialist for president, and Bill Buckley, conservative icon and Yale alum, debating why we needed nuclear weapons. The highlight of the semester was the colloquium, which lasted three days and brought together students from Yale and twenty or thirty other campuses, including many women. Carlos Romulo—the Philippine diplomat who was at the time president of the UN General Assembly—was one of our featured speakers.

Challenge was a glimpse of the sixties before the sixties. Our focus was on raising social consciousness among our fellow students. It was a remarkable time. Nothing seemed impossible. As an organization—a small group of young people determined to make something happen—we were completely anarchic. Challenge had no president, no one formally in charge. We had to designate a treasurer in order to open a bank account. We chose Danny Horowitz because his father was president of the local bank. We figured if his father ran the bank, Danny would have fewer problems with them—our idea of strategic organization.

Our trips to the Bowleses' place in Essex involved mostly singing songs and planning Challenge activities. But Sam, Ralph and I also talked a great deal about the future. We took the LSATs together. I decided to take another shot at the Rhodes, and Ralph applied as well. Sam applied to become a Fulbright Scholar in Nigeria.

As for Challenge, it was a big success. Four hundred students attended the fall colloquium. More than seven hundred attended in the spring—when we featured Thurgood Marshall, Bayard Ruskin, and Michael Harrington. It was a sort of teach-in, before there were teach-ins. And Yale students, without ever electing officers, sustained it for the next four or five years.

Looking back today from the perspective of a college president, I am struck by how spontaneous Challenge was and how little we knew about what we were doing. Student activism today is far more sophisticated and considerably more focused. By the time I became president of Colorado College, a student with a passion for environmental activism could lead an effort that actually put solar panels on the roof of a college residence hall. In addition to having a semester where students explore environmental issues, today's students start a campus garden. Beyond bringing in speakers to talk about the root causes of hunger and poverty, they arrange to take food left over in the dining halls to the local soup kitchen. I believe today's student activism is more effective, far more able to make change happen than was the case for us at Yale in 1959.

The political environment in which student activism takes place today is reminiscent of the sixties. In the sixties this country was at a boiling point over civil rights and the war in Vietnam. Today climate change, antiracism, and economic justice are galvanizing issues. Back then we sought to change the leadership of the country. While the vote for change is still important, today's students prefer to create a targeted nonprofit, build a socially responsible business, or mobilize a networked movement for change.

Challenge reminded me that volunteers need to be organized thoughtfully; they need specific responsibilities and recognition for the work they do. A good heart is important, but that alone won't get the job done. Challenge taught me how to recruit, deploy, motivate, and manage volunteers—a valuable lesson in years to come.

In addition, Challenge taught me that any activity—no matter how serious—also has to be fun. If you're not having fun, something's wrong. Challenge dealt in a serious way with vital topics, but the music and the party that followed the speeches and debates proved to be an essential part of the energy our colloquium generated. People came to hear Hubert Humphrey or Thurgood Marshall or Ayn Rand (that's right, Ayn Rand *was* one of our speakers). But after all the speakers and debates, a concert featuring Pete Seeger and Odetta really got people excited and eager for action.

A decade later, during my early campaigns, we would ask, "Are we having fun yet?" If we were not having fun together, we were missing something at a vital human level.

Even our T-shirts asked: Are We Having Fun Yet?

The first time I interviewed for a Rhodes Scholarship I was too tense to be sensitive to who was across the table from me. I did not make it past the state interviews. The second time, in 1959, I treated the process more casually but also more strategically. I had been encouraged to reapply by Prosser Gifford, a friend who had prompted me to apply the first time.

"Apply again?" I said.

"Think about it," he said. "A number of people get the Rhodes on their second attempt. You have finished your thesis, won a teaching prize. I'd give it another shot."

So I did.

I remember coming home from the cocktail party before the Ohio interviews and telling my parents I had met a future Rhodes Scholar. His name was Dennis Shaul, from Akron and Notre Dame, where he had been elected president of the student body as a junior. "He's amazing," I told them.

As it turned out, Dennis and I were both nominated from Ohio and went to Chicago for our regional interviews. I decided to find out what I could about the individuals who were going to be interviewing us—I learned that the representative from Kentucky was editor of the Louisville *Courier-Journal*; another owned a baseball team. Twelve of us gathered in Chicago to compete for four positions. The first candidate, a brilliant mathematician and almost certainly the smartest among all of us, went in. Forty-five minutes later he came out crying.

"What happened?" I asked.

"I don't know," he said, "the interview was going well, and then they asked me what I truly believed. I just didn't know how to answer. I froze up."

Shaul went in, and, after he came out, he said they asked him if being a Catholic and exercising academic freedom were compatible. Another question: "Do you believe in parades?"

Finally, it was my turn. The first question came from the newspaper editor. "Mr. Celeste, you're interested in politics and international matters. Wasn't it Plato who said that no one under thirty-five should be permitted to have a voice in public debate?"

I looked at him and said, "I don't know if Plato said it, but I can tell you why I disagree with that notion." Apparently, that endeared me to him. I got the scholarship on my second try. So did Dennis Shaul.

We were off to Oxford.

Chapter 3

Oxford

Just before I was due to leave for England, Peter Bergman, a Yale friend who had become active in Challenge and who lived on the east side of Cleveland, called: "Dick," he said, "I need your help."

"You need my help?"

"I've been trying to take out this Sarah Lawrence girl from Akron," he told me. "I've asked her three or four times, but she always turns me down. This time, when I asked if she wanted to go to the theater with me, she said, 'Maybe. But my college classmate is visiting and I've got to find a date for her.'"

"And you thought of me."

"Dick," he said. "Come on."

"Who's the girl?"

"I don't know anything about her," he said. "That's the truth."

I didn't know what to expect but told him fine. "I suppose," I said, "if it'll help you out."

"Thanks a ton," he said. "You won't have to pay for anything. We'll come get you at your house, no problem. It's all on me."

That Saturday he and the girls arrived to pick me up, and my blind date turned out to be absolutely beautiful—jet black hair, dark eyes, tan skin. I was taken with her before we'd exchanged a single word.

She introduced herself. "I'm Andrea Cousins."

We proceeded to have an incredible time, and at the end of the evening—I have no recollection of what play we saw—I asked if I could call her.

She said she'd like that.

That was how it started—with a blind date. We spoke frequently after that. I was getting ready to go to Oxford and volunteering on the Kennedy for

President campaign. This was September 1960, and the election was in full swing. I had attended the Democratic convention in Los Angeles with my father, who was then mayor of Lakewood, earlier that summer, and, though I was a firm Adlai Stevenson supporter, my father had been persuaded by Ohio's governor Mike DiSalle to back Kennedy. Once Kennedy won the nomination, I came on board.

In those days I had a motor scooter, and I decided to head east ahead of my departure for Oxford to say good-bye to friends at Yale and to sell the scooter. And, of course, to spend time with Andrea—now back at Sarah Lawrence. Andrea invited me to watch the first Nixon/Kennedy debate at her dorm. There was not a single Nixon supporter at Sarah Lawrence that night, and I have a dim recollection of Kennedy besting Nixon in the debate. The truth is I was focused on Andrea. By this time, I had realized that Andrea was the daughter of Norman Cousins, a highly regarded journalist, author, and peace activist. Maybe there would be a future for us, but it didn't seem likely.

I left the next day for New York, where my parents met me and wished me well on my journey. When I arrived at Exeter College, a postcard—a Modigliani painting—was waiting for me signed "love, Andrea." I sent her back a postcard, letting her know of my safe arrival.

I think a verse was included.

At Oxford I was never as focused on the academic side of things as I might have been. There was simply too much going on. Kennedy had been elected, and we celebrated. Early on, his administration found itself enmeshed in the failed Bay of Pigs invasion. This outraged many, including a group of us Rhodes Scholars, and we wrote a letter of protest and sent it off to Washington.

During a protest I attended in the fall of '61 put on by the Campaign for Nuclear Disarmament, I met Lydia Howard. She approached me with incredulity—not unlike the way that Steb Bowles had done—saying how surprised she was to find an American with such firm antinuclear convictions. Petite and attractive, with dark hair and dark eyes, she looked a little like Andrea Cousins, who was still very much on my mind. Lydia was vivacious and outspoken, and we were soon going to protests together. The New Left—both an intellectual and political movement—was gaining influence, and Lydia was part of it from the beginning. She was a strong, forthright, uncompromising woman.

While early on at Yale I had felt like a fish out of water and spent my first couple of years apart from the life of the campus, the opposite was true at Oxford, where I made friends easily. Most of my time was spent in political discussion—wrapped up in real-world concerns, ideological debates of the moment rather than academic study. In part, the fact that I was older than most of the students at my college—Exeter—contributed to the fullness of my social life. My five years in New Haven nurtured a poise and maturity that I sorely lacked when I arrived at Yale. The pervasive influence and romance attached to the Kennedy administration also didn't hurt. Many young Brits connected me as an American with the youth and energy of the president and his fresh-faced younger brother.

From an academic perspective I was still pretty much at sea after my first term, so I made an appointment with my advisor and described that I was basically covering the same ground as I had at Yale. I really wanted to focus on something that would move my academic career forward. At Oxford they offered a B-Phil program roughly equivalent to a US master's degree. Initially I was going to research the trade union movement in Ghana and made plans to visit there the summer of 1961. My particular interest in Ghana was due, at least in part, to the fact that I had become friends with a fellow Exeter College student named Kwamena Phillips. He had a relative in the Ghanaian High Commission in London who helped me make plans. It would be a chance to do the kind of firsthand study of the African situation that had seemed an impossibility at Yale.

Due to a complicated set of circumstances, I found myself alone—and lonely—in Paris for the Christmas holidays. One unexpected turn of events salvaged my holiday.

Danny Horowitz—cousin of the Botwinik brothers—had given me a contact for his parents, who were in Paris for the holidays, and encouraged me to give them a call. They were staying at the George V, one of the finest hotels in Paris. I told him I would try, though at the time I imagined myself having the sort of wild Christmas adventure that would leave little time for calling his parents. When no "wild adventure" materialized, I reconsidered.

Danny's folks were thrilled to hear from me and offered to pick me up and take me out to dinner. I didn't want them to see the seedy place where I was staying, so I said I'd make my way to their hotel. "As it turns out," said Danny's father, Bill, "we have another young friend joining us. We'd love you to meet her."

I went to the hotel that night in blue jeans, my shirt impossibly wrinkled. I had neither a jacket nor a tie, but the Horowitzes didn't seem to mind. They invited me in and introduced me to Marie Antoinette Robert. She was engaged to their friend, a journalist from Hartford, Connecticut, who had met her in Paris on assignment. He had returned to his job in the States. She expected to join him in a couple of months.

Danny's parents took us to a wonderful restaurant, Les Grenouilles, which turned out to be about ninety paces from my hotel. Miette, as she was called, and I hit it off right away.

After dinner, Danny's parents offered to drop me home, but I respectfully declined. Instead, we went back to their hotel, where I thanked them profusely. It had been a wonderful night. The food had been incomparable, we all got along famously, and Miette had, as we were saying goodnight, slipped me her phone number. "If you need someone to show you around Paris," she told me. "Give me a call."

The next day things brightened. I finally was able to get a phone call through to my parents and, buoyed by their voices, I decided to call Miette. She sounded genuinely pleased to hear from me and gave me directions to the metro stop near where she lived. I wanted to take her out for a meal but, having almost no money, offered coffee instead. After we walked around the park in her neighborhood, she asked if I was hungry. I'm not sure how exactly I managed to get it across that I had no money, but she offered dinner at her apartment.

While she was cooking, it began to rain like crazy outside. The dinner was simple but wonderful, and she produced a bottle of wine. As we ate, we watched the rain fall and talked.

A day later, I returned to Oxford, feeling my Christmas vacation had not been a complete disaster.

Not quite a month later I was invited to a march in London sponsored by the Campaign for Nuclear Disarmament protesting a planned Soviet Union nuclear test. A massive crowd gathered in Trafalgar Square. After a while the police demanded that we disperse.

Instead, we all sat down.

I found myself sitting next to Lydia Howard's aunt—a woman who had demonstrated countless times. As we sat there, she entertained me with stories of the many protests she had been at. Eventually the police began arresting people. When they reached us, they asked us to stand up. When we refused, they very politely—it was all most civil—carried us to the waiting van.

Hundreds of us got arrested that day. My fine was ten dollars. After a few hours in the police lockup, I signed a form and was on my way back to Oxford. Though I have not made a Freedom of Information Request, I suspect that the record of my arrest joined the envelope that contained our anti–Bay of Pigs letter as part of my FBI file.

I would do it again.

My plans to go to Ghana that summer fell through. When a general strike was called, Kwamena told me that his uncle in London had suggested it was not the best time for me to visit the country. It simply wasn't safe.

As a result, I decided to change my scholarly focus and again met with my advisor to discuss the possibility of studying the history of diplomatic relations in Africa. I had a fairly clear idea for my thesis. It was based on the Berlin Conference of 1884–85, where the colonial powers of Europe divided Africa. For a thesis advisor, the Exeter don suggested I talk to Prof. A. J. P. Taylor. "If that's what you're writing about," he told me, "you must speak to him."

A. J. P. Taylor was a legend in Britain at the time. Famously described by historian Richard Overy as "the Macauley of our age," Taylor was the author of the book *The Origins of the Second World War,* which began with his controversial Nuremberg Thesis arguing that the war had been the result of a criminal conspiracy put together by Hitler and a small group of close associates. Intractable, opinionated, banned several times by the BBC, Taylor had gained a wide popularity and influence through a television series during the war called *The World at War—Your Questions Answered.* Though of course I knew of him, I did not realize that his initial thesis had focused on the Berlin Conference of 1884–85. I called on him in the spring of 1961 and outlined my topic, telling him a little about the work I had done at Yale. He agreed to be my advisor.

As it turned out, that was the one and only time I saw him.

Looking back now, my lack of academic engagement at Oxford and with Taylor especially is perhaps the most significant missed opportunity of my life. I'm not quite sure how it happened. The Oxford system was opaque to me. I never fully engaged in the tutorial system. I needed a Wild Bill Emerson to tackle me early on and tell me specifically what to do. I sometimes wonder if Taylor would have turned me into an academic. Perhaps.

But missing the opportunity to work closely with a man who was one of the great minds of his time is a true regret.

For spring break, I asked Lydia if she wanted to share a ride to France on my new scooter. She gave me an enthusiastic yes and suggested that we travel south of Paris to the villa where her mother and father were spending a few months. Everything seemed set. Then the Berlin Crisis of 1961, a situation that escalated almost literally as Lydia and I took the ferry to France, cast its ominous shadow. We stopped in the first little town we came across for coffee and discovered everyone talking about the confrontation between Russian and American tanks in Berlin.

Lydia and I decided that this was it—the moment when the nuclear showdown was occurring. It could well be our last night. So, even though we'd had an argument, even though we were in a small town where we hadn't planned to be, we made up our minds to make the most of it.

The nuclear exchange, of course, did not occur. The two of us arrived, bleary-eyed and exhausted, at the villa where her parents were staying and had dinner with them. At the time Lydia's mother, Marghanita Laski—the prolific novelist and sometime panelist on *What's My Line?*—was working on words for the *Oxford English Dictionary*. In addition to refining definitions, she was in the process of collecting illustrative quotations, and the house was filled with books of all sorts. What I remember most clearly about that time is having my grammar corrected by Marghanita Laski, who leaned in and looked at me closely: "Do you say different from or different than?" she asked me. Then she waited eagerly to hear what I was going to say.

Lydia was staying with her parents, and I was headed south to Barcelona. As I got onto the highway, it was cold and rainy. A bad day to be on a Lambretta. Soaking wet and dirty, I ended up spending the night at a transport café in the south of France. The next day it was still cold and rainy, so I said to myself, if the sun comes out before I reach Barcelona that is where I'll stop. The sun came out some hours later when I was high above the coast north of Barcelona. Below me a little village—San Pol de Mar—huddled along the seaside. Without hesitation, I pulled into it.

What struck me was how quiet it was. It was late Sunday morning. No one was moving. I went to one small pension, then another, all closed. Then it dawned on me—I had arrived before the tourist season. Nothing was open. The more I explored the more worried I became, wondering whether I'd have to get back on my scooter. Finally, I happened upon a little place called Pensione De la Barca. It seemed empty too. As I looked in the window, beyond the chairs piled on top of tables, I spotted someone inside, and so I knocked.

I can't imagine how I must have looked—scruffy beard, soaked to my skin and covered in muddy road splash. I knew only elementary Spanish. A woman came out and said something to me which I didn't understand at first. When she repeated it, I realized she was asking if I was German. I told her no, American. Then she asked if I was a soldier. "No," I told her, "student."

She turned to her daughter standing behind her. I explained again that I needed a place to stay. The daughter somehow managed to communicate to me that they were closed, but that they would make an exception and prepare a room for me. It turned out to be beautiful with pristine sheets and a pile of towels. I must have spent an hour in the shower scrapping all the grime off.

When I came downstairs for the midday meal, I found that they had set up a small table for me. At the back of the restaurant the whole family was gathered for Sunday dinner around a massive table. I sat down to soup as they were talking and laughing at their table. Apparently prodded by the daughter, they soon invited me to join them. I proceeded to have one of the most memorable meals of my life.

It happened to be the Sunday before Palm Sunday, the Feast of St. Joseph, and every male in my host family—five in all—was named Giuseppe. This was their "feast" day—and a feast it was.

After the soup they brought out paella—delicious paella—and, thinking that this was the main course, I must have had three helpings. They were laughing at me. Then to my surprise equally delicious roast lamb and vegetables followed. After the lamb came salad. And wine throughout. Finally, they served a flan and Benedictine—the herbal liqueur invented by Alexandre Le Grande in the nineteenth century. This was not just any Benedictine, this was the real thing, distilled at the Benedictine monastery nearby.

We sat there for at least two hours, eating and toasting Giuseppes.

As the meal came to an end, they asked if I wanted to go to the movies later that afternoon. I said sure but I needed to take a nap first.

I woke up at eight o'clock—the next morning.

I stayed at Pensione de la Barca for another week. The big event during my stay was the football match between Barcelona and their arch rivals, Real Madrid. The folks at the Pension told me that, if I wanted to watch the match, I had to go to the neighborhood bar, which was the only place able to get the TV signal. There I was nursing a drink, waiting for kickoff and watching *Rin Tin Tin* dubbed into Spanish. Finally, at game time, a dour-faced announcer appeared, saying that, due to technical difficulties, they would not be able to televise the match.

Chaos ensued. The Barcelona fans were sure the "technical difficulties" were intentional.

As I walked back to my place, I could hear radios being turned on one after another. By the time I got back, the match was everywhere, coming from every direction, the cheers, the play-by-play in the most vivid stereo I had ever heard.

Barcelona won 1–o! Olé!

———

In the early spring of 1962, I met Dagmar Braun at a birthday party for my Australian roommate, Michael Smyth. Coming from a play rehearsal, I arrived late. In her memoir, Dagmar claims it was my birthday, but that was not the case. No matter what else might be said about me, I would not be late for my own birthday. Up the street from our apartment was the Oxford Language Academy, which attracted young men and women from around Europe and beyond who wanted to pass the Cambridge language exam for English. Mike was dating a girl who went to the Language Academy, and, apparently, she and some of her friends decided to have a surprise birthday for him. I came home from the rehearsal—I had recently been cast in a campus production of Turgenev's *A Month in the Country*—and I went around introducing myself to these women I had not met before. One of them was Dagmar.

Beautiful, with intense eyes and an intriguing accent, Dagmar exuded both innocence and a kind of worldly charm. She glommed onto me despite, I later learned, being engaged to a Hungarian fellow named Lajos. In order to delay the marriage, her father had offered to send her to the Language Academy for a year. He had offered to send her anywhere, so long as she delayed the wedding, in the hope that she might put off marriage entirely and instead go to law school in Vienna. Her fiancé had been active in the Hungarian Uprising in 1956, and that impressed me immensely.

We spent the rest of the party talking. I invited her to tea the next day—I thought it a very sophisticated thing to do—though I learned later that she felt it was forward, a kind of cheeky come-on. We talked over tea for maybe two hours. I suspect I did most of the talking since her English wasn't that good. I suspect that flattered me.

At that moment I was still keenly interested in Andrea Cousins, with whom I had continued to correspond. She was now spending her junior year in Paris, which I considered exactly the right place for a romantic like her. She also had a serious boyfriend, Peter, at Harvard. She had always been frank about Peter, which I understood was her way of putting a boundary on our relationship. Still, while we had not spent a lot of time together, we wrote each other often and affectionately.

There was something very strong between us, and looking back at her letters—I've kept many—this is plain. Andrea: "These words coming through your fingers are like music from the hands of a pianist. How long have you played the pen?"

I write back: "Since I was fourteen and could speak."

Later I ask, "Do I make life more hard than soft for you?"

She replies, "It is never soft, but life in love is bearable. If anything is hard for me, it is the simplest sort of self-restraint."

Another note: "Funny thing," she writes, "to be so in love with you, and for it to be so new, each time I see you."

My plan was to travel to Paris for spring break and see what happened when we were actually in the same room together. I began making plans that involved me going to Paris with my college mate Ian Capps, see Andrea, and then go from there to Florence. Overhearing us talking about the trip, Gina Thal—the girl who had introduced Dagmar and me at my roommate's party—began talking about how she wished she had seen Paris. Gina, from Venezuela, was sixteen at the time. When I learned that she was getting ready to return to South America, I expressed my disbelief that she could go home without seeing France.

"My mother would never let me go," was Gina's response. "I would need a chaperone."

"Find someone to go with you, and come with us," I offered. "Surely your mother will be okay with that."

Dagmar volunteered to be the chaperone.

Our plans changed. It would be Ian and me, Dagmar and Gina. The two girls would be going to see Paris. I was going to see Andrea. A week before we were to leave, however, Gina told us her mother would not let her go. I assumed that Dagmar was going to cancel as well. But she didn't.

So the three of us went to Paris.

I had not told Andrea that Dagmar was coming, figuring she and Gina would be off on their own. But with Gina out of the picture, I had no choice but to show up at Andrea's place with Dagmar in tow.

Andrea seemed almost jealous. That struck me as odd: in the first place I had no commitment to Dagmar, and in the second place Andrea had never suggested there was any sort of exclusivity between us. We ended up having an awkward three days, with Andrea letting me know that she would like to have some time alone with me and, at the same time, Dagmar being intent on all of us hanging out together.

Eventually it came time for me to take off with another pal, Jack McNees, driving to Florence. I suggested to Dagmar, without really thinking about the implications, that, since we were traveling through Switzerland, she could come with us, take the train to Vienna from there, and save a little money.

We left Paris in the Morris Minor convertible Mike Smythe and I bought together. We had the top down the whole way. It was a beautiful, sunny spring day, and Dagmar and McNees were deep in conversation about Nietzsche in German.

When we dropped Dagmar at the train station in Zurich the next day, I said, again on impulse, "If you want to meet me in Florence, we can drive back to Oxford together."

She said she'd like that. Without a more specific plan, we said good-bye. Neither of us gave a thought to what was required to meet up at an unfamiliar train station in Italy. We just set a date and went our separate ways.

A week later I found the platform where the train from Vienna was arriving and stood there watching the passengers get off. No Dagmar.

That's that, I figured. Fine.

I stopped for a cup of coffee at a café in the station, and, as I sat there, another train pulled in. The last person disembarking was Dagmar. It turned out that the train from Vienna had split at some point—half went through Milan while the other went through Padua—and by the time one train got to Florence, it had become two different trains.

If I hadn't stopped for coffee, we would never have connected.

We stayed in Florence for a day or two and then started driving back to Oxford through the French countryside. It was a magical time. Dagmar was brilliant and beautiful. Though her English was halting, it was good enough that she could understand everything. We slept together in the same bed. But all we did was sleep, nothing more. When we got back to England, we drove off the ferry and almost immediately got a flat tire. I changed it with difficulty in a heavy downpour. We arrived at the flat in Oxford with me soaked to the skin and filthy, covered in grease and grime. When Dagmar and I opened my apartment door, to my surprise, Andrea was waiting inside.

In Paris I had told Andrea that there was nothing going on between Dagmar and me—trying to let her know that she was the one I was interested in—so she decided to find out for herself. She was clearly upset, and I didn't know what to do. Sensing a crisis, my roommate Michael offered his bed—the only proper bed in the apartment—so the two girls could sleep in it. I crashed on the couch in the living room, where I usually slept. I told myself we would sort things out in the morning. Around midnight, someone was tapping on me. It was Andrea.

"Dagmar sent me here," she said.

I was confused.

"Dagmar said that I have right of first refusal," Andrea whispered. And stood there, looking at me.

"Andrea," I told her, "I'm too tired to do anything about this right now."
Slowly, she went back to the bedroom.

Things were over between us. I had rejected her, or so she thought, and there was no coming back from that.

As life would have it, I did get to see Andrea years later. Her nephew attended Colorado College while I was president, and she visited a couple of times. It was strange to see her after so long, to think about how my life might have been different if I'd invited her onto the sofa that night with me. Would she have remained engaged to Peter? Would I still have married Dagmar?

As it turned out, Andrea never married. Andrea was and is a remarkably bright and lovely human being. She earned two doctorates, one in philology and one in psychology, and has practiced mostly in and around Boston.

Was ours a near miss? Of this I am certain: none of the other women in my youth grabbed and held my affection the way Andrea did.

When Andrea returned to Paris, Dagmar and I began to get serious about each other. A plan slowly took shape to get married a year hence. I would return home after my second year at Oxford and then—after a year or so—we would get married. I had decided to return to Yale to pursue an MAT degree. I knew people who had graduated from the program, and it seemed like a practical direction to take. Then, if I chose, I could return to Oxford to work on the thesis for my B-Phil.

Though Dagmar and I had talked about marriage, about family, and about what we wanted out of life, I didn't want to rush into anything. We had known each other for perhaps four or five months by then. We were very young and had no idea what the future might hold.

Then one day at *A Month in the Country* rehearsal, I was pulled out to take an urgent call from Dagmar. She asked me to come to the police station. I told her I would come right away.

I arrived to find that she had been accused of theft. Money had been taken from another student's purse. Apparently there had been a series of thefts at the school and so they planted marked bills in a student's purse, which had allegedly been found in Dagmar's handbag. I was the only person she knew who had any "standing." You had to be a local property owner to be able to bail somebody out. As a student at Oxford, I was accorded an equivalent status.

After the accusation, Dagmar was dismissed from the language school. She came to stay briefly with Michael and me. Her mother soon came to Oxford, and I found them a place with friends. Her father's advice was to enter a guilty plea and get the hell home, but Dagmar refused and maintained her innocence.

One of my fellow actors—David Aukin, who would later go on to produce *Four Weddings and a Funeral*—suggested that we talk to his father, a leading member of the legal community in London. Though his father couldn't take the case, he gave us the names of lawyers who'd be willing to take it on pro bono since none of us had any money. He also advised Dagmar how to get started. Write down everything exactly as it happened, he told her. But also understand that, if you do go to trial, there is a chance you will be convicted. Probably, he went on, because it is a first offense, you are likely to get off with a fine. But you will also be sent home and not be allowed to return to England.

I was still working—or at least dabbling at work—on my thesis, traveling to and from London, making notes on the Berlin conference. Mostly, though, my time was spent learning lines for my role in *A Month in the Country*. We had a great cast and won excellent reviews. I was a so-so actor, but theater was never a career that I thought about pursuing. It was fun for me and nothing more. After the play I planned to return to the States and become a high school teacher.

Then two things happened that changed my plans.

First, our production of *A Month in the Country* was invited back for a summer appearance. This was a singular honor; each year the Oxford Theater would invite one student production for a two-week run during its professional season in late July or early August.

Second, Dagmar's trial was slated for late July. I decided that I would stay in Oxford and return to the States at the end of the summer. It felt like it was meant to be, as if fate had intervened in order to make sure we stayed together. The more we talked about it, the more it seemed to make sense to get married that summer. Why postpone marriage for a year, we said to each other, if we are here now?

The play's director, an American named Michael Rudman—who would go on to become a celebrated director in British theater—had a touch with the press, and he promoted a front-page story in the *Oxford Mail*, "a fairy tale couple," they called us. The story did not mention that Dagmar was going to stand trial.

When Dagmar did go to court, she was well represented. It turned out that, after she had been kicked out of school, another theft had occurred. The prosecutor did not tell us this, but we knew from Dagmar's friends at the school. It became a crucial piece of evidence. Additionally, the woman whose money was stolen was mean-spirited. When she testified, she came across as quite nasty. Dagmar, on the other hand, came across as thoughtful and kind. The jury quickly acquitted her.

The notion that I would marry Dagmar was distressing to my father. He expressed his opposition quietly in letters, but I later learned from my brother that, from the moment I wrote that we planned to get married in August until the wedding took place, he would leave the room at the mention of my name.

Why did I get married so quickly and not wait the year as we'd originally planned? It's a question I still ask myself.

Nevertheless, in mid-August I packed my things in Oxford and went to Vienna. Dagmar had warned me that her father—Vati—would try to put me off. He did. His pitch was that everyone would be better off if we waited, that there was nothing we wouldn't be able to do better the following year. This suggestion was not a surprise. After all, it had worked once. But Dagmar wouldn't hear of it. She was resisting him, it seemed. Just as I was resisting my father.

Thus, I found myself in late August 1962 exchanging vows in a strange land in a language I didn't understand. Not a single member of my family was present. I was marrying a woman I loved—there was no question in my mind that I loved her—but without having really thought about what it truly meant.

It has struck me on more than one occasion that perhaps the most fateful action of my life was largely the product of circumstance and, especially, isolation.

Dagmar was a devout Catholic, had experienced the war, had an especially complicated relationship with her father, all of which made her seem like an unlikely person for me to marry. It was an accident of the stars, the fact that we dated during this very intense time of crisis for her and when I was at a crossroads myself, not at all sure of what direction I was heading or who I was going to turn out to be. Our relationship seemed fated from the sight of her in April alighting on that train platform in Florence after I had given up on her. Wasn't the play being invited to reprise in July in Oxford another sign?

Looking back at one's life, some choices, those turning points when you may have taken a different direction, can seem less and less inevitable. What would have happened if I had not married so young? As I reflect on that impetuous and lonely act, I believe two impulses were at work. The first, I was keeping a commitment—as my father had taught me. I had promised Dagmar that I would see her through her crisis.

At the same time, I was asserting my independence.

To most people, of course—to our friends in Oxford and my castmates—our marriage did look like a fairy tale. The reality was quite different. The day after the wedding in Durnstein, with no car and little money, Dagmar carried her bridal gown and roses, and we stuck our thumbs out to hitchhike back to Vienna.

As we stood by the side of the road waiting for someone to give us a lift into the future—into the rest of our lives—we had no idea what was in store for us. There was no way to tell that Dagmar would be the best—and the most difficult—woman for me to marry. She would push me to be the best that I could be. But she would also leave me empty in ways that it would take me years to understand.

I was a good provider. I took care of the house and balanced the budget. In her memoir, Dagmar recollects my sitting at the kitchen table, head in hands, trying to figure out where the money was going to come from. We usually had just enough to get by, often through the generosity of our parents. I tried to be a good father. I set aside Sundays as family days and did my best to be present when our children needed me. We have incredible kids—accomplished and loving. But, through most of my years in public service, they knew the most dependable way to reach me was through my secretary.

In the final analysis, Dagmar and I achieved a great deal, both as a public couple and as husband and wife.

Was there something missing in our marriage from early on?

There was.

Do I own a major share of what was missing in the marriage?

Absolutely.

How does one add up the blessings that amount to a life? There is a part of me that wants to stack them up and measure them. In my case there is certainly an abundance of blessings.

Alongside these blessings I ask myself, what is there to regret?

Well, for one, that I was unfaithful.

Not knowing what the future held or even whether a car would stop for us, we had no way of knowing that there was a lift waiting for us just around the corner.

In less than a year, Dagmar and I would set off on a journey that would change our lives forever.

Chapter 4

India

When I got home from Oxford in the summer of 1963, I planned to enter the Yale MAT program. After a brief visit to Lakewood to introduce Dagmar to my parents and siblings—who were still getting used to the idea that I was married—we left for New Haven.

If things had gone differently that fall, I might have ended up a high school teacher. In my mind, education impacted, and was influenced by, the political process. I had come to the conclusion that the way to build a durable constituency for change was from the bottom up; education, as much as politics, can drive community action and renewal.

But teaching—a move toward a less public, more contemplative way of life—was a road not taken. This direction had an allure for me then and tugs at me still. It may sound strange, coming as it does from a person who has spent most of his life in one kind of fishbowl or another, but it is true. There has always been a part of me that has wanted to hang back—to be the campaign manager rather than the candidate. To sit back and observe the crowd rather than have to wade through it asking one person after another for support. This desire to carve out a private space never left me, even as the life I led became increasingly public.

Being back at Yale felt familiar. But married life in New Haven was anything but idyllic. We had very little money and were living in a rundown apartment in a questionable part of town. Dagmar had talked her way into a job shelving German language books at the Yale Library, and I was working part-time for the City of New Haven along with my studies. We were scraping by, though we told ourselves it was only temporary. Once I had my MAT, I figured I would find a real job.

One day in early October Dagmar told me she needed to see a doctor. Her breasts, she said, were feeling strange. Something was wrong. Could it be serious? We ended up in the office of Dr. Silvio Conte. She went in to be examined. Twenty minutes later the doctor came out with a big smile on his face.

"Well," said Dr. Conte, "she's pregnant."

"Pregnant?" I said, flabbergasted. "She came in for a breast examination."

He shook my hand. "And, based on my examination, your wife is built to have children."

Dr. Conte would turn out to be exactly right.

Not long after that news I got a call from Sally Bowles, Sam's sister. While I had been in Oxford, her father's political fortunes had been mixed. He had been appointed undersecretary of state by President Kennedy in 1961 but was summarily replaced in early December—part of a cabinet reshuffle that became known as the "Thanksgiving Day Massacre"—after Bowles's opposition to the Bay of Pigs invasion had been leaked. Bowles had been given the title of president's special representative for African, Asian, and Latin American affairs and ambassador at large, a hastily fabricated position meant to temper the shock of his removal from the undersecretary position. Sally Bowles was working for Sarge Shriver at the newly formed Peace Corps. She knew me and my work in Challenge and was calling to urge me to apply for a job.

"Dick," Sally told me on phone, "the Peace Corps needs bodies. Come to Washington, see how it goes."

Her call was timely. Going to school didn't seem like what I should be doing with a baby on the way. More than that was a chance to become a small part of Kennedy's Washington—the New Frontier, the future. I told Sally I'd come. During the interview, a position in the Division of Volunteer Support as a liaison for volunteers going to Latin America was suggested.

"You speak a little Spanish, don't you?" asked the interviewer.

"*Very* little," I told him. "I've never been south of the border."

He thought about it for a second but not much longer. "You'll pick the language up," he told me, "and as for the rest of it, we'll brief you." I was offered the job.

When I returned to New Haven I told Dagmar about the offer.

"What do you think?" I said. "We'd have to move, and there'd be traveling involved with the position. But it's a great opportunity—and we'd get health insurance to cover the cost of having the baby."

I don't want to say that sealed the deal, but it didn't hurt.

The basement apartment we moved into on Capitol Hill was better than our New Haven place, but not by much. Our landlord was Ben Bradlee, who was then beginning his tenure as executive editor of the *Washington Post*. The area around 504 D St. S. E. was very different from the gentrified place it is today. One night there was a shooting a few blocks away, and while my sister, Pat, visited, we killed a rat on our doorstep.

It wasn't safe for Dagmar to be alone when I was out of town, so she'd often stay with Chet and Steb Bowles, who lived on N Street in Georgetown. Sally was living in their carriage house at the time, and it was a lively place. Because Dagmar was so often there, she became something of a fixture in the Bowles household, attending dinner parties and other functions with Chet and Steb.

After I returned from one of my training trips, Dagmar told me about a dinner she'd gone to with the Bowleses, hosted by Drew Pearson, the syndicated journalist best known for his column "The Washington Merry-Go Round." At dinner Dagmar had found herself sitting next to an older gentleman with whom she got into a spirited discussion. It wasn't unpleasant, she said, but it was clear the two had not seen eye to eye.

"Who was it?" I asked.

"Who was who?" she asked me back.

"This man you were arguing with."

"It wasn't an argument," she said. "It was a discussion."

Dagmar told me a little more about this "discussion"; it sounded like it had turned into a bit of a debate. "Do you remember his name?"

"Chief Judge something or other."

"*Chief Judge* something or other?"

"I can't remember the last name," she told me.

"What did he look like?"

She thought about it. "Round face," she said, "white hair."

"Chief Justice Warren?" I asked.

"That's him," she said, without blinking.

She had no idea who he was.

"He is the chief justice of the United States Supreme Court," I said. "You got into an argument with *him?*"

"A discussion," she insisted.

I called Chet later, saying I hoped that Dagmar hadn't been too much of an embarrassment. Dagmar was—and still is—outspoken, and, back then, when she was still finding her way around the English language, she would say things in English—her vocabulary could be very raw—that she never would in German. There was no telling what she might have said to Chief Justice Warren.

"Don't worry," said Bowles. The chief justice had sent him a note the next day saying it had been a delight to sit next to such an opinionated and charming young woman.

"People," wrote Warren, "so rarely tell me what they really think about anything these days. She was a refreshing change."

Though I knew Chet from my trips to Essex with Sam, I do not recall ever having a one-on-one discussion with him until after I began working at the Peace Corps. But even in Washington, Bowles saw more of Dagmar than me, which is why it came as such a surprise when he invited me to lunch at the State Department.

I walked into his office to find a beautiful small table—white linen tablecloth, napkins, and silverware gleaming—set for just the two of us. A waiter stood by ready to pour tea and lemonade. Chet shook my hand and thanked me for coming. We sat down and began talking about the Peace Corps, politics, foreign policy, and how I found working for his daughter. Finally, he got around to the reason he had wanted to talk to me.

"Nothing has been announced," he said, "but President Kennedy has asked me to return to India as ambassador."

I congratulated him.

He gave a very short nod of acknowledgment. "I think Jack really just wants to get me out of town," he said, "but India is an important post, particularly at this moment, and Steb and I would welcome the chance to go back." He paused. "All the same, I've told the president that I'll only consider it if he agrees to certain conditions." He retrieved a letter from his desk and handed it to me. "I've spelled out those conditions in writing."

I tried to keep my wits about me. I was twenty-five, and this was a personal letter to the president of the United States. The history major inside of me couldn't believe it: I held in my hands a piece of paper that would soon be part of the historical record. I scanned it quickly and saw that it soon dispensed with formalities in order to detail the challenges and opportunities of the position. Most crucially it underscored the need for the ambassador to have direct access to the president. If Bowles was going to serve as ambassador, the letter stipulated, he would need a discrete channel of communication with the Oval Office.

"What do you think?" he asked me.

It was a lot to process. I mumbled a few things. (What, exactly, I mumbled will never be part of *any* historical record.)

"Assuming the president responds positively," said Bowles, "Steb and I will be going out in June. I would like you to consider coming out as my personal assistant."

I didn't know what to say. This was completely out of the blue.

"Don't give me an answer right away," he said. "You have a lot of things to think about. Dagmar's pregnant, and you need to discuss it with her. I think you both would enjoy India, and I need a young person to handle my schedule and correspondence, to help out writing speeches and organizing my travel. There are a variety of things, and we can get into more detail if you're interested. But let me say, I think you'd do an outstanding job." Bowles waited for me to reply, and, when I didn't, he went on. "Ask Dagmar to talk to Steb. She can give her a clear idea about life in India and what it's like to raise a family there. We had three of our kids with us in the fifties when I was Truman's ambassador, and they loved it. Cynthia's written a book about it, you know, and you might look at that as well."

I got home to find Dagmar eager to hear what the meeting had been about.

"You are not going to believe this." I told her about Bowles wanting to bring us to India with him.

"What did you tell him?"

I said I'd have to think about it and that the idea was simply overwhelming. "I *think* I know where India is," I said and went to the atlas to make sure. One memory came back to me as I did—the question about India at Yale during my orals, the one question I'd fumbled. Dagmar and I talked about it for perhaps two hours. As it turned out, I was the only one uncertain about taking the job.

"When would we leave?" asked Dagmar.

After the baby was born, I told her. "But we'd have to get there—or at least I would—fairly quickly afterwards."

"Look," Dagmar told me, "I moved to this country from Austria, then to New Haven, then Washington. Moving is not a problem. Not for me."

I called Bowles the next day. When he picked up the phone, there was something in his voice—I think he was worried I was calling back too quickly—and he pointed out that neither of us had talked to Steb.

"Okay, we will talk to her," I said, "but the answer is yes."

———

Before I could be appointed to the diplomatic service, I needed an FBI clearance. This was standard procedure and, in most cases, would have been nothing but a formality. It wasn't quite so for me. Apparently, I had earned my own file as result of the letter I'd signed with some of my fellow Rhodes Scholars protesting the Bay of Pigs. My arrest in London at the antiwar demonstration was likely part of it, too. On an early morning in May 1963, I presented myself at the State Department for my interview.

"Tell me about these radical students at Oxford," began the interviewer, flipping through the file.

"What radical students?" I asked.

"The students who were upset over President Kennedy and the Bay of Pigs," he said. "The ones who signed your letter."

"It wasn't my letter. We all agreed, and we all wrote the letter. Isn't it an American right to be able to speak your mind, even criticize the president?"

He couldn't disagree with that but let me know he was not letting me off the hook. "Do you know any Communists?" he asked next.

I told him, "As a matter of fact, I do."

"You do?"

I told him about Jack, the porter at my college at Oxford. He had been the secretary of the Oxford City Communist Party.

"How well do you know him?"

I thought about it. "We would talk almost every day."

He couldn't believe what he was hearing. "Really?" he said, adding to his note. "Every day?"

"I'd give him a copy of the *International Herald Tribune,* and he'd give me a copy of the *Daily Worker.* Then we'd argue about them."

"Have you stayed in touch with him?"

I told him no, I had not been in contact with him since leaving Oxford.

"Would you say you had a personal relationship with him?"

"We had a daily back-and-forth; that was it."

He made another note. Then he asked: "Have you ever had a homosexual experience?"

"I don't know," I said.

"You don't know?"

"I might have."

"I beg your pardon," he said, blinking. "You might have?"

"I'll describe it to you," I said, and told him that, when I was president of the National Student Methodist Movement, I had been the student leader at a citizenship seminar in New York and DC. I shared a hotel room with a minister who had come along to oversee the seminar. I had woken up in the middle of the night to find him sitting on the side of my bed, patting my shoulder.

I was startled, and he was dismayed. When he realized I wasn't interested, he apologized, and that was that. We both went back to sleep.

"Was that a homosexual experience?" I asked my interviewer.

"What did you do?"

"I didn't do anything," I said. "I wasn't interested."

"You didn't move to another room?" he asked. "It didn't bother you?"

"It didn't bother me as long as he didn't get into bed with me."

"What's his name?"

I wasn't going to give the FBI his name, and I said so. "You asked me if I had a homosexual experience. This is the closest I can come."

"Let me ask you a different question," said the interviewer. "What's the name of that guy wrote that book, *Tropic of* . . ."

"*Cancer,*" I said, filling in his blank.

"That's it," he said.

"Henry Miller," I said.

"Have you read it?"

I told him I hadn't. "But I've heard of it."

"What do you think about it?" he wanted to know.

"I can't really think about it," I said, "if I haven't read it."

He looked at me closely. "Do you think it should be sold in bookstores in the United States?"

I said I didn't see why not. "Nobody is required to buy a book."

"Do you know what's in this book?" he asked me.

I reminded him I hadn't read it.

This is how it went for forty minutes or so. I was frank and open. Completely honest. This was the advice I had been given, to not omit anything they might discover later and think it suspicious because I had not disclosed it.

The FBI stalled on my clearance.

A few days later Chet and Steb were getting ready to depart for India, and, as his personal assistant, I was taking care of many of the details surrounding their move. Dagmar and I were at their house for a farewell dinner, and Chet asked if everything was set for our departure. I said it was, although I was a bit concerned that I hadn't received my security clearance—and entertained them with the story of my interview.

"Don't you remember Eleanor Roosevelt's policy?" Steb asked when she'd finished laughing. Eleanor said, "When I'm asked to fill out those security clearance forms, I *only* put down the seditious stuff."

We had a good laugh about this. The next day Chet picked up the phone and secured my clearance, vouching for me personally.

In preparation for the baby's arrival, Dagmar and I had decided to go to Lamaze classes. We went every other week to the Washington Hospital Center. Another Peace Corps guy—senior to me, though not a whole lot older—named Charlie Peters was in the same Lamaze class with his wife. Dagmar's due date was June 15. It came and went. No baby. Charlie and Beth welcomed their son.

We were getting more and more anxious. We were packing for our move to India.

We tried to relax about it. On June 21 I took Dagmar out for a glass of wine at a bar at the top of a hotel overlooking the White House. Nothing. We came home, walked around the block twice—finally contractions began in earnest.

We drove straight to the Washington Hospital Center. Fifteen hours later Eric Celeste arrived. With a smile on his face.

As soon as we could, Dagmar, Eric, and I flew to Cleveland and introduced my parents to their first grandchild. As ambivalent as my father had been about my decision to marry Dagmar, his reserve disappeared—mostly anyway—with the arrival of his grandson. Leaving Dagmar in Cleveland, I returned to Washington for a couple of days and then flew to India to take up my new position with Ambassador Bowles. Eric, at two weeks old, was at that time the youngest person ever to have been issued a diplomatic passport. Shortly thereafter Dagmar and Eric flew to Vienna to stay with her parents for a couple of months.

I landed in Delhi in the late afternoon of July 6, 1963. A driver took me from the airport to the Bowles residence. Steb asked if I would be interested in going to a recital with her that night. I said of course. After dinner we were driven to a lavish home not far from the embassy where perhaps forty people were sitting on cushions, many nodding and some murmuring. At the front of the room on a slightly elevated platform a solitary figure sat tuning what appeared to be a large, misshapen guitar. Forty minutes later the guy with the guitar-like instrument was still tuning, adjusting, then adjusting again the pegs on the head of the instrument, tipping his ear every so often in the direction of the vibrating strings as if listening closely.

Steb appeared to be having a great time, but I was getting impatient. Who takes forty minutes to tune an instrument? It turned out, of course, that he wasn't tuning—this *was* the concert. I had never seen a sitar before and knew nothing about the instrument's movable frets or its microtonal range. I had listened to my first raga.

I clearly had a lot to learn about India.

My focus, initially, was on the ambassador and the inner workings of the embassy, most particularly on understanding my responsibilities and how to work effectively with Bowles. Though very much a public figure, Chet made it a priority to retain a modicum of privacy. When he and Steb hosted people for dinner, invariably around 9:30 he would excuse himself. That meant writing in his journal, ending nearly every day with a half hour—often longer—of reflective writing.

He encouraged me to do the same, and though I never developed his discipline, I did give it a try when I arrived in India. I still have that journal—an imposing volume: rectilinear, hardcover, green, the words "Federal Supply Service" embossed on its front cover. On the flyleaf of the first page I'd written my name, underneath it, New Delhi, India. The first entry is October 31, 1963. I had been in India for a few months and had been joined by Dagmar and Eric. I am in in a reflective mood:

"Now is an especially important time in my life for I must finally reach a vocational decision; I must continue to build the framework for a stable and satisfying family life; and I must learn as much as I can from my unusual opportunity of living and working here in India with CB. This record, then, should serve as an exercise in self-awareness and self-discipline as well as a chronicle of public and private events."

Though I don't say so in the journal, it's possible that my future was so much on my mind because I had suffered several health issues—a bout of dysentery and an attack of acute appendicitis.

The latter was treated at New Delhi's Holy Family Hospital. After an emergency operation I woke up and found myself looking at a nurse. "Thank you for a beautiful sample," she told me.

"A beautiful sample?"

"Your appendix was so close to bursting," she said, "we got it in the nick of time."

That was India. Never knowing what was coming next and always anticipating the unexpected. I was quickly getting used to a new boss and a new environment—both the Foreign Service and New Delhi. I was also getting the hang of the job—handling everything personal for Bowles, even his bank account. I would sign his checks with his blessing. Somewhere there were four years of checks with my "Chester Bowles" signature on them.

Bowles was particularly impressive for his sense of history. It informed everything he did. Most people think in terms of two or four years; Chet would think in decades and beyond. This was crucial in India where the time scale is dramatically different than in the United States. Though, as an American, Chet was often impatient to make things happen, he also believed that over time people of goodwill could solve nearly any problem. It distressed him when we couldn't stop the fighting in Vietnam or resolve the differences that made the relationship between India and Pakistan so contentious. A side effect, perhaps, of keeping focused on big-picture issues and the sweep of history was that he could forget the little things. When he would come out of his office on his way to the foreign ministry, his secretary Helen Marina would look him over carefully.

"Mr. Ambassador," she would often say, stopping him.

Chet would discreetly zip up his fly.

Along with Chet's correspondence and the projects he wanted me to track, one of my responsibilities was the ambassador's schedule, particularly his social schedule, which he didn't want to think about. This meant I supervised the social secretary at the embassy, conversing on a daily basis with a young woman named Bimla—or Bim—Nanda.

Bim was the eldest of three daughters, who all had earned master's degrees from the University of Michigan. When Bim came back to India, she had married—an arranged marriage to a man who turned out to be abusive. Bim would not put up with it—which was unusual in India in the 1960s. Even more unusual, her parents welcomed her back home and supported her decision to divorce.

Bim's father, Dr. Nanda, was then the veterinary general of India. As a young man he had been the world table tennis champion. I knew him as an elegant, gentle human being. The dynamo in the Nanda family was his wife, Sita, who had survived the devastating Queta earthquake in prepartition India. Though she lacked the formal education of her daughters, Mama was one of the shrewdest, smartest, most decent individuals I have ever met. She managed her household—just as she managed the family's finances—with an acuity and wisdom that was hard to match.

When I first arrived in India, I went to the Nanda house almost every night. Dagmar had not yet arrived, and I was living in a barely furnished apartment in the embassy compound. Bim would invite me to her family home in Defence Colony, promising that her mother would feed me and her father would send me home later in a car. Consequently, most nights I'd find myself eating dinner on the *barsati*—the garden-like space atop their home—with a number of other young foreigners, reporters for the *New York Times* and the *Baltimore Sun*, a Fulbright Scholar or two, artists who were visiting. It was a kind of salon, and it became my second home during my first few months in India.

A month before Dagmar was to arrive, Meena, Bim's youngest sister, took me aside and told me she was getting married.

"Is it an arranged marriage?" I asked.

"Of course," she said.

"Meena," I said, "you have a BA, you have an MA, you have a thriving business"—the three sisters had started a preschool in Delhi called Playhouse School that had become the place to send your kids if you were a mover or shaker in Delhi—"and you're letting your parents decide who you're going to marry?"

"Well," she said, "Daddy's getting old, and he wants to know I'm taken care of. And besides, it's time—I am twenty-five, after all."

"So," I said, "who are you marrying?"

"A man named Rajbir Singh."

"Do you know him?" I asked.

"I've seen him," she said. "He was a couple of years ahead of me at college."

"What do you think of him?"

She shrugged. "He was very popular," she said. "A good singer, a scratch golfer, a nice man."

"Meena," I said, "how can you let your parents choose who you're going to marry?"

"Dick," she said, "Mama and Daddy have been married for more than forty years. They know far more about marriage than I do. My parents love me, and they would never do anything—knowingly—to hurt me. Why shouldn't I trust them to make a good decision?"

Dagmar arrived a few nights before Meena's wedding, and her first impression of India was this incredible Punjabi celebration—a joyous explosion of singing, drumming, dancing, and drinking—along with wedding vows. The very next day Ambassador Bowles called me. He was at home and asked me to come over immediately.

"Of course," I said. "Do I need to bring anything?"

"No," he said, "No, just bring Dagmar and get over here right away."

We got to their home as quickly as we could.

When we arrived, we found Bim there along with a young American named John Bissell, as well as a Hindu priest. A small fire had been built on the ambassador's back verandah.

Bim and John were getting married. The only witnesses were Chet and Steb and Dagmar and me. It turned out John's father was a dear friend of Chet's and had asked them to stand in for the family. John had spent two years quietly waiting for Meena to find someone to marry because he knew that in India a divorced daughter could not remarry until her sisters had their husbands. It was an intimate introduction to the curious mix of tradition and change that characterized India, the striking way in which two opposite ways of thinking and being in the world could exist side by side, apparently without contradiction.

The three Nanda girls are like sisters to me now. My Indian family.

In addition to Bessie Louis, I have had only two true mentors. The first was my father, and the second was Chester Bowles, who believed strongly in young people, trusted them with serious responsibilities, and inspired them to carry out those responsibilities creatively and effectively. A deeply serious person, Chet would often tell stories that were meant to be instructive. One early story was about a personal assistant of his—two or three assistants before me—who Bowles had asked about his correspondence, because it had dropped off precipitously for no apparent reason.

"Charlie," Bowles asked the man, "how are we doing?"

"Doing fine," came the reply. "Just fine."

Bowles took him at his word, but then, a couple of weeks later, he happened to be in the office late one evening and needed a pair of scissors. He went to the nearest desk—Charlie's—and began opening drawers. What he found instead of scissors was a drawer filled—packed, literally—with unopened letters.

Charlie had been unwilling to admit that he couldn't keep up. Bowles cautioned me never to let that happen. "If I'm asking too much, you tell me," he said. "If you're falling behind, you tell me."

Bowles shared another story related to his narrow reelection loss for governor in 1950. It wasn't a presidential year, which meant that generating momentum was difficult. But he had also made the mistake of alienating a key democratic constituency.

My Indian family. *Front row:* Mama, Padma, and Bim. *Back row:* RFC and Meena.

"How did you do that?" I asked him.

"When we were adopting our budget," he said, "we put a tax on mixed drinks served in bars. Only after the election did I realize that over 90 percent of the bartenders in the state of Connecticut are good Irish Democrats—and they were really upset. Their grumbling probably cost me the close election."

The lesson: pay attention to choices you make; they have consequences, sometimes unexpected, down the line. More than a decade later, I ignored this lesson—and paid a price.

The most memorable piece of advice came as I was assisting him in crafting a message to President Johnson. I don't remember what the message was about, but I do remember him stopping and looking at me closely. "Dick, do you have a traffic signal?"

"A traffic signal?" I asked.

"Right in here," he said, pointing to his midsection, "each of us needs to have a green light and a red light, because there will be times when you're confronted with a decision and you don't have time to seek advice or ask for a set of options. Your signal has to flash green or red. I'm curious, Dick, do you have that kind of traffic signal? Because you're going to need it."

Over the course of my life, I have come to know that traffic signal very well.

Many years later, for instance, when I arrived on campus as president of Colorado College to find myself in the midst of a post-9/11 decision to allow a controversial Palestinian speaker on campus, campus security informed me that the Colorado Springs police wanted to post snipers on the roof of Armstrong Hall so they could get a clear view of the quad where demonstrations and counterdemonstrations were planned. "They want to put snipers on the roof," I was told, "to keep people safe."

I didn't have to ask anyone—my traffic signal flashed bright red.

The answer was absolutely "no." "You do not invite folks with guns—even police officers—onto a college campus. Period."

To be an effective leader—Bowles's central lesson—you must develop a set of values and a level of self-awareness that enables you, when required, to make a critical decision quickly. Your "signal" flashes.

Much has been written in recent years on the power and the accuracy of gut judgment—the insight that arrives in the blink of an eye—but this wasn't what Bowles had in mind. His traffic signal refers to values that you have cultivated and that inform your decision-making process at a fundamental level. It is crucial to have that traffic signal in place because as a leader you will face circumstances when you do not have the time to deliberate, gather more facts, or consult subject-matter experts. You must make the decision yourself. And it's not simply a matter of making the call—it is making the call and *owning* it. Bowles's traffic signal wasn't a reflex; it was a process of honing one's values so that you are ready to handle real events.

Of course, often your traffic signal is going to flash yellow, telling you to take some time, that there's more you can find out. But you cannot go through life—and you certainly cannot lead—always on the caution light.

Another lesson that had a direct impact on what followed my four years in India I learned from Chester Bowles's example. It didn't come from a story but from simply watching him in action. This was the importance of being able to speak to businesspeople in their own language.

This became evident to me when one of the annual Henry Luce/*Time* magazine tours—designed for a small group of carefully selected CEOs and business leaders—stopped in India. Taking two weeks to travel around the world, they would visit with ambassadors along the way. Chuck Percy, then CEO of the Bell and Howell Corporation (and later senator from Illinois), led the delegation that stopped in New Delhi.

As Bowles's personal assistant I was responsible for the logistics of the visit and had ample opportunity to observe the way that Bowles addressed the group. What struck me was how, instead of using bureaucratic or political terms, Bowles explained the relationship between the United States and India in a business context.

"Look," he told the CEOs, "we have a substantial investment here. Let's talk about the significance of India. You have made a serious investment with our USAID work, you have made a serious investment with Food for Peace—and Food for Peace provides a return on that investment. Not only are American farmers being supported . . ."

He spoke to them in their own language.

I was impressed. Few of these business leaders were Democrats; in fact, nearly all were Republicans. At that time, few had a nuanced perspective on international relations. I watched Chet walk them through the business case for what we were doing in India. The response was overwhelmingly positive, and many commented that his presentation had been much clearer than any of their earlier briefings. These leaders were not impressed by how often the ambassador saw the prime minister or how much he relished social protocol. Instead, they responded to language that connected our national interests in India to a return on the investments we were making there.

A few years later, preparing to leave India, I told Bowles that I was going home to work for my father in the family business. It would provide an income, but it would also provide a practical understanding of the world of business that Bowles exemplified. "If I'm going to go into politics," I told him. "I have to know how to engage the business community."

Bowles disagreed. "You're ready," he told me. "Go straight into politics."

As successful as he was in the business world—Bowles had built an advertising empire before entering politics—he came to feel that business was a waste of time. He couldn't recognize how much his business experience informed his public service.

Bowles was disappointed at my decision not to enter politics directly upon my return from India. But even my delay was a result of his mentorship. In this case, his actions spoke louder than his words.

This lesson remains relevant for young people entering politics today. Democrats in particular need to understand business culture and how people in business make decisions. Many individuals who enter politics—from both sides of the aisle—have little business experience. As a result, they are ill-prepared to weigh actions—on taxes or regulations, for example—that impact business and the economy. And they often become overly deferential when pressed by business leaders.

The eight years that I spent working with my father in real estate would prove to be invaluable in the years that followed.

An unexpected lesson from Chester Bowles.

Another of Bowles's protégés in India was Doug Bennet, who would go on to be president of National Public Radio and president of Wesleyan University. Doug and his wife, Susie, had arrived a little before me and were living in a small house in the diplomatic enclave. During our first year in India, both Susie and Dagmar became pregnant, and Susie delivered Michael—later the US senator from Colorado—two months before Dagmar delivered Christopher, our second son. Because we already had Eric—he was not quite two years old at the time—we were "experts" in the field of child rearing. We became coaches for Doug and Susie and would babysit for them when they needed it; they, in turn, would babysit for us.

One of our shared responsibilities was drafting articles and speeches for the ambassador. A major project for us shortly after we settled in behind our desks was to help Chet with a series of lectures at the University of Delhi. He was looking for a way to discreetly address the economic development challenges facing India in the mid-1960s. In the decade since Bowles had first served as ambassador to India, a more formal and protective coterie formed around Prime Minister Nehru. Lacking the personal access to the prime minister that had marked his earlier stint shortly after Independence, Bowles wanted to convey his thoughts in a friendly public forum.

An invitation to speak at Delhi University provided the forum to do so. He delivered a series of four lectures: "Five Essentials in Nation Building"; "Dynamics of Rural Development"; "Industrial Growth with Social Justice"; and "China and India—Problems and Prospects." Doug and I devoted weeks of hard work—research, outlining, gathering preliminary thoughts from Chet, drafting and redrafting—that resulted in a thoughtful and engaging lecture series. In order to broaden the reach of Bowles's observations, our information service published the lectures as a book, *The Makings of a Just Society*.

In his introduction to the book, C. D. Deshmukh, vice-chancellor of Delhi University, wrote of Bowles, "As U. S. Ambassador to India both at the beginning and the end of a critical decade of economic growth he has served not only his own country but India as an adviser and friend."

Deshmukh continued: "In (this) series of lectures Mr Bowles raised questions of immediate as well as long term importance. It is my hope that the issues raised by Mr Bowles in this book will stimulate as much discussion among his readers as they did among those who were privileged to hear him." Much of Bowles's thinking, especially the relationship of social justice to economic development, would influence my own policy perspective as I became involved in politics.

Doug's academic training had been in Russian history, and, from time to time, he would meet young Russian Foreign Service officers, most of whom would, sooner or later, try to tempt him into some kind of transgression. The Russians were always cultivating Americans, looking for possible recruitment. Doug spoke Russian, which seemed to make him a prime target.

"Doug," a Russian Foreign Service Officer would say, "I can get you any kind of woman that you would be wanting."

"You don't like the women" would be next. "You like the men? We can get the men too."

Doug was never receptive.

That was the Cold War in India in the early sixties.

I found myself faced with a temptation of my own when Dagmar's mother arrived from Vienna with her friend Gerti Grobauer—Schlange was her nickname—to stay with us.

About five years older than me, Schlange was a striking, voluptuous woman who had been recently divorced. I remember her sitting by the pool in the embassy compound shortly after we met and the look she gave me—the sort of look that made you think anything might be possible.

She was hard to resist.

I sensed that she was interested.

When Dagmar's mother was preparing to return to Vienna, Schlange decided to stay on with us a little longer. Dorli—Dagmar's mother—found that suspicious, and, just before leaving, accused Schlange of trying to seduce me.

I maintained she was imagining things. Of course she wasn't. Once Dorli left, I began slipping into Schlange's room in the middle of the night after Dagmar and Eric had gone to sleep. Dagmar had no idea.

There I was, less than two years into my marriage, betraying my wife with her mother's friend. Did I feel guilty? Yes. Did it stop me? No.

Sadly, it was just the beginning.

Much later in my life, when Dagmar and I were in the throes of our divorce, we talked about my infidelity.

"When did this begin?" she asked me.

I told her the truth. It began with Schlange.

———

In November 1963 I was in the process of planning for the arrival of Pete See-ger, the legendary folk singer. At the time Dagmar and I were living in a big house in Defense Colony, some distance from the embassy. It was our first real home together, much larger than anything we would be able to afford stateside. As newlyweds, living in India allowed us to feel far more estab-lished than we actually were.

One of my core duties as Bowles's personal assistant was to take charge of the schedule for visitors who were important to Steb—like Duke Ellington, Pete Seeger, those sorts of people—and use their presence to put on pro-grams that would appeal to Indians.

My routine in those days was to wake up early and skim the morning pa-pers. I would go through the seven or eight English-language papers quickly, noting anything that should be called to the attention of the ambassador. I was up especially early on November 23—it was Dagmar's birthday—and found the papers face down on our doorstep. After arranging birthday cards around Dagmar's place at the breakfast table, I turned over one of the papers and was stunned. In stark black print: Kennedy Assassinated.

My first thought was that someone was pranking me—a sick joke.

One by one, I turned over each of the papers.

I could not believe what I was seeing—only the untimely death of an im-mediate relative could have shocked me more. I read the headlines again. They were as simple as they were unbelievable. A part of me just couldn't process it. I stood absolutely still for what seemed like a long time as a myriad of implica-tions ran through my mind.

I needed to talk to someone. To wake Dagmar, to call Doug Bennet, to do something.

Bowles, at the time back in Washington, had been scheduled to meet Pres-ident Kennedy in the Oval Office November 25 to discuss the possibility of increasing military aid to the Indians in light of recent hostilities between them and the Chinese. Bowles believed such assistance would be a way of furthering our national interest and our relationship with India, and he thought Kennedy was amenable to the idea. But now Kennedy was dead. What would happen to this opportunity?

A week later I wrote in my journal, recalling that day: "Logic had deserted history in one cheap and unreasonable and brutal and all too human act."

As soon as I could think clearly, I called the embassy. The marine guard picked up the phone, and I asked him about the headlines.

"It's true," he told me.

I told him I'd be right in.

In some respects the State Department is at its best when an entirely unthinkable act like the Kennedy assassination occurs. They have a drill for everything; they know what to do at a time of crisis. By the time I arrived at the embassy, the flag was already at half-mast and the marine guards had been issued black armbands. A conversation was under way—which I joined immediately—about the condolence book that would be placed in front of the embassy, where people from all walks of life could convey their sympathies. A year and a half earlier, Jacqueline Kennedy had come to India to dedicate the new embassy and residence and had received an overwhelming welcome. There would be an outpouring of sympathy. We needed to find ways to manage it.

Still, there was no getting over the shock of it. Lyndon Johnson was president. How could a young person like Kennedy be dead? Who did this? What kind of madness was this?

We lived by the newspapers and news ticker, talked in hushed voices, and prayed for the best—especially that Lyndon Johnson would fight for the causes Kennedy had enjoined: civil rights, peace, and global development. Death cast Kennedy's shadow bigger than it had been in life, and the closeness of the Kennedy family (which had been much maligned during the election campaign) now made the loss seem somehow more acute, more palpable, more intimate.

We tend to be cynical about our politicians. But the youth, energy, and courage of Kennedy, his graceful and beautiful family, had seemed somehow to rise above that. In the words of his brother Teddy, President Kennedy sparked "a dream that would never die."

In the midst of the trappings of grief, Pete Seeger arrived. Because of the president's death, all public events we had planned were canceled. But he, his wife, Toshi, and their son Dan spent four days in New Delhi anyway. They grieved with the rest of us.

The overlay of my coming to terms with Kennedy's death was trying to entertain Pete and Toshi Seeger without totally depressing everyone. Pete's response to the tragedy was that he wanted to sing, believing that music would provide an emotional outlet for people. That was probably true, I told him, but protocol dictated that to honor the president's memory we had to observe a ten-day period of mourning during which there could be no official events.

Pete did sing, though. In our house. I have a vivid memory of him going upstairs each evening to sing Dan to sleep.

Finally, on Pete's last day, Steb and I agreed that we had to find a way for him to perform. "Maybe," I suggested, "we could do something informal."

We took Pete to an elementary school near the embassy, where he sat and sang to and with the children. He sang "Itsy Bitsy Spider" and a whole set of children's songs. The kids loved it. He loved it.

That evening, we gathered a few friends to honor John Kennedy. One of Prime Minister Nehru's aides, a talented traditional Hindi singer, joined Pete in our living room, along with perhaps a dozen people, including Steb—Chet was still back in Washington—Toshi, and Dagmar. Pete and our Indian friend traded songs back and forth for perhaps two hours.

It was intensely sad and intensely uplifting—a remarkable moment.

A month or so after the Seeger visits, Dagmar and I moved into the diplomatic enclave—near the embassy and a few streets away from the Bennets—because of a crisis at the boys' boarding unit of the American Embassy School.

The school was essentially a day school, but sixteen boys lived in a home not far from the school. Their families were posted in remote places—State Department parents, agency parents, USAID parents—families who wanted their kids to go to a good school and so had placed them in the boarding unit.

An older couple had been recruited from a middling prep school in New England to be house parents and had apparently come to India expecting an easy time—an idyllic getaway from their American lives in beautiful New Delhi. Instead they found themselves confronted by sixteen spoiled, disrespectful, unruly teenagers who were determined to make life miserable for them. Part of the job required that houseparents live in a small apartment in the house with the boys. There the couple fell prey to numerous pranks. The boys would steal things and hide them throughout the house, disregarding everything the "house master" told them. The most unnerving prank occurred when a kid lobbed a firecracker into the shower of the housemother. In the hot weather, as you showered, you had to open the window to let in fresh air. Someone took explosive advantage. A week later the houseparents flew home to the United States for Christmas. They never came back.

The ambassador called me into his office. "Dick," he said, "I've got an assignment for you." He told me about the boys. He made it clear that this assignment was not a choice. "The movers will be at your place in two hours," he told me. "We're moving you into the house."

So Dagmar, Eric, and I moved into the house with sixteen teenage boys!

Unlike the previous housemaster, Dagmar and I were tough. We set rules and made them stick. The boys were unhappy but ended up paying attention.

A cardinal rule: "no smoking in the house"—because it was dangerous in such cramped quarters. One day after school, Dagmar smelled cigarette smoke and went upstairs. She found one of the older boys with his back to the staircase, in his underwear, smoking. Coming up behind him, Dagmar pulled his shorts down to his ankles and told him to never again smoke in that house. Afterwards she told me she could hear his buttocks snap together.

Nobody smoked in the house after that.

After a month or two we had another emergency involving teenagers. This time Bowles called both Doug Bennet and me into his office. "I've just received a report that boys from the school have been stealing motorbikes," he told us. "They joyride them, then abandon them."

"Really?" I said.

He gave me a serious look. "This could cause a diplomatic incident," he told us. "I need it resolved." Bowles was not given to melodrama; it was, in fact, a serious situation. In India at that time, owning a motor scooter was like owning a Tesla today. There was a two-year waiting list just to acquire a scooter.

Living in the boarding unit, I had a hunch who some of these boys might be, so I gathered them and told them that the ambassador had heard about the joyriding. We needed to know the names of every boy involved. If we didn't get every single name, I said we're going to throw the kids we do know out of school. In twenty-four hours, we had a list, which I brought to the ambassador.

"Well, we need an appropriate punishment," he responded. "Here's what we're going to do. Number one, I'm going to read them the riot act. Number two, they're going to have to do community service, and it has to be *harsh*. Number three, I'm going to make it clear that if they put another finger on someone else's property, they'll be kicked out of school and their *parents* will be sent home. But *we* won't inform their parents—*they* have to do that. Make a careful note of this conversation, Dick, so that if we end up sending someone home, there won't be any question about why."

I told him I would assemble the miscreants.

"But what's the punishment?" asked Bowles. "The community service they're going to perform?"

I said that Doug and I had located a rural school under construction some twenty-five miles out of town—a bumpy, brutal ride by Jeep in what was usually sweltering heat. "We're going to take them there and get them dirty making mud bricks for the school walls every Saturday for eight weeks."

Bowles said he thought that sounded appropriate.

We started the following weekend. We had two old Jeep Wagoneers that would each fit eight or nine passengers. I was in one; Doug was in the other. Our job was to supervise them. The first Saturday, after about two hours, the boys were really struggling. They hadn't done much hard physical labor in their lives and had no clue how to make proper bricks. Little Indian kids stood around laughing at them. One of our boys approached me and said he was quitting.

"You can't quit," I told him.

"I just did," he said.

"If you quit," I said, "I'll tell you what happens. When we get back, I will tell the ambassador you've quit. Then you *and* your father will be sent home."

The kid looked at me and threatened to hit me in the face. He was a big guy, eighteen years old, about my height.

"Go ahead," I said. "That will expedite the departure of you and your family. You will be home before you know it."

I watched the kid make up his mind. Slowly he lowered his hand and went back to work.

That was the last rebellion we experienced.

The boys worked so hard that they slept the whole way home and didn't have the energy to go out that night. Just as we had hoped.

The work went on for two months. The kids spoke no Hindi and neither did we—though we had an interpreter. By the third Saturday, the boys began to take an interest in the village. When we broke for lunch, the boys wandered half a kilometer into the center of the village, where several of the older men were sitting around, sharing a hookah and conversing with each other. The kids listened and watched, taking in the scene. The fifth week, one of our kids brought his guitar and during lunch started noodling around on it. Soon an Indian youngster fetched his sitar, and before long they were playing together.

By week six, word about the disciplinary project had gotten back to the embassy school. Real work had been done in the village—the boys had started to tell their friends, proudly, what they were doing—and we started getting calls.

"Why do they—these kids who have misbehaved—get to do this and we don't? It's not fair!"

Yes, mandatory service could become a badge of honor.

———

Toward the end of my first year, as Chet and Steb were getting on a plane to head home for leave, Chet handed me an envelope. "Don't open this until I'm out of the country," he told me. "Until I get back, Dick, you're in charge." I laughed at that. There was no way I was actually in charge, and we both knew it. Still, I understood what he meant. I was to be his eyes and ears in his absence. "Remember," he said, "don't open this until I'm out of the country."

"What's in it?"

Bowles shook his head.

After the Pan Am flight departed, I opened the envelope to find two pages on which Bowles had confided in his characteristically cramped, almost illegible handwriting, that he had Parkinson's disease.

I had no idea. He had not shown the slightest symptoms.

The letter went on to say that he had not told anyone—other than Steb—but he had been diagnosed in 1963, shortly before taking up his assignment in India, and he was now about to have a surgical procedure that involved drilling a hole in his skull and using electronic probes to identify the seat of the problem in order to halt, if not reverse, the effects of the disease. He described the procedure in some detail and assured me that Steb would be in touch once the surgery was over. He wasn't worried, he said, and had every confidence in the surgeons and the care he was getting. He did think it important that I have the information so that I could brief Jerry Greene (the deputy chief of mission, the person who was *actually* in charge) once the surgery had been completed.

I had to sit on this news flash. I didn't know for how long.

Chet had the surgery shortly after getting home, and it went well. When they returned to India, Steb recounted how Chet came out from under anesthesia.

He had checked into the hospital under an assumed name, she explained, because he didn't want anyone to know that he was undergoing surgery. In the recovery room, as he was regaining consciousness, the doctor asked him his name, eager to make sure they hadn't done any brain damage during the procedure.

Chet looked at him blankly. He was clearly struggling. "What is my name?" he said, not quite to himself.

There was an exquisite moment of pure panic. Had the operation done irreparable harm? Did Chester Bowles not know his own name?

Steb piped up. "Chet," she said, "it's okay—just tell him your real name. He's the doctor."

"I'm Chester Bowles," he said without hesitation.

He came back in good shape, virtually asymptomatic for the next several years.

One of the visitors I was charged with showing around was Arthur Goldberg, who wanted to learn about the status of labor in India. At the time Goldberg was not yet the US ambassador to the United Nations, but Lyndon Johnson was trying to persuade him to step down from the Supreme Court and move to the United Nations. During the visit he discussed with Chet whether to give up his Supreme Court appointment.

Not long after his arrival, he said he would like to learn more about the centuries-old Jewish community in South India. So we flew from Delhi to Kerala—from the north to the south of the country—so he could visit the Paradesi Synagogue. Constructed in the sixteenth century by Spanish-speaking Jews who were driven out of Spain, it was then, and remained until recently, the oldest active synagogue in the British Commonwealth. As I walked with him and his wife Dorothy toward the synagogue through the quarter of Old Cochin known as "Jew Town," a pair of boys came running up to us.

"Excuse me," said the first boy to me, "are you Jewish?"

I told him I wasn't.

They looked at Goldberg.

"Are you Jewish?" asked the second boy.

Goldberg said he was, and the kid grabbed him by the hand. "Hurry," he said, "we need you for a minyan."

Another of our visitors was Vice President Hubert Humphrey, who came to India several times, usually for funerals. Each time I was his control officer. After Prime Minister Shastri's funeral, I rode with him back to the airport. We shook hands, and he thanked me for my help and boarded Air Force 2. I was relieved to get the vice president on his way without incident. But when I arrived back at the embassy, we had received an urgent message from the airplane. The vice president had left his Homburg in the car, and he needed it back.

I immediately called the motorpool, where our driver found the hat by the backseat. The problem was how to convey a Homburg back to Washington without it getting squashed. It could go in a box, but what would happen to the box in the diplomatic pouch? Was there any guarantee the vice presidential hat would even reach Humphrey?

Fortunately, the next day I found a CIA officer headed back to Washington for consultations. I gave him the hat and explained the seriousness of the situation. "The vice presidential Homburg," I told him, "must not be dented. It must be delivered, by hand, to the vice president's office in the old Executive Office Building."

It was.

Perhaps prompted by congressional visits—or the line of Americans passing though who were actively engaged in public life—I found myself beginning to contemplate a return home and to consider the prospect of entering politics.

One of the unexpected pleasures about writing the story of one's life is to discover the tricks of memory face-to-face, as it were. For most of my life when people have asked me about my decision to enter politics, I would describe it as almost unexpected, a vocation that snuck up on me. Writing this book, however, has forced me back in time, to fading telegrams, neglected snapshots, and most particularly forgotten correspondence that sometimes presents one with a version of oneself that is different, sometimes *strikingly* different, than the self that one remembers.

In my memory, when I recall what I was like as a young man in India working for Chester Bowles, I recall a Dick Celeste who was still holding on to the possibility of going to law school. Admittedly a legal career was mostly a placeholder for not knowing what I wanted to do. But I don't recall having a clear intention of pursuing politics at the time.

Imagine my surprise when I dug up a letter to my father dated November 20, 1965—HAPPY THANKSGIVING is scrawled, underlined twice at the top of the yellow legal paper—which begins by raising the question of my father's consideration of a run for governor: "I have just gotten out of bed—unable to sleep—thinking about my own future and about politics in greater Cleveland. We have often talked together about this—each encouraging the other to become involved. Ted wrote recently that you are still toying with the idea of running for Governor. It is surely a challenge cut to your size—although I am just far enough away to venture a guess as to the timing. I have a hunch that it may not be ripe but as I say, I am out of touch."

My father decided not to throw his hat into the ring, but it is striking to look back at that letter and see that it was a possibility. There is both delicacy and honesty in my reply. My political instincts told me that my father should *not* run and even now I am surprised by the clearheaded forthrightness that marked our relationship.

Soon, however, my Thanksgiving note tilts in another direction—toward my own political ambitions: "I really am writing about myself. Tonight I realized—almost suddenly, although it has been brewing for a long time—that

I am yearning to come home and enter into our national pastime at full tilt. I suspect that the thing that has driven this home has been the recent spate of Congressional visitors coming through Delhi . . . I realized that the time was fast approaching when I must 'strike out on my own. ' And ironically, in a sense, return home to Cleveland."

The letter goes on to describe the impulse to return home and enter politics as being the logical consequence of everything that has preceded it: "It is no wonder that I feel that politics is my 'calling.' You, thank God, raised all of us to think in terms of public life as the highest vocation. And you matched words with outstanding deeds. I suspect that is why politics is in my blood. My plan—such as it is—is to return to Cleveland in Sep/Oct 1966 and prepare to run for congress the following year. Whether I use teaching or National Housing Inc as my initial 'base' is uncertain. It would depend a lot on timing (I would prefer teaching, I think, if I could 'fit it in'—although if you get some low cost housing projects under way in Cleveland that might do even better.)"

The letter then concludes with a number of very specific requests for information about the feasibility of a candidacy—residency requirements, bio sketches of congressional incumbents in Cuyahoga County, and information about the Ohio Democratic Party. I even asked him to send me a few good histories of Cleveland and a biography of Tom Johnson, who was the thirty-fifth mayor of Cleveland and the 1903 Democratic nominee for governor of Ohio. I still have that biography!

A few days later—still going through my papers—I found my father's reply dated December 7, 1965. He begins by addressing the question of his gubernatorial bid: "Regarding my running for Governor, I believe this is just about out because, first, Rhodes has such a good press that it will be difficult for anyone to get any help from the papers. Second he is allegedly making such a good record that it will be difficult to find real issues to present. Third, the Democratic party is so fragmented and so disorganized that it would be difficult to get effective support. Fourth, the game at this point is not worth the candle. Fifth, the timing, as you so well put it, is not right."

There must have been a certain satisfaction in having one's son echo one's assessment of the situation so closely. More significant, perhaps, is his response to my broaching the subject of following him into political life: "This brings me to the question you raise about wanting to 'strike out on my own': and if returning to Cleveland seems the best avenue to strike out on your own then come back as fast as in good conscience you can."

It would not be for another couple of years. Bowles had in the meantime asked me to stay on and given me a promotion. It was another commitment that I had to honor. A number of things were on my mind at the time. First, what would life be like after India? Also, could I join the family business? With two small children and a wife to feed, I was starting to worry about money.

I was asking my father about my political future, to be sure. But I was also hoping he would offer me a job.

As a result of my promotion, I now arrived at the embassy early to sort the cables so that the ambassador could focus on the important ones. One morning I arrived at the embassy and Helen, the ambassador's secretary, told me Marlon Brando had called.

"Marlon Brando?" I asked.

"He wanted to talk to the ambassador," she told me.

"Helen," I said, "Marlon Brando didn't call. Are you kidding?"

"Whoever it was, he claimed to be Marlon Brando."

"I doubt very much it was him," I said. "It's someone pulling your leg. There is no way—no way—it's Marlon Brando. If this guy calls again, put the call through to me."

Half an hour later, she buzzed me. "Marlon Brando's on the phone," she told me.

"Mr. Brando," I said, picking up the phone, "this is Dick Celeste, the ambassador's assistant."

I remember the distinctive growl of his voice. It was definitely Brando. "Mr. Celeste," he said, "I need to talk to the ambassador."

I told him I wasn't confident it could be arranged. "The ambassador is really very busy," I said.

Brando explained that it was important. "I'm here on a UN mission," he told me, like he was making me an offer I couldn't refuse. "I really need to see the ambassador."

"Mr. Brando," I said, "I'll tell you what. The ambassador's not here right now. Why don't you give me your contact information, and I'll get back to you."

He told me he was staying at the Oberoi Hotel in room 833, then hung up.

I immediately called the hotel and asked if they had a guest named Brando. They did. M. Brando in room 833.

Later, when Bowles and I finished reviewing cables, I said, "Marlon Brando is in town, and he wants to see you."

Bowles looked at me. "Who's Marlon Brando?" Though politically astute, Chet knew almost nothing about popular culture post-1948.

"You don't know who he is," I said, "but Steb will. He's a popular movie star." I reeled off a series of titles: *A Streetcar Named Desire, On the Waterfront, Viva Zapata!*

Bowles looked at me without a glimmer of recognition. "Call Steb," he told me, "and if she thinks it's worthwhile, invite him over for a drink."

So I called Steb.

"Marlon Brando!" she said. "Absolutely! Dick, what time?"

I called Brando back and invited him over for drinks. I figured that I should probably oversee this, and, because it was Marlon Brando, Dagmar wanted to be there too.

It turned out Brando liked martinis. As the head bearer brought out drinks, Brando explained that he was in India as a UN spokesperson for family planning. He had spent two weeks in Africa visiting family planning programs there and was convinced the way to encourage population control was to provide free condoms to villages all over Asia and Africa. To do this, he told us, we should redeploy helicopters from Vietnam to drop condoms into third-world villages. Bowles cautioned that such a step was highly unlikely.

By the third martini, Brando was pretty loose. "The funniest thing happened to me shortly after I arrived here," he said. "I see someone's slid a note under my door."

He took another sip of his drink.

"The letter begins," said Brando, "'Dear Paul Newman. I'm so excited, I'm a big fan of yours. I especially liked you in *Shane*. Would you please give me an autograph, sincerely Mohan.'"

"Mr. Brando," asked Steb, "what did you do?"

"I wrote him back," said Brando.

"What did you say?"

"'Dear Mohan,'" he said, "'I'm so excited to find a fan of mine in New Delhi, especially one who liked me in *Shane*. Here's my autograph.'"

"How'd you sign it?" said Steb.

"Paul Newman," said Brando.

We all laughed.

"Not only am I not Paul Newman," added Brando, "Paul Newman wasn't in *Shane*."

———

In 1965 Dagmar and I stopped in Vienna during our home leave to spend time with her parents and introduce our son Christopher, who had been born at New Delhi's Holy Family Hospital in April. Christopher, by the way, arrived much more quickly than Eric. About eighteen months after that, Gabriella was born in October 1966, again at Holy Family Hospital.

Eventually we would return to the States with three kids under the age of five. India spoiled us because we had a full-time ayah. In India you seldom heard a child cry because the moment one did he or she would be picked up before another tear was shed.

Only when we got back to Ohio would we find out what having three very young children was really like.

Chester Bowles's concerns reached beyond his immediate responsibilities as ambassador to India. For example, he wrote often to President Johnson about Vietnam and our policy there. India was one of three members of the International Control Commission (ICC). When the French withdrew from Vietnam, they negotiated an agreement with the government in Hanoi to divide the country, creating a demilitarized zone—and that agreement would be overseen by the ICC composed of Poland (representing the Eastern Bloc), Canada (representing the West), and India (a neutral country, to tip the scales between the two when necessary). India, however, was reluctant to offend either side by taking a position, so the commission often found itself deadlocked.

Bowles—like many in the State Department—was concerned that Lyndon Johnson was going to be lured into bombing Cambodia because we had evidence that the North Vietnamese were infiltrating into the South through Cambodia. In 1965 Bowles was asked by the president to visit Southeast Asia to give Johnson firsthand perspective about the North Vietnamese use of Cambodia and to develop a persuasive case to put to the Indian government. I went along as Chet's aide. We traveled first to Thailand, a major staging area for us; then to Laos, right on the border; and finally to Vietnam. Mostly we dealt with the big-picture perspective, but we also had specific briefing sessions about the North Vietnamese infiltration.

After our return, I wrote a confidential report about the trip, which I shared with Ambassador Bowles. Looking at it now, it provides both an interesting perspective on how we were assessing the situation at the time as well as an insight into the person Dick Celeste was more than fifty years ago.

"August 8, 1966: After lunch we met at General Westmoreland's headquarters for an overall military briefing. Because we had expressed an interest in the infiltration question the whole briefing was geared to proving that Viet Cong (VC) and North Vietnamese (NVN) use Cambodia for supplies and safe haven and the Demilitarized Zone (DMZ) has been used for massive infiltration. These propositions are both undoubtedly true; the question is—as an Indian would say—what to do? The initial military response seems to be, 'bomb 'em.'"

After we left Saigon that evening, we switched to a small COD (carrier onboard delivery, a two-engine plane the navy used to ferry people and fresh food to aircraft carriers) and landed on the carrier *Constellation* in the Gulf of Tonkin. As massive as the ship is—about the size of three football fields—the experience of landing was genuinely scary. "I decided one thing that night," I wrote in my report. "No one, but no one, could convince me to land on a carrier at night."

During the trip, many of our hosts assumed I was with the CIA. At each stop, Bowles would stay with the resident ambassador, and I'd be assigned to stay with people who had vague titles like "political officer." One of my very good friends—he'd been a Rhodes Scholar with me—was a young Foreign Service Officer in Laos. "Why are you staying with the CIA station chief?" he asked. "Are you with the Agency?"

I told him no.

"Really?" he said. "You're not?"

"I'm not," I said. "Really."

"You can trust me."

"I am not with the Agency," I told him.

I don't know that I convinced him. Insisting that one is not with the Agency is exactly what someone who was with the Agency would do. No one believed me.

By March 1967 Dagmar and I were getting ready—at least emotionally—to leave India. We were starting to say our good-byes and had invited a group of friends over to the house—one of the rare times when we hosted a dinner party rather than attending one. Our guests had just arrived when the phone rang. It was Dave Blee, the CIA station chief, asking me to come to the embassy.

I told him about dinner. "I can't leave," I said. "Dagmar will kill me."

"Dick," he said, "you've got to come to the embassy right now."

"Dave," I said, "listen, please, I can't just leave."

"*Dick*," he repeated sternly, "come to the embassy."

I explained to Dagmar and the rest that I had to excuse myself. Our house was about two blocks from the embassy, so I walked. When I arrived a few minutes later, I was surprised to find the door locked. This was very unusual. Normally you'd enter the front door and show your credentials to a marine guard at a desk in the center of the foyer *after* you entered the embassy. But not that night.

I rang the bell, and shortly a guard opened up.

"What's going on?" I said.

He looked past me, over my shoulder at the empty street behind me and said, in a low voice, "A woman came here claiming to be Stalin's daughter."

"Stalin's daughter?" I said.

The marine nodded. "They're upstairs," he told me.

I went up to the office of the deputy chief of mission. Inside, Roger Kirk, a young political officer whose father had been the US ambassador to the Soviet Union, had joined Blee. They were sitting at a small conference table and quickly confirmed what the marine had said: about a quarter of an hour earlier, a woman had arrived at the embassy with a pair of suitcases asking for asylum. She had presented a Russian passport and claimed to be Joseph Stalin's daughter.

"Where is she now?" I asked.

"She's down in the consular office," said Blee, "being interviewed."

"Is she really Stalin's daughter?" I asked.

"She could be," said Blee. "We don't know. She could also be a provocation."

It didn't take much imagination to suspect the Russians were up to something. A few weeks earlier the Soviets had sent a new number two to their embassy in New Delhi, who, according to the agency, specialized in black propaganda. As Doug Bennet knew, there were regular efforts to recruit young American officers by Soviet intelligence. The Stalin daughter ploy might be another effort to embarrass us.

Her story was hard to believe. Not only did this woman say she was Stalin's daughter, she claimed to be the common-law wife of an older Indian gentleman who worked at the Foreign Language Press in Moscow. This fellow was the uncle of Dinesh Singh, the deputy foreign minister of India rumored to be Indira Gandhi's paramour. Her husband had died the previous November. She had promised to bring his ashes from Moscow to immerse them in the Ganges. Six months had passed. She—her name was Svetlana—had stayed in India after scattering the ashes. She now wanted asylum.

She was still downstairs, waiting. We did not want to expose more than one embassy officer to her. We worried that at any moment she might falsely accuse someone from the embassy of rape or that the Soviet embassy would allege we had kidnapped her. We would be ordered to produce her, and she would confirm whatever wild accusations had been made by the Soviets.

The truth is we didn't know. Maybe she was a provocation, and maybe she wasn't. There was no obvious course of action open to us.

Frankly, the idea that Svetlana Stalin could have arrived in India in November—and stayed until March—living in the home of Dinesh Singh the whole time—unknown to everyone, including India's aggressive mainstream press as well as the CIA, was highly implausible. Her story was that the Soviet ambassador in Delhi was on her case because Brezhnev was demanding that she return to Moscow. Finally, she told us, the ambassador traveled to see her and deliver an ultimatum, saying it was an embarrassment to the Russian people. "Brezhnev did you a favor," the ambassador told her, "letting you bring those ashes back to India. That was a privilege, and what you're doing now by lingering in India is wrong."

She told us she had come back to Delhi that weekend—March 5 was a Monday—and taken an apartment at the Russian embassy compound. The Russians expected her to take the Aeroflot flight to Moscow very early Thursday morning. The last straw, she alleged, occurred when the Soviet ambassador invited her to lunch that afternoon and served Polish ham. She ate the vegetables on her plate but didn't touch the ham.

The ambassador was offended. "What kind of a Soviet woman are you?" he asked. "This is the best ham in the world made by our comrades in Poland."

She wouldn't touch it.

"What's happened to you?" he asked. "You've become a vegetarian? A Hindu?" And he launched into a tirade about how she had become an embarrassment to herself, to her family, and especially to the Soviet people.

That lecture confirmed her decision to seek asylum in the United States.

She waited until that evening when the Soviet ambassador was hosting a party at the embassy for a senior military delegation visiting from Moscow. With the party in full swing, she simply called a cab and carried her suitcases to the gate. There was nobody around to stop her or even notice, she said, because they were all at the party. A few minutes later she walked into the American embassy just two blocks away.

We need to lay out options, said Blee, eager to confer with the ambassador. Bowles, who was in bed with bronchitis, was living in the same modest bungalow their family had loved when he was ambassador in the fifties, a comfortable home on Ratendon Road that backed onto Lodhi Gardens. That's where we would find him. The clock was ticking, and we knew it.

Arriving at Ratendon Road, we went directly to Chet's bedroom to brief him on the situation.

"Dave," Bowles asked Blee, "do you think this is Stalin's daughter or not?"

"We honestly don't know. She has given us an incredible story. If she has actually been here for the past five months, we should know. *Blitz*"—the communist newspaper—"would have run a story on her, something."

"What are our choices?" asked Bowles.

We outlined the three options we had agreed on earlier at the embassy. Diplomatic protocol dictated that we inform the government of India that we had a Soviet citizen claiming to be Stalin's daughter requesting asylum. Once they had been informed, we would make a formal request for their help in facilitating her departure.

This was the first option.

"This is problematic," said Blee, "because just a few months ago, a Russian sailor jumped ship in Calcutta and came to our consulate. When we informed the Indian government, it took three months before they permitted us to get that guy moved. That was someone with no political significance. What would happen if this *is* Stalin's daughter?"

We laid out the second option: turn her away. "If we really believe that she's a provocation," Blee said, "the right thing to do is to say, sorry, we can't help you."

"Third option," offered Blee, "we could give her a visa to the United States but buy her a ticket only halfway. There's a Quantas flight to Rome that leaves at one in the morning. We could put her in a safe house there until we sort this out."

"If we turn her away, whoever she is," Bowles told us, "that's not American. We respect people's requests for asylum. If we call the government of India, we're going to create a debilitating three-way tug of war between Moscow, New Delhi, and Washington. Give her the visa, let her know she has got to get on the plane on her own. We can drive her there, but she has to board the plane alone."

It seemed like the best of the options.

"Cable Washington," said Bowles, "and let them know what we propose to do."

We drove quickly back to the embassy and at 8:30 P.M. I sent a flash message to Washington: "Eyes only, Secretary of State, highest classification"—which of course guaranteed that at least twenty people would read it immediately—

"Individual claiming to be Stalin's daughter arrived at Embassy 1910 hours seeking asylum. Unable to confirm identity. Concerned that individual may be a provocation. Propose to issue a US visa but send her to Rome on Quantas ETD 0100 hours. Seek your guidance."

I—we—figured we would get a quick response telling us whether they approved our proposed course of action.

Half an hour later we received a brief acknowledgment: "Message received. Will respond ASAP."

That was it.

Meanwhile Roger Kirk had been sequestered in his office reading a manuscript the woman had brought with her when she presented herself. She had written a book, she claimed, about life with her father growing up in the Kremlin. Roger had been trying to figure out if it was authentic and thus if she was who she claimed to be. Kirk said he couldn't be sure. "I've scanned it," he said, "and it could be the real thing. But I have no way of confirming it without spending several days fact-checking it."

In the absence of certainty, we were guided by our internal traffic signals. Option three flashed green. She would have to get onto the Quantas flight on her own two feet. Toward midnight Blee drove her to the airport. I remember watching them leave. A nondescript woman—I didn't see her face—came out and got in the car. Blee closed the door behind her.

A Russian-speaking CIA agent had boarded the plane in advance but did not identify himself until after the plane had taken off. He didn't want to be accused of being a kidnapper.

It turned out the Quantas flight was delayed forty-five minutes.

The woman claiming to be Svetlana sat patiently on her own in the lounge through the delay. Finally, she boarded the plane.

The next morning we got several messages.

One was from Washington: "What happened?" They had never sent us instructions of any sort.

The second was a brief agency response. After the woman's appearance Blee had rung every bell he could in Langley asking if they could find some scrap of intelligence about Stalin's daughter. Contrary to their original response—nothing—they had discovered, tucked away in an obscure file, a low-level source reporting eight years earlier a rumor that Stalin's daughter was living with an older Indian employee at Foreign Language Press. It had been filed in DC and never forwarded to Delhi. Between this piece of intelligence and the fact that she hadn't blown the whistle at the airport, we were convinced the woman was indeed Svetlana Stalin.

Then we got confirmation.

Around 2:00 A.M. Thursday—the departure time of the Aeroflot flight that was supposed to take Svetlana to Russia—Blee was awakened at home by a call from his KGB counterpart in New Delhi.

"What the fuck did you do with Stalin's daughter?" demanded the KGB chief (or something along those lines).

"Stalin's daughter?" said Blee.

"You kidnapped her," he said.

"We didn't kidnap anyone," Blee said. "And I'm not sure I know exactly what woman you're talking about. But if this is the woman I'm thinking of, she came to the embassy claiming to be Stalin's daughter. She had a valid passport and said she wanted to seek asylum in the United States."

"This woman!" sputtered the KGB station chief. "She's in the States now?"

"We didn't take her there," Blee said, "because we didn't want to embarrass you, and we wanted to give her a chance to change her mind. But the truth is we thought that she was a provocation."

"A provocation?" he said. "Why did you think she's a provocation?"

Blee reminded him of his newly appointed deputy, the expert in black propaganda.

An already delicate situation became more delicate the next day when, at every post around the world, meetings between Soviet and American diplomats were called off. One of the reasons behind the Soviet ambassador's eagerness to persuade Svetlana to return home was that he himself was headed back to Moscow for reassignment. Even his farewell call on Bowles was canceled.

As it happened, that upcoming Friday I had a dinner—long scheduled—with Valerie Ostepenko, my counterpart in the Soviet embassy. We had been getting together, with Bowles's encouragement, every three or four months to talk about matters of mutual interest such as Vietnam and the International Control Commission. Gradually we'd gotten to know each other and had become friends of sorts.

Our visits were reciprocal. He and his wife would come to our place for dinner; Dagmar and I would go to theirs. I called him Friday morning, saying I assumed our dinner was off.

"But why would you assume this?" he wanted to know.

"Because everywhere they're canceling things," I said.

He knew what I was talking about. "No," he said, "our dinner is on."

"Is it really?" I asked.

"See you at seven," he told me.

After I hung up, I began to worry. I didn't want to get snatched and held. I asked Bowles whether I should go and what I should say about Svetlana's departure. Bowles's response was that I should keep the dinner and if I was asked I should describe exactly what happened.

"Tell him the whole story just as she had told it to us, exactly as you experienced it," said Bowles. "And make sure you leave a message with the marine guard here," he added, a moment later, "so that if you're not back by a certain time we can, well, make inquiries."

Inquiries. The word did not reassure me.

Dagmar and I arrived for dinner at the Soviet compound around seven on Friday, and his wife offered us the usual vodka and caviar. I declined, wanting to be careful about what I ate and drank, still worried that we might find ourselves hostages. Time passed and there was no sign of Valerie. My nervousness increased. Finally, he arrived at eight, very apologetic. "I'm really sorry," he said, "there are so many things going on. But this you know."

We sat down to a delicious dinner. Eventually over dessert he said: "Dick, let me ask you, why did you kidnap Svetlana Stalin?"

"Valerie, we didn't kidnap anyone," I said. "I'm going to tell you exactly what happened."

And I did.

"She's in Europe," I said, though I didn't say where. "We want to make sure she considers everything carefully before she comes to the United States."

I realized it was almost midnight and knew I had to get back to the embassy. I didn't want the marine guard raising an alarm with the Indian government, so I told Valerie I was expecting a cable I needed to see and respond to. I asked him if I could go briefly to my embassy and then come back to finish dessert.

He drove over to the embassy with me. I went in and assured the marine guard that everything was fine. Then we returned for dessert.

Later we found out that the Soviets had decided that Svetlana's departure was an Indian, not an American, problem. The Indians had simply not taken proper care of this very important visitor. The Soviets went very hard at the Indira Gandhi government. After a couple of weeks LK Jha, the principal secretary to the prime minister at the time, was sent by Indira Gandhi to meet Svetlana in Switzerland, where she'd moved.

Jha tried to talk her into returning to Moscow, saying that her defection was harming relations between two countries she loved and because her children wanted her back in Russia. One of her children was a doctor and the other was an academic, and she talked to them on the phone with Jha observing. The children urged her to return, but she refused, saying that she simply would not return to Moscow under any circumstances. "I've made up my mind," she said. "I'm going to the United States."

From Switzerland Jha traveled to Moscow, where he met with the deputy foreign minister and apologized for what had happened, admitting it was an embarrassment for the Russians and for the Indians. He explained that he had met with Svetlana and done his best to persuade her to go home, but she had refused.

"How did you let this happen?" was the question the Soviet asked.

"What do you mean," said Jha, "let this happen?"

"Well," the deputy foreign minister said, "according to Dick Celeste . . ."

"According to Dick Celeste?" said Jha, "What's that supposed to mean? Who is this Dick Celeste?"

"Celeste," said the deputy minister, "the assistant to the US ambassador in New Delhi."

"I don't know this Celeste," said Jha.

"Well," said the minister, "he's obviously a senior person there, who spoke with one of our officers in Delhi." He then described, in detail, what I had told Valerie Ostepenko after dinner.

The first thing Jha did when he got back to New Delhi was pick up the phone. "Get to my office right now," he said to Bowles. "Who in the world is Dick Celeste?"

I suspect Jha, like others, may have assumed that I was CIA. Bowles had to go through a long explanation with Jha as to who I was and how I came to be in New Delhi.

Eventually Svetlana Stalin left Switzerland and came to the United States. The brouhaha in Delhi subsided.

Richard Nixon visited India near the end of my tour. Though Bowles differed politically from Nixon, he was a thoughtful host. The ambassador was always willing to do what his role called for. Not once did I see him be anything but gracious, even when those he hosted did not share his view of the world.

Steb, on the other hand, knew she was going to have to restrain herself. She was, therefore, on her best behavior.

The night Nixon arrived, he was invited to the ambassador's house, along with his two sidekicks, Bob Ellsworth and Ray Price—one the former senator from Kansas and the other the editorial writer for *Time* magazine. After greeting them, Steb offered drinks. Soon the head bearer handed a martini to Nixon. Before he could set it down, one of Bowles's several Springer spaniels bounded across and jumped on him.

The martini spilled over Nixon.

Steb, mortified, apologized profusely.

"Don't worry, Steb," said Nixon, "it's fine. I have a dog too."

"Of course," said Steb, "that Ch-, Ch-, Ch-." Everyone in the garden knew that Steb was, despite her best efforts, thinking of the so-called "Checkers" speech that Nixon had given in the fall of 1952 after having been accused of financial improprieties. Checkers was an important figure in the Nixon saga.

Nixon spent four days with us in Delhi with me as his control officer. The day before his departure he asked Bowles to arrange a press conference. Chet was reluctant, remembering the disaster of Nixon's California postelection defeat press conference when he had said infamously, "You won't have Dick Nixon to kick around anymore." But that had been years earlier. Nixon was in the process of rebuilding his image after that ungracious step back from politics.

The Indian press, Bowles knew, did not cut politicians any slack. In those days, left-wing and Communist Party newspapers would critique anything a visiting American might say. In fact, most of the media had inherited a rather British disdain for all things American. These journalists were not going to be a receptive crowd for Nixon. Bowles did what he could to discourage Nixon, who remained determined. "I'd like to know what you would say," Nixon said to Bowles.

Bowles outlined three points. "You could say that China is the model of central command development," he said. "India is the model of liberal democratic development, and we have a great stake in the success of India. Second, you could say that you've looked at the way that the people of India have used our foreign assistance and the Food for Peace we've provided and you are most impressed. Third, mention that you've sensed a growing tie between young Indians going to the United States to study and young Fulbright Scholars coming to India; this is the sort of thing that we'd all like to see flourish. You view India as a model for developing countries in the future and as an important partner to the United States."

Nixon didn't take a single note. That did not inspire confidence in any of us.

The next day, after Bowles introduced him at the crowded press conference, Nixon began by saying that he had three observations to make. He then repeated Bowles's three points. Almost exactly—to the word. Nixon delivered his three observations with such conviction, such apparent spontaneity that the members of the Indian press were so taken aback that they didn't ask a single difficult question.

I was with him as we drove out to the airport. "Dick," he told me, "I want to thank you for helping me during my visit and for showing me around."

I thanked him.

"I get the feeling," he went on, "that you're interested in politics, and I just want to encourage you because, for all its ups and downs, it really is a noble calling. Even though I sense you may be the other party, I hope you think seriously about a career in public service."

After I had returned to the States, I received a letter from him thanking me for putting together a visit that had been helpful to him and during which he had learned a lot about India. And at the end of the letter, he reiterated his encouragement to think about a career in public service—that people like me were needed. This was 1967, a year before he was elected president.

In 1970 I ran for state representative and featured that letter in the newsletter I distributed just before the general election.

I had the endorsement of the president. In those day Nixon was riding high.

The rest is, as they say, history. Except that the Svetlana story didn't end for me in India.

Dagmar and I finished our diplomatic life in June and planned to head separately to Europe. She was taking the kids to Vienna to visit their grandparents. I was heading in a different direction with Valerie Ostepenko's help. Months before the Svetlana episode, he had arranged at my request a four-day visit to the Soviet Union. I wanted to visit Moscow University, see a collective farm, get a feel for what was going on in the Soviet Union. Nearly all of our foreign policy in the mid-1960s was defined in juxtaposition with that aspiring superpower. It would, I thought, be an invaluable experience.

Resigning from the Foreign Service meant that the day I was leaving Delhi, they replaced my diplomatic passport with a standard passport. I was no longer a member of the Foreign Service. So I arrived on June 5, 1967, in Moscow, was met by an Intourist guide, checked into the hotel, and then spent that afternoon on campus talking to students.

The second day the tour guide picked me up and said, "Unfortunately, our visit to the collective farm is not going to be possible."

"Why not?" I asked.

"The road is being repaired," she said quickly. Then changed the subject. "You expressed an interest in urban planning," she said. "I am going to take you to meet one of our urban planners."

"Fine," I said as we drove to an office in downtown Moscow.

We arrived at a building with a distinctive brass plate by the door with a design I had seen before but could not place. We walked up two flights of stairs, and she led me into a large room that was sparsely furnished with a desk and two chairs. And shrouded in cigarette smoke. Behind the desk a man sat, cigarette in his hand.

"I'll see you when you're finished," said the Intourist guide, closing the door behind her.

"Mr. Celeste," said the man as soon as the door closed. "I'm afraid we've brought you here under false pretenses."

This was not what I wanted to hear.

"I'm not an urban planner," he continued. "I don't even like cities. I wouldn't live in a city except for my work, which requires me to live in cities."

An uneasy feeling crept into the pit of my stomach. "Could you tell me what sort of work you do?"

"I'm a journalist," he said. "With TASS."

That was the logo I had recognized. The Russian News Agency.

"I need," he said, "to talk to you about the Middle East."

It dawned on me that what became known as the Six-Day War was under way. "I know nothing about the Middle East," I told him.

He said, "But I need to tell you about the Middle East."

"You don't understand, I'm not a professional diplomat."

He said he knew that as well.

"I don't think you understand. I was in India working for Chester Bowles as his personal assistant. I was not a career diplomat. I am not who you think I am."

"This is a very important conversation," he told me, and reached into the desk, bringing out a yellow pad. "Take careful notes."

For the next hour and a half he talked about what was going on in the Middle East. He explained that the Israelis had captured large numbers of tanks the Soviets had provided and said that we needed to reach some kind of understanding that would avoid an escalation. A secret delegation from Cairo was in Moscow, he told me, anxious to persuade Soviet officials to replace the equipment that had been lost. The Soviets would rather not resupply them. An understanding that the Americans would not be giving more military equipment to the Israelis would help the Soviets in their refusal.

It was a fig leaf—a reason for the Kremlin to say no to the Cairo delegation.

He then spent quite a bit of time describing the case for restraint on both sides, referring to a series of articles that he had written while he had covered the United Nations.

When the "urban planner" concluded I had several pages of notes. My Intourist guide reappeared. As we were getting into the car she said, "I assume you want to go to the American embassy."

I told her that was right.

We arrived and, as at every embassy, a marine guard was posted at the entrance. Roger Kirk had given me the name of a fellow diplomat he knew, telling me that if I needed anything while I was in Moscow to give this guy a call.

Roger's friend came down five minutes later and asked how he could help.

"I've just had," I said, "an unexpected and important conversation." I told him about the chain-smoking fellow from TASS who hated cities. His name was Oleg.

The embassy guy couldn't believe it. "How the fuck do you know Oleg?"

I explained how the tour guide had taken me to his office.

"His office?" he said. "We've been trying to find Oleg for the last three days."

I said I knew nothing about that.

"We've got to go to the bubble and talk," he said, referring to the room in the embassy designed for secure conversations.

I told him I didn't want to go to the bubble.

"What do you mean?" he said.

"Where is the place they are most likely to listen to our conversation?" I asked him.

He thought about it. "Our cafeteria," he said.

"Then let's go there," I told him. "I want them to know that I've given an accurate account of the conversation with Oleg. I'm not telling you anything they don't know. So there's no reason to act like they shouldn't hear what I'm telling you."

Thus my experience with Svetlana Stalin concluded. Clearly, my careful report about what had happened when she walked into our Delhi embassy was remembered in the Kremlin.

As for the *other* question, the one that had echoed through the hallways of the Indian government after the Svetlana Stalin incident—"Who is Dick Celeste?"—that remained to be answered.

Chapter 5

On to Columbus

Coming home to Ohio, I was worried about the future. I had loved working for Chester Bowles and loved India. And the State Department had provided Dagmar and me with a comfortable living. I knew coming home would be a rude awakening.

But the ambivalence I felt went beyond that. I needed to figure out my future and a way of supporting my substantial family. I had learned from Bowles an important lesson about gaining experience in the business world but had not thought through seriously the practicalities of what this would entail. Before India I had only considered becoming a teacher or a lawyer. Now I set my sights on going into the real estate business with my father.

When I broached the subject with him he was supportive, saying that he and my brother Ted had been talking about how great it would be to call the company Celeste, Celeste, and Celeste. There remained the awkward question of how much he would pay me. In the end we settled on $10,000 a year. It wasn't a lot. I had been earning $13,000 as a Foreign Service Officer and the government provided housing, travel, and an excellent health plan. Returning to the States I had done my best to arrange a soft landing, but there were limits to how soft it could be.

This concern about money would be perennial. For a number of reasons, Dagmar wouldn't—or couldn't—manage the family budget, so I did. When I asked her recently about what she remembered about our early years together, she said that her most vivid image was that of me hunched over the kitchen table, head in my hands as I stared at the bills trying to figure out where the money would come from. As I was preparing to return home in 1967, Ambassador Bowles had surprised me with a personal check for $10,000. He said that he wanted to make the first contribution to my future campaign as a way of thanking me for my work with him. I was totally stunned as well as deeply grateful. I thanked him profusely—and wondered what to do with such a sum.

My father and I had exchanged thoughts about politics in advance of my return, and much of our correspondence of that time focused on the shape our respective political futures might take. One possibility was to run for Congress, which had prompted me—a couple of years earlier—to ask him to mail me maps of congressional districts. I wasn't sure, though, if this meshed with my deeper ambition to bring about social change. As I was sitting in India wrestling with my political ambition, Dad was in Cleveland being romanced by the local Democratic leadership to run for mayor of Cleveland. The incumbent mayor, Ralph S. Locher, was considered mediocre and vulnerable in the 1967 election. In contrast, my father had proven to be a highly popular and effective mayor of Lakewood who had won reelection handily in a Republican town.

A number of contrived scenarios had been proposed to Dad that would conclude with him being mayor. One, urged on him in late 1966 by Louis Seltzer, editor of the *Cleveland Press,* and relayed to me in a letter, involved the notion that the mayor's law director would get an appointment with the Johnson administration. My father would be appointed law director to replace him. Then, if the mayor should *also* be appointed—again by the Johnson administration—Frank Celeste would automatically become mayor. He would have gained the office without ever having to run for it.

I thought it was a bad idea. In my November 1966 reply to my father I expressed strong reservations:

> Remember this might just be Seltzer. What other indications do you have that the offer is serious? If it is a serious offer, what assurances do you have that they will stand by the offer and not leave you hanging as law director? More importantly, what assurances would you have of continued support after you were installed . . . they are not doing you a favor by offering you the job—I am sure you would get elected whenever you chose to move into Cleveland and campaign. Moreover, there are real disadvantages to this method of taking office—less popular support, exposed to the charge of outsider, built in conflict with party leaders, etc.

In the end, no appointment merry-go-round occurred. However, the idea of Frank Celeste running for mayor of Cleveland persisted. In early 1967 several key Democrats urged him to run. Their pitch was that if Frank agreed to run, everything would be taken care of. He would move into a Cleveland apartment and declare his candidacy. He'd have the support of the key players: the newspapers, the business community, and the Democratic Party. The business community would raise the money, the party would discourage the incumbent from running, and endorsements from the papers would see him through the general election.

Again I was unconvinced. One thing that made me skeptical was the likely candidacy of Carl Stokes, a state representative who had run for mayor before. Stokes was a magnetic figure, the sort of person who could speak with passion at a political meeting and also hustle a game of pool anywhere in the city. He had built a strong political organization in the predominantly Black neighborhoods on Cleveland's east side. If he ran against my father, he would be a formidable opponent, particularly if—as likely—the election became polarized along racial lines.

Martin Luther King Jr. had come to Cleveland in early 1967 to promote voter registration on behalf of Stokes. Then-mayor Locher had refused to meet with King and declared that he, like two other recent visitors to the city—Floyd McKissick, national director of the Congress of Racial Equality, and Alabama governor George C. Wallace—was an extremist. This inflammatory statement deepened the growing rift between Black and white voters. Though my father had strong ties in the Black community, I couldn't see Frank Celeste garnering much support in a polarized contest.

Nevertheless my father bought the optimistic scenario. By the time I returned from India, my father had a headquarters staffed by three people. One was Jim Nolan, a gadfly Irish politician from Cleveland; another was a young woman named Carol Frode, my father's campaign secretary. The third was a young man named John Kealey, who seemed to be volunteering mostly because he had his eye on Carol.

It was a bare bones operation. My father had hired a PR fellow whose experience did not include much politics—particularly partisan politics. When my father entered the race, he lacked a core of strategic advisors who would give him candid advice—or who would be able to take swift and decisive action on his behalf. Nor did the race seem about to be handed to him in the way it had been promised.

This became clear to me almost immediately. The very first event I attended with him—within days of my return to Ohio, before I'd set foot in National Housing Associates, my father's real estate business—was a meeting of a group of Italian American city employees. A candidates' meeting was being held, according to an anonymous tip Dad had received. He decided to go and asked me to come along. The two of us drove to the small Sons of Italy Hall in Collinwood.

We arrived to find the place plastered with signs for the incumbent, Ralph Locher. Presiding over the meeting was none other than Bronis J. Klementowicz—Locher's law director, known widely as the "Polish Falcon." The event had been advertised as a "Candidates' Night," and Klem was at the podium extolling the virtues of the mayor.

After he had finished, one of the members of the club stood up and suggested that since no other candidates were present they endorse Locher.

I stood up. "Wait a minute," I said, "there is another candidate here."

"Who are you?" I was asked.

"My name's Dick's Celeste. This is Frank Celeste. He's a candidate."

"He didn't sign up in advance," was the reply. "He can't just show up."

"What do you mean?" I asked. "He is an Italian American candidate. You should give him a chance to speak."

I was ignored. "Motion to endorse Locher. Second? All in favor?"

It was unanimous.

"Okay," said a guy at the front. "Who wants a beer?"

I went up to the biggest guy in the place—I don't remember his name, just that he was a couple of inches taller and a lot wider than me. "This is supposed to be a candidates' night. How can you do that?"

"It's not a political meeting," he told me.

"How can you say it's not a political meeting? Look at all the signs on the wall. You think I'm stupid? Not a political meeting?"

By this point he was in my face.

I kept at him. I was outraged at the way my father had been treated.

"You get out of here right now," the guy told me. "If you don't walk out of here standing up, I'll send you out lying down."

My father pulled me away. That night was the first indication that this was not going to be a campaign for the faint of heart.

A few weeks later the Cuyahoga County Democratic Executive Committee met to decide who to endorse in the mayor's race. Three people were nominated: Ralph Locher, Carl Stokes, and Frank Celeste. This was supposed to be greased—arranged—the moment when the hammer falls and Locher decides he won't seek reelection because he doesn't have the support of the party.

It didn't work like that. Promises had been made, yes. But that was it—no follow-up. The Democratic chairman was the county engineer, Bert Porter, who understood that the executive committee was largely composed of city or county patronage employees—people who, because they want to hang onto their jobs, only vote against incumbents when told to do so. The outcome was predictable, though not the one Frank Celeste had been promised: Locher first, Stokes second, Celeste a distant third. No one, it turned out, had done any arm-twisting for my father.

The treasurer of the county organization was a man named Joe Mull. He had been at the meeting when my father was promised the party endorsement. Mull resigned when Locher got the nod, saying that he hadn't come from Lithuania to the United States to find democracy and then simply just stand by while the political party he loved went back on its word. The next day—and every day thereafter—Joe joined us in my father's mostly empty campaign headquarters.

When it became clear that both Carl Stokes and Ralph Locher were in the race for keeps, the same people who had urged Dad to enter the race began asking him to get out. They didn't want Stokes to win and were worried that my father would split the white vote.

My father refused, however, telling them that he had entered the race counting on their support and was going to see it through. Influential Democrats said they would support him but didn't. The editor of the *Plain Dealer*, who said he was going to endorse him, didn't. The only person who kept his word was a leading Cleveland lawyer named Jack Reavis. He agreed to raise $60,000 for Dad, and he did. Late in the campaign, one of the Democratic Party kingpins visited my father and asked how much it would take to get him out of the race. My father refused. "People are counting on me," he said. There weren't that many of them, unfortunately, but he still felt responsible to them.

"Is it fifty thousand?" he was asked. "A hundred? What will it take to get you out of the race?"

My father steadfastly refused.

As Election Day neared, it became clear to everyone—Dad included—that Frank Celeste was not going to win. The final event was a three-way debate between my father, Carl Stokes, and Seth Taft, the Republican candidate for mayor. Ralph Locher wouldn't bother to show up. My father didn't want to go either.

"I'm losing my voice," he said. "Why don't you go in my place?"

I was dismayed to see my father that disheartened, so I agreed to stand in for him and make the case for why Frank Celeste was the most qualified candidate for mayor.

It was my maiden political speech.

Afterwards Carl Stokes said to me, "It's a damn good thing your father didn't send you to every one of these debates."

My father had not done his homework as he had when he'd run successfully for mayor of Lakewood. Even though he had real friends in the city's different constituencies, including Black churchmen who were ready to support him (a few even with Carl Stokes in the race), he hadn't worked the Slovak community or the Italian community, or even the Black community for that matter. The results said as much: Stokes won, Locher finished second, and my father was such a distant third that his votes didn't amount to the margin that separated the top two.

It was a tough defeat, but my father took it well. He liked to say that he had received fewer votes but made more friends than anyone else in the race. That was probably an exaggeration—though not the fewest votes part.

I learned a great deal from my father's ill-fated campaign. One lesson was never enter a race unless you have a clear idea where your votes are coming from. Instead my father had counted on others and their empty promises. And that was the second lesson: take private assurances with a grain of salt. Only public support really counts. In planning his run for mayor, Dad had assumed that his qualifications plus others' assurances were the road to victory. People quietly pledged their support, told him they would deliver endorsements or votes, and he believed them. By contrast, Carl Stokes knew where his votes were and mounted a well-organized effort, energized by Martin Luther King Jr., to turn them out.

The final lesson from the Cleveland mayor's race was this: politics is a very tough business. It touches people's lives in many ways, and some people involved have a lot at stake. Elections can cost people jobs, influence, and, in some cases, fortunes. Just how devastating a loss could be was driven home to me by Joe Mull. On election night my father's loss was evident early. Frank Celeste was among the first to congratulate Carl Stokes. Dad would later say that the best thing to come out of his campaign was the marriage of Carol Frode and John Kealey.

It would, however, turn out to be Joe Mull's last campaign. He had watched the way it all unfolded, watched his beloved Democratic Party chairman break promises, watched the newspapers encourage my father and then back away, watched my father's distant finish. It hit him hard. The real tragedy of that election wasn't the Celeste loss. Two days after the election, Joe went into the woods behind his home and shot himself.

My father and I never talked about Joe's suicide, perhaps because neither of us knew how to process it. Dad had been trying to do the right thing and was disappointed that the right thing as he saw it was not what people wanted. Still, politics for him was never life or death. But for others it was. And still is.

Don't get me wrong. My father loved the campaign trail. He really did make many friends. He was always positive, had fun, and inspired hope. I saw and savored all of this. That has stuck with me. Still, in the years to come, the memory of Joe Mull made me mindful of the need to weigh carefully what I promised and how I would deliver.

By early 1968 I was working full time in real estate, still uncertain about my political future. Riots had inflamed Cleveland's Hough neighborhood in 1967. And racial tensions were high as civil rights demonstrations spread across the South. Black Democrats in Mississippi announced they were going to send a "freedom delegation" to the National Convention because no Blacks could be elected on the regular party slate.

Thanks in part to the "Dump Johnson" movement, Gene McCarthy had by this point become the "Pied Piper" of the antiwar movement. Young people all over the country were volunteering in his campaign.

Around this time I was contacted by John Nolan, whom I had met when he visited India on behalf of the attorney general. John wanted my take on the prospects of Bob Kennedy's presidential candidacy in Ohio. Our convention delegation had been selected early in 1968, pledged to Steve Young, the popular US senator from Norwalk, as favorite son. Young had made it clear, however, when he accepted the favorite son designation—and in spite of his early opposition to the Vietnam War—that the delegation would be loyal to Johnson after the first ballot. As I outlined in my memo to Nolan—written before Johnson left the race—these delegates were pledged to LBJ through Young. But their pledge might not match their "private inclinations." The memo suggested a series of strategies for moving delegates from LBJ to Kennedy and speculated about who might support the effort. My conclusion was that moving the delegates to Kennedy after the first ballot was a possibility but not a sure thing.

Nolan was a fascinating man. He was an assistant attorney general and had visited India at Kennedy's request to take the temperature of student leaders around the world. I had arranged for us to meet a group of young leftist activists in Calcutta, and that led to our friendship. He was an Irish Catholic, smart, gritty, and straightforward, the guy Bob Kennedy would send to Alabama when he needed a firsthand report on what George Wallace was doing.

John once told me a story about working for Bobby, who had called him in one day saying he had a special job for him.

"What's the job?" asked Nolan.

"The president wants you to go to Cuba," said Kennedy, "and negotiate the release of our prisoners there. Sit down with Castro and get them out."

"If that's what you want me to do," said John, "I'll do my best."

A few days later he was contacted by the State Department, who said they had a gift for him to take to Castro. It was a wet suit; Fidel was a diving enthusiast in those days. John said fine and continued his preparations for the trip, which included calling Bill Donavan—a fellow Irishman who had run the Office of Strategic Services during the war and helped create the CIA—whom Nolan knew. "Would you mind if I came up to New York?" Nolan asked, hoping to get the benefit of Donovan's advice.

Donovan was happy to oblige. A few days later the two met and discussed the president's mission and what Nolan might expect. Near the end of the meeting Donovan asked about gifts. "Have they given you anything?" he said. "Anything to give to Castro?"

Nolan told him about the wet suit.

"That's interesting," said Donovan. "When you get back to Washington, courier that wet suit up to me. I'd like to have a look at it."

Nolan sent the wet suit to him and, a few days later, Donovan sent it back. Nolan took it with him to Cuba, gave it to Fidel, who was thrilled. The two of them went diving together and had a great time. Negotiations had been positive, though not conclusive. When he got home Nolan hung a picture in his basement of him and Castro in their diving gear, smoking big cigars.

Not until 1976 when the Church Committee held its hearings on assassination attempts by the US government did Nolan learn that he had been given a poisoned wet suit. Apparently Bill Donovan, suspecting this, had secured a substitute wet suit, which he had sent to Nolan. The hearings revealed that the CIA had been perplexed by the failure of the poisoned wet suit; Castro had worn it—they had the photographs from Nolan—but he was still alive, somehow.

Another Bobby Kennedy story that I had heard in India came from Brandon Grove, the elegant man who had been in charge of the front office under Chester Bowles when I first arrived in New Delhi. Grove was a career Foreign Service Officer whose first posting had been to West Africa, where Attorney General Kennedy visited. Several months later, Bobby was sent by President Kennedy on a tour through Asia to meet key foreign leaders. The attorney general asked the State Department to lend him Brandon to staff his trip. Grove was about an inch and half taller than me—over six feet five—and quite distinguished looking—like he could be a US senator or the maître d' at the Ritz.

In each of the countries Kennedy visited, he would invariably visit a university so he could interact directly with students. In Tokyo, Kennedy had gotten into a fascinating back-and-forth with a group of leftist students. This was what Bobby loved; he fed off the energy of young people and was utterly charismatic. Once he got into a discussion, it was hard to stop him. He and his party next went to Indonesia, which was particularly sensitive at the time. Diplomatic relations between the United States and Indonesia were suspended, which meant the visit required a special arrangement; Kennedy's plane would land at a designated time, and, twenty-four hours later, it had to depart.

After landing in Jakarta, Kennedy spent time trying to improve communications with government leaders. The next morning, as in Tokyo, he met with a student group. He soon found himself immersed in a thoughtful, highly animated question-and-answer session. On it went, showing no signs of stopping. Brandon was nervous because he knew that it took an hour to get to the airport—and the plane had to wheels-up at 11:00 A.M.

As 10:00 A.M. approached, Grove took it upon himself to stand up in the back of the room: "Mr. Attorney General," he said, "we have a plane to catch."

"One more question," said Kennedy.

After answering the question he seemed about to take another when Brandon popped up again. "Mr. Attorney General," he said, "I just want to remind you, we live in a *real* world with *real* people, and there's a *real* airplane that's going to have to take off in an hour. We have to be on it."

That did it. Kennedy excused himself, and off they went. After several more stops, Kennedy returned to Washington, and Brandon Grove went back to his post in West Africa. Two months later he received a small package from the attorney general. In it was a pair of gold cuff links. One was inscribed "real world," the other, "real people."

That was Bobby Kennedy. There was no question in my mind that he would make a strong candidate, but Johnson seemed determined to run for reelection even if few wanted him to. Then in March—after the New Hampshire primary—Johnson stunned the country, announcing that he would not seek another term.

Soon afterwards, Bobby Kennedy declared his candidacy for president.

Memorial Day weekend 1968, Dagmar and I took the kids to Connecticut for the annual gathering at the Bowleses' splendid home in Essex. We would see the two of them and their family and spend time with the "Chet Set"— three generations of folks who had at some point worked for Chet. By the end of May, after a whirlwind campaign, Senator Kennedy had emerged as the front-runner. He arrived in California in early June, hoping to secure the nomination with a victory there.

Kennedy had won my respect when I saw him speak in the aftermath of Martin Luther King's assassination. When King was shot in Memphis, Kennedy had been campaigning in Indianapolis, where he gave an unforgettable impromptu speech. As I watched on television, Bobby climbed onto the roof of a car surrounded by angry Black youth. He talked about how he understood their pain, how it felt to lose his own brother to an assassin's bullet. The next day he came to Cleveland and spoke, just as eloquently, in my hometown. The pain and outrage he shared with us had been visceral and intensely personal.

We were sitting in the Bowleses' home late at night as Bobby addressed his supporters in the ballroom of the Ambassador Hotel after his California win. "And now it's on to Chicago," said Kennedy, "and let's win there."

Hearing him gunned down was like getting hit in the stomach.

In shock, we sat—many of us in tears—around Bowles, who quietly told us this story: Bobby Kennedy had been his adversary for much of his time at the State Department. Bowles had opposed the Bay of Pigs, and he believed that Bobby had urged his exile to India for that opposition.

"But you know," he told us, "I had come to respect Bobby Kennedy."

I was astonished to hear Chet say this. I had only heard him describe Bobby Kennedy as impetuous, someone who didn't quite understand how the world worked.

"During my exit briefings when I returned from New Delhi," Chet confided, "I was walking down the corridor in a Senate office building, and Bobby Kennedy was coming the other way with an entourage. He stopped, approached me, and said, simply, 'Chet, you were right, and I was wrong. I owe you an apology.' Then he moved on." Chet paused. "Bobby Kennedy won my respect that day."

Many of us felt compelled by Robert Kennedy's death to do something, convinced that we could not just have more of the same. More of the same was Hubert Humphrey, the obvious choice to be Johnson's successor. Or, of all people, Richard Nixon. We needed to act.

I needed to act.

Shortly after I returned from Essex, a friend from Yale named Allard Lowenstein called. Al was one of the architects of the "Dump Johnson" movement, which had played a key role in convincing LBJ to withdraw from the presidential race. And he was, perhaps more than any other single person, responsible for organizing Gene McCarthy's campaign as an antiwar protest. Al had come to believe McCarthy couldn't carry the Chicago convention. He had been among those who had approached Bobby Kennedy—discreetly—to urge him to run. On the phone, Lowenstein said he wanted to meet the director of the Ohio Democratic Party. A few days later he was sitting in our living room with Pete O'Grady, who ran the ODP.

Al shared his view of the situation with O'Grady. McCarthy had been strong enough in the early primaries to convince LBJ to forgo reelection. But he wouldn't be strong enough to win the nomination. And Humphrey was damaged goods because of his connection to Johnson and Vietnam. Only Ted Kennedy could win in November. Would O'Grady keep an open mind?

O'Grady seemed interested but wary. After he left, Lowenstein said he had a proposal for me. "Dick," he repeated, "Johnson is out, Bob Kennedy is dead, Hubert Humphrey is going to get the nomination unless we do something dramatic. We need to draft Ted Kennedy. But to do that we need to start loosening up delegations."

He knew the Ohio delegation was composed of Johnson loyalists, and the issue was how they might be redirected.

"Do you think you could mount a primary here in Ohio?" Lowenstein said.

"What do you mean?"

"Another primary," said Allard. "A privately sponsored primary where Democratic voters could cast their ballots for a range of candidates. I believe ordinary voters would indicate a preference for Ted Kennedy. I can raise the money—if you will handle the organizational side."

Dagmar and I, eager to help reenergize the Democratic Party, agreed to put together what we would call the August primary.

Within a few days Al began feeding us checks and volunteers, McCarthy activists now looking for a way to open up the convention. Picking up the Bobby Kennedy line, our mantra became "On to Chicago." For people who had been field organizers for McCarthy, or active in the antiwar movement, Ohio's August primary became where the action was in the final weeks before the convention.

We knew there would be substantial antiwar sentiment in Chicago against Humphrey—a genuine liberal Democrat who had been tarred with the Lyndon Johnson brush—and the idea was to turn that momentum in the direction of Ted Kennedy. So out of our modest house in Cleveland we stitched together a statewide vote as if it were a primary election for president. On the ballot were Hubert Humphrey, Ted Kennedy, Gene McCarthy, and George McGovern. Fifteen or twenty young volunteers were sleeping on our floor.

Periodically the one television reporter who took us seriously, Bob Franken, would stop by and check on our progress.

An early logistics challenge was, literally, polling places. We needed somewhere to station our ballot boxes that was public and secure.

One of our volunteers was an older Cleveland party regular named Paul DeGrandis, and it was Paul who solved this problem. "Let's get the fucking fire stations," he said.

"What do you mean, get the fucking fire stations?" I asked.

"I work with the Ohio Firefighters Association," he said. "Let's just get the fucking fire stations. We can put the polling booths there."

It was a great idea. We got the fire stations.

We set up nearly two hundred polling places across the state and had volunteers in about a third of Ohio's counties, including all the major cities. When the polls closed, we flew the ballot boxes back to Cleveland, where they were counted in the basement of St. Agatha's Church on Euclid Avenue. Father Finian Murphy—a politically minded priest who would become a close family friend—supervised the tabulation of results and bestowed his moral authority to the proceedings.

Ted Kennedy won the August primary but not by a lot. Humphrey did better than many of us had expected, mostly because of his long identification with the civil rights movement. Black voters tended to stick with Humphrey. In any event, we sent the vote tally to each Ohio delegate, urging them to keep an open mind.

About a week before the convention, I got a call from Mike DiSalle, the former governor of Ohio, asking if I would come to Chicago to help him with a project.

I figured what the heck.

Jerry Austin, later my campaign director and close friend, was also on his way to Chicago. Originally from Brooklyn, Jerry had been raised in a trade union family and graduated from City College in New York. He likes to say that, at least in that regard, Colin Powell followed in his footsteps. After graduating from college, he had become a VISTA volunteer, then came back to teach high school in Cleveland. He'd met my brother not long after Ted returned from the Peace Corps, and the two of them ended up living in the same apartment in Cleveland. Ted introduced us and, though both had been involved in Dad's mayoral race and the tail end of the August primary, the Chicago convention was the first time Jerry and I worked closely. He had been helping the McGovern campaign, and McGovern asked Jerry to travel with him to Chicago. I got there on my own, the plan being to meet in Mike DiSalle's suite in the Palmer House.

When I arrived in Chicago, I saw that the noisy demonstration in the park not far from where we were staying was growing by the minute. Mayor Daley had police everywhere trying to stop delegates from being accosted. Confrontation was in the air.

Mike DiSalle told Jerry and me that he and Jesse Unruh, the California state treasurer, were mounting a "Draft Ted Kennedy" effort and wanted our help. He needed nuts and bolts guys. We recruited a handful of August primary folks and put out a call on the local radio for "Kennedy volunteers." We needed bodies to man an intense, highly improvised effort to swing delegates to Ted Kennedy.

As a first step we posted people where the delegations were housed and asked delegates to sign petitions supporting Kennedy. Many did amidst a growing sense of excitement. People who had heard the radio appeal came to the hotel wearing Kennedy buttons, eager to help. Jerry and I realized that Kennedy campaign materials never used a first name.

To keep other volunteers busy, we asked them to make signs. Soon we had 250 handmade Ted Kennedy signs. But getting them into the convention hall posed a problem. Mayor Daley had sealed off the floor in order to keep demonstrators out. However, I remembered that a *Plain Dealer* reporter named Jim Naughton, a good friend from Cleveland, was on the floor covering the action. I called the press center and asked to speak to him.

It took a while, but eventually he came on the line.

"Jim," I said, "if you got some packages, could a group of delegates pick them up?"

"What's in the package?" he said.

"You don't want to know."

"Are they going to get me in trouble?" he asked.

"If you don't know what's in the packages, they won't get you in trouble. I will get a couple of delegates to come down and ask for them."

He paused for a moment. "Okay," he said.

We bundled up the signs and sent them to the press center for Naughton. Soon delegates we had identified as Kennedy supporters were alerted and showed up to collect them. By eight that evening, television commentators

reported seeing signs spreading across the convention hall and were specu-
lating about nascent draft Kennedy sentiment.

As we talked to delegations, we were getting serious traction. For example,
a delegate named Marie McGuire from Pennsylvania came in and said she
was for Kennedy, asking what she could do to help. We had made enough
signs, we told her. An hour later she came back with Milt Shapp, the governor
of Pennsylvania, who handed Jerry $500.

In the middle of this frenzied activity, Bill Josephson, a friend of mine from
my early days at the Peace Corps, called. I didn't know he was in Chicago. He
asked me to join him for lunch at a club nearby. Almost as soon as I arrived,
Bill began telling me Teddy Kennedy didn't want any of this going on.

I told him that all Kennedy needed to do was to call Mike DiSalle to stop
it. In the middle of lunch, Bill got a call from Paris. I had a hunch it was Sarge
Shriver, our ambassador in Paris at the time. I put two and two together and
realized Bill was hoping to get Shriver on the ballot rather than Kennedy.

From our petitions we had a vote count, and to this day I am convinced Ted
Kennedy could have won the nomination. But apparently Kennedy advisors
gathered nearby in the merchandise mart assessed the delegate count differently; Mike DiSalle got the call. Ted Kennedy was out. Hubert Humphrey won
the nomination but was badly damaged by the violence of the Chicago police
against the demonstrators gathered near the convention hotels.

Al Lowenstein later described the draft Kennedy effort to me as "a trapeze
act that missed by inches." Austin and I returned to Ohio and set to work to
do what we could for the Humphrey campaign. That effort also missed by
inches.

Using the money that Chester Bowles had given me, Dagmar and I had
made a down payment on a home in Cleveland, a congressional district and
a state House district held by Republicans. My pal Paul DeGrandis had approached me to run against the incumbent Republican congressman. By that
point, however, I had decided I wasn't interested in going to Washington.
With three young kids, I didn't find the idea of commuting back and forth to
Washington appealing.

But my decision not to run for Congress was also influenced by my early
focus during the MAT at Yale on the challenge of urban education. My belief
that schools were cornerstones of urban change lingered. Finally, there was
the influence of Chester Bowles, who had loved state government and been

disappointed by Washington. His enthusiasm for what he had been able to accomplish as governor was infectious. That enthusiasm stayed with me.

I began to give talks to various groups in the community. The Jesuits, particularly, would invite me to talk to high school students about my experience overseas with Bowles as well as my time at the Peace Corps. Dagmar would often go with me to the schools. During one of these discussions a young man asked why I wasn't in public service myself. "If you feel so strongly about these issues, Mr. Celeste," the boy inquired, "why haven't you run for public office?" I hemmed and hawed.

On the way home Dagmar said, "That was a good question. You need a better answer."

One of the curious things about running for public office is that one has to figure out how to actually do it. There are no easy-to-follow handbooks, no user manuals to guide you through the process of declaring your candidacy. Having decided in late 1969 to run for state representative, I had no clear idea about how to actually tell people I was running. For advice I called Carl Stokes's press secretary, whom I had met during my father's unsuccessful mayor's race.

"You need a press release," he told me. "A one-page statement about why you want to run and why you think you're the best candidate for the job." After much effort I came back with two and a half pages. I couldn't limit my many qualifications and plans to a single page. He produced a blue pencil, crossing out one paragraph after another. Eventually he got it down to a single page.

"Now what?" I said.

"Take it to the *Sun Post*, the weekly paper in your district. Sit down with the editor," he said. "Tell him why you've brought this press release and why you're interested in running—and that's how you'll announce your candidacy."

I did exactly that.

The editor read the release, nodded, and gestured beyond his office. "See that young man out there," he told me. "Give him your press release, and he will do an interview." The reporter was named Chuck Austin, and he would write the first story covering my maiden campaign.

Later he would become a Celeste volunteer.

My classmate Jim Asbeck—who had defeated me for senior class president at Lakewood High School—became my campaign manager. Jim was a manager for BF Goodrich and approached the campaign in a highly systematic manner using something called a PERT chart—short for Program Evaluation Review Technique. Originally developed by the US Navy, Asbeck's PERT chart facilitated the process of thinking backwards from Election Day. With a background in finding efficiencies in manufacturing, Jim had a unique understanding of the way *time* is often the most underappreciated resource in a political campaign.

It may seem like a small point, but it isn't. Indeed, the role that time plays as a resource in a campaign is something that few politicians fully grasp. Money is an obvious resource. Everybody knows that. Where the money will come from—and how much—is a key consideration. So is the question of campaign volunteers. They are a crucial resource, but most folks running for office are aware of the importance of volunteers.

Time is more elusive, however, and the role it plays in a campaign is sometimes difficult—particularly for fledgling politicians—to grasp. Candidates think about what they need to do today or tomorrow, but not where they want to be on Election Day. Most crucially, candidates need to frame the question they want voters to focus on as they enter the voting booth as clearly and compellingly as possible and work back from that question.

As I worked with Jim, we also adopted the notion of a vote budget. How many votes did we need? Where were those votes going to come from? We looked closely at voting patterns from previous years and developed precinct-by-precinct targets that we needed to be successful.

Jim and his wife, Virginia Waldheger—yes, the same Dee who was my coeditor of the high school yearbook and the girl my father thought I should marry—were essential members of the team. Dee brought her own brand of precision to the campaign. She organized all of our volunteers into a file— using cards with holes punched in them. Each card represented a supporter or a potential supporter. Through the cards Dee punched holes that had been aligned in particular ways so she could identify people systematically. One "pull" organized people by geography, another by age group, another by expressed interest, yet another by the type of events they had attended. Today, of course, she would have all of this information and more in her laptop.

Another young woman who volunteered—Peggy Donovan—was deaf. She became one of our office managers. An excellent lip reader, she had a day job at American Greetings. She welcomed people when they arrived for evening phone banks. The key to my campaign for state rep—and this would be true of all my campaigns—was extensive citizen involvement. From the start I made it clear I didn't want people simply to cast a vote for me—I asked them to become part of the process. More than just knocking on doors or taking people to the polls, I wanted them to become part of a growing constituency for change.

We created an attractive storefront campaign office and turned to our babysitters to help recruit volunteers. Our most faithful door-knockers were young women from St. Augustine Academy—the local Catholic girls' school. These enthusiastic campaigners also proved keenly interested in learning more about the political process.

Every Saturday, John Kealy—the same young man who had worked in my father's campaign—led neighborhood canvasing. John, now married, was living in my district. He became known as "Coach" and, together with his team of faithful young volunteers, knocked on the door of every registered voter—twice—during that campaign. "Coach" would get the girls and me pumped up; then at the end of our canvasing he would pick up fresh Kelly's doughnuts, and we would have a feast.

In the general election, my opponent was George J. Usher, a member of Lakewood City Council who had never lost an election. Usher owned an insurance agency—and his name was everywhere. His company sponsored about three quarters of the teams who played Little League baseball. All that summer I had to look at kids walking around with T-shirts that read: George J. Usher Insurance Agency.

Part of me worried that those Little Leaguers were walking signboards for Usher, believing they were prompting people to vote for my opponent. As it turned out, however, those shirts were not persuasive. Another early lesson in the reality of politics: signs don't vote. No matter how many signs you put up, they will not win you an election.

You have to engage people on a personal basis.

Over the years, beginning with that state representative race, I have employed a number of guerrilla tactics in campaigns. One of my favorite examples in that first election occurred at the old Cleveland Stadium where, each year, the Browns would hold a preseason NFL doubleheader. There was always a massive crowd—98,000 people packed in the stadium. On that day in 1970, my brother called stadium security and said he had an emergency message for Richard Celeste.

"We have an emergency message for Richard Celeste," said the announcer. "Will Richard Celeste please report to security?" We knew that George Usher was at the game with his pals from the local Rotary Club. Afterwards one of the Rotarians, a Celeste supporter, told us: "We razzed the shit out of George. 'Come on now,' we asked him, 'who's going to page *you*?'"

Later we applied a similar technique when I was running statewide. Every time I traveled, we made sure I was paged at the airport. Wherever I was going, whenever it was even slightly plausible for me to be in the airport, we would arrange to have me paged. Did it win me votes? Probably not. But it was our version of lawn signs, and it was fun and free—and it kept our team enthusiastic.

Another innovation of that first campaign involved a Shakespearean performance. Each summer the Great Lakes Shakespeare Festival mounted productions in the Lakewood High School Civic Auditorium, and we asked what it would cost to buy out a performance. They quoted a good price, and we persuaded a friend of ours, Larry "J. B." Robinson—the "Diamond Man," a prominent Cleveland jeweler with a classic radio voice—to emcee the evening. We recruited a dozen or so sponsors to cover the cost of the show and then filled the theater with supporters who bought ten-dollar tickets. In the end we netted over three thousand dollars for the campaign.

Serious money for a state rep race in 1970.

During the very early days of that campaign, a young fellow named Dennis Heffernan knocked on our door. He had decided he wanted to get into politics and had asked advice from a congressman named Charlie Vanik. "You want to get into politics," Vanik told him. "You have to work on a campaign."

"You know of any campaigns?" asked Dennis.

"There's this young guy, Dick Celeste," said Vanik. "I know his father, who used to be mayor of Lakewood. His son is running for state rep."

"What are you doing now?" I asked Dennis.

He was working as a roofer. It was probably the worst summer job you could have—in the hot sun, day after day, backbreaking work.

He got involved in the campaign immediately. Enthusiastic and charming, Dennis became my best friend, prepared always to hold me accountable and to ask me the hard questions few others do.

Our association began in earnest when I managed to find every excuse to stay at home rather than go out and knock on doors. First, it was the winter weather. Then we hadn't prioritized the precincts. Finally, we didn't have the campaign literature.

One Saturday in April after our leaflets arrived, Dennis said, "Okay, pal, we've got the literature, let's go." He literally dragged me out of the house that beautiful spring morning.

We went to the most intensely Democratic precincts in a heavily ethnic neighborhood known as "Birdtown" for its street names—Lark, Robin, Quail.

There I began personally campaigning for the first time. "Hi. My name is Dick Celeste. I'm running for state representative." Only once was I truly stymied. As I made my pitch to a fellow carrying his groceries home, he looked puzzled and shrugged. "You're a Democrat, aren't you?" I asked. "No," he responded, "Romanian."

What I quickly came to love most about running for office was meeting people of all sorts. This would remain true throughout my career. During that first race for state representative, we had house party after house party where I would meet new folks. Their names went into Dee's card files.

One early party that stuck with me was at the home of a firefighter's widow. She was about seventy and was living on her husband's pension. That pension was so small that she would walk five blocks from her house to buy groceries, and when she got home she'd review her bill religiously to see if she'd been overcharged. She told me that the week before our party, she had walked all the way back because she'd been overcharged a nickel. Five blocks for a nickel!

Talking to her that night, this personal connection made the pension issue come alive to me. A few years later, as a young legislator, I helped win approval for improvements in Ohio's fire and police pensions with that widow very much on my mind.

I learned and grew from getting to know people from diverse backgrounds. The experiences I had grown up with—picking up garbage and digging sewers, working in the library—had shown me how distinctive and interesting people could be. They all had their own stories. Pietro Zyzpyk, for instance, who was a garbage collector with me, had emigrated from Poland and mined coal in Pennsylvania. It was big step up for him to work aboveground. A celebration for him was whiskey with a beer chaser and pierogi on Friday night at the Slovak Club. He was half my size and could pick up twice my weight in garbage. Unbelievably strong. We would talk about everything. Pietro was deeply authentic. And connections like these were what energized campaigning for me.

Meeting new folks and hearing their stories would put fresh jump in my step because someone had given me the gift of sharing. It is hard for me to understand how anyone could be in politics and not love this part of the job. Above all else, politics involves listening to and engaging with people, often literally reaching out and touching them. I realize that this isn't always appealing to those who would like to hold public office. For example, my friend Jack Gilligan, the former governor of Ohio, was charming and funny in a small group but could come across as uncomfortable and aloof in a crowd. Not me. I loved everyone. Labor leaders. Business guys. Young, old. Black, brown, white. Men, women (sometimes a little too much). And especially kids.

In my statewide campaigns, the Ohio Democratic Women's Club became big fans of mine and worked hard for me. They were the backbone of the party, women for whom politics meant the world—the way a "garden party" might be for others.

I visited their convention in Steubenville toward the end of my second term as governor, I was making my way around the room, shaking hands, saying thanks. I kept getting asked why I was there.

"Because I'm not going to run again," I said.

"What are you going to run for?"

"I'm not running for anything," I said.

"You can tell us," was often the reply. "What's next?"

"Nothing's next," I'd say. "I'm just here to say thank you."

Perhaps three hundred women were arranged in tables of seven or eight. I approached a table where the women were giggling like little girls, looking at one of them.

As I went to shake her hand she said, "Do you want to see my ass?"

Turning red, I had no ready response.

She tugged her blouse down to reveal a large donkey tattooed on her breast. The rest of the women were howling. "Thanks for sharing," I sputtered.

This was Bob Kennedy's real world with its real people. It is hard to convey how much fun we had campaigning. Yes, it is a serious business. But it also nurtures friendships—both old and new—especially when you engage with people authentically.

By that first Election Day, our vote budget showed where we needed to get our votes, so we had assigned our youthful volunteers to pass out literature at those precincts and later report vote totals. I had encouraged our young canvasers to get permission from their teachers to work at polling places on Election Day.

When my opponent discovered so many young people passing out Celeste literature, he complained to the Lakewood truant officer. Almost immediately our office received a call from one of the kids who had been picked up. She reached me from the board of education, where she had been brought. "Mr. Celeste," said the weepy girl, "what are we going to do?"

I called the school superintendent who was not sympathetic—at first.

"Listen," I told him, "I expect to be your next state representative and you're going to ask for my help with education appropriations. All of these students have permission slips. If you want my help, I want you to apologize to them and have them taken back at once to their polling places." Which he did.

And I won.

That was my first election.

In 1970 two other liberal Democrats from Cleveland won as well: John Sweeney from Cleveland Heights, an economics professor at John Carroll University, and Harry Lehman, a lawyer from Shaker Heights. We carpooled together to Columbus.

The three of us were summoned for a caucus in early December. We Democrats were in the minority—forty-three out of ninety-nine seats in the House.

Judge Ann McManamon swearing me in as state representative in December 1970

Presenting my credentials as a state representative to Speaker Chuck Kurfess, January 1971

Of those forty-three, fifteen were from Cuyahoga County. We represented by far the biggest delegation. Immediately there was a contest to choose a Democratic leader who would have access to patronage and other perks from newly elected Gov. John Gilligan.

Two candidates were contesting: A. G. Lancione from Bellaire, along the Ohio River, and Don Pease from Oberlin. A. G. was an attorney and Pease, a newspaper publisher. A. G. was a traditional Democrat, not a bad guy, but old school. Don Pease, on the other hand, was a liberal Democrat, a kindred spirit. And I learned—discreetly—that the governor was supporting him.

I received a personal phone call from Lancione asking for my support. "I'm an Italian American," he told me. "You're an Italian American, and we should stick together." He was the current Democratic leader.

I told him I wasn't ready to make a commitment.

I talked to my fellow freshmen, John and Harry, and we decided that if we could hold Cuyahoga County together as a block—fifteen along with the votes from Lorain County—Pease would be close to securing the leadership. We would just need five or six additional votes. I talked to Mayor Stokes in advance, and he agreed to encourage the Black members of the Cuyahoga delegation to support Don Pease. Between them and we three liberals, we had a majority of the Cuyahoga caucus.

We met as a county delegation, and a few veteran legislators—among them Lenny Ostrovsky, who liked to spend his time at the racetrack, and Tony Russo, a very sly old-timer—made it clear they preferred Lancione. They made the pitch for him, and we made the pitch for Pease. "If we're going to have any influence as Cuyahoga County," I said at the end, "we should adopt the unit rule. Let's vote and then be bound to support the winner." There was agreement on this point. We voted. Pease won.

A week later, on a crisp December day, Harry, John, and I showed up in Columbus with Democrats from across the state to choose our leader. Most of the members we had never met. It turned out a third candidate, Myrl Shoemaker, an old hand from outside Chillicothe, threw his hat in the ring.

Lancione called the caucus to order. Shoemaker stood up and argued that it wasn't fair for Lancione to preside. "You're a candidate after all," he said.

"Fine," said Lancione. "I'll give the gavel to Vern Riffe."

Riffe—a legendary figure in Ohio politics and someone who will figure prominently in the pages to come—was from New Boston in the southern part of the state. That set off alarm bells for Shoemaker. "A. G.," he said, "now wait a minute. Vern is your right-hand man."

"Look," replied Lancione, "the rules of the caucus are clear. If the senior member can't preside, the next most senior member does. That's Vern."

That seemed to settle the matter. The rules are the rules, after all.

As Lancione came down from the podium, Harry Lehman—our lawyer—said, "Gosh, Mr. Lancione, it would be really helpful to see the rules. Are they written down?"

"Written down?" asked A. G. "Hell no, I make them up as I go along." He took his seat behind us. We should have known.

As Vern Riffe called us to order, Lenny Ostrovsky stood up and said, "Mr. Chairman, I move that we vote by secret ballot."

Yes, we really should have known something was up.

The secret ballot was quickly adopted. Votes were cast and counted. Don Pease received just nine votes. So much for Cuyahoga County's "unit rule." Shoemaker got a handful. The rest went for Lancione. This was my first lesson in counting votes. The key was knowing who you can depend on when doing so.

After announcing the results, Vern invited all of us to a reception that he and A. G. were hosting at the Neil House across from the statehouse. As we arrived, Vern was standing at the door shaking hands.

I hadn't been properly introduced to Vern, so, as I took his hand, I said, "I'm Dick Celeste—and I don't know what kind of schools you have in New Boston. They might not teach you how to read or write, but they sure as hell teach you how to count."

Vern roared with laughter. And often during the time we worked together—the next twenty years—he'd say, "They sure as hell taught me how to count." It became his favorite line.

"Listen, Dick," Vern told me that evening, "I hope you know that we're going to do our best to give you the committees you want." And he did. He could be both a rival and a friend. I knew he was likely to be both.

And I respected him as both.

Each time I ran for governor, Vern talked about running. I was convinced that Vern would never run because he had too much power as a legislative leader. He went on to become the longest-serving Speaker in Ohio history. I named the new office tower in Columbus after him. But that's another story.

Early on, a group of rookie legislators was invited to lunch by Lenny Ostrovsky, a character more at home at the racetrack than on the House floor. "I've got a live one," he told us. I had no idea what that meant.

He led us—four or five freshmen—to lunch at the restaurant at the top of the Sheraton. When we arrived, we discovered our host, "the live one," was a fellow named John Babka, who lobbied for the Ohio Coal Association.

"I can't stay for lunch," said Jim Mueller, a staunch environmentalist in our group, "if that's who's picking up the tab."

Ostrovsky looked at him. "Listen kid," he said, "nobody ever bought a vote with a lunch."

I remember wondering: what have I gotten myself into?

The question of who paid for what and what they expected in return would confront me from time to time during my public service—as it must for any public official. It began early, when Sam Bradley, one of my contributors and a friend of my father's, gave me a call. Sam was then the biggest supplier of kitchen equipment in northeast Ohio—he did industrial supply for kitchens, bars, and hotels—and he asked me to come and see him in his office. We arranged to meet the following Saturday morning.

"How's it going in Columbus?" he wanted to know.

I told him I was learning a lot, and after more small talk he shared why he had wanted to see me.

"Last fall I bid on a kitchen contract," he said, "for one of the state universities. The contract was supposed to be awarded by the end of last October."

I nodded, not sure what the problem was.

"By way of background," he said, "I do very little business with the state. But once every three or four years, I bid on a public contract just to keep myself sharp. So I submitted my bid."

"All right," I said, still not sure where this was going.

"Two weeks before the scheduled bid opening, I got a call from a guy—he didn't identify himself—who asked me if I was the one who had made the bid. When I said yes, he said, 'For $250,000 you can have the contract.' I said, 'Sorry, I don't do business like this.' And I don't, Dick," he told me. "I only bid occasionally on this sort of contract, and I'm almost always the low bidder. So I was willing to wait—but the guy was insistent. 'If you want the contract,' he told me, 'it's going to cost you.' I hung up the phone."

"How can I help?" I asked, more interested.

"Dick," he said, "they never awarded the contract, and now we have a new governor. I'm worried there's some hanky-panky going on that could leave me out in the cold. Could you take a look at it for me?"

I said I would be happy to do so. "I'll need the details," I said.

"Not so fast," Sam told me. "Let me make sure you understand the situation. If I get this contract, I'll make $400,000. That call convinced me that I've got the best bid."

I told him I understood that. "I'll look into it," I said. "Just give me the specifics."

"Dick," he said, "if I do get the bid, I want you to get 25 percent."

I could do the math in my head. That would be $100,000—a lot of money back in 1970. "Sam," I said, "you don't need to pay me anything. Just give me the information, and I'll find out what I can."

He gave me a look. "Now wait a minute," he said. "I'm not asking you to do anything wrong."

"I'm not saying you are."

"Then what's the problem?"

"You hired me to be your state representative. My job is to work for you. This is an important matter, and I want to help out."

"I want you to be compensated. You're making me feel like I'm asking you to do something wrong," he said. "And I'm not asking you to do anything wrong."

"I understand," I told him. "I'm just saying you don't have to pay me to look into this."

"Dick," he said, "I've never done anything in the public arena where I didn't pay someone. Whether it's a curb cut at a restaurant, whatever it is, somebody gets paid." He shook his head. "Look," he said, "if I don't pay you, I'll have to hire a lawyer in Columbus, and he'll charge me $150,000."

We went back and forth for fifteen minutes. Sam never gave me the details.

The whole exchange had been so disconcerting that, when I got back to Columbus, I sought out a lawyer who served on a House committee with me. "If someone offers me a commission to get something done with the state of Ohio," I asked him, "am I violating a law?"

"Actually, you would be violating a law," he told me, "because under Ohio law you can't accept a contingent fee if you're a legislator."

"What about all the lawyers here?" I asked.

"They don't do the work personally, their law firms do," he said. Lawyers as legislators could always bring business to their law firms without a conflict of interest. So could insurance brokers. But not the rest of us.

Not long after my exchange with Bradley, I was sitting in the members' lounge at the statehouse when a page told me that I had a phone call. It was from Paul Corey, a former teacher who had risen to be a union official. He would soon become a member of Jack Gilligan's cabinet. Paul told me that a friend of his, a midlevel state employee, had asked him for help. This fellow had taken a civil service promotion exam two years earlier but had never received notice of the result. Could I check on this for Paul and his buddy?

I said sure, and Paul gave me his friend's information.

I had a few minutes to spare, so I called the Department of State Personnel and outlined the situation—an exam taken by so-and-so but no results were conveyed.

"He never got a result one way or the other," I said. "Could you check on it?"

The woman at the other end of my call promised to look into the matter— and to my surprise—called back less than half an hour later. It turned out that this man had passed the promotion exam and should have been promoted. He was entitled to two years of back pay for the difference in salary.

I called Paul in Cleveland. "I've got an answer for you."

"That was fast," he said.

"I just happened to have time and so did the woman I reached at DAS. Your friend passed the test two years ago." I forget the actual amount to which he was entitled, but it was substantial.

"Are you kidding me?" he said. "That's fantastic—can I tell him?"

"It's going to be in his next paycheck."

Ten days later Paul Corey called again. His friend wanted to *do* something for me.

"Paul," I said, "he doesn't have to do anything for me. All I did was find out what he was entitled to."

"But he wants to say thank you."

"Fine," I said. "Have him write me a thank you note."

Paul said, "I think he wants to do more than that."

"Just send me a thank you note," I told him.

That was May. In November Dagmar told me she received a $200 gift certificate to Higbee's, a department store in Cleveland, in the mail—no name and no return address. I remembered that Paul Corey's friend was determined to say thank you. My guess is that he bought a gift certificate and sent it to my wife.

This type of thing happens in politics. Many people believe—even *expect*—there to be a transactional aspect of the work we do as public officials. And perhaps too often there is. I wonder what I would have done if I hadn't been fortunate enough to have a father and father-in-law who made sure we were able to make ends meet.

As it was, when soliciting campaign donations—even those in the $100,000 range—my only promise to donors was the same promise I made to Peggy O'Reilly and the other young people who volunteered on my first campaign: if you have a concern, you have a right to express it to me directly. But I can't promise to do what you want.

Perhaps my most memorable encounter with an effort to buy influence occurred years later, during my second term as governor. One of my major contributors—and a very good friend—was a coal mine owner from southeastern Ohio. His access consisted of a quarterly one-on-one breakfast with me at the governor's residence. We would talk about what was happening in the coal industry and what the upcoming issues confronting our Public Utilities Commission looked like. This fellow was free with his advice, often in very colorful language. Occasionally it was even good advice.

On this particular morning we were winding up our conversation, and I was preparing to go to the office. This person said he wanted to take an extra minute to discuss a matter on behalf of a friend. This friend owned a trash operation in New Jersey and had purchased a shut-down deep mine in southeastern Ohio, planning to ship trash from New Jersey to bury it in Ohio, apparently claiming this was safer and more environmentally responsible than dumping it into the New York harbor or a local landfill. Landfills in the East were overflowing. The story had been in the news after the Ohio EPA refused to issue a permit for the proposed dumping due to concerns about groundwater pollution.

"Would you," this contributor asked, "be willing to urge the EPA to reconsider?"

I asked him what he thought my answer would be.

He responded, "Just tell me."

I told him, "The answer is no."

"That's what I told my friend." He paused, then went on. "But if I told you there's a million dollars in this for you, would you reconsider?"

"Listen, my friend," I said, "you know what the answer is."

"Well, tell me anyway," he persisted.

"The answer is still no."

"That's what I told my friend you would say," my visitor said with a smile as we left the house.

Years later, this same guy took Jacqueline aside at our wedding and said, "You know, you are marrying the dumbest son of a bitch I know." When Jacqueline expressed surprise, he went on, "I had a briefcase with a million dollars in it, and he turned it down."

Jacqueline said she had no idea what he was talking about.

"Well," said my gravelly-voiced contributor, "you have to ask him."

That night he paid for the band at our wedding.

Lest I leave you with the sense that I did not benefit from my time in public office, I should acknowledge how I could afford to raise six kids and send five through good private colleges on my public service salary. The answer is quite simple: I couldn't. If it had not been for the generosity of my father and Dagmar's father at key moments during those years, I would have been unable to serve—and might have found it harder to say no to Mitch.

In fact, three especially close friends—now all deceased—helped enable my younger children to go to college. Each of the three took responsibility for providing the financial aid that helped one of my children through school. None of the three—a Cleveland businessman, a Dayton businessman, and a Cleveland civic leader—ever asked me for a favor. They only wanted to know how the kids were doing at school.

Of all the pressures one faces in public life, the one least well understood and most widespread is the financial pressure that confronts honest and well-meaning public servants. Whether it is generating enough income to support a family or resisting the inclination of some to try to tilt the system in their favor, a young politician will often face difficult choices. And in recent years, the growing cost of campaigns has only multiplied the pressures and temptations.

I recall once being in a car with Hubert Humphrey during the 1968 presidential campaign. I was a year back from India—with three small children and a wife to feed—which may be why the moment stuck with me. I remember Humphrey talking to his travel guy—always at his side during the campaign—and berating him because he hadn't made sure the mortgage payment on the family home in Minnesota had been taken care of. Humphrey was a small businessman—the family owned a pharmacy—and here he was in the midst of a presidential campaign struggling to find the money and make sure his mortgage payment wasn't late.

In my first state representative campaign in 1969 my total budget was $9,000. The biggest individual contribution was $100; we got perhaps five or six. As I was running for state representative (and becoming a father for the fourth time), I had to work hard to balance our bank account—as well as my campaign finances—at the end of each month. My annual salary (as a part-time legislator) was the magnificent sum of $6,000.

After eight years as governor, I left office with a net worth of about $80,000, basically the equity from our home.

It is incredibly difficult—if you don't have an independent income or family wealth—to stay focused on the public interest. At the same time, a sea of money is being invested in politics—in campaigns and in politicians. The result is that these two realities—financial strain on political families and a plentiful supply of dollars from those interested in tilting public decisions in their favor—converge in ways that invite corruption.

We need an equitable and thoughtful system of public finance for elections if we are to insure a healthy democracy in the decades ahead. And we should pay public officials salaries commensurate with their responsibilities—as they do in Singapore, for example.

I need to share more about one super-volunteer from that first state rep campaign: a high school student named Peggy O'Reilly. I had been in office for about two months in 1971 when she called me in Columbus to ask what I was "planning to do about Apple Creek." Throughout the campaign she had heard me talk—repeatedly—about building a constituency for change. She had listened to my message about why politics was important. She continued, "Someone needs to do something about Apple Creek.

"What do you mean, Apple Creek?"

"It's one of the state institutions where they keep kids who are retarded. What are we going to do about it?"

"Peggy," I told her, "I'm not sure I understand what the problem is."

"Yesterday we watched a documentary at school about what happens at this place. It was awful. It made us sick, and we have to do something about it."

She went on to explain how Apple Creek did not have attendants on its wards at night. As the afternoon shift left, many patients were made to stand up against the pillars in their wards while their arms were tied around the pillars. This was the only way the staff could make sure the patients would not hurt themselves or each other overnight. When morning shift arrived, the first thing they had to do was untie these people and clean up puddles of urine. "It was just terrible," said Peggy.

"Why don't we get a group together and find out more about this?" I said.

Two weeks later Peggy and some fellow students accompanied me to Apple Creek and met with the superintendent.

"I don't have a budget for twenty-four-hour care," he explained. "Unless we can get more money into the state budget, this is the best we can do. We try to keep people from harming themselves."

I said to Peggy, "This is why we need a state income tax."

With passage of the income tax in late 1971, Apple Creek and other state institutions were provided twenty-four-hour staffing. In the 1972 election, the income tax Gilligan had insisted on instituting was on the ballot for repeal. Peggy was one of those who worked with me to defend the income tax. The politics of change had become real for her. Peggy went on to Miami of Ohio to study social work. But she never stopped calling me.

When I became lieutenant governor, she would call my office and ask me what I was going to do about one or another problem. And when I became governor in 1982, she was running a senior facility in southeastern Ohio and would lobby me on issues associated with the elderly. Around that time she became pregnant and shortly thereafter was diagnosed with a brain tumor. Not long after delivering her son, Peggy O'Reilly died. Over and over again in later campaigns, I would tell people—particularly young people—that I wanted to introduce them to a hero of mine.

Peggy O'Reilly.

Peggy understood that when you work to elect someone, you have a claim on them once they're elected. She never relinquished that claim. The world is a better place for Peggy and her grit.

Her son called me a couple of years ago and asked to see me. "I want you to tell me about my mother," he told me.

Being state rep was like middle school in politics for me. Elementary school was observing my father and other politicians. Middle school was stepping into the arena myself. A state representative, especially in the minority, didn't have to do much heavy lifting. You worked on selected issues important to you or to your constituents. But I could not even get a hearing for my bills.

So I focused on constituent services. During my first term, I was called one day by a fellow who lived in my district to discuss his son, who was in one of Ohio's juvenile institutions. He came asking for my help because his son was being abused in prison.

I asked him for the details and said I'd see what I could do. I called the superintendent at the facility and said I understood this kid was having a hard time.

The superintendent said he'd check on it and get back to me.

Meanwhile, the father would call me every four or five days, often in tears. "My son is beautiful and fragile," he would say. "He's being taken advantage of by these boys. Please do something."

I explained that I was doing my best. I understood how worried he was.

After a couple of weeks, the superintendent called. "Representative Celeste," he said. "I'd like to see you to discuss this matter."

I assured him I would make time.

"It's just," he said, then stopped. "There are aspects of this I'd rather not put on paper."

A week later the superintendent and I met in Columbus. "You're right," he told me. "This boy is very vulnerable, both emotionally and physically. He's not a strong boy, and there are tough kids in our place. He's also very pretty, which has caused problems for him. We're trying to provide better protection for him, so he's not hassled by the other residents in our facility."

The boy's father, I said, was going to be happy to hear this.

"But I have to tell you something," he said. "You've told me his father is very eager to get him home." He paused. "I talked to this young man, and he does not want to be released to his parents."

"He doesn't want to be released to his parents?" I asked. "His father seems genuinely concerned about him."

"His father has been abusing him sexually," said the superintendent, "for at least six years. He would rather be locked up than sent home."

I was stunned. "What would you recommend?"

"If you can find a facility—maybe a foster home—that would take him, I'd recommend that we release him. But, knowing what I know, we cannot release him to his parents."

This was not what I expected. I asked the father to see me in my Lakewood office. There I told him I'd met with the superintendent. "I think I can probably persuade him to release your son."

"That's wonderful," was the reply. "I can't wait to have him home."

"But," I said, "the superintendent will not release your son if he comes home to you."

"What do you mean?"

"Because of the abuse that has occurred in your family," I said. "Your son is vulnerable, and he would rather stay in that facility than come home to you. So you have a choice. You can keep your son in that facility or agree to have him placed in Lutheran foster care, where he will be safe."

Reluctantly, he agreed to have the son released to the Lutheran facility.

In public life you engage the real world. And real people. Sometimes all too real.

For my first two years in the legislature, I lived mostly on the couch in my brother's house. I was in the minority, which meant my work was usually over early. After committee hearings—which would end about nine-thirty in the evening—I would go to the Neil House bar and sit with the old-timers, most of whom were Republicans, asking them about their experience as legislators and listening to their stories.

Two of my favorites were Lloyd George Kerns and Carlton Davidson. Lloyd George Kerns was chairman of the House Finance Committee, and he eventually helped put together the bill that instituted Ohio's income tax. He came from Marion, home of Warren G. Harding, the twenty-ninth president, and was a country lawyer, quiet and unassuming. Carlton "Pappy" Davidson was a bachelor, a schoolteacher, then school superintendent in Ironton, along the Ohio River.

Pappy and Lloyd George Kerns roomed together and loved to talk. Over beers I'd sit with them and listen as they recalled historic legislative fights and the sometimes complicated, sometimes surprising relationships that existed between various legislators.

I once asked Kerns about his law practice. He was working hard on the finance committee, and it was difficult to see how he would find the time. "Do you practice much law these days?" I asked.

"Dick," he said, "when I was young, I wrote wills for all of my friends. I did it for free. They couldn't afford a lawyer, and I needed to keep busy. So I did their wills and put them in my safe. They became wealthy farmers or businessmen. Now those friends are dying. A couple of probates a year and I'm all set."

They told me about a night after they'd been doing some rare heavy drinking. I'm not sure what the occasion was, but they returned to the room they shared in the Neil House. Lloyd George entered first and went immediately to the bathroom. When he came out, Pappy was peeing out the fifth floor window.

A few moments later a police officer pounded on the door. "Someone was seen pissing out the window," he said. "From this room."

Introducing themselves as members of the legislature, they said that they had no idea who it could possibly have been.

"Could you at least identify this person?" they asked the cops.

"I couldn't really see, but some guy was up here pissing out the window."

"We just got back here," said Lloyd. "Sorry we can't help you." A near miss.

Carlton told me a story that had just happened—it was late 1971—when a place called the Playboy Club had recently opened in Columbus. Carlton said that a couple of weeks earlier he had urged Lloyd George to join him and check it out; Lloyd wasn't enthusiastic, but Carlton persisted on the grounds that they should at least know what the attraction was.

"So we went," said Carlton, "and I'll be dammed if there wasn't a line at the front door. I went up and said that I was with Lloyd George Kerns, chairman of the Finance Committee and asked if we could get in.

"No, you can't," said the woman at the door.

"What do you mean, no, I can't?"

She persisted, "No, you can't—Lloyd George Kerns is already inside."

"What do you mean?" said Carlton. "I know him. We're in the legislature together. He's standing back there, and he shouldn't be made to stand back there."

"He is not standing back there," she said. "He's at his table. Inside, right now."

"How do you know he's at the table?"

"I seat him there every night," she said. "Let me show you." She turned to the desk behind her and took out a business card that said, "Lloyd George Kerns, Chairman of the Finance Committee." "See," she told them, "he's here already."

"I don't care who gave you this card," said Carlton, "but the real Lloyd George Kerns is back here with me. He'll show you his driver's license."

Some guy had gotten his hands on the chairman's card and was passing himself off as Lloyd George Kerns.

During my first race for governor, I went to Ironton, Pappy's hometown. A couple of times when I had been lieutenant governor I had cast deciding votes on issues, one being a pay raise for local public officials. I wouldn't be a beneficiary—anyone who voted on a pay raise bill had to wait until they were reelected to benefit. But, knowing how tight family budgets were for office-holders, I believed public officials deserved the raise. Pappy took me around the solidly Republican county courthouse. "You have got to meet this guy," Pappy would tell people. "He's a Democrat, but he's our kind of Democrat. When there was a tie vote on your pay raise, he voted for it. So I just want you to remember his name."

After our courthouse tour Pappy invited me back to the modest house he shared with his sister to have some lemonade. We chatted, and his sister was very pleasant. "Does Carlton behave himself up there?" she asked me. I assured her that he did.

As I was preparing to leave, he said, "Come out and see my birds."

Birds? I asked myself. *What's he talking about?*

He took me behind the house where there was a long coop. He was raising fighting cocks, which he would take across the river to Kentucky for cockfights.

How much can we ever really know about our friends and colleagues? I was thinking to myself.

That was how I spent my first two years in the legislature. I couldn't pass a bill of my own. I voted in favor of the income tax. I voted against the death penalty, and we lost on that; it remained in the Ohio Revised Code. Then I ran for reelection. Yes, I could get along with Republicans in the statehouse.

But I was determined not to lose my seat to one.

In the midst of my 1970 state rep race, I was painting a bedroom in our house, with the radio on, when I heard the news that Ohio National Guardsmen had killed four students on the Kent State University campus.

I was stunned and angry. It was one thing for young people to be dying in Vietnam in a war we shouldn't have been fighting. It was another thing altogether to have it happen so close to home—young people in the Ohio Guard killing young students on a university campus.

In 1971, antiwar demonstrators gathered on the steps of the statehouse, and I—along with a handful of fellow legislators—went out and met with them. As we returned to the House floor, we heard a Republican legislator denouncing us as treasonous for meeting with demonstrators who were not supporting our boys in Vietnam.

In 1972 my opponent, Tony Sinagra, was from a family I knew well. Tony's father, Nate, had a wonderful grocery store in Lakewood. In fact, it was my father's favorite. Young Tony was a member of city council. People were worried that it was going to be a tight race, and Tony did everything he could to gain an edge—including playing the "treason" card—citing my meeting with protesters on the statehouse steps.

It was a desperate act by a desperate candidate. I won handily. Ironically Sinagra went on to become, like my dad, mayor of Lakewood.

After my victory I decided to test my political muscle. I told Harry Lehman and John Sweeney, as well as Mayor Stokes, that I would like to become the Cuyahoga County delegation leader. A fellow named Jimmy Celebreeze—no relation to either former mayor Tony Celebrezze or state senator Tony Calabrese—had been the leader and had done next to nothing. I reached out to members of the delegation, and most committed to me. Unlike my father or Don Pease, I counted my votes carefully. I knew who would back me and who wouldn't.

As soon as I announced my intention, the chief justice of the Ohio Supreme Court, Frank Celebreeze, the older brother of Jimmy, called me at home.

"I'm calling," he said, "to ask you not to run for delegation leader."

"Chief," I said, "I'm running."

"No," he said, "I'm telling you not to run for delegation leader."

"I'm not prepared to back out," I told him. "I have the votes, and I believe I will be a good delegation leader."

"Listen," he said, "sooner or later you're going to need me. And I'm telling you I don't want you to run."

I insisted that I was running.

"You little shit," he said. "You can't do this." And on he went. Dagmar could overhear him he was shouting so loudly. I finally said, "Look, Chief Justice, I don't have to listen to this. I'm going to stand for delegation leader, and I'm going to win." I hung up.

Elected delegation leader, I went to Columbus and sat down with Vern Riffe. We had won a majority in the House. "I want to be part of the team," I told him. "We shouldn't have a divided party here."

He made me majority whip.

This was more title than job. Still, I was part of the leadership team.

This was another lesson I learned along the way: you don't burn any bridges. Yes, I had supported Don Pease against A. G. Lancione. Yes, I had been on the other side. But they could help me, and I could help them. This was something I needed to keep in mind.

To an extent, Vern Riffe felt a kinship with me. His father had been mayor of New Boston—he was actually Vernal Riffe Jr.—and, if you went down to New Boston, you didn't talk about Vern, you talked about "Jun." That was

Joining state representative Pat Sweeney (*left*) for a bill signing by Governor Gilligan in 1973

his nickname. My father had been mayor of Lakewood, of course, and knew Riffe Senior. When I arrived in 1971, Vern knew who I was.

We would become allies who never fully trusted each other. It was one of those situations where he had his fish to fry, and I had mine. In those situations where we were frying the same fish, we were fine. On occasion there were conflicts. He was like my father in a lot of ways. Vern wanted to be governor, but he didn't want to have to run for it, just as my father wanted to be mayor of Cleveland without having to run for it. Unlike my father, however, Vern was shrewd enough to know where the votes were. He understood that if he ever had to run against me in a statewide primary, I would win.

While I ran for reelection for state rep and continued to represent my district, I wasn't an enthusiastic legislator. I was more interested in what was going on in the executive branch of government. I was already thinking about statewide office, and at the beginning of 1973 I had a conversation with the core team that I had assembled: Jerry Austin, my brother, Dagmar, and a handful of others. It was a time of transition. I was in the leadership of the general assembly, but my head was elsewhere.

Thinking about a statewide race.

Chapter 6

The Awkward Challenge

In the late 1970s I was approached by Jim Stanton, then president of the Cleveland City Council, asking if I had any advice about running statewide. I told him the most important thing to understand is that Cleveland is not Ohio. Cuyahoga County, our home county, is crucial for a Democratic victory, but you need to experience the diversity of the state. Get in the car, I told him, and drive south through Akron and Canton, Dover and New Philadelphia. Then head east on I-70 and spend a night in Belmont County. Move on to Marietta and Portsmouth along the Ohio River, and finally return to Columbus through Chillicothe, the first capital of Ohio. When you get back to Cleveland, ask yourself if running statewide is something you really want to do.

"Why not Dayton?" he asked. "What about Youngstown?"

Because, I told him, Dayton and Youngstown are going to feel more like Cleveland. To get an idea of what it means to run statewide, you need to have a sense of the rest of Ohio—which you have to take seriously if you want to win. Perhaps Washington County and places like it won't be where most of your votes come from. In fact, you may only carry sixteen of Ohio's eighty-eight counties. But you have to reduce the margin by which you lose in the other seventy-two counties. On election nights in my statewide campaigns, the vote budgets we put together were just as closely watched in counties that we didn't carry as in the ones we did.

Mansfield author Louis Bromfield famously described Ohio's place in our nation this way: "Where exactly is Ohio?" he asked. "It is the farthest west of the east, and the farthest east of the west, the farthest north of the south, and the farthest south of the north, and it is probably the richest area of its size in the world."

In the spring of 1973, nearing the end of my second term as state representative and considering my first statewide run, Ted and I took the sort of trip I later recommended to Jim Stanton. We wanted to get the feel of a statewide campaign, so we traveled from Columbus to Youngstown and then down along the Ohio River, through Steubenville, Bellaire, over to Scioto County, and finally up the highway through Chillicothe. This was long before I announced my candidacy, even before I had assembled the team that would help decide what office—secretary of state or lieutenant governor—I would seek. (At the time, the governor and lieutenant governor ran separately, which is how we ended up with a Democratic governor and a Republican lieutenant governor.) After that trip I realized that I needed to introduce myself to the rest of Ohio beyond Cuyahoga County.

For a start I volunteered with the Ohio Democratic Party, saying I would speak at party dinners anywhere they needed a speaker. My first invite was for the Ross County Democratic dinner in Chillicothe, and the ODP assigned a young woman to help arrange my visit. When Ted and I pulled up to the Holiday Inn where the dinner was held, the sign on the marquee read: "Welcome State Representative Richard Celeste."

"Find out who got my name up there," I told my brother.

That person turned out to be Jan Allen, the person assigned to me by the ODP. Diminutive, energetic, possessed of a highly organized mind, Jan had grown up in Chillicothe, where her dad, Gib, had a pharmacy. She had a modest, small-town way about her, and she bubbled with enthusiasm for politics. She welcomed the hard work required to thrive in the excitement of campaigns.

One meets people like her on the campaign trail, individuals for whom politics is a passion. But Jan was special. I had never seen a schedule so detailed and complete. She treated me like a serious politician, not just another state rep. Ted and I knew that to be successful I would need people like her—intensely loyal, driven, highly competent.

Jan Allen became my first paid campaign staffer.

The primary for lieutenant governor was crowded, and most of the candidates possessed greater name recognition than I did: William O'Neill, J. W. Brown, William Sweeney, James Williams, Lucille Huston, Henry Eckert, Don Hanni, and Tony Calabrese, who had been the unsuccessful lieutenant governor nominee in 1970.

I believed—despite my relative youth—I could do well in the general election. But getting there was not going to be easy. I knew that if we were going to win, we needed a creative strategy. Jerry Austin, who was living near me at the time and would become my campaign director, identified step one. "Look," he said. "Your first election is won with just one vote."

"A single vote?" I said.

"We've got to persuade Governor Gilligan to endorse you," he told me. "That's the first election."

We contrived a number of tactics to secure the governor's support—many of them off-beat, innovative tactics that would become our trademark. One of our first moves was to simultaneously drop our campaign literature in Gilligan's home precinct in Cincinnati and the precincts of a half-dozen political reporters across the state. Our aim was to convince Gilligan—and Ohio's political pundits—that we had a savvy grassroots campaign organization. If the Celeste campaign machine was delivering literature to his doorstep and the doorsteps of those who wrote about the race, the assumption was that we must be doing this across Ohio. We weren't, of course, but for the time being that didn't matter. What mattered was that influential individuals thought we were.

Next, we mapped out the circle of people the governor might ask for advice on the lieutenant governor's race. Once we had identified the "influentials," I personally met with each of them so that, no matter who Jack Gilligan consulted, they would mention Celeste.

Finally, I spent time with him directly, telling him I expected to win the primary and I wanted to do it with his support. "I want to be your strong right hand," I stated.

Time was of the essence because the party was going to meet to consider an endorsement, and Gilligan had to make a decision before that. As we were waging our one-vote campaign, Tony Calabrese had gone before the Ohio AFL-CIO Executive Committee, hoping to win their endorsement. One of AFL-CIO leaders, a Machinists Union officer named Ed Fire, related how Calabrese had appealed on grounds of being a strong ethnic candidate.

"I'm an Italian American," he said. "You need to support me."

"Wait a minute," said Ed, "isn't Celeste an Italian American, too?"

"He's not Italian," Tony replied disdainfully. "He's a Methodist."

Gilligan's one vote—and the endorsement that followed—would not assure a primary win, but it would boost my chances. Gilligan's people were worried that the primary voters would nominate Calabrese. Chair of the Italian Americans for Kennedy in 1960, Italian Americans for Johnson in 1964, and Italian Americans for Humphrey in 1968, Calabrese was a "dese, dem, and doze" kind of guy—an Italian American in his late sixties who had been in politics for most of his life. He was famous for the rhetorical question: "Whattya want? Good grammar or good government?"

Though Calabrese was a longtime state senator, he was often confused with Tony Celebrezze, who had been elected to an unprecedented five two-year terms as mayor of Cleveland. But Ohio's dominant political name was Brown. In the previous election, Calabrese—not Cleveland's mayor—had been beaten handily by Republican John Brown. And Ohio's secretary of state was Ted Brown. Three elected members of the state's supreme court were named Brown.

As governor, Gilligan had to replace Sen. Bill Saxbe when he resigned to become ambassador to India. Seeking Gilligan's nod were John Glenn, Howard Metzenbaum, A. G. Lancione—Speaker of the House by that time—and Jim Stanton. After heavy lobbying on all sides, Gilligan chose Howard Metzenbaum.

It was an unexpected decision. My hunch is that John Glenn didn't get the appointment because Gilligan hoped John would be his running mate in the 1974 election. It would be an unbeatable ticket, Gilligan's advisors believed. Their hope: that in 1976 Gilligan would run for president. That was the pitch to John Glenn: "Join me on the ticket, and in '76 I'll run for president and you will become governor."

Glenn was entirely uninterested. Above all he did not want to be anyone's number two. He truly aspired to be a US senator. Still resentful about Gilligan's decision, he ran in the '74 primary against Metzenbaum. That race would conclude with a famous confrontation between the two candidates at the City Club in Cleveland. During that debate, Howard Metzenbaum sensed the electorate's strong antiwar sentiment and kept referring to John Glenn as "Colonel Glenn." He claimed that he would be a better senator because of his business experience. To drive his point home, Metzenbaum said to Glenn, who had spent his adult life in the military: "You have never once met a payroll."

John Glenn—not known for a quick response—shot back: "Tell that to the Gold Star mothers."

Just like that, Howard Metzenbaum's hopes of victory were history.

As we were focusing on winning Gilligan's vote, I worked to become known throughout the state. To begin, I set out to meet as many county Democratic chairmen as I could. As I traveled the state, I met an unforgettable cast of characters who made up Ohio's Democratic politics in the mid-1970s.

One of the first was Jack Sulligan, the Democratic chairman in Mahoning County—Youngstown—an old-time Party stalwart who presided over a daily card game in a room above the party headquarters where various county officeholders gathered over the lunch hour. He led a tight-knit Democratic organization that could deliver the votes.

Sulligan agreed to see me but was more than a little skeptical. When I came into his office, he looked at me as if to say, "Who is this thirty-five-year-old kid?"

I asked for his support anyway.

"Kid," he told me, in his raspy voice, "I can't do it."

I explained why I thought I could win. I was confident that the governor was going to endorse me and that we would be a powerful team. A strong and unified team at the top of the ticket would help his local candidates.

"Yeah, well," said Sulligan, "you might be a good candidate, but I got an asshole of my own in this race."

"An asshole of your own?"

"This guy," said Sullivan, out of the side of his mouth, "he used to be a city judge, Don Hanni, and he's running for lieutenant governor. I've got to support him."

I persisted and reminded him that I had been in the legislature for four years. I was young but understood statewide issues. Ohio needed someone like me—who would bring a strong margin out of Cuyahoga County. If I got the nomination, I promised, I would campaign hard in Youngstown.

"Listen kid," he responded, "I'd like to help you, but I can't. I got to carry my county for Hanni. I can't let someone from Youngstown lose Mahoning County. The guy is a sonofabitch, sure, but he's my sonofabitch."

It seemed there was nothing to say.

"But I'll tell you what," he added. "I'm not going to hurt you. I'll give you Patti Cataline."

"You'll give me Patti Cataline?"

"She's a fireball," he said. "She's with the young Dems. I'll tell her and some of the others to work with you and we'll see how you do. We won't hurt you too bad."

So Patti Cataline was assigned to work with the Celeste campaign. And she worked hard. When the primary votes were counted, Hanni carried Mahoning County by two hundred votes. I ran a close second.

That was Jack Sulligan. A man who knew how to deliver the vote.

———

Visiting Ohio's small counties was something few Democratic candidates did, just as they passed up most county fairs. Democratic voters tend to be urban, which meant slim pickings at county fairs. I took a different approach. I aimed to improve my share of the vote even in counties I would not carry.

I still recall with a laugh my experience in Vinton County, a county so small that it didn't even have a full-blown fair. Instead, it had a junior fair—one that took place in a single grandstand that could hold perhaps a hundred people. Our county chairman was the sort of rough-edged guy one tends to underestimate, and I did exactly that. When he explained the fair—"not actually a fair"—I insisted on going. I planned to go to every county fair; I wasn't going to miss this one.

As we arrived, the frog jumping contest had just ended.

Early on in my campaign, I had been warned by old-timers not to bid on animals at county fairs. It's a tradition to auction off the animal that wins the blue ribbon, and that can turn into an expensive proposition. The blue-ribbon calf at the state fair, for example, once went for $90,000. It is not the kind of thing that you bid for on a state representative's salary.

In addition to potentially being expensive, it's not an especially good move politically. You make one person happy and five people unhappy. Therefore, I stayed away from auctions. But this was not even a "real" county fair, and these were just frogs. I figured that I could afford a frog.

"Hey," I said to the chairman. "Let's bid on the runner-up." The winner had fetched four dollars.

He looked at me and shrugged. "You want a frog?"

The bidding started.

It began at a dollar, then a dollar and a half, pretty soon it was four bucks.

Then five.

Then seven.

Then twelve.

The county chairman gave me an elbow. "Dick," he said, "Get the hell out of here. Let me take care of this."

"Take care of what?" I said.

"Somebody recognized you," he told me. "You're busted."

I went looking for the port-a-potty. When I got back, he had bought the frog for eighteen bucks.

After winning an auction, it's a courtesy to offer the animal back to the kid who raised it. "Listen," I told the kid, "this frog is something. You must want him back."

"No, thanks," he said.

I kept smiling. "This is a heck of a frog," I told him. "Runner-up in the jumping contest. You don't want him?"

"Nah. It's not my frog," he said. "I just picked it up on the road on the way to the fair. You keep it."

Joe Ujhelyi was the Democratic chairman of Lorain County, just west of Cleveland. Joe had been a standout football player at Ohio State in the late 1920s—and became an attorney. He was a legendary figure and, unlike many of the older party leaders, seemed genuinely happy to meet me.

"I am always eager to get young people involved in politics," he told me.

"How did you get started?" I asked.

"I came back to Lorain to practice law," he told me, "and was interested in politics. In the early 1940s I started doing voter registration drives among local Democrats. Interestingly, we registered more voters in Lorain County than any other county in the nation in 1946. I got a little bit of notoriety from that."

Joe was just getting warmed up, I could tell.

"In early 1948 I got a call from President Truman—I was forty-one—and Truman said he wanted me to run a statewide voter registration drive for his campaign. I said, 'I'd love to, Mr. President, but I can't.'"

"What do you mean you can't?" the president demanded.

"I can't do it," said Joe, "I'm forty-one years old; I'll talk to these county chairmen and they're going to tell me to go fly a kite." Typically, county chairmen like to control voter registration so that they know exactly who the new voters are and how they are likely to vote.

"This is going to be close election," said President Truman, "and you and I know it. Voter registration in Ohio may well be the key to my victory."

"I agree," said Joe, "but I don't see how I can do the job for you."

Truman said, "I know you can do this job, and I want you to do it. Tell me what you need to be successful."

"Here's the problem," said Joe. "I have to start in Cleveland with Ray Miller, the chairman there. When I talk to him about voter registration for Cuyahoga County, he's going to throw me out of his office. He's going to say, 'Get your ass out of here, kid. I don't need your help.'"

Truman said, "If he says that, just pick up the phone and call me."

"How do I pick up the phone and call the president?" Ujhelyi asked.

"I am going to give you a special number," said Truman. "Call it, and you will get me. It may take a few minutes." Then he gave him the number. "Use it carefully," said Truman, "and don't share it with anyone else."

"Fine, Mr. President," he said. "I'll do my best for you."

A few weeks later he went to see Ray Miller. Miller kept him waiting for an hour and twenty minutes. When Joe finally got in, he found him behind the desk smoking a cigar. "Whattya want, kid?" Miller asked.

"I just want to introduce myself," said Ujhelyi. "I'm going to be running the statewide voter registration campaign for President Truman, and I wanted to figure out the best way of working with you."

"What do you mean, voter registration?" was Miller's reply. "This is Cuyahoga County, and you're from Lorain County. Go back to Lorain."

"The president has asked me to do this statewide," began Joe.

"Get your ass out of my office," said Miller. "You're wasting my time."

"Mr. Miller," said Joe, "with all due respect, are you going to say no to President Truman and his plan for voter registration?"

"You know what?" said Miller. "Tell President Truman to kiss my ass. I'll take care of Cuyahoga County."

"Would you permit me to use your phone?" asked Joe. "For one minute?"

Miller told him to go ahead.

Joe dialed the number that Truman had given him. When someone picked up, he said, "This is Joe Ujhelyi. I'm calling from Cleveland, and I would like to speak to President Truman."

Miller was rolling his eyes, chewing on his cigar.

A few minutes later Truman came on the phone. Ujhelyi said, "Mr. President, I'm in Ray Miller's office in Cleveland." Then a pause. "Yes, sir. I have explained, sir." A third pause. "He said exactly what I told you he would say. Yes, sir." Then a much longer pause. "Just a moment." He put his hand over the receiver. "President Truman wants to talk to you."

"Give me the fucking phone," growled Miller. Grabbing the receiver, he put it to his ear. There was a long pause. "Yes, Mr. President," said Miller. "Well, yes, of course, Mr. President. Well, of course, I do understand it's important, Mr. President. If you insist, Mr. President. Thank you, Mr. President."

He hung up and turned to Joe. "Get your ass out of here," he said. "You can do the voter registration drive, but I want to know when you're in my county and exactly what you're doing."

"And that's how I got started in politics," Ujhelyi told me.

———

I spent a good deal of time on the road, usually staying in people's homes wherever I went. Once I met with the party chairman of a small county along the Ohio River for morning coffee. He seemed supportive. As we were leaving the diner, he said that he'd like to take me over to meet his secretary because she knew almost every Democrat in the county personally.

I said great.

"Do you mind if we stop at the drugstore along the way?" he asked.

I said fine.

He opened the door of his car, and a buzzer went off.

"Do you always leave the keys in your car?" I asked him.

"Oh yeah," he said. "Around here there's only one person who steals cars, and everyone knows who it is."

"You mean there's no crime here?"

"Dick," he said, "I'm glad I'm not a defense attorney. I'd have almost no one to defend."

We walked down the street, and I noticed a beautiful Rolls Royce. "What's a Rolls doing here?" I asked. "That belongs to a local trial lawyer," was the reply. "He won a big black lung settlement."

"Does that guy leave the keys in his car, too?"

"Sure."

I had a good chat with his secretary, and then I went on my way. About eight months after I was elected lieutenant governor, that county chairman called me. "Dick, remember that Rolls?" he said. "It was stolen."

I asked, "Did they find the guy?"

"Sure," he told me. "The Rolls was parked in the driveway of the only guy in the county who steals cars."

What's not to love about the business of politics?

Though I traveled to every part of Ohio, my home base of Cleveland was crucial. No matter how far away I might find myself, Cleveland remained my home. I went to Yale and Oxford, then came back to Cleveland. To India, then back. Politically that was important since I hadn't gone to college at Ohio State or John Carroll. Cleveland was always my home and key in my statewide campaigns. In fact, as part of my 1982 campaign, I asked folks in my hometown, "Isn't it time for a governor from Cleveland?"

In that first 1974 effort I did win Governor Gilligan's endorsement. And went on to win the primary by over a hundred thousand votes. The runner-up was Tony Calabrese.

Dennis Heffernan went with me to my first county Democratic dinner as a party nominee. I made a point of going around the room shaking hands with everyone there and, finishing up, felt I had done a good job. Dennis didn't think so. "That was a waste. You didn't connect with a single person," he told me. "Go around and do it right."

That stopped me. Upon reflection I understood what he meant: there is a difference between merely shaking hands and genuinely connecting. The people you meet on the campaign trail—those you ask to vote for you—can tell the difference. If you're going to persuade an individual to vote for you and to tell others, your connection needs to be authentic.

I am often asked how I was able to convey that kind of personal touch. The answer is I just plain enjoy people. But to convey that personally requires an intense emotional focus. And that act of engaging deeply, even for a moment, has a kind of reverence about it.

Bill Coffin, my chaplain at Yale and good friend, used to describe enthusiasm as "the spirit in us." When we truly share enthusiasm with someone, we experience a sense of the Holy Spirit.

Often when I was meeting people at a political gathering—listening, touching, hugging—the enthusiasm I felt, the energy I shared, the affection I experienced were like a gift, a blessing. These moments seemed to fuse my youthful faith and my adult action. They were deeply intimate and nearly impossible to communicate.

Dennis understood the importance of a genuine connection. That is what he demanded of me that night, just as Wally Smith knew a great speech and demanded it of me. During my life I have been blessed to have around me people who set high expectations for me—beginning with Bessie Lewis. Her mantra, "From those to whom much is given, much is expected," echoes to this day.

Among those who would demand my best was the team that grew around me during the lieutenant governor's race. It was a tightly knit, committed group of volunteers who came together quickly, organized efficiently, and formed the core of each of my future campaigns.

Jerry Austin became the chief campaign strategist. My brother, Ted, was campaign director, as he would be in the governor's campaign in four years. Ted and his wife, Bobbie, had served in the Peace Corps in Fiji, and he was working in the Welfare Department for Jack Gilligan. When I was in Columbus during the campaign, I usually slept on their living room couch, just as I had when I was a state rep.

As highly organized as we were, it was also intensely personal. These folks became close personal friends. Often couples, they loved spending time together even when they weren't campaigning. In later years, there would be considerable discussion in the press—some of it sardonic—about "Celestials," the individuals at the heart of my organization. I have never particularly liked that term because it conveyed a sense that they were cultish (as the press would have it) rather than the reality—strong-willed members of the constituency for change that we were building. The "Celestials" never followed me blindly; if I took a stance on an issue which one of my team didn't like, I would hear about it. We all simply relished working hard together to achieve a victory and make change happen.

One such "Celestial" who came on board in the lieutenant governor's race was Gayle Channing. Gayle was a social worker then married to a hospital administrator with two young daughters. She constantly wrestled with health issues, but she was a dynamite organizer who was a relentless advocate on children's issues. She inspired volunteers and found them meaningful roles. She was just right for me and what I wanted to achieve.

Another was Bill Flaherty, who, like Gayle, was about my brother's age. Originally from New Jersey, he had come to Ohio in the McGovern effort. Bill was recruited by Ted to organize our election day effort. In 1972 he and Jim Ruvolo had run Lucas County for McGovern—one of just two Ohio counties he carried. This, I knew, was because the county chairman—Bill Boyle, a former cop with one good eye—encouraged them as they put together a rare unified party effort for McGovern. Flaherty and his wife, Cindy, worked hard for me in the lieutenant governor's race. They would play key roles for me over the next fifteen years.

Bill learned early on how to influence my decision making. He would make a strong case on an issue, and, if I disagreed, he would appear to accept it. But if he felt strongly enough about the matter, he would wait a while, then make the case again. Often when Bill made the case a second time, I would find myself agreeing with him and wondering why I disagreed in the first place. Bill was the best sort of "Celestial" because of the spirit of open and frank exchange that characterized our relationship, a willingness to ultimately join together to act.

Another early "Celestial" was Dave Hetzler, along with his wife, Nappy. David was the office manager for us, taking the evening shift. The campaign would run from morning until about eight or nine in the evening. At the end of the day, Dave would sort out the evening call sheets, then prepare materials for the person running the office the next day.

Our media consultant for the lieutenant governor's race was David Milenthal, who would also stay with me through my later races. His father was an old-style liberal Democrat, an activist schoolteacher who came out of the Jewish labor movement. Co-owner of an advertising agency in Columbus, David was a friend of my brother who came to politics more out of curiosity and a desire to be where the action was rather than deep convictions about issues. He produced the minimalist media of that campaign. We ran a single TV ad in which I was featured pushing a lawn mower. Since no one running for lieutenant governor in Ohio had used TV before, it made our ad a novelty and increased its impact.

Like Jerry Austin, with whom he had a productive though often intensely competitive relationship, David understood that there needed to be a strategic framework behind an effective political pitch. To move people and build our constituency for change, we would need to find new and creative ways of energizing voters. It began in that lieutenant governor's race—with a modest spot featuring me and a lawn mower.

In 1974 we stuck with the Jim Asbeck approach—planning our campaign from Election Day backwards. We tracked volunteers and we tracked money, but we also kept close watch of the calendar, concentrating on what we wanted voters to be considering as they entered the voting booth in November. Our focus was twofold: first, we wanted voters to see an effective leadership team for Ohio. In those days—before the governor and his running mate ran in tandem—candidates often did not put their party affiliation on campaign literature. We did. Our message was clear—a vote for Dick Celeste was a vote for unified leadership—Jack Gilligan's "strong right hand."

My second focus was to contrast myself against a long-standing incumbent with a strong political name. Our theme in this respect was "more than just a name." We put together our vote budget based on how many votes Gilligan had received in earlier statewide races. The more votes I needed from a county, the more time I would spend there. At the same time, I resolved to visit every county in the state. I was determined that nowhere in the state would people be able to say Celeste failed to ask for their vote.

After I won the nomination, Dagmar and I began taking the kids around the state in an RV. By our very first stop on day one in the RV we realized that laundry was going to be a problem—we needed clothes that were comfortable and easy to clean. We found a place called the People's Store, and Dagmar spotted bib overalls in all sizes. They would be comfortable and would make trips to the laundromat a snap. So bib overalls it was for all the kids.

During that campaign in 1974 I received what I still think of as the greatest introduction ever, from state senator Bob Secrest.

Secrest had been a legendary member of the US Congress who resigned three times and had later been reelected to the same seat. He resigned first to fight in World War II, then to accept an appointment by President Truman, and, finally, to accept an appointment by Governor DiSalle. Secrest was known for having sponsored virtually every bill related to veterans' affairs while he was in Congress. Rawboned, maybe an inch taller than me, Secrest was a guy who could start playing poker Friday night, well lubricated with vodka tonics, and finish Sunday morning ready, after gargling mouthwash, to deliver an amen-evoking sermon in one of the small churches in his district.

The occasion was the Democratic dinner in Washington County where Secrest was the emcee. The big town in the county is Marietta, along the Ohio River. But the dinner was held in Churchtown. (Churchtown because that is where the Catholic Church was located. It happened to be the only precinct in Washington County that went for George McGovern in 1972, probably because the nuns thought he was Catholic.)

Perhaps three hundred Democrats gathered in the school gym to eat fried chicken, mashed potatoes, and corn bread. The head table was on the stage at one end of the gym. Bob Secrest was sitting in the middle and had the county officials on either side of him. Though I was the main speaker, I was *behind* the curtain because the stage curtain couldn't fully open. Few people could see me.

When it was time to introduce the guest of honor, Secrest began: "You know," he told the crowd, "the trouble with us Democrats is that we're always nominating old men from Cleveland."

Heads nodded.

His voice rose. "We nominate old men from Cleveland, and then they never leave Cleveland, and we lose the damn election."

More assent.

"Well, this year," he declared, his voice rising, "we did something different. We nominated a *young* man from Cleveland, and, guess what, he's left Cleveland." Secrest was speaking even more loudly. "Now I *know* he's traveled all over the state because he arrived in my hometown with his wife and his five kids. In their bib overalls. Why, they stayed in front of my house in their motor home the whole night." He paused, then shouting: "This young man, he's left Cleveland. He's campaigning all over the state." Another pause: "Why, if we keep this up, we'll have him chewing Mail Pouch Tobacco. I give you, Dick Celeste."

By that point everyone was on their feet cheering. Secrest had said nothing about Yale, nothing about a Rhodes Scholar, not even anything about my two terms as state rep.

Just Mail Pouch Tobacco.

Once when I was presiding over the Senate as lieutenant governor, a bill to regulate fox hunting came to the floor. While the bill had easily passed the Ohio House of Representatives, for some reason it was in trouble. At that point Senator Secrest rose and asked to be recognized. As always, he held his Maxwell House Coffee tin that he used as a handy spittoon. And, as always, when word went out that Secrest was going to speak, the Senate galleries quickly filled.

Slowly, he began:

"I know a number of my fellow senators are wondering what the hell fox hunting is all about. Let me explain it to you. You start with some good old boys and their dogs. And the men and their dogs like to have fun. So they let this little fox loose, and after a few minutes the men and their dogs go out looking for that fox. And one man will hear 'woof' and say 'that's my dog!' Another will hear a 'yap' and say 'that's my dog!' Soon the boys need to pause and refresh themselves. Then they hear more barking. Then more woofing. Then they refresh themselves. After a couple of hours, the good old boys are drunk as skunks, the dogs are confused, and the fox is home safe."

Bob Secrest concluded, and the Senate chamber was roaring with laughter.

"Shall the bill pass?" I asked.

"Aye," with one voice.

Politics attracts some remarkable characters. For me, one of the most unforgettable Ohio originals was Bob Secrest.

Contemplating the lieutenant governor race, I had believed that the main challenge I faced was the primary, figuring that I could win the general election running on Jack Gilligan's coattails. Not only was he the incumbent, he was running against Jim Rhodes, the governor who had sent the Ohio National Guard to Kent State. Early polls showed him trailing Gilligan badly.

Gilligan believed he retained the goodwill of the voters after the income tax he had fought so hard to institute had been upheld in a referendum in 1972. Faced with a Republican House and a Republican Senate who resisted establishing an income tax, he had vetoed a series of budgets until my friend Lloyd George Kerns eventually put together a budget with an income tax that received just enough Republican support to pass.

When the repeal issue was framed on the ballot in 1972, you had to vote *yes* to abolish the tax. It was counterintuitive, and I suspect many voters made the erroneous assumption that voting *no* would kill the income tax. The Gilligan team misread the failure of repeal to mean that Ohioans were fine with the income tax. Many were not.

To make matters worse, in the spring of 1974, the Republican Speaker of the House announced Ohio was going to have an eighty-million-dollar budget surplus. He argued that this proved that the Gilligan tax was too high. Gilligan asked his staff if this was true. They told him no. So Jack Gilligan accused the Republicans of "chasing moonbeams."

It turned out that the Speaker was right. And Gilligan's staff knew it. They should have realized that the tax commissioner would have to document the state's revenue. In early June, the tax commissioner announced that Ohio had an eighty-million-dollar surplus.

With that news, Jim Rhodes spent the summer declaring it was time to defeat "Governor Moonbeam." "He doesn't even know what's going on in his own state."

This was a classic case of staff trying to manage an elected official. Jack Hansen, Gilligan's chief of staff, was later asked why they denied the existence of the surplus. He responded that if Gilligan had been told, he would have informed the legislators—and they would want to spend it. Jack Gilligan was undermined by his staff. They misinformed him by holding back information he needed before going public on the issue.

Charlie Peters, my friend from early Peace Corps days, wrote a classic article for his *Washington Monthly* called "Bad News Doesn't Travel Up," following the *Challenger* disaster. It made this point exactly: in all organizations there is a strong tendency to resist passing bad news up the line. In the case of the *Challenger* disaster, those who suspected problems with the O-rings were unable to get their concerns to those in the position to call off the launch. Later, as governor-elect, the first question I asked my budget director was whether I could count on her to relay bad news. "I need someone who is going to let me know what I need to know," I told her. "I don't want to read about it in the papers."

I had no desire to become another Governor Moonbeam.

As Election Day neared, Gilligan sensed that the tide was turning against him. In late September, Jack pulled me aside and said, "I need help from Howard Metzenbaum." Howard had very good relations with organized labor, and Gilligan felt Metzenbaum could energize their support for his campaign.

I needed to see Howard anyway for help in my campaign, so I met him a week later in Cleveland. He was licking his wounds from his primary loss to John Glenn. I asked him for help in my race, and he agreed. I then said that Jack wanted his help.

"Why would I help Jack?" Howard asked me.

"Howard," I said, "he appointed you to the United States Senate."

Howard looked at me and said, "He didn't have a choice. Labor made him do it."

I was dumbfounded. "But he did appoint you, and he needs your help."

It never happened.

The election came down to the wire. Jim Rhodes went to bed election night thinking he had lost, but the Gilligan people knew how close it was going to be and never claimed victory. Someone woke Rhodes at two in the morning and told him he had been elected governor for a third time. Out of more than three million votes, Jack Gilligan lost by 11,500 votes. About one vote per precinct.

Meanwhile, I won by 90,000 votes. I did not realize that Gilligan had lost until the next morning.

A couple of weeks after the election, I visited Jim Rhodes in his office in downtown Columbus. Rhodes, from Jackson County, graduated from high school and got into politics almost immediately. He had been mayor of Columbus, state auditor, and already a two-term governor. Rhodes understood Ohio and enjoyed the support of a powerful and wealthy circle of friends who looked after him when he was out of office. Socially and intellectually he and I were opposites. I had gone to Yale and Oxford, and he had graduated from high school and taken a few courses at Ohio State. I had grown up in a comfortable, middle-class family, and he had come from a family who struggled in Jackson.

But he and I shared a deep affection for Ohio and loved the diversity of its people. Rhodes seemed to sense this early on, and after we had run against each other twice he came to consider me a kindred spirit. But not at that moment.

After congratulating him on his victory, I said I would do whatever I could to help. "I think that's what the people of Ohio expect," I said, "and I'm committed to working together."

He looked at me and said, "Do you play golf?"

"No," I said. "Why?"

"Take it up," he told me, "because you're going to have plenty of time. I'm not going to give you a damn thing to do."

And that was it. He didn't say it in an unfriendly way. But it was apparent he didn't want me as a strong right hand.

———

I went to see John Brown, the outgoing lieutenant governor, and asked for his help providing insights into the operation of his office. Brown refused outright. "You can come into this office after you've taken your oath of office," is how he put it. "Not before."

I persisted. If I was going to be effective as lieutenant governor I would need a clear understanding of the budget and staffing of that office, however modest. After getting the cold shoulder from Brown, I approached Jack Gilligan, explaining that I wanted to hit the ground running when I took office. He put me in touch with Pete O'Grady, now one of his cabinet members. O'Grady signed off on placing several folks in state agencies while they worked as my transition team. When I took office, they'd been working in the statehouse for perhaps six weeks.

About a month later, a *Plain Dealer* reporter stopped by my office. "Tell me about the phantom employees," he said.

"Phantom employees?" I asked. "What are you talking about?"

"I understand there's a grand jury investigation into the matter of phantom employees."

I told him I didn't know what he was talking about. "A grand jury?"

"Did you put Jan Allen, Jerry Austin, and others on the state payroll?"

I explained the situation. "They weren't phantom employees. The administration knew about it, and they were doing real state work helping to prepare me for the office of lieutenant governor."

The reporter seemed to think there was something comical about this—the idea that anyone would take the office of lieutenant governor seriously was about as novel as someone running a television spot for a lieutenant governor campaign.

Not long after my conversation with the *Plain Dealer* reporter, I was called to appear before the grand jury. I sought out Paul Ward, an experienced Columbus lawyer. "Tell me how a grand jury operates," I said to him. "What do I need to do to defend myself?"

He explained the process. You testify, but you're not allowed to bring witnesses or evidence. On the strength of your testimony, a decision is made about whether to indict or not. I explained the situation of how the employees had come to work for the state, and Ward seemed unworried.

"Look, Dick," he said, "the truth is the best defense. Explain what happened. You're not trying to hide anything. Tell them *exactly* what happened, and they'll make a judgment. And I think that the judgment will be that there's no criminal behavior here."

He was right. The grand jury tossed out the case. However, Tom Ferguson—the state auditor and a fellow Democrat—issued an audit finding saying there was no basis in the Ohio statute for transition expenses. While there had been no illegality involved, the employees had been improperly hired; they therefore had to repay their wages.

I felt it was wrong to ask my people to do this. So, with the help of my father, I repaid the $7,000 on their behalf.

I emerged from my first "scandal" unscathed, and a little wiser. It was a reminder that politics is a serious contact sport. The so-called "phantom employee" scandal was Jim Rhodes and the Republicans serving notice. "You, Celeste, are a rising star in the Democratic Party," was the message, "and we will not hesitate to cut you off at your knees."

They had tried to do that and had not succeeded. But it was a serious reminder, a hardball to the head, underscoring the scrutiny one is under in public life and the sharp side of politics. For all the joys that come from meeting people on the campaign trail, for all the blessings of being able to make a difference on the behalf of one's constituents, there remains a tough side to politics. It can be a harsh business. I remind myself of Joe Mull.

Was I anxious? Here's the truth: I wasn't. I believe that I wasn't anxious then—nor was I during some tense moments that were to come—because of the sense that my work as a public official was an important expression of my faith. In my heart of hearts, I felt that I was called to public service. I was responding to my grandmother's admonition: to whom much is given, much is expected. Throughout my public service, each night as I went to bed, I offered the same simple prayer: "God I am going to sleep for the night. I'm turning my problems over to you," I'd pray. "They're in your hands."

Whether I was going before the grand jury, preparing a crucial campaign speech, confronting a tough decision, or wrestling with a family problem, this simple prayer brought me untroubled sleep. Yes, I experienced some very hard nights as governor, for example, when flash flooding killed people in northeastern Ohio or when considering whether to close the savings and loans during the 1985 crisis. But my faith helped me keep things in perspective—and sleep soundly.

I also benefited from a gifted and devoted team. One of the best joined me not long after I was elected lieutenant governor. Soon after the election, as I was walking through the statehouse, Paul Corey, my Cleveland friend who had become a member of Gilligan's cabinet, stopped to congratulate me. "I have one piece of advice for you," he said. "Just two words."

"Okay," I said. "What are they?"

"Dora Globe."

"What's Dora Globe?"

"Not what's Dora Globe," he said. "Who is Dora Globe. She is the best."

Dora Globe was an experienced state employee who turned out also to be an extraordinary executive secretary. I hired her soon after that conversation and knew immediately that I had found an essential member of my team. In the years that would follow, if anyone—including any of my children—needed to get hold of me, they contacted Dora. If the kids needed a check, or a permission slip signed, if there was any real emergency or serious request, Dora managed the situation. Everybody who met Dora became a devoted fan. For good reason.

Dora was the best.

With the exception of Jack Gilligan, Democrats had done well. Statewide we had won auditor, treasurer, and attorney general. We had strengthened our majority in the House. I was viewed as one of the upcoming leaders with a strong claim to be the next candidate for governor. As the press became less interested in the brouhaha surrounding the "phantom employees," I turned my attention to what lay ahead—the task of defeating Jim Rhodes in the 1978 election.

I had plenty of time for this effort. Lieutenant governor did not require the heavy lifting I would have faced as secretary of state, for instance. The lieutenant governor presided over the Senate (a duty I took seriously, but which only infrequently asked something of me), was head of the Ohio navy (which did not exist), and was responsible for whatever else the governor delegated. Since Rhodes gave me nothing, that freed me to travel the state.

It also left time to challenge Rhodes. I assumed this role as the most vocal opponent of his 1975 bond proposals. Rhodes had always loved bond issues—he'd borrow money for highways, college buildings—and obligate future governors to pay with general revenue funds for decades to come. His four proposed 1975 issues totaled billions of dollars. The issues were endorsed by most of organized labor, the Ohio Chamber of Commerce, and many newspapers across the state.

With the Celeste team, I decided to fight the issues. We developed a strategy that involved two key allies who also opposed the bond issues: the League of

My fan club at my swearing-in as lieutenant governor in January 1975. *Left to right:* Chester and Steb Bowles, my mother, me, Dagmar, Governor Gilligan, and my father.

My father, Frank Celeste, administering the oath of office of lieutenant governor to me

Women Voters and the United Auto Workers. The UAW contributed $60,000 to finance a campaign, which was not much of a war chest. Rhodes and the Republicans had at least $2 million to invest in their PR campaign.

In the end, we defeated all four 1975 bond proposals. The key element was a clever television spot that Jerry Austin and David Milenthal produced. Set in a seedy sandlot baseball diamond, dark shadows and trash dominate the opening—this is not a place to be late at night. Suddenly, a weaselly-looking guy in a trench coat appears. "Psssst," he hisses to the camera, "vote yes on Issues 2, 3, 4, and 5. And if you like them, have I got something for you." He opens his trench coat, and you see a string of watches inside. Then the words: "Vote NO on 2, 3, 4 and 5. UAW and League of Women Voters."

The unexpected defeat of the issues helped establish me clearly as the leader of the Democratic opposition and cemented my status as Gilligan's successor. When I wasn't presiding in the Senate, I was already on the campaign trail, speaking at Democratic dinners whenever I could—including the Jefferson-Jackson Day dinner, the Ohio Democratic Party's most popular annual event.

One of my original thoughts on running for statewide office was the conviction that either outcome would be good for my family. If I lost, I'd move back to Cleveland, and the family would be together; if I won, we'd all move to Columbus. We had started looking for a house shortly after the election and found a house on the Scioto River in rural Delaware County. Dagmar had wanted to try country living, and the house on Riverside Drive—about forty-five minutes north of downtown Columbus—certainly qualified.

We had 6 acres next to a 250-acre soybean farm. We resided in the Buckeye Valley school district, among the most geographically dispersed and poorest in the state. A bus took our kids to school. I drove into Columbus daily to preside over the Senate, and Dagmar soon found a job in town at the Center for Tomorrow, a think tank and research center. She was going to college at the same time.

The kids basically took care of themselves. Perhaps not always as well as I thought they were taking care of themselves.

In some respects, it was a good place to grow up. The schools the kids went to were small, which meant they could play the sports they wanted. They were left free to pursue whatever esoteric interests they chose. Our eldest son, Eric, discovered computers at the Delaware Public Library. In those days most computers would take up a whole room and hardly anyone had one in their home. Going to the library, Eric taught himself how to program when he was just thirteen; then he discovered the computer center at nearby Ohio Wesleyan. He hung around outside, asking students whether they needed help. "I can show you how to use it," he'd say. Then he'd assist these kids five or six years older than him. In return they'd share their passwords. Eric came home one day and urged me to buy stock in a company called Apple.

I didn't listen to him. That was a mistake.

Our eldest daughter, Gabriella, played softball. She was a great pitcher and a tough competitor. She still is. Christopher played basketball and was a determined athlete. We bought a donkey to placate Noelle, who wanted a pony. I had heard that ponies needed a lot of care. Donkeys, on the other hand, were reputed to be virtually carefree. Dagmar and Noelle saw an ad for one, so we all went to buy him. The kids asked his name.

"Senator," the farmer selling him told us.

We decided we couldn't have two politicians in the family, so we changed his name to Dink-Donk.

Along with a new donkey in Delaware, we kept our home in Cleveland and rented it to an organization as the first battered women's shelter in the state. Designed to accommodate five kids, it worked well as a shelter—though we never publicized the fact because the location of the shelter had to be confidential.

Domestic abuse was an issue in which Dagmar had a serious interest. As lieutenant governor I sat in on several hearings in Cleveland about the issue. Once the woman testifying was the wife of a labor leader, a big supporter of mine. These hearings awakened me to the pervasiveness of domestic violence, a concern that remained with me throughout my public service.

On rare occasions there would be a tie vote in the Senate. In the mid-1970s, most bills were handled on a bipartisan basis. During my second year, a bill to decriminalize possession of an ounce or less of marijuana came to the Senate floor. I'd been alerted to this bill by Peter Lewis, a longtime friend and contributor and also a strong advocate for legalization of marijuana. When it came time to vote, one senator decided to take a walk. The tally stood at sixteen to sixteen. Lacking a majority of votes, the bill would have failed. So as the presiding officer I exercised my constitutional right to cast a vote. The legislation passed.

A year later, a bill to raise pay for state and county officials came to the floor. This legislation was considered every eight years or so and was always touchy. Under Ohio law, if you voted in favor of a pay raise, you could only receive it after you were reelected. The same Democratic senator who had taken a walk a year earlier did so again. Once more, the tally was sixteen–sixteen. Again, I cast a vote in favor of the legislation.

Voting as the lieutenant governor was, of course, controversial. Some folks held that I was wrong to exercise my constitutional authority on any issue. It had been years since a lieutenant governor had done so. But I believed in taking responsibility, and, like Chester Bowles, I respected the operation of state government. I was not going to watch a good piece of legislation fail because the lieutenant governor was unwilling to vote.

Some predicted that these issues would haunt me in future statewide elections. They never did.

In 1976, Jerry Austin and I pulled together a group of volunteers to attend the Democratic National Convention in New York City. During our 1968 effort to draft Ted Kennedy, we had learned that people at conventions are like water bugs on the surface of a pond. They go skittering in many directions, and on the surface there's lot of activity. But most delegates—except those running the convention—have little idea what is actually happening. We decided to go to the convention for several reasons—among them to help draft John Glenn for vice president, to cultivate the Ohio delegation, and to raise my profile and a network of contacts.

During the 1976 presidential primary, I had stayed neutral. As the Ohio's senior Democrat, I wanted all candidates to feel welcome in our state. My brother, Ted, wasn't neutral, however, and he ran the vital win for Jimmy Carter. Ted had earned considerable respect in that campaign. (My parents would attend the Carter inauguration with Ted and Bobbie.) The Ohio delegation continued to play an important role—during the roll call, Ohio clinched the nomination for Jimmy Carter.

It was a historic convention, and I wanted to participate. Was I already thinking about a presidential run and what it would entail? Were we already laying the groundwork for it? The thought was probably not far from some minds.

We mounted two attention-grabbers at the convention. The first involved buying peanuts wholesale—hundred-pound burlap bags. Somehow Austin wrestled those huge bags into a taxi. At our hotel we divvied the peanuts into smaller containers and took them around to the convention hotels. The peanuts were a salute to Jimmy Carter. A sign attached said, "provided courtesy of the Lieutenant Governor of Ohio, Richard F Celeste."

People loved it.

The second ploy was to deliver daily copies of the *Plain Dealer* to the Ohio delegation with a note from the lieutenant governor. These Carter supporters were often new to politics but determined enough to become convention delegates. It seemed like a good idea to reach out to them.

Our antics were captured in sardonic detail in Richard Reeves's book *Convention,* which came out in March following the convention. I recall being surprised by the tone of the book. Reeves had been friendly, and it came as a shock to find myself skewered in his pages. Though Reeves had not coined the "Celestial" term, *Convention* did give it prominent play:

At 11:00 P.M. on Sunday, 24 people, most of them quite young, crowded into suite 2018 at the New York Sheraton, the rooms of Ohio Lieutenant Governor Richard Celeste . . . Jerry Austin, William Flaherty, and Jan Allen were three of the five members of Celeste's staff—the lieutenant governor of Ohio has almost no governmental responsibilities—and most of the rest were volunteers who had come in from Ohio on their own. Celeste groupies, Celestials . . . When the others left, after midnight, Celeste and his wife, Dagmar, sat down to finish addressing 600 invitations to a cocktail party.

Later Reeves characterized the impression we made at the convention. Let me say that a key attribute of anyone who hopes to survive public life is a thick skin and the ability to laugh at oneself. I was reminded of this by the Reeves book, which, I confess, still makes me wince:

Dick Celeste's big party was scheduled from 5:00 to 7:00 P.M. in the large Sheraton suite of the Ohio state chairman, Paul Tipps. At the last minute Celeste got nervous and told his assistant, Jerry Austin, that he needed something extra to make sure that people would remember the party. Austin went to a wholesale house at Sixth Avenue and 42nd Street and spent $65 for another 100-pound bag of peanuts. "This is the fourth bag I've sold this way in three days," said the man behind the counter. "What's going on?"

Reeves had a point—I stuck my head up higher than I should have at that point in my career. I was just a lieutenant governor. Who was I to show up in New York as if I were running for president?

In August 1977 Dagmar gave birth to our sixth child—Stephen—an unexpected bonus baby. In early October, Dagmar suffered a psychotic break. It was, in part, postpartum depression. But I am sure it was also the growing stresses in our family.

Eric, who was at the house, called me while I was presiding in the Senate and described Dagmar's bizarre behavior. I drove home immediately. I found Dagmar in a state that is hard to describe. She was in a different place entirely, speeding it's called—speaking with frenetic speed, jumping incoherently from one topic to another, switching randomly from German to English—and hallucinating wildly. She had not eaten or slept properly for a couple of days. Impossible to reason with, she began issuing dire predictions and said she saw angels hovering nearby. As a mother, she had stopped functioning. She couldn't breastfeed Stephen or cook dinner for the kids or even have a coherent conversation. It was deeply disturbing. How could we help? Would we ever get her back to normal?

I decided that she needed to be somewhere safe and away from family pressures. So I drove her to Cleveland to consult our good friend Roberta Steinbacher, a professor at Cleveland State with a background in psychology, who also happened to be an ex-nun. I hoped that she'd be able to help slow Dagmar down. Roberta volunteered to have Dagmar stay with her. But after several days, Dagmar's condition worsened. Recognizing that Dagmar needed to be hospitalized, I took her to the Cleveland Clinic, where unfortunately her male doctor was unsympathetic to the Catholic symbolism of her hallucinations and couldn't understand much of what she was saying, since it was often German. He recommended electroshock therapy, which Dagmar and I adamantly refused.

Fortunately, I found a psychiatrist in Columbus at Mount Carmel Hospital, a woman who spoke German. When she agreed to treat Dagmar, I brought her back to Columbus. In the meantime, her mother came from Vienna to look after the children—especially Stephen, who was just a few months old. Eventually, as a small baby, he would live for a time with her in Vienna.

With this going on, I wasn't sure if I should proceed with a race for governor. The expectation was that I would run against Rhodes. But given all that Dagmar and the family were going through, I wondered if I should call off the campaign. Deeply uncertain about the right thing to do, I sat down with my old pastor at Lakewood Methodist Church and asked for his counsel. I had launched a major campaign, but my wife was seriously ill. Should I withdraw from the race?

"Dick," he said, "let me tell you what my experience has been. If a person's mental health issues cause another family member to change plans or careers, it often places a burden of guilt on that individual as they recover. Dagmar will recover; we have treatments and medications now that can help her. It's a matter of time and healing, and I think if you decide not to run, your decision will become a burden for her."

With the holidays near, I took some time out from the campaign trail. For several months, my main task was trying to reconcile the space for Dagmar to heal with the demands of a governor's race.

In the end, I decided to run.

With Jerry Austin in a supporting role, I chose my brother, Ted, to be my campaign director. Knowing that a gubernatorial campaign was around the corner, Ted had approached me early on. I had a confidence in him and gave him the job without hesitation. Ted was totally loyal, and, though he lacked some of Jerry's brash creativity, he was more measured and unlikely to say something about the candidate or the campaign that would cause ripples in the press. Above all, Ted was my brother—blood—and I probably needed that comfort level for my first big-league campaign. It was a safe choice. For his part, Jerry worked with David Milenthal on communications and sat in on strategy meetings.

I felt that the focus of the campaign was that Jim Rhodes had failed to live up to his many promises. Ohio received national attention as school districts went into receivership, taken over by the state when local funding proved insufficient. Rhodes raised taxes once and then a second time. I believed that the voters wanted a fresh start.

I had campaigned—successfully—when I was lieutenant governor to change the law that provided separate elections for governor and lieutenant governor. Having been locked out by Jim Rhodes, I argued that teamwork should be a consideration when thinking about the governor's office. If the governor died or ran for another office, the lieutenant governor should become governor without party considerations complicating the transition. The 1978 election marked the debut for tandem elections.

I chose Mike Dorian as my running mate—someone who would inspire confidence among traditional Democrats. I wanted somebody who had a record of public service and had endured the scrutiny of public life.

Mike was a county commissioner in Columbus who had won by massive margins. His brother was the city auditor. They were a respected political family in Franklin County, the third-largest county in the state. Mike was a

Campaigning with the Democratic ticket in 1978. *Left to right:* Paul Tipps, Mike Dorrian, Nancy Echenrode, Tony Celebrezze, Margie Pizzuti, RFC, Gertrude Donahy, Tom Ferguson, Ted Celeste, Pat Leahy, and Jerry Austin.

wonderful, decent guy, not fancy or charismatic but a competent and devoted public servant. However, on Election Day, I was reminded that the second spot does not bring many votes to the ticket.

We nearly won. We waged a strong campaign against an incumbent governor who was one of Ohio's most canny vote-getters. We lost by twenty-two thousand votes—a narrow defeat. But a defeat nonetheless.

Only years later did a student in the class of political science professor Herb Asher at Ohio State University unearth the fact that nearly 150,000 ballots in that election had been disqualified because individuals had voted for governor twice. One reason may have been confusion since this was the first election in which governor and lieutenant governor ran as a team. Tantalizing in retrospect was the fact that most of these mismarked ballots were cast in heavily Democratic counties, using a punch card system that did not lock out double-voting.

So perhaps we had, in fact, won. But, as strange as it might sound, when we lost, a part of me was not surprised. Somewhere in my gut I didn't feel ready to *be* governor. I was hungry but couldn't take the last bite. Perhaps that was hinted at by my indecision on the education issue, notably how we were going to pay for the reforms I wanted to enact. I hadn't framed a compelling answer to that question.

I fumbled on my first rule for a successful campaign: you must frame the question you want voters to be thinking about as they enter the booth on Election Day. And provide a convincing answer. At that time, school districts were literally shutting down because of lack of funding. It was Jim Rhodes's vulnerability. As a candidate with experience as an educator, I should have embraced a bold program to reform education and its funding. But I waffled on the funding. Looking back, I'd say this to myself: if you believe in it, go for it!

Everything that happens to a public official is harder for the family than it is for the candidate. Victory, defeat, scandal, whatever, the experience is more intense for the family. As a candidate, you consider possible outcomes and mentally rehearse a victory speech and a concession speech. But you can't share what you're thinking. Your dress rehearsal is for one person only. Everyone else has their hopes and dreams hanging out there.

This was certainly true for my brother, Ted, who wept openly the night of my defeat. He felt that it was his defeat as much as mine. I didn't believe that was the case. While many people are involved in a campaign, ultimately the candidate has to own the outcome. Our results came in late. We had an enthusiastic crowd convinced we were going to win. My family and inner circle were tracking results from the field, and the numbers gradually became clear. I had let that old fox Rhodes slip back in, I thought.

I loved the people who had gathered that night in anticipation of a victory. I have old audiotape of my concession speech, with Dagmar, Ted, and the family on stage with me. You can hear folks shouting in dismay, some of them calling for a recount. It was essential for me to acknowledge the loss to these supporters but more important to convey what I thought we needed to do in the months ahead.

"We must build. And build. And build again," I proclaimed as I made it clear I wasn't going to leave Ohio. We had built a gifted and enthusiastic team. I wanted them to know I valued what we had built together.

Growing up, Ted had been more politically involved than me. He had worked in all of my father's campaigns and moved down to Columbus to work in the Gilligan administration. After Gilligan's loss, Ted and his wife, Bobbie, stayed on, and he opened a real estate business. He would end up getting a bum rap for running a losing campaign.

The truth is that he was an excellent campaign director and an astute political operative. He was observant and smart, and, most crucially, he was candid with me. If he thought I wasn't doing something well or I'd made a wrong decision, he would say so. Few people saw that aspect of our relationship. Indeed, most people believed that he lacked the ability to be frank with his older brother—because Ted just made a point of taking me aside privately. It was always just him and me.

The most insightful account of that election night may have been provided by my nine-year-old daughter, Noelle, who presented me with the report she'd written for school the next day:

What happened!!!!
1. I sat in the room for an hour eating watching TV etc
2. Reporters are all over and my dad couldn't get out to do his speech
3. ————
4. Everybody was there, republicins and Demercrats
5. This one republicin came up to us and said I'm sorry I'm a repuilcin
6. My Dad lost. to bad.
7. My Dad went up on stage and made a small speech and we had to stand on the stage too.
8. We had to squeeze through the crowd to get to our room.
9. We sleped over at the niel house and left for school around 6:30 and I went to bed at 2:30 so I didn't get lots of sleep. But I still got to school as you can see.
10. My Dad had a small speech for all the people upstairs and I started crying really hard
11. But my dad is not a quitter he's going to run again.

I have kept that note with me ever since. It remains close to my heart. How do we want our children to talk about us? I could not have wished for more. "My dad is not a quitter," she wrote. "He's going to run again."

I could not have put it better myself.

What happened !!!!

1. I sat in the room for an hour eating watching TV. ect.
2. Reporters are all over and my Dad couldn't get out to do his speech.
3. ~~[crossed out]~~
4. Everybody was there republics.ns and Demercrats.
5. This one repuicing came up to us and said I'm sorry I'm a repuiicn.
6. My Dad lost To bood%
7. My Dad went up on stage and made a small speech and we had to stand on the stage too.
8. We had to squeeze through the croud to get to our room.
9. We slept over at the niel house and left for school around 6:30. And I went to bed at 2:30 so I didn't get lots of sleep. But I still got to school as you can see.
10. My Dad had a small speech for all the people upstairs and I started Crying really hard.
11. But my dad is not a quitter hes going to run again.

Good Luck next time !!!!!!!!!!
Noelle

Noelle Celeste had to write a report for her fourth-grade class because she missed a day of school to be with me on Election Day 1978. This was her report.

Chapter 7

Peace Corps

After losing the election, the family moved back to our Cleveland home, and I returned to my old job, working alongside my father and my brother in National Housing Consultants, focused on senior citizen housing.

I was disappointed, of course, that I had lost. But I was not distraught. Frankly, I didn't see it as a setback so much as an essential step on a longer political quest. The tradition in Ohio was that a statewide candidate lost at least once before winning. I was no exception to the rule. Like my daughter, I knew that I would run again. And I was confident that I would be a stronger candidate.

I looked forward to the next four years to consolidate my support in northeast Ohio, to build my profile statewide and to restore some financial security for my family. With this in mind, I went back to my desk in the office I had shared with my father and Ted and set to work.

But, again, serendipity overtook my expectations. Before the year was out, I received a phone call from Washington, DC. I was surprised to find myself speaking to Mary King, deputy director of ACTION. ACTION was an umbrella agency composed of federal volunteer programs ranging from VISTA and Foster Grandparents to the Peace Corps. She was calling out of the blue to ask if I would interview for the position of Peace Corps director.

"I think you've got the wrong Celeste," I told her. "You must be looking for my brother, Ted. He's the Celeste who served in the Peace Corps—the Celeste who ran President Carter's campaign in Ohio."

"Are you the Celeste who ran for governor?" she asked.

I said that I was.

Reassured, she said, "Then you're the Celeste I'm looking for. We would like you to come to interview for the position of Peace Corps director."

After a long pause—my mind racing back to Chester Bowles's unexpected invitation to join him in India—I said I was willing to consider it. My father and my brother were both in the office that day. "I just got a call from Washington," I told them. "I was asked to interview for Peace Corps director."

Ted rolled his eyes. "You?"

"I thought they were looking for you, Ted," I told him. "But for some reason it was me."

The next week I was on a plane to DC.

At the time I didn't have a detailed knowledge of what was happening in the Miatico Building where I had worked almost fifteen years earlier. I had heard that there were problems but only what had been reported in the newspapers. Carolyn Payton—the former director—had resigned in a dispute about the status of Peace Corps within ACTION. In addition, she had clashed with ACTION director Sam Brown over his proposal to send volunteers on short overseas assignments and then bring them home to use the skills they had acquired to fight poverty here.

While there may have been more personal reasons behind her resignation, Payton had been very public about what she resisted as a significant shift in the mission of the Peace Corps. She told the *Washington Post* that Brown was trying to turn the corps into an "arrogant, elitist" political cadre intended to "meddle in the affairs of foreign governments."

Payton also chafed at what she described in the papers as "the peculiar administrative structure under which the Peace Corps operates." The Nixon administration had submerged the Peace Corps into ACTION, depriving it of its ability to act independently. This concern about the status of the Peace Corps I did understand—and share.

I was surprised that the agency was still so severely constrained within the Carter administration. President Carter's mother, Miss Lillian, had served as a Peace Corps volunteer, and the expectation among the Peace Corps community was that Carter would restore its independence. Instead, Sam Brown had lobbied successfully to be "double-hatted" as director of ACTION and director of the Peace Corps. Carolyn Payton had never held the director title; instead, she was "deputy director of ACTION responsible for the Peace Corps."

The extent to which this lack of independence had adversely affected morale was reflected in the questions I faced in my interview. There were perhaps ten people gathered in a small conference room with Mary King presiding. We had a wide-ranging discussion about the role of the agency and its future. Would I strive to make the Peace Corps autonomous? What did I think of short-term volunteers?

Despite having been so abruptly plunged into this brouhaha, I could sense an undercurrent of resentment and frustration. As the interview progressed, I became convinced they did not view me as a serious candidate. I had been a name on a list, someone they had to interview. It seemed a bit surreal for all of us. Certainly for me. I had spent the past four years strategizing to become governor of Ohio—and now I was expected to offer serious thoughts about what I might do as director of the Peace Corps.

The search committee fairly represented an agency deeply concerned about where it found itself, facing serious questions about how direction and morale could be restored. How could the Peace Corps recapture its spirit and identity? Would the Peace Corps once again enjoy an independent budget? Its own congressional liaison? Its own general counsel? As it stood, the agency was being run by people who answered to Sam Brown.

When the interview ended, I had a much clearer understanding of what they hoped for in a director but felt that they were unlikely to offer me the job. This impression was reinforced as the interview ended. "Do I have to fill out anything?" I asked. "No," I was told. "Do you need any other information?" I asked. Again the answer was no.

I arrived back at National Housing Consultants assuming that I was a straw candidate and that some Washington insider would get the appointment.

To my surprise, Mary King called a few weeks later to say that President Carter wanted to appoint me the next Peace Corps director.

"Now," she said with a chuckle, "there are forms to fill out."

I was nominated on March 29, 1979, and by April 3 I was on the payroll in consultant status so that I could begin to work. Things moved quickly. In the three weeks or so that followed I had two critical tasks. The first was to map out a road forward for the Peace Corps that would move forcefully toward an independent agency. And second, to bring in a couple of people whom I could trust and who would work well in the Peace Corps environment.

To accomplish the latter, I reached out immediately to ask Dora Globe and Bill Flaherty to join me in Washington. Dora would serve as my executive secretary, and I wanted Bill to be my chief of staff. Bill was one of the few people who knew I was being considered for this appointment and had hinted that he had an interest in joining me in DC. He was an ideal fit not only because he had firsthand experience in domestic poverty programs but,

Conferring with President Carter in the Oval Office in 1979 when I was the Peace Corps director

more important, because I could trust him completely and count on him to understand the political crosscurrents in Washington and Ohio—and to tell me whenever he felt I was on the verge of a wrong decision.

When I called Bill to tell him that I had the job and wanted him to come with me, he sounded as surprised as I had been, then said, "Let me talk with Cindy"—his wife. Within a day he called me back to say yes. Dora said yes, too.

The first challenge, however, would provide the essential foundation for whatever I could achieve in the less than two years that remained of President Carter's term. Therefore, when I met with the president in late March to discuss the appointment, I stressed that I felt the independence of the Peace Corps needed to be restored. The president listened sympathetically but pointed out that Sam Brown felt just as strongly that the Peace Corps should remain part of ACTION.

I had expected the pushback, so I outlined what I thought was a workable compromise. The Peace Corps would become an autonomous agency within ACTION. My title would be director of the Peace Corps. We would have independent budget authority, our own congressional liaison and legal counsel. The president asked that we draft an executive order laying out this understanding to be signed as I was sworn in as director.

Vice President Fritz Mondale swearing me in as Peace Corps director in the spring of 1979

Thus, on April 27 my paperwork was amended. I moved from an "expert" being paid a per diem to appointment as director of the Peace Corps. In fact I had two titles: I was *also* an associate director of ACTION. The White House formally announced my appointment at the beginning of May, and I was sworn in by Vice President Walter "Fritz" Mondale on May 23. Mondale could not resist noting the preponderance of Ohioans among the several hundred guests in the East Room. "We picked one state at random . . . Ohio," he said with a grin. As the ceremony was winding up, President and Mrs. Carter joined the crowd (many of whom, like my brother, Ted, had campaigned hard for his victory in Ohio).

I should note that drafting the executive order was not an easy task since at the time we had no independent lawyer for the Peace Corps. Faced with this difficulty, I reached out to Bill Josephson, a longtime friend who had been the original general counsel at the Peace Corps. He agreed to help on a pro bono basis. Actually, I think it was a labor of love for Bill, who was devoted to assuring a strong and successful Peace Corps. As someone who had worked side by side with Sarge Shriver in creating the agency in the early days of the Kennedy administration, Bill was eager to restore as much of that original legacy as possible.

I was the beneficiary of his skill and dedication. So too was the Peace Corps—for the second time in thirty years.

Almost immediately after my confirmation I flew to the Philippines to meet with volunteers in the field. I wanted to reach out to the PCVs at their work sites and gain a firsthand sense of how they perceived our mission and the direction they were receiving from headquarters. As is often the case with Washington politicians who lose touch with the folks back home, I sensed that the volunteers felt a gulf between the ACTION headquarters and their lives in-country.

I was not the only one to recognize this. A number of talented individuals within the organization in Washington were thinking creatively and strategically about the Peace Corps. I learned a lot from John Chromy, David Levine, and David Downs, to name several. Still, I knew that if I was going to be successful, I'd have to spend as much time as possible with volunteers in their villages.

While I had worked for the agency briefly in the early Shriver days under Sally Bowles, that assignment had never taken me abroad. I had relied on letters from the field to characterize the kind of experience volunteers were having. Only during my time in India with Ambassador Bowles did I visit PCVs in the field. Visiting volunteers where they lived and worked would help me connect with Peace Corps realities on a deep personal level. It was akin to my experience in 1974 at that Democratic dinner in Wayne County, where Dennis Heffernan prodded me to go around the room a second time and make an authentic connection with each person. I knew that PCVs needed and deserved a strong connection with their director.

I also understood that to restore the morale of the agency I had to honor its center of gravity. For the Peace Corps, that center of gravity was (and remains) overseas—volunteers and country directors who are on the ground every day living out the mission initially articulated by President Kennedy. My focus on the volunteer perspective served me well throughout my brief tenure. When I traveled, I would call on our ambassador, but I would stay with our country director and volunteers.

I was determined to reinvigorate the constituency for the Peace Corps. That effort required listening carefully, articulating its mission clearly, and building a constituency devoted to advancing that mission.

The Peace Corps has always been allergic to politics. Visiting volunteers in the field is different from shaking hands at a Democratic dinner or asking for a vote. But there *are* similarities: both require cultivating genuine engagement. You had to listen closely and let people know you valued what they had to say. Without an investment of time and attention at the front end, strategic initiatives were likely to run into resistance. I needed to engage our volunteers early in order to achieve change in Washington.

Though I was in the Philippines to learn from the PCVs and lay the groundwork for change at headquarters, the volunteers themselves had their own plans for me. This was their opportunity to put me through a boot camp of sorts.

I arrived in Manila in the late afternoon after an eighteen-hour flight, eager for a quick shower and perhaps even a little rest. No way, Mr. New Director.

The country codirectors (a husband-and-wife team) immediately loaded me into the back of a "jeepeny" for a seventy-kilometer drive on incredibly bumpy roads. Like the experienced statewide campaigner I had become, I fell asleep during the first kilometer. My ability to sleep soundly while gripping an overhead crash bar as we bounced along was the source of both wonder and plenty of kidding. Photos documented the director's remarkable posture, snoring away. After overnighting with a group of PCVs in their village, we bounced back to Manila for a raucous pig roast in our directors' backyard. These codirectors were one of the first such teams we had credentialed, and I was pleased to see the arrangement working well.

And the volunteers seemed pleased with me.

While the team there may have seen this trip as a kind of hazing for me, I welcomed it. Traveling over those roads to a remote village reminded me of heading out with Doug Bennet and our misbehaving kids in India. Without an inkling of what the future held for me, Chet Bowles had somehow prepared me for this newest and most unexpected chapter of my life. It felt familiar, almost as if it was meant to be.

After my return to Washington, I spent considerable time with our regional directors, former volunteers, and early Peace Corps staffers in order to get as many insights as possible. These perspectives—an understanding of where the Peace Corps had been, where we were, and where we ought to be headed—along with the voices of PCVs in the Philippines, helped shape my goals for the next couple of years.

One of the many volunteers I visited was a woman from Chicago posted to a remote village in Ghana. Her host was the family of the village headman. At the end of my visit, I sat with him to ask him about the experience of having a PCV in his community. In a very formal way, he stood and began a speech thanking me and the people of the United States. "I want to thank you for sending Anne, whom we call Fante, to our village," he began. "If you had told me, before she came, that an American would travel to live and work here, I would have told you that that is not possible."

He went on. "And if you had told me that this person would come here and live as a member of my family, I would have said that is not possible."

I continued to listen. "If you told me that a woman would come from the United States, live with my family, and help the women of my village build a health clinic, I would have told you that is *not* possible."

I began to respond, but he held up his hand. "But," he said, "I have seen Fante come to this village, and I have seen her become a member of my family, and I have seen her work with the women here to build a clinic. I know now that when we all join hands together, we can do things we cannot imagine."

His message has stayed with me ever since.

On the same trip to West Africa, I visited a young woman named Helen DesRobbiers. Helen majored in biology at Boston College and loved gardening. Her assignment was working in a Senegalese village on the edge of the Sahara to help a women's co-op develop a community garden.

I visited Helen about eighteen months into her service. Over a homemade lunch, I met five or six of the women who were part of the co-op. After the meal Helen and the women were eager to show me the project they had been working on together. We walked a couple of kilometers to a dried-out riverbed, which they had turned into a small vegetable garden. Though the plot was modest, the women and Helen were very excited because the vegetables growing there would supplement millet, until then their only crop. Their sense of achievement was palpable.

As we walked back to the village, I took Helen aside. "Helen," I asked, "how do these women feel about having a blind volunteer in their midst?"

As capable as Helen was, she was legally blind. She had to kneel to get close enough to examine the plants growing in the new garden, and her mother's letters were written in large block letters that Helen would hold close to her nose to read.

"Oh, Dick," she smiled. "They don't know that I'm blind."

"What do mean they don't know you're blind?" I was astonished.

"I just felt that it was never important to tell them." Again, she smiled. "In fact, I am teaching two girls how to read, and I've noticed they hold their papers against their noses when they read."

I then asked her the question I asked every PCV I met. "What has this experience meant to you?"

Her response stunned me. "It has given me the gift of new eyes."

She paused for a moment, letting her words hang there in the air. Then she continued, "If I had stayed in Boston, I would have no idea how these women live here on the edge of this great desert. It has given me new eyes to see my country more clearly, too. I know now what I love about my country—and what I would like to change."

A longer pause: "And it has given me the gift of seeing myself in a new way. If you had told me back in Boston what I would find myself doing here, I would have never come. So," she concluded, "that is the gift of new eyes."

Helen's story became—and remains to this day—a kind of parable I share with people when enlisting their understanding and their help. We are so used to seeing things from a single perspective we often think that this is the only way our community or our state or our nation can be.

We all need the gift of new eyes.

Two aspects of my work as Peace Corps director would serve me well when I became governor. The first had to do with money. The second had to do with people.

In the legislature our tendency is to focus on one or two elements of the state budget, subjects of special interest to us. If you are interested in education, as a legislator you pay attention to the line items that impact education. If you are interested in horse racing, or the coal industry, you will master the parts of the budget that bear on your area of interest. This narrow focus obscures the larger context of budget making. How does the overall budget address the key goals of the state—or the agency? What are the tradeoffs? How might funds be redirected?

When I arrived, my first Peace Corps budget was buried inside the much larger budget of ACTION. The challenge was to decipher that budget and understand how to make the resources of Peace Corps go further. Since I was commuting each week from Cleveland and living in the basement of the Heffernan townhouse, I had every evening free. I spent many hours each night in my eighth-floor office untangling our budget numbers from those of ACTION—determined to figure out where Emerson Markham, the ACTION budget officer—had squirreled away money. I knew that every budget chief wants a "cookie jar" so that when his boss needs funds for an urgent crisis or a new initiative, he can respond positively.

To master a budget, you have to be willing to ask what may seem like dumb questions. If something does not make sense, ask about it—even if you risk looking foolish. I first learned this lesson almost a decade earlier as a young legislator. In committee hearings I was often the one who asked what sounded like an obvious, even naive question. Equally often fellow legislators would thank me for asking the question they were unwilling to ask for fear of seeming dense.

So each night I added to my list of questions for Emerson Markham. "Why do we carry these funds in a special account?" I asked after I had been on the job for a few weeks.

I could see him fidget. "Well," he explained, "technically that money was not appropriated by Congress."

"And what does that mean?" I continued.

"Well," Emerson repeated, "that means that this money can be used at the director's discretion." I wondered when he might have told me had I not asked.

My "night school classes on budget making—and money hiding" would serve me well in the years ahead.

The second valuable lesson from my Peace Corps days involved the challenge of cultivating a diverse talent pool. As soon as I became director, the White House began to send a stream of candidates for my vacant deputy director position. I rejected one after another. One of my top goals was increasing the diversity of the agency—beginning with my deputy. The White House pushed would-be diplomats who happened to be white (and often recently unsuccessful political candidates). I did not want a clone.

We were also eager to increase the diversity of our country directors and had in place an office called "Talent Search" started by Sam Brown and run by Nancy Graham. Our recruitment and selection process needed to be based on merit and not simply political connections. The central takeaway from Nancy's operation was that you cannot cultivate a more diverse and inclusive organization if you just wait for whoever walks through the door. You must cast a wide net. And she did.

At the Peace Corps we had a cardinal rule: The three finalists in every search had to include racial and gender diversity. This rule dramatically widened our talent pool. This experience in recruiting diverse talent helped me in 1982 when I assembled a cabinet with more women and African Americans than the cabinets of all of my predecessors combined.

Eventually the White House recommended someone I could hire with confidence as my deputy. Bill Sykes, who had a wry sense of humor, once (after Ronald Reagan was elected president) described himself as a "short, fat,

Black Republican." In fact, Bill was a highly gifted public administrator who was liked by all of his colleagues. And he was certainly not going to be mistaken for my clone.

On December 12, 1979, as I sat at my desk, I received a call informing me that PCV Debra Loff had been detained by young rifle-toting radicals at her work site in the municipal market in San Salvador. It was a distressing call—one no Peace Corps director wants to get.

Almost three years earlier, Richard Starr, a PCV in Colombia, had been kidnapped by the Fuerzas Armadas Revolutionaries de Colombia (FARC), and he was still being held for ransom. I worried that this might result in the same grim situation.

Debbie had spent fourteen months in El Salvador working in the San Jacinto Market to educate women vendors about health and nutrition. She and the market manager were taken captive and held in the manager's office by a group of Salvadorian students who styled themselves after the February 28 Popular Front. At the same time, ten other Salvadorians were being held hostage at another public market in town.

This was one of the most challenging moments during my leadership of the Peace Corps. I felt personally responsible for Debbie and resolved to bring her home safe and sound. Fortunately, unlike the Starr case, Debbie's captors did not demand a ransom.

Of course, everyone in Washington—especially in the White House and at the State Department—wanted information. I believed that our country director and Debbie's fellow PCVs had the clearest picture of what was going on—and the best access to the women in the market. That first day I was even able to speak to Debbie briefly from a phone in the market office. And Bill Flaherty and I were in daily contact with her family.

Tensions were high in El Salvador. Within a few months, Archbishop Oscar Romero would be assassinated as he said mass in San Salvador. I wanted to reassure the Loff family without being overly optimistic. We did not know how dangerous her captors might be. We were particularly concerned about her safety at night when the market was closed. Later we learned that the women Debbie worked with took turns sleeping outside the office to make sure that no one harmed her.

Fortunately, after ten days of negotiations with the municipal officials, the hostage-takers freed Debbie and her colleague. Debbie arrived home in Newark in time for Christmas with her family.

The public policy debate sparked by the Loff kidnapping was predictable. A few days after her release, our ambassador in El Salvador suggested that it was time for the Peace Corps to withdraw from the country. In response I sent a sharp rebuttal to the secretary of state stressing my firm belief that withdrawal of all PCVs was an overreaction and would be detrimental to both the long-term effectiveness of the Peace Corps and the interests of the United States. To remove volunteers because of a single incident was arbitrary and self-defeating. It would halt the important work we were doing alongside those most in need. Moreover, such a withdrawal could indirectly jeopardize our programs in other countries. Here is an excerpt from my memo to the secretary:

> The fundamental premise which sets the Peace Corps apart from our embassies, AID, and other foreign policy instruments is that the Peace Corps is not to be used as an instrument for leveraging immediate foreign policy goals . . . the proposed action of withdrawing all volunteers from El Salvador, when many believe they should stay, may do fundamental damage to the perception which has protected our Volunteers in the past—their unique role as Americans who are not representatives of our government's interests, but of our people's good will. In Santo Domingo the sign said: "Gringo go home. Cuerpo de Paz stay."

Debbie, of course, had to come home. I met her upon her return and was both surprised and inspired. I had formed a picture in my mind's eye from her voice as we talked on the phone when she had been under a lot of stress. Consequently, I was unprepared for the fresh, freckled, enthusiastic face I encountered. This woman had just been held hostage by heavily armed youngsters, but I would never have guessed it as I looked at her. Her first words to me were, "When can I go back?"

I had to tell her that wouldn't be possible. If we sent her back, she would have been more a celebrity than a volunteer—which would put her in danger. Instead, she and her fiancé ended up in graduate school at Ohio State University preparing for a career in overseas community development and health work. As for the Peace Corps, the murder of Archbishop Romero finally forced us to pull our volunteers out of El Salvador early in 1980.

Debbie Loff's happy ending was not the case for all of our PCVs. On more than one occasion a Peace Corps volunteer died, most often in traffic accidents, and I felt a responsibility to call the parents to give them the news personally. Every time I had to make one of these calls, I would sit in front of my phone, overwhelmed with empathy for the parents, thinking about my own children and how I would feel getting a call like the one I was about to make. Yet I picked up the phone and made the call.

I grew in important ways during my tenure at the Peace Corps—even though it was less than two years. We promoted volunteering for the Peace Corps, calling it "the toughest job you'll ever love." My stint as director certainly toughened me. During my first gubernatorial campaign I felt a nagging doubt about my readiness for the job.

After the Peace Corps I knew I was ready.

The Peace Corps Act sets out three goals. First, to assist developing countries. Second, to personify America's values. And third, to bring the experience home and enrich community life here.

I believe that the Peace Corps is most successful in terms of the second goal. Our volunteers like Anne, Helen, and Debbie served in an exemplary fashion—living humbly and working side by side with ordinary folks in their host communities. The American values of optimism, generosity, curiosity, pragmatism, and the can-do spirit were personified by PCVs in Latin America, Africa, and Asia. Seeing men and women of all ages from the rich and privileged United States willing to get their hands dirty to help improve the lives of ordinary families, often in remote settings, sent a powerful message—and still does.

With respect to the first goal, our impact is more complex. Peace Corps programming has changed from an emphasis on education, often teaching English as a second language in the early days, to a more nuanced set of projects—women's health, agriculture, small business development. Host countries must request a program and play a key role in its design. Often what looks good on paper in the nation's capital is quite different out in the villages. Thus, many volunteers have to improvise, responding to needs that only become evident after months on site: a tutoring program for kids, fish farming to supplement a family income, building a well for safe drinking water. In the end, almost every successful volunteer will say that they received far more from the people with whom they worked than they were ever able to contribute in sustainable change.

As for the third goal, the impact of the returning volunteers has grown as the "alumni" numbers have grown. When I testified during my confirmation hearing, there were two RPCs serving as US Senators—Paul Sarbanes and Chris Dodd. A fellow Ohioan and former volunteer, Tony Hall, was a member of Congress. Still, the returned volunteers tended to be at best a loose-knit group, more apt to identify with those who served in the country where they had worked than with RPCVs as a whole. In fact, one of my initiatives was to encourage the development of The Peace Corps Institute in order to give a voice to returned volunteers who wanted to have an impact on Peace Corps policy development and congressional budget decision making.

Today former volunteers are the backbone of our international agencies. They are ambassadors and Foreign Service Officers; they fill the ranks of US-AID; they lead and labor in virtually every US-based NGO working in the development field. RPCVs teach and write textbooks. They promote international education and global conflict resolution. But often this is done without attribution to their Peace Corps experience. Efforts to fulfill the third goal tend to fly under the radar.

Shortly before the election of 1980 I asked my old pal (and landlord) Denny Heffernan to join me for lunch at the Hay Adams Hotel around the corner from the Peace Corps and across Lafayette Park from the White House. Dennis and I talked presidential politics. Our conclusion was that President Carter's reelection was a long shot.

"I am going back to Ohio in January," I said.

"Well," Denny said in his usual colorful fashion, "if the president is a lame duck, let's go around the world while we can."

I was game. I wanted to end my term as director as I had begun it—engaging with volunteers in the field.

Our first stop on that farewell swing was Tunisia. I had warned Denny that this was going to be a Peace Corps trip—not Club Med. He would pay his own way and stay with me wherever our Peace Corps hosts put us. In other words, there would be no Palm Beach hotels (Dennis and his wife owned one). That was clear from the moment we arrived in Tunisia. As soon as we landed in Tunis our country director corralled us and took us to meet two PCVs working some distance from town.

The volunteers were working on an agricultural income enhancement project, teaching farmers to raise chickens to supplement their traditional crops. We were in rural Tunisia, far from the tourist beaches. The farmers and our volunteers described their efforts and answered our questions. Then we had dinner and a couple of beers.

Growing drowsy, Denny asked, "Where are we going to sleep?" One of the PCVs smiled and pointed to the corner of the small room where we had been sipping on beers. "There."

"Okay," I said. "Do you have any mattresses?"

"Maybe a couple of sleeping bags" was the response. He pointed to a water faucet and said we could use it to brush our teeth and then gave us directions to the latrine. As we finally tried to get comfortable, Denny's thoughts turned to Ohio. "You know, you are going to have to get started soon. This race is going to be a lot harder than the last one—starting with a *real* primary."

I said that I thought I would need to raise $3 million.

"Double that," Denny said. "The next campaign is going to be just like this floor. Really hard!"

As Dennis dozed off, I thought to myself how Denny had pushed me in 1970 to begin knocking on doors. Now he was going to push me to ask folks for serious money. The floor seemed especially hard as I fell asleep.

As I prepared to leave the Peace Corps in January, I experienced what I came to think of as "pre-nostalgia." I was going to miss my colleagues. They were highly talented and dedicated individuals, and we were doing good work together. Much remained to be done. We had achieved significant autonomy for the agency, but the Peace Corps still needed to reclaim its independence. I began to draft the memo to my unnamed successor that I would leave on my desk when I vacated the Miatico Building on January 20.

We almost never talked politics at the Peace Corps. Still, I was a political appointee with a political resume. And I had brought a couple of Ohioans, Dora and Bill, with me. So inevitably I was the butt of Ohio jokes, and, as my departure drew near, colleagues began to express curiosity about my plans.

On January 16, 1981, the staff held a farewell roast for me; getting roasted was a long tradition for outgoing Peace Corps directors. Great fun was made of my thinly disguised political ambition. Bill Lafarge, my legislative liaison, and the "Peace Corps Tabernacle Choir" sang an original song. Dan Moldea from Mary King's office went on at hilarious length about why "there are few people in this world less deserving of praise and accolades" than Dick Celeste.

One person noted that I raised budget issues constantly and found obscure arithmetic errors in budget documents. So she had introduced a few errors into each submission just to see how long it took me to spot them. Bill Flaherty rose to disavow any connection with me whatsoever and to swear that he was a career federal employee with no interest in Ohio politics. Raucous laughter ensued. A number of roasters commented on my tendency to wear blue button-down shirts, khaki slacks, and penny loafers (much like Chet Bowles's wardrobe). For some reason the penny loafers came up es-

The Peace Corps leadership team. I am in the back row on the right. Two members of this team—Bill Sykes, deputy director (*far left*), and Chris Sale, budget chief (*front center*)—will go on to join my first cabinet, Sykes as director of the Department of Administrative Services and Sale as budget director.

pecially often. So did the observation that younger staffers had a marked tendency to dress a lot like a former lieutenant governor of Ohio.

And what about the rumors that said the former lieutenant governor was contemplating a second run at governor? My colleagues were intrigued by the rumors. But their real concern was to keep the Peace Corps headed in a positive direction—eagerly anticipating the twenty-fifth anniversary celebration planned for later that year.

On my wall today I have a picture of all of my staff crowded into the director's office with a very young Stephen standing in front of the team. It is a family picture—my Peace Corps family. It was going to be hard to leave that family behind. But as Dennis had pointed out on that mud floor in Tunisia, a tough challenge lay ahead. The next campaign would not be for the faint of heart.

I needed to get to work if I wanted to win this one.

Chapter 8

Landslide

My friends in Ohio expected me to run again. Dagmar and the children were ready for it; my parents and Ted were supportive; my inner circle was impatient to get going. Even as I commuted to Washington and the Peace Corps, we kept in touch with the campaign team through regular newsletters. I was ready. They were ready. And we all understood that the campaign would not be easy.

As always, I faced the challenge of how to run for office while at the same time supporting my family. I needed a job that provided time to reenergize the statewide organization required to forge a victory. This quandary often forces candidates to depend on a few individuals with deep pockets who expect something in return. I was fortunate. There was one person I could count on—my father. His only expectation was that I would be a fine governor. And perhaps one day fulfill his youthful rejoinder to his civics teacher in Monessen: "No, but my son can."

"What do you need?" Dad asked. I explained the situation—I was going to teach an urban economics class at John Carroll University for a semester, but that would not meet our family's needs. Could I come back to National Housing? "That means doing real work," he said, half-smiling.

"I will do my best to carry my weight," I responded. "But I hope I will be able to do some traveling and speaking." Requests to speak at county Democratic dinners were already coming in.

"I understand," he told me. "You still have an ownership interest in National Housing. But you will need to deliver on our projects." I assured him that I would. My father was obviously strongly in my corner. After just a few months, my father and I discussed my thoughts about the upcoming campaign. He wanted to know what lessons I had learned from the last effort—a question that set the stage for perhaps our most difficult conversation.

I said, "Based on my conversations the last few weeks I have had to make a very tough decision—and I am not sure you are going to want to hear it."

"Then you had better tell me now and get it if off your chest," he said.

"Dad, I can't have Ted run my campaign this time around."

He tried not to betray his displeasure. "I don't see why not. He is your brother. No one will work harder or be more loyal. And you know he is counting on it." I knew he was right about Ted. This was about blood—the family legacy.

I tried to explain my decision to him as best I could. "Dad, you know there are twelve key county Democratic chairmen. To win the primary I will need all of them—well, nearly all—in my corner. The reality is that nine of those twelve blame Ted for my defeat in '78. You and I know that that is not fair. But that is what they believe. If I bring Ted back to run the campaign, they will conclude that I haven't learned from my defeat—and they do not want to back a loser. As unfair as it is, I need to signal that I have listened to them and I am willing to make the tough call."

Dad did not like it one bit. "You know that is not fair. Ted is your brother." But he knew that I had made up my mind.

I also had to tell Ted, which was harder than telling my father. We were working in the same office. Ted was doing a great job. We both knew he was carrying my weight on our housing projects. Telling him that he would not run the '82 campaign would be a serious blow for him and for our relationship.

"I want to do this," Ted said. "And I can do it. This campaign will be better, and you know it!" I tried to explain. It was not about his ability or what happened in the last race. It was about perceptions and my ability to instill confidence in my judgment. I hoped that he would understand. His support was enormously important to me.

Looking back now, it occurs to me that I may have imagined some of the conversations I had with Ted. Perhaps I had spoken in a less direct way. A lot remained unsaid in our relationship until long after I had left the governor's office. Only after I had time to reflect and he and I began to share our feelings much more candidly did I come to see my decision clearly. I feel that Ted took on more of the burden for my defeat than he should have, not only quietly holding himself responsible for it in some way but also taking the fall publicly when I passed over him in 1981. Still, even with the benefit of hindsight and healing, my decision to appoint Jerry Austin as campaign director rather than Ted was the right call.

The 1982 primary was not going to be easy. In 1978 I had no serious opposition. By '82 some Democrats felt that my time had passed. I'd had my turn, the thinking went, and now it was someone else's turn. Bill Brown, Ohio's incumbent attorney general and a conservative Democrat, and Jerry Springer, who had been the "boy wonder" mayor of Cincinnati and an outspoken liberal, both had announced their candidacies. Brown was a proven statewide vote getter, and Springer, though a bit unpredictable, was charismatic and a strong fundraiser. Neither was a pushover.

Early in the primary season, an unexpected trial balloon was floated. Vern Riffe and Marvin Warner held a press conference to announce that they were planning to run for governor. When asked who would head the ticket, however, they hemmed and hawed; each saw himself at the top. My team was shaken by this prospect. After all, Vern Riffe was the most powerful sitting Democrat as Speaker, and Marvin Warner could bankroll a statewide race on his own.

I told Jerry and the team it would never happen. Vern would not risk the Speaker's gavel and Marvin would not risk a defeat. Soon their trial balloon deflated. At that point I devoted myself to winning their backing. I also worked hard to woo C. J. McLin, a colleague of mine from the state legislature who was president of the Black Elected Democrats of Ohio and a good friend of my father. By early 1982 all three were on board.

Money has been referred to as the mother's milk of politics. And my first real test in this regard came toward the end of 1981. I had not been able to do any political fundraising while I was Peace Corps director. And, like virtually every person I know in politics, asking for money—while vital to my success— was one of my least favorite activities. I put it off as long as I could. Therefore, as the first reporting period for the governor's race loomed in late '81, Jerry Austin and his right-hand guy Larry McCartney confronted me with a critical issue. That report was about to disclose that both Bill Brown and Jerry Springer had more than $1 million in the bank. I had perhaps $50,000. Such a fundraising gap would raise serious doubts about whether I was a viable candidate.

McCartney, who later would become my patronage chief, said he had an idea for how to avoid getting blown out before the race had really begun.

"You need a big number in the bank," he said.

"How big," I asked.

"At least three-quarters of a million," he responded.

"And here is the thing," he added. "It only needs to be in the bank over the weekend. Once you have filed your campaign report you can return the money to the donors. We just need to get through this reporting period."

The following Friday our filing showed that we had nearly $800,000 in our campaign account, almost all of it contributed in the week of the filing. When reporters asked how I felt about being outraised by Brown and Springer, I pointed out that it had taken them a year to gather their money. "I had raised mine in a week."

The press corps was impressed.

What they did not know is that the following Monday I repaid three loans of $250,000 each to Frank Celeste, Dennis Heffernan, and Ted Bonda. Nor did they notice, because three months later, by my next filing, I had outraised both of my opponents. I believe this is a fine illustration of "smoke and mirrors."

Of course, once the loans were repaid, I had to get to work raising serious money. My goal was $5 million. And my first call was on Milton Wolf, a previous contributor and a prominent leader in the Cleveland Jewish community. Wolf, the son of a Cleveland policeman, had become a successful real estate developer. A major fundraiser for Jimmy Carter, he had served as ambassador to Austria. Because of my work in an embassy in the 1960s and Dagmar's roots in Austria, he sought our perspectives prior to accepting the offer from the president. That conversation cemented our friendship.

Distinguished, thoughtful, and good-humored, Milt was very approachable, unlike many wealthy individuals. Early in 1982 I sat in his home on South Park Boulevard and asked him to serve as my finance chair. I explained why I felt I was the best candidate, how I could win. It would cost $5–6 million, and I wanted to start with a group of ten guys who would each give me $100,000. (This was before Ohio set political contribution limits.) "I need your help," I told him. "I would be proud if you would be my finance chairman."

Milt sat quietly for a few moments. Then he said, "Dick, I am frankly worn out. I worked hard trying to help John Glenn when he ran for president. I worked hard for Jimmy Carter. I like you. I will give you $100,000. But I can't be your chair." I was crestfallen and tried to persuade him, but he was firm. "Why don't you talk to Albert Ratner?" he suggested. "He thinks highly of you, and Albert would be a great finance chair."

Albert Ratner was CEO of Forest City Enterprises and another highly respected leader in Cleveland's Jewish community. I made an appointment to see him the following week and went through the same pitch as I had made to Milt. Why I was running. Why I expected to win. How much it would cost.

I wanted to start with ten guys at one hundred thousand each. And I really wanted him to serve as my finance chair.

"Dick," he said, "I have always liked you. And I know how much Milt thinks of you. But I am in the middle of a big project here in town, and we have a Republican mayor. I just can't be your finance chair."

And the contribution? I asked.

"I will do the hundred thousand, just not a high-profile position."

I saw Milt Wolf a few days later. I told him that I thought I was doing something wrong. First he had said that he wouldn't be my finance chair and now Albert.

"What about the hundred thousand?" he asked.

"Albert will do one hundred," I said, "but I still need my finance chair."

Milt thought for a moment and then said: "Go see Bob Tomsich. He likes you, and he wants to be a player."

I knew Bob. He was the CEO of NESCO—a company he had built from scratch. Perhaps I could convince Bob to step up on my behalf. A few days later I went to see him at this office.

"Dick," he said, once I had finished the same spiel about why I was an excellent candidate—the winning candidate—and how I needed his help, "I am not your guy. I don't want to be a finance chair. I will do the hundred thousand, but that's it."

I returned to Milt Wolf's living room. "I'm worried. I don't have a finance chair," I said, after describing Tomsich's turndown.

"And the hundred thousand?" Milt asked. I told him that Bob was committed.

As I explained how distressed I was that I still did not have my finance chair, Milt said that I should ask Peter Lewis. "Look," he said, "Peter is a liberal Democrat. More than that, he's your contributor and good friend. It is time for him to step up."

A few days later I sat across the breakfast table from Peter in his penthouse apartment on Cedar Road. I repeated my pitch with an edge of urgency. "I really need you, Peter."

"Dick," Peter responded, "I would be terrible as your finance chair. I am a giver, not an asker. But you need one—you didn't even ask me for enough. I will do one hundred thousand now," he said, taking out his checkbook and writing a check, "and I will do another hundred in the general election. I want you to win."

Six weeks had passed since I had first asked Milt Wolf to serve as my finance director. I must have looked desperate as I sat down with him once again.

"How did it go with Peter?" he asked.

"I must be doing something wrong. He turned me down."

Milt inquired, "What about the hundred thousand?"

"Well, he gave me a check for a hundred and said he would be good for another one in the general."

"Dick," said Milt, "I'll be your finance chair."

I realized that the last six weeks were the "Milt Wolf test." He had devoted a great deal of time and effort on behalf of John Glenn's presidential campaign. In that effort John had proved to be an attractive candidate but a poor fundraiser. Sitting down with a potential donor, John would engage in warm conversation—about orbiting the earth, serving as a military test pilot, and working in the Senate. Apparently, he may have felt that people's admiration would automatically translate into contributions; he found it hard to make the ask.

While Milt never said so in so many words, I felt that he wanted to make sure I would make the ask.

Few politicians really enjoy asking for money. And today, as the costs of campaigns have skyrocketed, elected officials spend an obscene amount of time "dialing for dollars." While I was reasonably good at it, I never truly enjoyed the process.

People have various reasons for contributing. You have to be clear in your ask about what a contributor—especially a major contributor—can expect in return. For some, it is a matter of conviction and shared values. These contributors expect only that your public service will make them proud—and they will be invited to lunch or dinner once in a while. Others contribute because they want access to power. They want to be able to bring friends to the governor's residence. Or go on a trade mission with the governor. Or watch an Ohio State football game from the governor's box.

Finally there are those who want something more—those who want influence, a chance to tip the scale in their direction. Unless you speak very directly to contributors at the outset, the distinction between access and influence can blur and lead to serious misunderstandings. My rule was to state clearly to all major contributors that they would have access—I would always be prepared to listen to their case—but that they could not count on my acquiescence. I reserved the right to make a decision on the merits, even if it went against their wishes. In my experience, this distinction was respected by all of my major contributors.

Shortly after I won the primary, Tony Garofoli, then the Cuyahoga County Democratic chairman, called and said that he had someone he wanted me to meet. Tony said that his name was Sam Lucarelli, founder of a very successful temporary staffing company. Apparently Lucarelli was interested in learning more about the political process and had asked Garofoli for advice.

I agreed to meet, and Garofoli came along to make the introduction. "You said you were interested in politics, Sam," Tony said. "Dick Celeste is, in my view, the most talented politician around, and you ought to find a way to help him."

As we began to talk, it was clear that Lucarelli was a tad naive. He seemed a bit overwhelmed that he had the former lieutenant governor and now governor hopeful in his office. "Well, how can I help?" he asked after a while. I told him that one of my critical needs was money for the general election.

He did not seem surprised. "What are other people doing?"

I said that my top contributors had each committed $100,000. He thought about it and then asked, "If I contribute a hundred, can I get an invitation to the inaugural?"

Tony and I both chuckled.

"You bet," I said, "and to a small reception that evening as well."

"I'll do fifty now and fifty later," he told me—and wrote a check as we sat there.

Not once did we have a discussion about his business. In fact, I did not realize at the time that during the tax season each spring the State of Ohio hired some of his temporary help to open the flood of envelopes containing tax returns from our citizens.

But Sam's contributions would come back to haunt me—and him. Several years into my first term, Sam Lucarelli was busted by the FBI for a gambling game that he was running. While this after-hours activity had nothing to do with me, the headlines in the local paper, the Cleveland *Plain Dealer*, proclaimed "Celeste Supporter Arrested by Feds." Sam was convicted and sent to a federal penitentiary in Pennsylvania.

Years later, after serving his time, Sam called to say that he had a story he wanted to share. Apparently, shortly after going to prison, Sam was visited by two federal agents saying that they had come to talk about Celeste.

"What about him?" Sam asked.

"Look, it's simple. Just give us Celeste, and you can walk," they said.

"What are you talking about?" Sam said he asked them.

The agents said that they knew he had given me a big contribution. They wanted to know what he got in return.

"Nothing," was Sam's response.

The agents did not believe him and pressed him.

"You want to know the truth." he told them. "I'm doing *less* business with the State of Ohio today than under the guy before him."

"Come on," they persisted. "We know you had to pay to play."

Again, according to Sam, they offered to reduce his sentence to time served in return for testimony against me.

"Hey," Sam said, "Celeste never asked me what my business involved, and I never asked him to do me any favors. And he didn't do me any!"

At that point, Sam related to me, one of the agents said something like, "Look, we know all about this omertà business. Just give us Celeste."

Sam said he exploded. Pointing to the cell across from him, he said, "See that scumbag? I got more respect for him than I got for you two. Get the hell out of here and don't come back."

Sam was a major contributor. All he wanted was an invite to a party. What he—and I—got instead was headlines in our hometown paper with the veiled implication that I was corrupt. It reminded me of the "phantom employee scandal" in my early days as lieutenant governor. When people talk about politics as a contact sport, this was one kind of body blow.

During the primary, the state's financial crisis and taxes were front and center. Interestingly, Jerry Springer—the outspoken liberal—made a point of saying that he would raise taxes. Bill Brown—cautious and conservative—promised not to raise them. I found myself positioned in the middle. I said that I would do all I could to avoid a tax increase, but I could not rule it out. My theme was to focus on putting people back to work; that would guide my decision on budget and tax policy.

I also literally tried to stand between my two opponents as often as possible, particularly next to Bill Brown, who was considerably shorter than me. Looking back, I was unkind to him, taking advantage of being a foot taller. Whenever we appeared at the same event, I made a point of grabbing the nearest photographer and putting my arm around Bill. After two or three unflattering photos appeared in papers around the state, Bill made sure that we were never in the same room at the same time. It was more than just a mind game. I was taking advantage of research showing that voters favor taller candidates over shorter candidates and even that presidents tend to be a good deal taller than the rest of their generation.

The truth is that I always liked Bill Brown. He came from the small town of Lisbon, Ohio, and graduated from law school at Ohio Northern in Ada, another small town. Like Jim Rhodes, another successful small-town politician who became a statewide powerhouse, Bill was feisty and smart. He surrounded himself with good people and pursued a progressive agenda as attorney general—especially on consumer affairs and environmental protection. Years later Brown would say that losing the 1982 primary saved his life. It turned out that he had an undetected heart problem. I think Bill felt that if he had persisted in a grueling statewide campaign, he would not have survived.

Jerry Springer was not that much shorter than me. Still, I beat him, too. Two decades after that primary I ran into Jerry in Chicago's O'Hare airport as I was changing flights. He thanked me profusely for beating him—and opening the door to his immensely colorful and successful career on TV.

Springer was one of a kind. I got to know him when he was elected in 1971 to the Cincinnati City Council. Jerry resigned in 1974 after admitting he had visited a prostitute in Kentucky (famously paying by check). Apologizing for letting his family and his constituents down, he ran again for council in 1975 and won handily. Jerry had supported me in both my race for lieutenant governor and in my 1978 run for governor. With a gift of gab and a disarming self-deprecating charm, Jerry was uniquely able to turn writing a check to a call girl into a political plus.

Party insiders, however, viewed Springer as problematic—just too unpredictable. So he had to build a campaign largely on his own. And he brought his unique skills to the task—especially when it came to fundraising. For example, Jerry realized that people who owned private planes tended to have substantial resources. Their ownership was a matter of public record—and so he began to tap a whole new set of contributors.

When the dust settled after the primary, Jerry had not raised enough. He was $60,000 in debt. I persuaded Marvin Warner, who knew Jerry well, to help get that debt paid. I wanted Jerry's help in the general election rather than having him out trying to raise money while I was doing the same. Jerry Springer became an active Celeste campaigner.

Even before I left the Peace Corps, Bill Brown made fighting crime a cornerstone issue in his campaign. Describing himself as a "hard line law-and-order advocate," Brown told the press that he would make sure that voters knew where he stood on crime in contrast to a liberal governor who would be soft on crime. Our pollster singled out this issue as one that could hurt me. Austin was on the phone with me immediately, urging me to make a strong statement on crime.

I was reluctant to spend money on any ad that didn't relate to my focus on jobs and putting Ohioans back to work. Jerry persisted: "I know that you have the endorsement of the Fraternal Order of Police, and that will help. But you also want to end the death penalty, and Brown will use that against you."

I continued to resist.

"Hey, didn't your house get burgled?" Jerry asked. It had happened a few months earlier. "How did you feel?"

I told him that our family felt violated and vulnerable.

"That's the spot," he said. "Just sit with your family, explain what happened, and say you will make sure that anyone who commits a crime is caught and serves time."

That spot, shot on the back steps of our home, surrounded by my family, disarmed the Brown campaign.

Nearly every feature of my campaign advertising was distinctive. For a start we had a campaign song, "Care about Ohio." Dagmar had commissioned Joe Ashley (a copywriter in Milenthal's company) to write a song as a wedding anniversary gift for me in 1977. Sung in Joe Ashley's tenor with his acoustic guitar in the background, it sounded like a cross between James Taylor and Jim Croce—and it truly resonated with people.

Have you ever seen the sun rise in Ohio?
Have you ever seen Ohio in the fall?
The farmlands and the towns
The busy city sounds
Seems to me Ohio's got it all.

Lately I've been thinking 'bout Ohio
Thinking what Ohio means to me
I'm proud to have it known
Ohio is my home
I want it to be all that it can be

Do you care enough to care about Ohio?
Are you proud to say Ohio is your home?
Do you believe we can do together
All the things that we can't do alone?

Don't you think you should do
Something for Ohio?
Do you want to see Ohio be the best?
If you care enough to care about Ohio
Then come on out and vote for Dick Celeste.

The song served as the background for an early biographical ad that reintroduced me to Ohioans. And it featured almost as a tagline in most of my campaign spots. Toward the end of the primary, people could recognize a Celeste TV spot just by the music, even if they happened to be in another room.

Most of my campaign ads featured an interaction between one or more voters and me in an issue-related setting—a farmyard, a factory gate, a kitchen table. My theme became "Stand up for Ohio." The policy of the Reagan administration, which was supported by the likely Republican standard-bearer, had put ten of thousands of Ohioans out of work. "If we don't stand up for Ohio," I asked, "who will?"

Perhaps my favorite spot featured Debbie Loff, talking straight to the camera—not an actor, not on teleprompter. Describing her experience of being kidnapped while serving in the Peace Corps and my efforts to secure her release, she concluded: "I trust Dick Celeste." Her authenticity made those words hit home.

Together, the voices of Joe Ashley and Debbie Loff, raised the campaign's media impact far above that of my opponents. To this day I wonder why political campaigns do not make more of an effort to use original music. Songs connect with voters at a fundamental, positive level. Perhaps this will prompt political spouses to imagine a whole new category of anniversary gifts.

For the 1982 race I chose Myrl Shoemaker as my running mate. I wanted someone who could work comfortably with Vern Riffe and knew how to appeal to rural voters. Myrl had been in the Ohio legislature for more than thirty years. He and his wife, Dorothy, had eight children, and he was a natural storyteller. Bill Brown, with legitimate small-town roots, selected Charlie Vanik, a highly respected former congressman from Cleveland—hoping to gain traction in my backyard.

I had carefully vetted Myrl's background before asking him to join the ticket, but he could still surprise me. It first happened on the day we were formally kicking off the campaign, starting in Cleveland and then traveling to his hometown, Bourneville, to meet with volunteers who were going to circulate

The Celeste-Shoemaker team on the trail in 1982

our petitions. Three TV stations and the Cleveland-area print media covered us as we thanked our team in advance and they disbursed to gather signatures. Then we boarded a KingAir for our flight to Chillicothe, the airport nearest Myrl's hometown (and named after Myrl).

It was a beautiful April morning, not a cloud in the sky. The air was crystal clear, and our pilot, Hy Rosen (we affectionately dubbed him Ho-rizon), kept the plane at four or five thousand feet so that we had a clear view of the farms and small towns that passed beneath us. I looked across at Myrl and realized that he was clutching the armrest, literally white-knuckled.

"Myrl," I said, "is this your first plane ride?"

It was. I was astonished. "You're kidding me, aren't you? I mean, you are sixty-four years old."

He looked at me and said with all seriousness: "Dick, I have never been in a vehicle where sooner or later I didn't have to get out and push."

That was Myrl's first—and last—plane ride. For the rest of the campaign, one of his sons would drive him to his appearances.

As I have said, you plan a successful campaign effort from Election Day backward. The overriding goal should be to understand and articulate the question that you want voters to have in mind as they enter their polling place. In 1982 the campaign was all about putting people back to work. The Reagan recession had hit Ohio hard; Reagan's advice to unemployed steelworkers in Youngstown was to move to Texas or California. By the time I would take my oath of office in January 1983, Ohio's unemployment rate stood at 14.2 percent. From the moment I announced my campaign—in the living room of an unemployed factory worker in Cleveland—until the conclusion of the general election, I ham-

I could sleep anywhere and usually did. Here I am on the King Air flying home from a campaign event.

mered on the importance of creating jobs for Ohioans. In the primary, I had to convince Democratic voters that I would be the strongest standard-bearer in the fall—and that I better understood what it would take to tackle Ohio's economic woes. And I convinced them.

In many respects the primary turned out to be more challenging than the general election, though that was not what I had expected nor was it how I treated it. The Republicans nominated Clarence (Bud) Brown—yes, another Brown—a small-town newspaper publisher from southwestern Ohio who had been a longtime member of Congress. Intelligent, popular, and courtly, Bud Brown had never campaigned beyond his congressional district. Furthermore, he had no firsthand experience with state government. So, early on, we decided to focus the question "who do we trust to put Ohioans back to work?" in two dimensions: first, experience, and second, vision.

We defined experience in terms of Ohio versus Washington, DC. All of Brown's history had been in DC, so we contrasted his voting record there, say on Social Security, with work that I had done for senior citizens in Ohio. A series of TV spots showed Clarence Brown in Washington with the segue "meanwhile back in Ohio." In this context the drumbeat of "Stand up for Ohio" began to bite and bite hard.

My vision for our state, which was articulated in the long introductory bio spot, called for recapturing our inventive spirit and reinvigorating our economy. During the course of the general election, I laid out an "action agenda" promising, among other things, to replace the Public Utilities Commission (PUCO) members and institute a "buy Ohio" program on my first day in office.

As I challenged voters to stand up for Ohio, I could sense that this struck a responsive chord—and our polling bore this out. As we entered the last two weeks of the campaign, we were confident enough to move some of my funds into a couple of tight state Senate races. I promised my supporters that there would be "no more business as usual." From the ghost loans that got my campaign off to its start to the investment in close Senate races as we came down the stretch, that mantra was true for the governor's race. Soon it would be time to deliver what "the constituency for change" we had built expected of me.

On the day I took office I wanted to be able to announce that I had received the resignations of all three members of the PUCO. I had realized that legislation passed the previous year expanding the PUCO contained a provision that would prohibit its members from representing clients before the commission for two years after stepping down. Current members, however, were not subject to any "revolving door" limits. In the days after I won the

At at a Democratic Party rally with Sen. John Glenn and my running mate Myrl Shoemaker (*far right*)

Annie Glenn, wife of Senator Glenn, feeding me pizza as we wait for returns in 1982

election I met individually with the two Republican members—both law-yers—and pointed out this provision, stressing that I would enforce it firmly. If, however, they tendered their resignations (despite a provision that they would be reappointed in the reform law), I would remember that gesture of goodwill and they would be free to represent their new clients before the PUCO immediately. Eager to practice utility law, they saw the merit in my request and provided resignation letters.

The Democratic member was another matter. Mike DelBane had served in the legislature with me. He was an old-time politician—an Italian Amer-ican from Trumbull County who went to 6:30 mass every morning. He had chaired the state government committee on which I had served as a freshman house member. I admired him as a role model and friend; Vern Riffe saw him as his right hand.

Mike and I met, and I explained that I had obtained a commitment from the two Republicans on the PUCO to resign. Now I needed his resignation.

"Wait a minute," Mike said, "I don't want to resign."

"Mike," I said, "I need all three of you to step down—so that I can keep my promise to our citizens."

"But I am a good Democrat and your friend," Mike protested.

"Here's what I have in mind, Mike," I explained. "I will announce all three resignations. Then I will appoint a new five-member commission as required by the legislation. One of them needs to be a senior citizen representative. And that will be you."

Mike gave me his letter of resignation.

Just two days before my inauguration—as our festivities were getting under way—I received word that Governor Rhodes (who could not run for a third consecutive term) planned to issue a contract for a new state office tower on a corner directly opposite from my swearing-in on the statehouse steps. I was irate. I knew the state did not even own all of the land involved. Nor were there construction plans for the building. Yet Rhodes wanted to reward some crony of his with a contract. I was determined to block it. And I knew that there was just one way to do so.

I called Vern Riffe, the only person in whom I had confided my plans for the PUCO. "Mr. Speaker," I said, "I am sorry but I won't be able to reappoint Mike DelBane to the PUCO."

"What do you mean? You made a commitment," Vern responded.

My kids the night before the inauguration in 1983. *Left to right:* Eric, Natalie, Noelle, Stephen, Gabriella, and Christopher.

"I know I did, but something has come up." I went on to outline what I had heard. I considered any action on the proposed state office tower (which was to be named after Vern and the Republican Senate Leader Paul Gillmor) a deliberate affront and an invitation to expensive litigation.

"What does this have to do with Mike DelBane?" Vern asked.

"Vern," I said, "you are the only person who can persuade Jim Rhodes to reconsider. He's a good old boy from Jackson County, and he needs to hear from his good buddy from Scioto County that this is not a good idea. If you are persuasive enough, Mike will get his PUCO appointment—and I will name him chair."

Early the next morning my phone rang. "Governor," the Speaker said, "don't worry. There is no construction contract, and no bulldozers will bother your swearing-in."

Following my oath-taking in frigid weather and a two-hour receiving line to meet well-wishers in the cabinet room, I got down to business. With the press looking on, I signed the Buy Ohio Executive Order. Then I signed an executive order banning hiring discrimination based on gender or sexual preference. And, finally, I announced that I had the resignations of all three members of the PUCO. Members of the press were astonished. How had I accomplished this, they wondered—especially since two were Republican appointees. Little did they know the backstory.

I also swore in my very diverse cabinet. Their average age was forty-three; under Jim Rhodes, it had been fifty-two.

The new state office tower did get built, but not as Rhodes had envisioned it. He had bragged about a sixty-story tower without any idea what would fill that space. Early in my term I asked Marvin Warner to become chair of the Ohio Building Authority with the task of overseeing this project. "I want you to make sure that this building is well designed, right-sized, and delivered on time and under budget." It was just the sort of challenge that Warner relished—and for the next two years he devoted himself to it.

I also met with Paul Gillmor—after the landslide the previous November he was now the minority leader in the Senate—and told him that I was recommending to the Ohio Building Authority that the new tower be named for Speaker Riffe alone. After all, he was already the longest-serving Speaker in Ohio history—and house offices would be in the new building, whereas Senate offices would be in a renovated historic building that had once housed the state supreme court. Gillmor was, of course, upset. But he did not have the votes.

My relationship with Jim Rhodes had become a complicated one. During the campaign, my brother had found himself in a delicate role working as he was on our fundraising. Folks knew that he was close to me and sought him out for that reason. Early in 1982 Ted started to be approached by Republicans who wanted to donate to my campaign. While not an organized or publicized effort, it happened with enough frequency that Ted began to realize people who were close to Jim Rhodes were quietly helping the Celeste campaign. Ted was sure that they also hoped that this generosity would be remembered.

Ted was cautious, not wanting to be set up by our opponents. So he was especially careful about accepting donations and ensuring that they were properly reported. As suspicious as we were at first, it soon became apparent that Rhodes himself was encouraging this. Perhaps Rhodes held me in higher regard than my opponent. Or perhaps he smelled a landslide in the wind. In any event, Ted—who had run the campaign against Jim Rhodes—became the backdoor for his support.

When I entered the governor's office with my family on the morning of my swearing-in, Governor Rhodes stood there alone. The office is a grand, high-ceilinged room with a fireplace that had long since fallen into disuse.

The oversized desk was clean as a whistle. Later we learned that Rhodes and his people had removed every scrap of paper (including some official records "missent" to the dump that very morning).

We had a few minutes before the ceremony was to begin. Rhodes was not one for small talk. "The teachers are your friends, aren't they? Well, you'll never satisfy them. Remember this—your enemies won't be your problem. Your friends will." He pointed to my family. "See these folks. When it's all over, they are the only ones you can count on."

Then he pulled me closer. "You got a lot of PhDs in your cabinet. Keep an eye on them. That is not the right kind of smart."

Jim Rhodes was right on both counts.

Chapter 9

First Term and Other Crises

We had won an amazing victory—the 20 percent margin was the largest achieved by any Ohio Democratic governor in the century. Not even the silver-tongued Frank Lausche, who had mesmerized me years before, had done as well. But reality smacked me in the face even before I took my oath of office.

For years I had been an admirer of Peter Drucker, a highly respected leadership guru. Drucker argued that a leader must be prepared to both initiate and react. An effective leader, according to Drucker, must confront and surmount crises, sometimes predicted and often unforeseen. A successful governor, I knew, would have to find ways of dealing with both. My first crisis would occur within days of my election, without any warning.

It involved Morris Jackson, the former deputy Senate minority leader, who aspired to be a leader in the new majority. Morris learned that Sen. Harry Meshel, from Youngstown, had the votes to become the next Senate president and did not have a place for Morris in his team. As a consequence—not quite two weeks after the votes had been counted—Jackson stood at a press conference and announced he was going to cross the aisle to support Paul Gillmor. Jackson's resentment was palpable. Though he was second in seniority, the Senate Democrats were going to leave him, as he told the press, "the low man on the totem pole."

I could not let this happen. We had just won a sweeping victory—including a one-vote majority in the state Senate. I needed to mobilize the African American political leaders with whom I had worked closely in my campaign. I asked John Coyne, the mayor of Brooklyn, Ohio, who I had tapped to become Democratic chairman in Cuyahoga County, to convene the key players.

Six of us met on a bright Saturday morning in Brooklyn City Hall. Coyne and I were joined by Congressman Lou Stokes, city council president George Forbes, my associate campaign director Arnold Pinkney, and Walter Burks, a member of the Cleveland School Board. Though he kept a low profile, Burks was a valuable presence that day. Soft-spoken and thoughtful, he was an ardent supporter of mine, remembering perhaps that when Arnold Pinkney ran for mayor of Cleveland, I hosted the very first house party for him in my home on Cleveland's predominantly white west side.

The meeting was the first time that Congressman Stokes had sat down with John Coyne after Coyne became Democratic county chairman over Stokes's objections. Stokes felt that the mayor from a small white suburb would not understand the issues impacting Black citizens in Cuyahoga County. Mayor Coyne quickly disarmed the congressman, describing how twenty years earlier he chose a Black contractor to build the Brooklyn firehouse next door to where we were sitting. Stokes expressed his surprise learning that John Coyne had been a longtime quiet but effective supporter of the Black community.

Coyne was a political institution unto himself, the mayor of Brooklyn for fifty-two years until he was finally defeated years later. He was known in those days as Hubert Humphrey's favorite mayor, and they campaigned enthusiastically for each other. A true innovator, Coyne promoted the country's first mandatory seatbelt law in his town.

Everyone was aware of the situation. Morris Jackson's nose was out of joint because he wanted his pal Oliver Ocasek to be leader. But Oliver didn't have the votes in the Democratic caucus. Both of them were going to be shut out. Our bottom line was that we could not afford to lose our majority in the Senate because of a personal grievance. When I mentioned Morris Jackson, they all rolled their eyes. "We can't have him going over to the Republicans," I told the group. "I need your help to get him in line." They readily agreed. Jackson did not need me in his corner, but he did need the backing of everyone else in that room. Without Stokes, Forbes, Pinkney, and Burks behind him, Morris Jackson would be history.

After some conversation around the table, they concluded that it boiled down to helping Morris find a job. The legislature was a part-time position, and they assumed that the deal he had struck with the Republicans involved a job of some kind. The meeting adjourned with the assurance it would be taken care of. They would need a few days, I was told, but I could count on them.

I considered this a test of our relationship. I had enjoyed strong support from the Black community both in the primary and the general election. These leaders knew that Jim Rogers had been appointed to my transition team and that I was committed to having women and minorities in the cabinet. They had made a significant investment in me with their votes, and they had high expectations about what we could accomplish together. The Senate majority would play an essential role in those accomplishments.

They also knew that I would stand unflinchingly on social justice issues. They had *seen* me do it in the past. For example, during a teachers' strike when I was lieutenant governor, my young (and even-then vocal) daughter Natalie asked me to support her teachers by picketing alongside them. I was more than willing to go with her.

Late that afternoon some of the striking teachers decided to occupy the school board offices. As I took Natalie's hand to head home, she insisted we join the demonstrating teachers, who were about evenly divided between Black and white. Since most of the folks working in the offices had gone home, the sit-in did not cause much of a stir. Perhaps an hour later, Congressman Stokes appeared. He looked around and spotted my daughter and me. "Governor," he said, with a laugh, "what are you doing here?"

Lou Stokes—and Arnold Pinkney—never forgot.

A few days later Morris Jackson was back in the Democratic fold.

The Morris Jackson crisis was dealt with almost offstage. Few people knew that I had a hand in turning him around. The next crisis was different: it was totally predictable and very public—Ohio's budget shortfall.

Jim Rhodes had left Ohio—and me—in a serious mess. On the day I was declared the governor-elect, Ohio's budget was between $268 million and $469 million under water. We needed to get a handle on this problem. The Ohio Constitution mandated that the budget be balanced every biennium. I had less than six months to fulfill that requirement. I remember sitting in the Sheraton shortly after the election and going over the numbers with Jan Allen. "I want to know the true dimensions of the problem," I told her, "because we're not going to go through this twice."

While I had come to like Jim Rhodes for the original that he was, some of his team could not resist making things difficult for us—for example, sending their records to a landfill as he left office. Overcoming the lack of reliable information, our budget folks were able to calculate just how deep the sea of red ink was—far deeper than Rhodes had claimed. I would have to make a number of decisions quickly.

The first was whether to renew the income tax surcharge (a 50 percent increase in paycheck withholdings for everyone in the state) imposed by Rhodes the previous July and due to expire March 31. Extending it through

June would raise $110 million—not nearly enough to get Ohio back in the black. Substantially more had to be done, not just for the current fiscal year but also for the foreseeable future.

A decision to raise taxes is never easy for anyone who will have to face re-election. Still, part of me was absolutely ready to make the call. I felt that the public had given me a mandate not only to do what was needed but also to tell the truth about things. I look back on it now as a case of landslide hubris. I thought I knew what needed to be done—without asking Myrl Shoemaker (or anyone else) for his perspective

After all, I had pledged no more business as usual. I was determined that we were not going to use any of the usual tricks to balance the budget. In the past—and still today—legislators employed an array of gimmicks to present the appearance of a balanced budget. For example, if the state waited for 120 days instead of 60 days at the end of the biennium before paying nursing home bills, it can push that burden into the next budget.

Another popular gimmick to seem to balance the budget was to slide the final biweekly payroll from one year into the next so that the state has only twenty-five payrolls to meet in the second year of the biennium and twenty-seven in the next. Rolling payrolls forward into the next biennium did not actually save the state money, but it could reduce the year-end deficit by more than $60 million back in the early 1980s.

But savoring an overwhelming victory, supported by Democratic majorities in both the House and the Senate and determined to be a different kind of governor, I was not going to resort to the old shell game. I was so firm that we were going to pay every bill in thirty days that I proposed to pay interest on any payment that took longer.

No more business as usual. We were going to do things right and tell the truth.

In addition to tackling the budget crisis, we needed to put people back to work. Getting Ohio working again had been the crux of my campaign. In order to help me think through new ways of approaching this problem I called Rube Mettler, then chairman and CEO of TRW Inc.—the aerospace and automotive company that had started off as the Cleveland Cap Screw Company in 1901.

Though I did not know Rube well, I had a deep respect for him as an especially thoughtful leader in the private sector. During the transition, I invited him to meet with me in Cleveland. I had a specific question I wanted to ask. "Rube," I said, "what could a state government do that would get your attention and incline you to invest in that state?"

He sat and thought silently for perhaps three or four minutes. It was a Zen-like moment. Here was a man with enormous experience taking my question seriously, carefully weighing what he was going to say. As I waited for his reply, it occurred to me that this was not the sort of question that he, as a businessman, would normally face. As much as politicians know they need to engage the business community, the idea of asking for their input on issues that transcend their own company was all too rare.

"Dick," he offered, finally, "there are two things that would attract me to a state. The first is long-term versus short-term thinking."

I gave him my full attention.

"Politicians tend to think only until the next election, which means that, if they have any plan in mind, it lasts two years and that's it. Under rare circumstances, three or four years. In the political world, that view may make sense. But business leaders put a premium on certainty. We have to take a longer view. For me that is at *least* ten years. So I would take seriously a state that had a strategic plan that looked well beyond the term of the governor."

Then there was a pause. He waited another long moment before going on.

"We at TRW are very involved globally"—he was at that time the chair of the US/Japan Business Council—"and I know there are a great many people who think that Japan is innovating more than we are. But that is not true. Japan's competitive advantage is that they move new ideas into the marketplace more *quickly* than we do. That's the key. I would be very interested in a state that had a strategy specifically aimed at moving the best new ideas in universities and research labs into the market as quickly as possible."

After an hour or so exploring his two suggestions, I thanked him for his time. He had given me a lot to think about. A strategic plan that looked beyond the electoral cycle and a way of moving promising ideas into the marketplace.

Sometimes the job of a leader to is to pose the right question to a wise individual and to take the response to heart. Rube Mettler's advice informed my jobs agenda. I failed to do the same thing with my first budget. And I paid a price.

An early heads-up about a potential crisis—before I was officially on the job—came in a call from Dick Lamm, then governor of Colorado. Almost immediately after the election, I had attended a training session in Aspen for new governors of both parties sponsored by the National Governors' Association and hosted by Lamm. I was given one of the handbooks designed for all newly elected governors and got to know Lamm as well as my fellow freshman governors.

"Dick," he said, "I want to alert you to a potential problem."

He had my attention.

"I'm calling several incoming Democratic governors," he told me, "to point out a change in the federal job training law. The old program called CETA—Comprehensive Employee Training Act—has been changed to JTPA, the Job Training Partnership Act. The feds will audit every state program as part of this conversion. I believe they're going to focus on states with new Democratic governors in an attempt to embarrass them. You should have your team be prepared for what might come at you."

I had already named Dr. Roberta Steinbacher, a professor at Cleveland State University, as head of the Ohio Bureau of Employment Services (OBES). Roberta was a trusted confidant and one of Dagmar's closest friends. As soon as I got off the phone with Governor Lamm, I urged Roberta to get up to speed on the workings of OBES and be prepared for pressure from the feds on JTPA. To assist, she brought on as deputy Donald McConnell, a Democrat with a deep knowledge of how the department functioned from having worked there during the Gilligan administration. Roberta came to rely on him heavily, particularly in those early days when she was still learning the ins and outs of OBES.

Dick Lamm turned out to be right about the feds. Just weeks after the inauguration, a representative from the Labor Department's Chicago office showed up to claim that the State of Ohio owed the federal government $254 million for improper accounting of CETA funds. It did not matter that all of this so-called improper accounting happened under Jim Rhodes or that the audit was timed to hit us just as we were struggling to fix a half-billion-dollar budget deficit. The Reagan administration was determined to do everything they could to make life difficult for rookie Democratic governors like me.

"Tell them," I told Roberta, "we will fight them for every single dollar of it." I was angry.

She reached out to Jerry Hultin—a smart, tough lawyer (who would go on to become president of Polytechnic Institute at New York University) who had volunteered on my campaign and could be trusted to stand up to the Department of Labor thoughtfully. After Roberta and I described the situation, he persuaded Ernst and Young to provide pro bono accounting services. Together they basically reconstructed the paper trail for nearly every one of the audit exceptions that the feds had brought against us.

It took a year and a half. In the end, we settled with the federal government for $2.3 million. The call from Dick Lamm—and our determined response to the feds—saved Ohio's taxpayers one quarter of a billion dollars!

Still, I found it unbelievable that the federal government would come after a state in such a political and punitive way. After all, the Department of Labor had never properly supervised the programs. Then, for political purposes, they decided to try to nail me for the years of poor management by my predecessor. Thankfully, it didn't work.

So much for crisis number two.

For all the pomp and circumstance of the inauguration and the great spectacle it turned out to be, I most clearly remember one moment when I was embraced by my mother and father just after taking the oath of office. There's a photo of that day, and the joy in their faces is palpable. That joy stays with me. Even now. My father beaming at me. The embrace of my mother.

After the inauguration festivities had ended and I had announced my first actions as governor, my team and I assembled at the governor's residence and got to work, brainstorming about how to address our budget crunch. Everyone

My proud parents with me at my inauguration as governor, January 1983

Dressed to celebrate at the inaugural ball, January 1983, with Dad (*center*) and my brother,
Ted (*right*)

offered ideas as we talked through different approaches. In the midst of our
vigorous discussion, I realized I was starving. I had not eaten since that morning. Neither had anyone else.

"I'm going to order pizza," I announced.

Everyone thought that was a good idea. They looked as hungry as I felt.

"Keep working," I told them and went into the kitchen, where I knew there
was a phone.

Though Rhodes had lived in the residence during his first terms in the
sixties, his wife refused to move back after he won in 1974. Instead, the grand
rambling house where we were to live had been used for visiting trade delegations and large parties. During my family's early days in the residence, it
was not uncommon to find an empty takeout container or coffee cup that
had been used as an ashtray hidden in a corner.

The house felt abandoned as I moved in that evening. Oh, well, I thought, Dagmar and the kids will give it some life very quickly. I dialed Domino's.

"I need five pizzas," I said, "delivered to the governor's residence."

"Yeah," said the guy who answered. "Right."

"What's the matter?"

"To the governor's residence?"

"That's right," I said. "This is Governor Celeste."

There was silence on the line. "Yeah," he said a second time. "Right."

"Okay," he said, after a moment. "Give me your phone number and I'll call back to confirm."

I realized I didn't know the new phone number. Or the address for that matter. There was nothing on the phone. Here I was trying to order pizzas, but I had none of the necessary information.

"I really am calling from the residence," I said lamely.

"Yeah," he said again, and hung up.

For a moment I just stood there. Then I called the highway patrol officer who was stationed outside the house. "Listen," I told him. "I need the phone number of this place and the address. I'm trying to order pizza."

"Governor," he said laughing, "tell me what you want, and let me order it."

The pizza arrived quickly. It was the first hint of the governor's ability, sometimes, to get things done. Eventually, I learned my new phone number and address.

In anticipation of Mettler's suggested strategic plan, even as we cut several state departments and increased taxes, we dramatically increased funds for higher education and created innovative programs such as Eminent Scholars to attract nationally recognized research talent and Thomas Edison Centers that focused on research aimed at spurring the state's growth in high-tech jobs. Many of the dividends from these investments did not become evident until my second term, but a single thoughtful conversation held during the clamor of the transition set in motion actions that eventually helped get Ohioans working again.

We did resolve the budget crisis and reformed the state's accounting practices as well. But I didn't get much credit for it. In fact, the interim budget turned out to be the source of blame instead. Headlines (and Republicans) claimed that I had hammered through a 90 percent tax hike. We were absolutely going to be facing a shortfall. Rhodes had enacted a temporary (and insufficient) tax increase that was about to expire. If we were to balance the state budget by June

Speaking at the
Edison Welding
Institute in 1988

30 (as our constitution required) and do it without gimmicks, I would not only have to *extend* the Rhodes tax but also *increase* it. Consequently, in addition to ordering a series of spending cuts, we enacted tax increases that amounted to about $300 million, boosting Rhodes taxes by 40 percent.

This meant that most Ohioans would pay 90 percent more in taxes more than they had a year earlier. But, in reality, it was only a 26.8 percent tax hike from what they had been paying under Rhodes. Yes, it was an increase, though nothing like the 90 percent increase headlined in papers across the state. The situation was not improved by my reluctance to promise that the taxes could be reduced if the state's economy improved in the next couple of years. I felt that such a promise was just more business as usual.

So I became the author of the 90 percent tax increase. In my eagerness to be bold, I had let the message get away from me. Factually, a 26 percent increase became indelibly Celeste's 90 percent tax hike.

I should have made three points as clearly as possible. First, we were maintaining Rhodes's so-called temporary taxes—which were insufficient to begin with. Second, we should have clarified what the increase was going to represent for every Ohioan's tax bill at the end of the year. Finally, I should have committed to review all tax increases in light of future revenue with the hope that the tax increases could be reduced.

I said none of those things.

Though the public did not see that truly balanced budget as one of our important accomplishments, I maintain that it was. Over the eight years I was in office, Ohio moved to generally accepted accounting standards, instituted annual reports on state finances, and passed balanced budgets on time. We even established a rainy day fund for the state that proved more helpful for my successors than for me.

Looking back, my failure to enlist budget advice from trusted advisors like Myrl Shoemaker and to communicate effectively about the nature of the tax increase was an early misstep that could have been avoided. It a was a lesson learned—the hard way.

One of my campaign promises had been to support legislation creating a State Employment Relation Board (SERB) and enabling public employees to bargain collectively for wages and working conditions. Within months the new Democratic majorities in both houses passed this landmark legislation, and I signed it into law.

We had ninety days to get the SERB operating.

To get moving, I named Prof. Ted Dyke chairman of the board. He was tasked with establishing the rules and procedures before the act came fully into force. Without clear rules and regulations, if a public employee group went on strike, we would have no structure to deal with it. I appointed Ted on the recommendation of Martin J. "Marty" Hughes, leader of Ohio's Communication Workers of America. Marty was an early Frank Celeste supporter and one of five senior labor leaders who had backed me early on. Ted Dyke taught employee law at Cleveland State. Marty assured me that he could get this delicate job done. I don't think we even considered other people. Dyke looked good on paper, and we were moving fast.

About forty-five days after Dyke was sworn in, Jan Allen came into my office and said that Ted had missed our deadline to submit draft rules for the SERB. When she asked him about it, he had hemmed and hawed.

I decided to give him a call myself.

"I'm working on it," he told me.

I asked him to get me something in seventy-two hours. But at the end of seventy-two hours, still nothing. I called Larry McCartney and told him Dyke wasn't up to it. "We have to have someone who can pull the trigger," I told him.

Next, I called Marty and explained that his guy was not doing the job. If he could get him in gear, this was the time. Another twenty-four hours came and went.

So I called Dyke in. Larry and I confronted him. He avoided our questions. It became clear that he was completely at sea. He could not even offer, say, ten pages of a twenty-page draft. Apparently the academic, faced with a real-world challenge, was in totally over his head. I asked for his resignation.

Suddenly he was decisive. "I'm not going to resign," he said, "you appointed me."

"Yes, I appointed you," I said. "Now I'm asking you to resign."

"You can't do that," he told me.

"I have the power under the law to dismiss you," I said. "I can fire you for misfeasance, malfeasance, and nonfeasance. You can choose, but I'm going to come at you if you don't give me your resignation."

"I have to think about it, Governor," he told me. "I'm going to get this job done. You've asked me, and I'm going to get this done."

When he left the office, I turned to McCartney and said that I needed to talk to Bill Brown, the former AG I had beat in the primary.

"Dick," said Bill, when I asked for his help, "I love this kind of assignment."

"Explain to him what malfeasance, misfeasance, and nonfeasance means," I said, "because he doesn't think he can be fired. I don't want to do that, but I will if he doesn't walk."

Within two hours Bill called back to say that I could expect Dyke's resignation on my desk first thing in the morning. Sometimes you have to let them hear what Camus called "the whisper of the guillotine."

Shortly thereafter, I asked former judge Jack Day, a highly regarded labor lawyer, to lead SERB. Within a month, he had the rules and regulations in place. Jack did a remarkable job.

The drumbeat of crises—small and large—continued.

One piece of advice Jim Rhodes gave me before we walked out together for my inauguration was especially prescient. "Your problems," he said, "won't be with your enemies; they'll be with your friends."

Two of those friends turned out to be David Milenthal and Margie Pizzuti, both of whom had been with me since my lieutenant governor's race. In our initial brainstorming we had determined that tourism, especially encouraging Ohioans to vacation in the state, could yield quick economic benefits with a modest investment. Al Dietzel tasked Margie—who was in charge of communications in his Department for Economic Development—with mounting an ad campaign. While I was on a family holiday on Kiawah Island in South Carolina (sparking criticism since we were encouraging Ohioans to explore the attractions in our own state), Margie awarded David Milenthal's firm a $7.4 million "sole source" contract to promote Ohio tourism.

I was dismayed. Any contract like that should have been competitively bid.

When I got back, I chewed out Margie. And David. This is public money, I told them, and that means we must invite competitive bids. It is as simple as that. We are now responsible for taxpayer dollars. My guess is they chose a sole source contract because they wanted to move swiftly. But sole source contracts smacked of business as usual.

I felt let down because I was getting criticized for something that I had not been aware of. The headline read: "Governor gives fat contract to friend." But I should not have been surprised that the press was coming after me so harshly; after all, I had set high expectations. I felt that it was one thing to be criticized for the budget—I owned those miscommunications completely—but what I had to learn was that, like it or not, I also owned missteps in which I had no direct involvement. As governor, I realized that any one of 54,000 state employees could do something that would land on my doorstep.

As upset as I was at the time, I did not dwell on something that I couldn't change. In fact, as I have observed along the way, this is one of my defining characteristics. Once a thing is done, I don't dwell on it. I deal with it and move on. It is ironic that as a student of history I spend so little time thinking about the past. Nearly all of my energy and passion is focused on what lies ahead and how to shape that future constructively.

Despite my dismay, I continued to work with David and Margie. I valued them as loyal members of my team. David and his firm ended up doing an outstanding job. The "Ohio, the Heart of It All" campaign was nationally acclaimed. And Margie proved to be a gifted leader as well as communicator.

Rube Mettler's suggestions about putting people back to work influenced two key cabinet choices.

First, the secretary/treasurer of the state AFL-CIO, Warren Smith, one of the most senior labor leaders in Ohio, became my director of transportation. That surprised everyone because Warren was the first non-engineer to hold the post. I felt that civil engineers seemed preoccupied with designing highways—not necessarily getting them built. With each new administration, a new director of transportation—a civil engineer—would announce his intention to review all of the planning work in progress. That was exactly what I wanted to avoid.

I told Warren, "I want you to put people to work."

I wanted as much highway construction under way as quickly as possible. I did not want to waste time redoing plans. Warren understood: orange barrels meant people in the construction and building materials industries were going back to work. Over the next four years we delivered on a half-dozen major highway projects promised by Jim Rhodes during the previous eight years. But never built.

That first biennial budget included a small gasoline tax increase, which generated nine dollars of federal highway funds for every dollar Ohio invested in a project. Folks began to call my administration the "Orange Barrel Administration" because of the proliferation of orange barrels marking highway construction across the state.

Even our highway engineers became enthusiastic fans of Warren Smith as the plan gathering dust in filing cabinets were actually getting built. To my mind, Warren's appointment was inspired.

My second key choice was Al Dietzel, a Republican who moved from president of the Columbus Chamber of Commerce to become director of economic development.

Al was a great guy—a lovely human being—who coincidentally lived next door to the governor's residence. That very first night in the residence, after my state troopers ordered pizzas, I wanted a shot of bourbon, but there was no liquor in the house. Dietzel, in on the budget talks, said, "Hey, I've got some next door." Within minutes he was back with Jack Daniels for me and beer for the others—an all-purpose cabinet member.

I dispatched Dietzel and Smith together on a tour of the state to meet with business and labor leaders, educators, and the various stakeholders whose perspectives could help us shape a Rube Mettler–style strategic plan for Ohio. After six months on the road, they reported back, and together we developed a long-term strategic plan focused on job development. When I took office on that cold January day in 1983, Ohio ranked dead last in the country in job creation. Unemployment was over 14 percent. When I left office eight years later, Ohio had climbed to number five in the country in job creation, and our unemployment rate was 5.3 percent, below the national average.

The story of job creation within a strategic framework is one that, in a lot of ways, is still being told.

Joe Sommers, Vern's right hand in the House, became my chief of staff. Originally from Canton, born and bred a Democrat, Joe had moved from county government to state government as part of the Gilligan administration—and then joined Vern. I thought of Joe as the grown up among the young people who made up my team. Most of us were in our thirties and forties; Joe was well into his fifties. Joe had deep historical knowledge both of issues before the legislature and the people in it. He and Myrl knew who stood where on certain issues and who around Capitol Square could influence votes.

With House Speaker Vern Riffe (*right*) and Senate President Harry Meshel (*left*) when I was governor in 1983

Joe was cautious where I could be impetuous, someone who would pull back on the reins and urge me to take time to think things through. On occasion my crew could get a little foul-mouthed. Joe was never that way. I don't recall anyone ever having a bad word about him, which is remarkable given that he had spent twenty years in Columbus and did not always say yes to people.

Joe knew where to seek help in any situation. For example, when I hurt my back, Joe saw me bent over with pain and asked what was wrong. I explained, and he referred me to Ernie Johnson at Ohio State, a doc who handled all the Ohio State athletes. Ernie examined me, gave me a set of steps to take proper care of my back, and supplied me with a "butt-board"—a stiff piece of wood to sit on while at my desk that would prevent more back aches.

Joe could help me fix my aching back. Or get a bill passed.

My lieutenant governor, Myrl Shoemaker, was wonderful. He had been a real trouper on the campaign trail, and I wanted him to assume a cabinet post. Although Myrl's first love was the state budget, I asked him to serve as director of natural resources. Myrl would be an effective advocate for the parks, and the cabinet post ensured that Myrl was at the table in a significant way.

Myrl also served as a conduit to Vern Riffe, along with Joe Sommers. If I needed someone to get a message to Vern discreetly, Myrl could do it. They knew and trusted each other.

I persuaded Jan Allen to join the team as my deputy chief of staff. I had initially reached out to her during the previous summer just a few days before she took the bar exam. She had already been hired by Jones Day, but after my call she talked them into letting her join the campaign for a few months. That was Jan—my earliest and most dependable supporter.

When the campaign was over, Milt Wolf, who was chairing my transition, asked Jan if she was prepared to stay on.

She did not have to think very long; the answer was a prompt yes.

Though I had three chiefs of staff during my time in office, Jan was a consistent and crucial presence. I could rely on her to get things done—to keep me, the rest of the staff, and the cabinet focused. If a report was due in ninety days, Jan would make sure it got to my desk on time. Conversely, if a cabinet member had a problem with another agency or our Washington office or our lawyers, she could ask Jan for help to get the response that she needed. Or if there was something that I absolutely needed to see, Jan was the person that people entrusted it to.

In hindsight I can see clearly that there must have been times when my initial chief of staff, Joe, felt himself the odd man out. My inner circle—Jan and Larry and, from the outside, Jerry, Bill, and Ted—would often go around him and speak directly to me. When I asked Carolyn Lukensmeyer (who was facilitator of our cabinet retreats and would become my COS in the second term) to take a look at how to improve my office operations, her top recommendation was to either give Joe real power or replace him. She knew that Joe felt out of sync with the informality of the rest of the office. And it wasn't Joe's style to confront me.

In those early days we sought a visual image of how we worked as an organization. Was it a hierarchy or spokes of a wheel? We were very much spokes of a wheel. Everybody had access; everybody had a chance to make his or her case. Being called chief of staff was misleading. I am sure Joe found this frustrating, but I never heard a peep from him. It was Lukensmeyer who forced that important personnel decision for me. Joe moved over to a cabinet position. He became much happier—and more effective.

Ray Sawyer had initially come to Columbus to oversee the formation of the Ohio Housing Finance Agency (OHFA) a new entity created by the passage of a 1982 statewide ballot initiative. As a supporter I was eager to get the agency into action as quickly as possible to provide another shot in the arm for Ohio's economy. We needed someone who knew how to structure a public agency with significant bonding authority. As I was wrestling with this, Jerry Austin called to say he believed that Ray Sawyer wanted to play a role in the administration. Ray, a terrific lawyer with strategic vision and public finance experience, moved his family to Columbus. With incredible speed and savvy, he had the OHFA up and ready for business—with people sleeping on sidewalks outside OHFA offices to be first in line for a mortgage loan.

Shortly thereafter, Ray became my chief of staff.

The lack of hierarchy in the office did not seem to bother Ray in the way it had Joe. We tried to create a modest hierarchy without much success. A strong egalitarian streak was shared by all of us, starting with me. Dora had the same amount of influence as Ray. So did Jan. So did Jerry. Ray was very effective because he focused on the big things—like the savings and loans crisis—and did them well. By the end of my first term, he was ready to move back to Cleveland. Like others who worked with me, he had put his very successful legal career on hold and had given up substantial income to serve in the Celeste administration.

By the time I was elected governor, Eric and Christopher were off at college. When they could carve out time, the two boys had worked on my campaign, but most of each year they were at school. Gabriella, soon to be a senior at Magnificat High School in Cleveland, refused to give up her senior year and move to Columbus with the rest of the family.

"No way," she said. I knew Gabriella was strong-willed enough that it was not worth arguing with her.

Dagmar and I had decided to rent our Cleveland house to a group of Ursuline nuns, and I offered to give them a break on the rent if they allowed Gabriella to stay with them. They agreed, and I found it a reassuring arrangement. My daughter would be living with a group of nuns—what could be more protective than that? Many years later I learned that it was not as innocent as it seemed.

The three youngest kids moved into the governor's residence, excited that each would have his or her own room. Barely used for so long under Rhodes, the house now became a lively place with young kids in and out, boisterous parties, and occasional exhibits of Ohio artists. The attic became a space for staff working on projects for Dagmar or me.

It did take some getting used to. The kids had grown up in tight circumstances in Cleveland. Now they found themselves in a sprawling mansion (though we banned that word). It was also a change for Dagmar, who had to figure out the complexities of managing a staff—a house manager, a cook, gardeners, and her own chief of staff. While we didn't do a lot of formal entertaining, we had our fair share of dinners and receptions.

The first thing that our five-year-old Stephen wanted was a treehouse, so we built one in the backyard. The other excitement for him was the presence of Ohio Highway Patrol as our security detail. A shed by our garage served as the office for the two officer shifts who provided twenty-four-hour protection. We put up a basketball hoop, mostly for Christopher when he was around, but I think the OHP shot hoops as often as he did.

Mostly it was Stephen who occupied the troopers' attention. He would come home from school and look for the officers. The lock for the state patrol office was a punch-code lock, ostensibly secret. Despite their best efforts, he would watch them punch in the code and let himself inside. He was that kind of five-year-old—brilliant, sociable, indefatigable. As a consequence, he spent a lot of time with the troopers yakking or just getting in their way.

Noelle, Natalie, and Stephen could walk to their schools, and they made friends quickly, often inviting them back to our house after school. It was, after all, the Residence. Who would turn down that kind of invitation?

Things became more challenging when the girls started dating. When a boy would come to take one of them out, it was not simply a matter of pulling up and knocking on the door. The boy would be greeted by a uniformed state trooper—pretty intimidating, very different from my experience simply shouting at Gary Strong's front door.

We all spent a good deal of time with the members of the state patrol assigned to protect us. One of the more curious, little-written-about aspects of public life is the unusual intimacy that develops between a public official's family and their protective team. Lt. Bob Strine was in charge of my security detail, but a dozen state troopers would cycle through over the course of eight years. We got to know all of them, spending a lot of time together in cars. They knew that I would usually nap or be talking to staff. But we still found time to discuss everything from how the Ohio State football team was faring to the best ice cream places in Chillicothe or whether Bob had been to the Bratwurst Festival where we were headed.

"I've been," I remember Bob telling me. "Lots of bratwurst—and beer."

Our troopers were as discreet as they were fun to be with. They would make sure my meetings weren't interrupted. Occasionally—if I was hosting something we needed to keep under wraps, like meeting with the commissioner of baseball or having lunch with someone who did not want to be put on the spot—they respected the need to keep it in confidence. It was a trust relationship.

For her senior thesis at Yale, Noelle examined the experiences of children from other political families who had grown up in similar "fishbowls"—as she called it in the title of her thesis. She discovered that there were striking similarities between the experience of her and her siblings and those in other political families. As extraordinary as her experience felt, her research showed it to be surprisingly commonplace for families in the public limelight.

Occasionally I found myself reminded of Jim Rhodes's comment that PhDs did not have the sort of smarts needed in public life—each time one of my PhD cabinet appointees got into trouble.

The first was Jim Rogers, a person I liked and respected a great deal. Jim had not one but two PhDs (one in organizational development and one in library science). He had been very involved in my campaign, particularly handling Election Day money. He had done an impeccable job of what could be a slippery task, accounting for every dollar. I was proud of that work. I had asked him to serve on my talent search team with McCartney and Stein-bacher. Later, when I offered him a cabinet position, he refused, saying that he couldn't complete the personal disclosure form.

I sat down with him and asked why.

"There something I've never revealed and I don't want to reveal," he told me.

"You have to tell me about it," I said. "Even if you don't put it on paper."

"I'm an illegitimate child," he told me. "I can't vouch for my family."

"That's not a disabling matter," I told him. "Not as far as I'm concerned."

We proceeded with the appointment—without his having filled out the disclosure form. At the time, all seemed fine. However, early in my second year we began to hear rumblings about Rogers and his Department of Youth Services. Larry McCartney had no specifics, but we felt that we should take a careful look at the situation. Larry hired a private detective. When the investigator did not find evidence of wrongdoing, we figured we had done our due diligence.

We soon found out how wrong we had been. Rogers—who turned out to have a gambling addiction—had been taking kickbacks from construction contractors hired to do work at the department's facilities. He was tried and convicted. I never spoke to Jim Rogers after that. I heard that he became a pastor while he was in prison, but I have never been successful in tracking him down.

I believe that being a good mentor involves delegating substantial responsibility and letting your mentee learn from his or her mistakes. Chester Bowles let me make my fair share of mistakes along the way. But I came to learn that there are times when good people can find themselves in holes that are just too deep. That is exactly what happened with my OBES chief, Roberta Steinbacher.

OBES had not been a well-run agency. Not only the job training audit matter with the Labor Department but many other legacy issues confronted Roberta and her colleagues. She did her best to address those issues and get the agency headed in a positive direction. But one of the individuals she relied on most heavily, Don McConnell, was prosecuted for soliciting campaign contributions—a profound betrayal of her trust. And she and her agency were taking an almost daily shellacking in the press.

My respect for Roberta led me to keep her in place longer than I should have. Only when she began to have a physical response to the stress did I urge her to move on. She had become blind in one eye and to save her other eye—to spare herself from the daily pounding—she needed to resign. Her health was more important than any state agency. Finally, she reluctantly agreed.

Roberta returned to Cleveland, and we did not talk for some time. Partly, I suppose, because I was busy but also, I am sure, because our parting was so difficult. I told her when I asked for her resignation that I felt I had made a mistake in letting her hang on longer than I should have. Asking someone you respect and care about deeply to step down, when for whatever reason they are no longer able to perform, is extremely difficult.

This was for me a very hard lesson: good people can get into bad situations. When that happens, you must step in early. I feel certain that had I acted more quickly and found a graceful way to replace her, she might have her eyesight today. I am less certain that the problems at OBES would have been resolved by a change of leadership.

In the case of Rogers, I only regret that we weren't able to uncover his criminal conduct ourselves and hold him accountable. Situations like this are the reason that every organization needs an internal auditor. You have to expect the best of people, but even smart, highly motivated people can get themselves into a jam. But, as I knew, bad news tends not to travel up in any organization.

Jim Rhodes understood that effective governance required more than a PhD.

Not every initiative during the first term went sour.

For example, the passport program was developed in our human services department to package several benefits for seniors available from different state agencies. To assist elderly Ohioans who often became confused about what they were eligible for, the program was designed to combine housing, medical services, and counseling into a "passport" to coordinated care.

The champion for this program was Joyce Chapel, who had been serving as the parks director in Toledo when my talent search team found her. Joyce was a gifted public administrator with a wonderful, unflappable, upbeat personality. Her favorite saying was "Governor, nothing beats a try."

Joyce understood that an agency needed more than good intentions. It had to track delivering services and assess the actual experience of clients. While her Ohio Department of Aging would celebrate the inauguration of ten new members into the Senior Citizen Hall of Fame, that did not help seniors struggling to stay in their homes or looking for nursing care. Joyce understood the challenge of translating policy into meaningful services at a community level. Joyce's successor, Carol Austin—Jerry Austin's sister—a PhD gerontologist, carried on Ohio's highly recognized efforts on behalf of older citizens that Joyce Chapel had commenced.

While our mental health reform was not fully adopted until my second term, it was a priority from Inauguration Day. It was a personal as well as a public priority for me because I'd experienced the system firsthand when Dagmar had her mental breakdown. Her crisis got me thinking about the problem more widely, especially the limited options available and the propensity to institutionalize people who suffered a mental breakdown.

For decades, folks with severe mental illness were placed in large, underfunded state hospitals. The Gilligan income tax had helped to address staffing issues, but I believed we needed to change fundamentally our approach to treatment for the mentally ill. As I learned with and from Dagmar, good therapy and proper medication could enable individuals to recover and fully function in the community. We could do a better job with a modest increase in resources but a radical shift in how we deployed them.

Unexpectedly, I chose the youngest member of my cabinet, Pam Hyde, to lead this initiative. The transition team presented me with the usual three choices, including at least one woman and one minority. Pam, thirty-two at the time, made the short list. She was a lawyer who had spent her career suing the State of Ohio on behalf of families of people who were mentally ill. When I interviewed her, I was very impressed.

She reminded me of my tough Italian grandmother: square-shouldered, looking me straight in the eye, not afraid of anything or anyone. Pam was the sort of person who made you think she could do anything she put her mind to, from cleaning the office to sitting behind the CEO's desk. She had that kind of presence, despite her youth.

From the first, she was clearly interested, but I had a concern.

"Are you sure you're ready," I asked her, "to come over to our side? You've been suing us—and, if I might say, successfully. I want to change this system, but it's not going to happen quickly or easily. Are you ready to take this on?"

Pam assured me that she would welcome the challenge.

My last question to her was standard but more personal. "Is there anything you think I should know about you that we haven't discussed?"

"There is one thing," she said.

I asked her what it was.

"I'm gay," she said.

"I appreciate your telling me," I replied. "That doesn't matter to me. But I want to emphasize that I'm hiring you to lead the Department of Mental Health, not to be my spokesperson on gay and lesbian issues. I want you to stay focused on mental health reform. If at any time the fact that you are gay becomes an issue, I'll stand by you. Completely."

It never became an issue. And Pam Hyde would go on to change things in a big way.

Occasionally a public official with a pet peeve can do something about it. In my case, the peeve involved Ohio's so-called rest stops. Campaigning for lieutenant governor with our kids in the RV, I had experienced firsthand how antiquated and filthy they were. Soon after I was elected, I pulled Warren Smith aside to say that I wanted to replace every one of these awful rest stops. I told Warren that he had ninety days to come back with a plan. Less than sixty days later, Warren was back. "Believe it or not," he said, "I found drawings on the shelf" for reconfigured rest areas.

"No kidding," I said.

"They're very good," he said. "We can use them."

This, I remember thinking, is what you get when you appoint someone eager to put people to work to a cabinet post. "You build them into the land so that they're mounded—you minimize heating and air conditioning that way. If we put a couple of solar panels on them, we could manage the electricity at very little cost. To replace every single one will take about three years. It will cost about $90 million."

"And," Warren continued, "I have a way to fund the project using our vanity plate money"—like a plate that says GOV RFC—"which is just enough to cover the rest stops. By the way, we also have a way to staff them. I've been talking to Minnie Johnson, our director of [the Department of] Mental Retardation. The county mental retardation boards are eager to find work for their clients who are incredibly reliable workers. So," Warren concluded, "we can replace the rest stops, and we can keep them clean."

"Okay," I said. "Let's do it."

Late in 1985 I went to a spot on I-71 near Mansfield and took a sledgehammer to the last of these old crappers (the only accurate description). Since we had a bunch of cameras watching the action, we had a tractor hidden behind it, ready to pull the decrepit thing down if my blow wasn't sufficient. Down it went.

Not long after we completed the replacement project, I started getting letters from travelers complimenting me on the quality and cleanliness of Ohio's rest stops.

Orange barrels and rebuilt rest stops meant Ohioans were going back to work.

Yes, there were women. However, I am not going to get into gossipy detail on this subject. This is not a tell-all, mostly because I don't think it is anyone's business. By the time we moved into the governor's residence, Dagmar had come to realize that I was not a faithful spouse. My behavior pained her, and I was never proud of it. In her own book she has shared her story. I respect her feelings and am grateful for our time together and for the wonderful children we share.

When people ask if I want to tell my side of the story, I am not sure I have a "side" to tell. The fundamental point I need to emphasize about my infidelity is that I must—in my everyday life as well as within the precincts of this memoir—own my own behavior. It was my responsibility then, and it still is. I can't excuse or erase that aspect of my conduct. Owning what I did has been essential to moving on and living a different kind of life.

I would go to marriage retreats, try to patch things up with Dagmar. But that was it. I did not take the time required for sustained self-examination or self-reflection—especially not the sort that I feared might erode my sense of self-confidence and purpose.

Earlier I described learning the serious effort it took to connect with people—I mean really connect. Part of this connection is a sense of familiarity, part is trust, and part is excitement. You can feel that connection as you move through a room, shaking hands and making eye contact. I could feel it as well during a speech. I developed a ritual that helped me to connect with folks when I was speaking—whether to a small group or a packed ballroom. I began by taking off my jacket and rolling up my sleeves as if I was saying that I am getting down to business and going to level with you.

Next, I would tell a story that would get a laugh at my expense—like my story about Knockemstiff, Ohio, that I had borrowed from Myrl Shoemaker. It helped people feel comfortable with me.

I was a decent speaker to start with (thank you, Wally Smith), but I got better with practice on the stump. By the time I was running for governor, I was in good form. I could bring people to their feet, ready to go out and do battle on behalf of me and the Democratic ticket. And, for a lot of people, that was the litmus test. They wanted to hear something that made sense (put Ohioans back to work), but they also wanted something that moved them (Stand up for Ohio). Faithful party members hear so many similar speeches, dull and poorly delivered, that they recognize and respond to someone who connects deeply with them and gets them excited.

In Wally Smith's class, a good speech had the ability to convince a listener—to think a certain way or feel a certain way or to take action in a certain way. Volunteer, write a check, canvass a precinct. Yes, cast a vote for Celeste and Shoemaker! And sometimes you convince someone to want to get closer to you.

I am not sure what would make me respond. As I say, the reconstruction of that mindset—my mindset—is not something that I have wanted to do. That is not who I am now, and I am better for it.

It was not until I had left politics—more than ten years later—that I took a hard look at myself. Perhaps my life would have taken a different turn if I had examined myself unblinkingly earlier. But I didn't. I guess when I was at the height of my political career, I was unwilling to ask myself a question so deep that it might throw me off my chosen path.

In a strange way my misbehavior kept me humble. I knew that I was flawed. I was never going to run for sainthood, but I wanted to be seen as a principled politician—not perfect but honest when it came to my commitment to the public. I felt it was essential to take strong, well-defined positions so that people could hold me accountable. Voters might feel good or bad about me, but they knew where I stood on public policy—if not on personal behavior.

That behavior would burden me later. But that was later.

In 1982 Dick Lamm shared a handbook prepared by the NGA with us rookie governors. This handbook outlined, among other things, the importance of your first budget. It offered tips and tactics for rolling it out effectively. It underscored the challenges of managing personnel and of dealing with the press. Gov. Dick Thornberg had even written about what to do when the unexpected occurs, based on the Three Mile Island disaster. He cautioned that at some point during your four years, the phone is going to ring, setting in motion a scenario that no one could anticipate. Maybe it's a leak in your nuclear reactor. Maybe it is a tornado. Maybe a cosmetologist has come down with Ebola.

That, we were told, is part of the job. My first term was not without crises—some of my own making.

Controversy around taxes is to be expected, especially if one's actions are poorly communicated.

Controversy around public spending is to be expected.

High-profile audits can also be predicted.

Probably every administration has to deal with an individual who doesn't measure up and causes an odor that's hard to shake.

Then there is the crisis that no one can predict. Perhaps, in hindsight, I should have seen it coming. I did not.

I had to deal with it all the same.

Chapter 10

Savings and Loans

At 5:00 A.M. on Wednesday, March 6, 1985, my phone rang. I picked it up immediately. "Governor," Marvin Warner told me, "we have a problem." This was Ohio's precursor of the financial meltdown that would eventually be known around the world as the Savings and Loans Crisis.

Marvin Warner didn't have to introduce himself. I had put him in charge of the Ohio Building Authority, in part to oversee the construction of the Riffe Office Tower, where Jim Rhodes had tried to break ground during my inauguration. Warner tossed out the Rhodes plan and oversaw a design both more attractive and more efficient than the sixty-six-story monstrosity the previous administration had proposed. Marvin was tough and smart. He was also one of the few people to have my personal number, and it was clear he was worried. "There's been a failure of a financial institution in Florida," he told me, "and it's going to affect our liquidity at Home State."

Wide awake now, I told him to go on.

In a few hours, he told me, the *Cincinnati Enquirer* would publish a story revealing his savings and loans—Home State—had deposited a substantial sum of money with a securities firm in Florida named ESM Government Securities, Inc., which had just declared bankruptcy.

"We need help," he told me.

Warner was not the sort of person to confide in you for no reason. His doing so indicated the severity of the situation. Anything less, he would have gone to Vern Riffe or Stanley Aronoff, both of whom were considerably closer to him than me. In fact, I suspect he had reached out to Vern, who told him to contact me. I know he tried to enlist the help of Stan Aronoff, who was vacationing in Israel when he got the call. In any event, Warner was now calling me.

I cut him off before he could get too far into his appeal. "Look," I said, "I'm going to have Ray Sawyer get back to you. And we can go from there."

Then I hung up and tried to go back to sleep.

I knew Marvin Warner. He was one of my major supporters, and I trusted him enough to appoint him to a key position. While some folks assume he had me in his pocket, it was never the case. Despite our association I was always careful to keep him at an arm's length. My first contact with him had come through Jack Gilligan. After I won the nomination for lieutenant governor, the governor had given me a list of potential financial contributors. Warner's name had been on that list. I went to see him, ironically, at Home State, where I hemmed and hawed before finally asking him for a contribution. He had expected the ask, of course, and responded by handing me an envelope.

I thanked him, but once outside I opened the envelope to discover ten $100 bills. A thousand dollars cash.

I could not take it. After all, I had sponsored the bill that limited cash contributions to $100. I got out of my car and went back into the building.

It was a generous contribution, I told Warner, "but I can't accept it." Marvin was nonplussed and asked the reason. I explained my legislation that had put the cash limit in place. He took back the envelope and wrote me a check instead, folded it in half and handed it to me. I thanked him again.

Once in my car I unfolded the check. It was for $500.

From that moment on, Marvin Warner and I understood each other.

I respected him as a successful business and community leader who had been a very strong supporter of Jimmy Carter and who was providing strong leadership at the Ohio Building Authority.

It was clear when Marvin called that he had a problem. What was not clear is why he had called the governor.

Being governor means there are literally thousands of people who want their problems to become your problem. Ohio was then a multi-billion-dollar operation with thousands of employees and hundreds of departments and divisions and with citizens constantly pressing for attention. A governor has to make quick decisions about what's important and what can look after itself. What would turn out to be a grave crisis initially seemed to me to be something that could look after itself. It was a banking problem, one that the banks should and would resolve on their own. What did Marvin know that I didn't?

That morning there would be no going back to sleep. As it would turn out, few of us would get much sleep for the next few months.

The first person I called was Jan Allen, who had heard nothing about the situation. If Marvin Warner was that concerned, we needed to get up to speed on it. Next, I called my chief of staff Ray Sawyer and filled him in. He would get in touch with Warner, get the details, and report back to me.

A couple of hours later we had at least some idea of what was going on. A securities firm in Fort Lauderdale called ESM Government Securities had gone under. While fraud had been alleged, there was little concrete information. It was also difficult to tell whom it would impact—other than Home Savings. What we knew was that ESM Securities owed Home State millions of dollars and would not be able to pay. The savings of Ohio depositors had evaporated.

By the time Ray Sawyer got back to me later that morning, he had also heard from Ken Cox, the newly appointed director of the Ohio Department of Commerce. Cox had found out about the Cincinnati situation independently when calls started to come in to his office. Sawyer agreed with Cox that Home State was exposed; the two seemed to think that might possibly be the extent of the problem. There had been an initial run on the bank, but it had not been devastating. The instinct of bankers is always to let a run continue, "to put cash in the window" and in that way reassure depositors. What people care about in a circumstance like this is getting their money back. For the moment Home State seemed able to do that. The question was: if the run continued, how long would Home State be able to meet its obligations?

To answer that question, Cox and Sawyer called a meeting with Thomas Batties, interim head of the Division of Savings and Loans within the Ohio Department of Commerce, and Ken Elshoff, head of the Ohio Savings and Loans League. They concluded the situation was serious but not desperate. Home State funds were covered by a private insurance association called the Ohio Deposit Guarantee Fund, and they were ready to step in. Much depended on the Ohio Deposit Guarantee Fund—ODGF, for short—having the liquidity needed to cover the Home State shortfall.

We realized quickly that a problem ODGF posed was its name—which implied that the State of Ohio stood behind it, perhaps even that the state was guaranteeing their deposits. It was, after all, the *Ohio* Deposit Guarantee Fund. In truth, however, the ODGF was a *private* insurance arrangement. The S&Ls insured by ODGF were state-chartered institutions who had decided not to be part of the Federal Savings and Loan Insurance Corporation (FSLIC)—based in Washington and charging a considerably higher premium. A typical customer entering an S&L could see for him- or herself that the safety of their money was guaranteed by the Ohio Deposit Guarantee Fund; its seal was right there on the front door.

The general impression that the state insured these S&Ls led Ray Sawyer and others on my staff to decide to issue a statement expressing confidence in the system. Panic was to be avoided at all costs because a run on the banks might prove catastrophic. Cox issued a statement that afternoon saying that the system was sound. So did Karen Horn, the newly appointed president of the Cleveland Federal Reserve.

That evening I went to a basketball game. Michigan crushed Ohio State. It was not a great day. The basketball defeat would prove to be the least of it.

Thursday—the next day—began with Ray Sawyer, who told me that the Federal Reserve had sent examiners to Cincinnati to inspect the Home State books in order to get a handle on the extent of their exposure. One quick option would be to find a buyer for Home State. The $1 million question—or in this case the $250 million question—had to do with understanding how much the bank owed above and beyond its remaining assets, and, further, how covering those losses would affect the liquidity of ODGF itself.

After meeting with Ray, I spoke for the first time to Karen Horn. Tall and reserved, a native Californian and graduate of Johns Hopkins, Horn had just been elevated to president of the Cleveland Federal Reserve. She was the first woman in the country to have risen to that rank, and it was clear to me that she enjoyed the confidence of the Fed chairman, Paul Volcker. He was willing to go the extra mile to support her.

Horn was frank about the uncertainty of the situation. "We don't have enough information at this point," she told me, "but we do have people." The Cleveland Fed had been monitoring the situation, and the goal was to make a decision about how to proceed by the end of the day. She asked me to send her a copy of the statement I had made earlier that day in which I stated that my top priority was to make sure none of the depositors would lose money. Though she did not say so outright, my statement stressing the priority of ordinary depositors clearly made her uncomfortable.

Almost from the beginning the Fed viewed Home State as a lost cause and were having a hard time seeing a situation in which depositors didn't lose money. Hers was an understandable response. When you do not know how bad things are, it is difficult to give that kind of categorical assurance. Horn was looking at the bottom line. I had a different set of priorities.

I next talked to the people at the ODGF, who told me they had also been in touch with the Federal Reserve. They assured me they had enough money to get at least through the day. The Feds had provided them with some twenty-two million based on collateral. However, they were reluctant to devote all of their cash to one S&L because they felt the problem could become bigger. They felt that the real issue wasn't Home State—which was, they seemed to be saying, beyond repair—but that other savings and loans were vulnerable. ODGF had to liquidate significant investments and were paying substantial penalties. ODGF seemed to be asking us to do what people *thought* we were doing already—guarantee deposits with taxpayers' money.

There was no way this was going to happen. We were willing to help but not back the fund entirely. That afternoon I had lunch with Vern Riffe and Paul Gillmor, both of whom made it clear they were not prepared to write a blank check to cover undetermined shortfalls. They were worried about the other institutions ODGF backed. All that day depositors had been lining up at Home State to get their money, taking out the front door the cash that ODGF had delivered through the back. That was the problem. If Home State used up everything that ODGF had, all the other institutions it insured would be at risk. The situation was extremely delicate.

There was an undercurrent in our legislative discussions. Because both Vern Riffe and Stan Aronoff were so close to Marvin Warner, they didn't want their fingerprints on whatever happened next. Consequently, they ceded the initiative to me. I was to figure out the state response, and they would assist in making it happen in the House and Senate. For that reason I reached out to two Republicans, Bill Batchelder, a state rep from Ashland, and Dick Finan, a state senator from Cincinnati.

Jan and Ray were in and out of my office all day as new information became available. Jan urged me from the outset to not talk to Marvin Warner. My own instinct from the moment I finished our early morning conversation was to let Ray Sawyer handle him. Jan also shared my distrust of Washington and agreed that we couldn't expect much help there. Her suggestion was to tap quickly people outside the administration for their advice about how best to handle the situation. Jack Kessler, a friend and a member of the Cleveland Federal Reserve Board, was one. So was Bob McAllister, a lawyer who I would later appoint "savings and loans czar." They were invaluable as informal advisors. The most unexpected crisis of my administration was turning out also to be the most threatening.

Ray Sawyer tackled the problem from a different perspective. He was looking for a deal to resolve the Home State situation quickly. Ray thought that, if we could get together with the Federal Reserve, the result would be a deal. He focused on that because he truly believed it could happen, and at the time it did hold promise.

The problem with that approach, we quickly learned, was that everyone involved wanted an absolute guarantee. They would step in only if none of their money was at risk. Some banks expressed an interest right off the bat—on the condition that the state provide an open-ended guarantee of their investment. They wanted a check that the legislature would never write. Nor did it help that the more we learned about Home State's situation, the worse it seemed. If we were to find a buyer, we needed to do so quickly.

In the meantime, I was doing my best to stick to a "normal" schedule. The last thing I wanted to do was give the impression that the Home State situation was something to worry about. I attended a meeting with representatives from Mitsubishi, went to a Hispanic reception, and by seven that night I was home for dinner with my family. I got a second call from Karen Horn that evening. She still did not have enough information to make a final decision. "There's no easy way out," she told me. "What we do know indicates the situation may be beyond repair for Home State."

Friday morning found me still optimistic, hoping to find a buyer for Home State as the most expeditious resolution. After an early morning meeting with Sawyer, I received another call from Karen Horn, who told me that we were going to need the assistance of the Federal Reserve. If the crisis had only involved a single banking institution, she said, the Feds would stay out of it. But the possibility that the crisis might widen meant they had to engage. She talked about potential steps, which included passing legislation and/or bringing in the US Treasury.

Just before noon I had another meeting with the legislative leadership. Stan Aronoff was fully supportive, as was Paul Gillmor. They assured me they would support anything reasonable I proposed. But any deal had to be one they could sell to their caucus.

Though I had not been in contact with Marvin Warner, I heard through Ray that he had identified a potential buyer for Home State, Oliver Waddell, chairman of the First National Bank of Cincinnati. Though I would eventually speak to Waddell myself, Ray handled most of the conversations with him. The two got along well. Oliver was a silk stocking banker; Ray was a silk stocking lawyer. Waddell's interest was tentative and conditioned on the state providing needed financing. Home State served Waddell's attractive Cincinnati market. Still, his interest was tempered by two things. The first was his vague distrust of Marvin Warner. The second was the lack of a solid estimate of the exposure at Home State. As a consequence, he insisted that the State of Ohio needed to come up with $250 million. I knew that there was not a legislator in Columbus who would approve that commitment.

I suppose if I had presented Waddell with a blank check, he could have been persuaded. The problem with the state putting up cash was the banks' resistance to treating public funds as a loan or an investment.

That afternoon Karen Horn called again to tell me the Fed had made a loan that would take Home Savings through today but not beyond. If Home State had undisclosed problems, the appetite for helping would evaporate. Another serious question was how to protect the depositors and prevent the funds that did remain from going to insiders.

I then touched base with Bobby Goldberg, another informal advisor. Bobby, an up-and-coming leader in the Jewish community in Cleveland, owned a highly respected federally insured S&L. Goldberg was not optimistic. He believed that nothing could save Home State and that the industry as a whole felt that ODGF was doomed. He argued strongly that we should not use any state dollars to bail out a private insurance fund.

In yet another call, Karen Horn summarized her call with Chairman Volcker that afternoon. Unfortunately, she had nothing reassuring to report. Based on their information, it seemed that the big money had already fled Home State. The less sophisticated depositors were almost certainly lost. The Fed's attention had moved toward other state-chartered S&Ls. With ODGF resources draining away, they were now in danger. Horn mused that the state should require the other S&Ls had to pursue federal insurance and that institutions that did not qualify for that insurance should be required to merge.

There was no easy way out.

I left the office around five so I could attend the wake of Anthony Russo, the former state legislator and longtime Cuyahoga County politician. At about the same time in Cincinnati, David Schiebel, chairman and president of Home State, announced that the bank would not open on Saturday. He was buying time. He knew as well as we did that a continued run would prove disastrous.

Saturday morning began with a call from Karen Horn reporting on the status of the other state S&Ls. Eleven, out of seventy, were rated number four (the worst) in terms of assets and exposure.

I was still trying to find a buyer for Home State. That afternoon we convened a group of five Ohio bankers to hear a presentation by the officers of ODGF. After four and a half often contentious hours, nothing had been accomplished.

My Sunday started off as usual with me making pancakes for the family. It's a long-standing tradition in the Celeste family to spend Sundays together. After pancakes, we would go to church and then spend the day together, often going to a bookstore. The afternoon would include a family meeting at which we would discuss things like who was responsible for dinners each evening and the chores for the week. Sundays were a day on which we would do our best to forget the fishbowl in which we lived.

That Sunday was far from ordinary. At the breakfast table was Rocky Morris, an attorney with the firm Porter Wright Morris and Arthur, our independent counsel. I flipped pancakes, and he briefed me on the situation.

When breakfast finished, I called Milt Wolf to get his sense of the situation. "Milt," I asked him, "what are the main things to worry about?"

Milt wanted to find a solution that would save Home State. After all, he was a builder who had probably secured loans from an S&L in Cleveland. At the same time, he understood the complexity of my position—and that any resolution I came up with would have to command legislative support.

Sawyer was skeptical about whether Home State management had the tools to manage the situation. We needed a conservator to keep the bank closed while we figured out what could be done. We needed to pin down what was happening with Home State's remaining assets, and we needed time.

My press secretary, Brian Usher, arrived at the residence, and, with Jan Allen, we started crafting a statement that emphasized I would be focused on finding a buyer for Home State who would provide the maximum protection to depositors. Whatever else happened, we needed to be sure that the savings of ordinary people were protected. That was my focus from the beginning, and it remained so throughout. The statement went on to say that a necessary part of the process was keeping Home State closed on Monday. While Jan and Brian read the statement to the papers, I made a checklist. On it there were three main items.

First, we needed to find a conservator who could stop cash from going out the front doors of Home State and get us hard information about its financial status.

Second, I needed to get the Federal Reserve involved and somehow find a buyer for Home State on the right terms.

Third, we needed to put in place legislation that would allow for the formation of a new insurance fund. I had managed to persuade Richard Finan, the Republican who chaired the Senate Ways and Means Committee, to help draft a bill that would involve a substantial state contribution or loan. Having the legislation in place was another attempt to win back the confidence of the depositors and get a lid on the situation.

The most pressing problem was finding a conservator who was knowledgeable about the savings and loans business, honest, and very conservative and who would let the federal examiners in and oversee a proper accounting.

I called my father for suggestions.

He proposed Arlo Smith, who I only knew by reputation. Retired in Florida, he had been a respected savings and loans executive in Cleveland and a national leader.

I called and told him what we needed. He said yes. And arrived the next day.

A lot depended on how people reacted to the news of the Monday closure. Karen Horn had people on the ground in Cincinnati watching the other ODGF-backed institutions. They sat in their cars outside the S&Ls, counting how many customers were going in. The Fed had eyes on our situation.

As for legislation, the most obvious course of action was to let the banks sort out their own problems. The last thing the banking community wanted was state intervention. If we did have to step in, one option was allowing only partial withdrawal. People would have access to only a certain amount of their money each week. The goal would be to make sure the run didn't go too deep. This option, however, would be hard to put in place and monitor.

A second option was requiring the state S&Ls to secure insurance that would *actually* guarantee their deposits. That meant legislation requiring the ODGF institutions to move under the Federal Savings and Loan Insurance Corporation (FSLIC) umbrella in Washington. To pursue this process, I was advised to call someone named Ed Gray, president of the Federal Home Loan Bank Board. I had never heard of him, but Jan made some calls, and soon I got the picture. Gray was a Reagan appointee—very political—not an experienced S&L guy. I needed to talk to him all the same.

With the benefit of hindsight, Ohio's problems, triggered by Home State, should not have surprised anyone. Examinations of Home State revealed that it was overinvested in ESM. They were required to disclose this information, and they had done so. During previous administrations, the bank had been repeatedly ordered to unwind some of those investments. They would agree, then do nothing. This went on from the early seventies until Marvin Warner's 5:00 A.M. phone call. Apparently, the state regulators worried that stronger action would cause depositors to flee. Home State had taken advantage of the absence of effective regulatory enforcement.

The chosen option, suasion, proved to be ineffective. No safeguards were put in place. This only became clear after we had closed Home State. About ten days after the crisis hit, an FBI agent confided to one of my staff that they had been investigating ESM for years. We should have known. Another example of bad news not traveling up.

Despite the urgency of the situation, Ed Gray was not returning my calls. "Leave him a message," I was told repeatedly. "I'm sure he'll get back to you."

He did not.

In order to get his attention, I enlisted our congressional delegation—Mary Rose Oakar, congresswoman from Cleveland and the ranking minority member of the House Banking Committee, and Chalmers Wylie, the Columbus Republican who chaired the committee. They put in calls to Gray. He remained unresponsive.

"So that option is cut off," said Ray Sawyer. "At least for now."

At a quarter after three I got a call from Karen Horn. "The good news," she told me, "is that there's not *total* panic."

The bad news, she went on to say, was that a number of things were still making the Fed nervous. In the first place, there seemed to be more large withdrawals than usual. She said that the Feds had set up a war room and that they were keeping people at key posts throughout Cincinnati, monitoring the situation.

By 5:30 she called back. "There's no serious damage," she said, "but there's also no end to the worry." She went on to offer me some advice. "Governor," she said, "I've been talking to Chairman Volcker, and we agree it may be helpful to you to have a lawyer experienced in major bank reorganizations."

I agreed and asked if she had any suggestions. She had three, she said, and she gave me names and phone numbers. Ray and I began to go review the list when the phone rang again, Karen Horn calling back.

"I just want you to know," she said, "that the number I gave you for Rodgin Cohen is wrong—he's at his Long Island home. So if you did want to call him, here's where he can be reached."

I might not know much about high finance, but I can recognize a signal.

I hung up the phone and turned to Ray. "Okay," I told him, "I *think* the signal is Rodgin Cohen."

Cohen was expecting our call and had been briefed. He was brilliant and self-assured, the best sort of New York lawyer, not slick but confident. He was well known as the man who had put together the Continental Illinois Bank bailout. The respect he commanded stretched across several constituencies: he could talk to legislators from both sides of the aisle; bankers and the business community would listen to him. Cohen told us he had already booked his plane ticket. "I'll fly to Cincinnati tomorrow," he said, "and talk to the bankers there in order to appraise the situation. Then I'll come up to Columbus and sit down with you."

At 7:45 I picked up the phone and found myself talking to Paul Volcker, chairman of the Federal Reserve. "I want you to know," he told me in his New Jersey drawl, "that we have an interest in this situation, and we are watching it carefully."

He went on to offer his perspective: "We can handle one of these institutions closing," he told me, "but not more than one. I understand that you've been in touch with Rodgin Cohen. He's a very good man, and we know he will be of help to you in this."

I thanked him for the referral.

"By the way, Governor," he said. "You have been able to do something that I have wanted to do, and been unable to, for some time."

I asked him what it was.

"You are bringing the dollar down in Europe," he told me. "This is something I've been endeavoring to do with little success. You're succeeding—though this is not the way I would choose to do it."

I still laugh about that today.

By Tuesday I was at the Federal Reserve offices in Cleveland, calling out-of-state banks to see if one would be interested in acquiring Home State. This had been Rodgin Cohen's initial recommendation. My assignment was to call eight different firms. I would dial the number, ask for the chairman, and then say more or less the same thing: we had a troubled financial institution that was in three of the prime markets in Ohio with about half a billion in core deposits and thirty-four branches.

Just about everyone I spoke to knew about the Florida bankruptcy and Home State's struggle. While there was some interest, our discussion always boiled down to getting a clear picture of the gap between Home State's assets and liabilities. One after another, I made the same pitch. I got no takers.

By Wednesday, March 12, significant lines had begun to form outside Mollitor and Charter Oak. Executives from those banks had gone to Washington and tried without success to get help. Any assistance would have to come from Ohio. Karen Horn still had people outside S&Ls tracking the lines. She called that afternoon to say that they had identified five that they believed were experiencing significant runs.

The Federal Reserve was watching all of this very closely, she said. The failure of that many institutions would have serious consequences.

I began calling the CEOs of the hardest hit institutions. I needed to know from them, personally, whether they had enough cash to stay open until the weekend. Speaking to some of the strongest and some of the weakest, I asked each executive the same series of questions. Could they survive what was increasingly a run? Could they get through tomorrow? What about Friday? Could they make it to Saturday morning?

Three of them said no. They would not be able to make it past tomorrow.

Total withdrawals were approaching $60 million. I would have to take a decisive step soon. The reports of general unease and the spreading lines in Cincinnati meant that I could not simply close the two or three most affected institutions. That would precipitate a run on all the state-regulated S&Ls. I called Chuck Thiemann, president of the Federal Home Loan Bank Board in Cincinnati, who told me that if we closed the ODGF-backed associations, they would "expedite" applications for FSLIC insurance. That sounded helpful.

But what did expedite mean? The state would need to pass legislation that required the institutions to be covered by FSLIC, but getting that done quickly depended on the goodwill of people in Washington like Ed Gray— who had still not returned my calls.

To the public we stressed that we were working on a solution, particularly the new fund that the legislature was creating—with $50 million dollars from the state and $40 million dollars from the ODGF associations. It was an extraordinary step meant to restore confidence. The bill was approved, and we called a press conference at six that evening just before I was scheduled to appear at a Chamber of Commerce dinner. We aimed to make the next day's headlines as optimistic as possible.

As it happened, a reporter asked whether Marvin Warner would continue to serve as chairman of the Ohio Building Authority? Without thinking, I said that Warner had called Ray Sawyer an hour earlier to tender his resignation. That became the next day's lead story, burying the headline that we'd just labored to put in place—the most unprecedented step taken by a state to protect its own financial institutions.

In other news that night, Provident Bank and Eagle Savings—a federally insured institution—announced they would refuse to honor checks drawn on ODGF-backed S&Ls.

Out of the frying pan into the fire.

There were two lead stories the next morning. The first was the Warner resignation. The second was an account of an S&L contingent making the trip to Washington in order to speak to the folks at FSLIC—and getting turned down.

By that point, runs at ODGF branches were spreading. Word reached me that there were two hundred people lined up outside Charter Oak and that a television crew from ABC News had arrived to cover the story. The situation was made worse because there was no clear message from the ODGF. Into that vacuum swirled rumor and fearmongering. I got a call from Charlie Meacham, chairman of Taft Broadcasting, who advised me to get someone there ASAP to represent the governor's office. After a hastily called meeting, we decided to send Ken Cox with Brian Usher, my press secretary.

Everyone was nervous about the situation, but Brian seemed the worst. He was a serious journalist with a love of politics. All of a sudden, we were confronted with *Nightline*, CBS News, the ABC morning show, CNN. In the next twenty-four hours he would be dealing with about a hundred national and international correspondents. It was a zoo.

From Brian's standpoint, this was absolutely big time. We had to make sure we did it right. His anxiety wasn't groundless. Brian felt one mistake could undermine "the whole thing"—the financial stability of the nation.

Meanwhile I was on the phone.

I called Volcker.

I called Karen Horn.

I called the governors of Massachusetts and Maryland to warn them, telling them to be ready in case the panic spread. The run in Ohio was prodded by a guy named Bill Cunningham who had a late-night radio show that could be heard across the East Coast.

Mike Dukakis was out of town on a trade mission, so I talked to his chief of staff. Dukakis's aide was attentive, saying he would take a careful look at their situation. Governor Hughes, on the other hand, said that his supervisor of state savings and loans had assured him that what was happening in Ohio could not possibly happen in Maryland. I urged him to treat any assurance he received with skepticism. Maryland soon experienced what is known as a "silent run"—people quietly withdrawing their money. The authorities did not realize how bad it was until they had a $250 million problem.

By Thursday afternoon—March 14, 1985—I knew that it was decision time. I began calling the people I could trust and who would be calm and clearheaded despite the pressure.

The first person I called was Jack Kessler, member of the Cleveland Federal Reserve Board. "Jack," I told him, "I have a big decision to make, and I need you to come sit with me." He said that he would get to Columbus that night.

Next, I called Don Shackleford, president of a very well-run S&L in Columbus. I didn't know Don as well, but each time I had dealt with him he impressed me with his capacity for independent thought. I needed to avoid a herd mentality, and Don had never been someone who ran with the pack. I told him what I had told Kessler: "I need you to help me make a very difficult decision."

Then I called my father.

Frank Celeste had worked with a number of S&Ls over the years. He understood the business. More than that, my father had been more responsible than anyone else for putting me in the place where it was up to me to make this decision. I wanted him beside me.

Up to that point I had been largely talking to lawyers. But there is often a difference between lawyering and deciding. A lawyer is trained to present you with choices. Now I needed people who knew how to make up their minds.

Before making the decision, I went home for dinner with Dagmar and the kids. As we were finishing, Jerry Austin came by. Jerry understood the political implications of the situation and the pressure I was under. Like me, he was concerned about the depositors at risk. But he was also thinking about the next election, which would be under way in less than a year.

"Tonight I'm going to have to make a decision on this savings and loans thing," I told him. "It could cost me the election."

"Whatever you decide," he said, "it needs to be *your* decision—one you are ready to defend to Ohio's voters when you run."

By 8:30 that night I was back at the office. On the way there, I had the state patrol stop for ribs—for the staff. I knew they weren't going to eat much that night.

Kessler, Shackleford, and my father gathered in the office, and I described four options. "You tell me what you think," I said, "especially if I'm missing anything."

I outlined each option with pluses and minuses.

The first was to allow the institutions to remain open but limit withdrawals. Each individual would be allowed to take out, say, up to $500 a month.

This option seemed politically safe insofar as it avoided having to shut the banks. On the other hand, the process would be hard to monitor; computers were not what they are today. It was an enormous logistical gamble.

A second option was to allow the institutions to stay open and let the run continue. This was the traditional route—a banker's solution. The strong S&Ls would survive; the weak would go under. The problem for many depositors— ordinary people who had put their faith in a private insurance firm that used the word "Ohio" in its name—was that they would lose their money.

A third option was to allow the strong S&Ls to open and to close just the weak ones. But this might precipitate a wider run that would exacerbate the crisis.

The final option: close them all and require them to secure FSLIC insurance.

"What do you recommend?" I asked my three wise men.

None offered an opinion.

"Dick," said my father, "I know you're going to do the right thing."

One thing was clear: they all agreed with my fundamental thesis that our priority was to protect the depositors. More than anything else, my duty was to protect these ordinary Ohioans and their savings.

As to which option was best, they did not have a recommendation.

It was my decision.

I put in a call to Paul Volcker, but couldn't get him. I wanted to get his opinion. While he could not legally point me in a particular direction, I would recognize a signal if he wanted to send one.

But I couldn't reach him. He was traveling. His assistant was apologetic but could not connect me.

"Listen," I said, "if I don't get to talk to him tonight, I'm going to come to Washington tomorrow and say that the message we're getting from everyone there, including the chairman of the Fed, is *Ohio, drop dead*"—a not-so-subtle reference to Gerald Ford's 1975 speech denying federal assistance to save New York from bankruptcy that led to the headline in the *Daily News:* "FORD TO CITY: DROP DEAD."

I was pissed.

At 11:00 P.M. Senator Finan called from Cincinnati. He reported radio host Bill Cunningham was whipping people into a frenzy, telling them to pitch their tents outside the banks or they risked not getting their money at all.

"What do you think?" I asked.

"Close them all," was Finan's reply, not a trace of doubt in his voice.

Thursday became Friday.

Volcker called me just after midnight. He had been getting on a plane in California, and they literally stopped the plane as it was taxiing out so he could call me. It was his turn to be pissed.

"Listen," he said. "They just pulled this plane back. I don't have time to talk now. I will call you when I land at 3:15."

I was clearly imposing on him.

The clock was ticking, and the tension was palpable. The Girl Scouts had come in the previous day, and I'd bought several boxes of cookies. "Is there any milk?" I asked. If we were going to stress-eat cookies, we needed milk.

Volcker, true to his word, called me back just after 3:00 A.M.

His first words were: "Governor, as you know, I have no authority over savings and loans. My interest is in the soundness of the banking system. I care because what's happening in Ohio is raising questions about the stability of the American banking system. I want to help to the extent I can. But I have no direct authority."

I said I understood.

He went on. "Let me share with you two important lessons about banking."

This was Banking 101 with freshman Celeste in the front seat. There would be an exam.

"The first lesson," he told me, "is that the system can always withstand one bank failure. It is the next failure that causes real problems."

"The second lesson is this," he said. "No matter how bad a bank looks from the outside, it looks a whole lot worse when you get inside."

With those two vivid lessons, he asked me what I was considering. I began to outline the four options that we had framed. "Before you go on," he reminded me, "I cannot recommend an action to you. I can simply tell you what I think are the positives and negatives of any course of action you have in mind."

I again said I understood and proceeded. "The first," I said, "is to let the run continue. As you know I've talked to Karen Horn."

"I know what Karen is doing," he said.

I told him I had reached out to the CEOs of the five institutions in the worst shape. None were confident they could make it through the next day. "I'm mindful," I told him, "of your comment that the system can withstand the failure of one bank, but when multiple banks fail it's another matter."

Volcker didn't reply.

I proceeded to outline the limited withdrawal strategy. "In the meantime," I said, "we can go into these institutions to determine their soundness."

He agreed that, while technology might be able to help, in that untested approach there could be serious problems. "It's a logistical challenge," he said. "Still, it is more appealing than banks failing or being closed."

I went on to the third option, just closing those institutions that were worst affected. The problem, he pointed out, was in knowing where to draw the line. The final option: "I sign an executive order to close all the S&Ls and give them seventy-two hours to demonstrate that they're viable so that we can reopen with confidence."

"Let me just tell you what happens when you close the banks," said Volcker. "In order to prevent the runs from resuming when they reopen, there would have to be convincing evidence that the banks were safe. I think the only convincing evidence is that they go through an examination and secure FSLIC insurance."

This was a lot to weigh.

"If you do that," he said, "It's likely to take six months to two years to get all of them reopened, and you'll have to invest as much as $250 million to cover the shortfall of the troubled institutions. Because there's no doubt in my mind that some of these institutions are very troubled."

That was the bottom line: six months to two years and $250 million that we didn't have.

A recipe for losing an election.

"I don't know if any of this has been helpful," he said, "but I stand ready to do whatever I can to be of assistance. I will ask Karen Horn to accompany you later this morning to make whatever announcement you intend to make. She will say that the Federal Reserve will do all that it can to insure the liquidity of these institutions."

I thanked Volcker and hung up the phone. It was four in the morning.

I turned to my advisors. They'd heard what Volcker said. I asked them again to make a recommendation.

My father turned to Jack Kessler. "You're on the Federal Reserve Board," he said.

Kessler turned to Shackelford. "You're a savings and loan guy."

Shackelford looked at my father. "Frank, you've had a lot of experience in S&Ls, and you love your son. You probably know best."

My father repeated that he knew I was going to do the right thing.

The long and the short of it: no one was going to make the case for one of these options. This was my decision and mine alone.

I had to be prepared to live with it.

I chased my three wise men out of the office, telling them I needed time to think.

Around five in the morning I got a call from someone who had seen the first edition of the *Cincinnati Enquirer* that morning. The front page featured two pictures. One was of a state-regulated savings and loans with a line of people surrounding it. The other was of a federally insured institution where there was no one to be seen. No lines, no anxious depositors.

From the outset of the Home State crisis, we had sought out other states that had confronted something similar to assess how had they responded. While Rodgin Cohen was working hard to mobilize the banks, Jan was researching the experience of other states. One was Mississippi. Their solution had been to close the S&Ls until they could get federal loan insurance. This action was similar to Karen Horn's early thinking.

Sitting in the governor's office, I thought: "Okay, Dick, you're a historian. The only precedent that comes to mind is Franklin Roosevelt. When FDR faced a banking crisis during the Depression, he vowed to protect the depositors. He did that by closing the banks and passing a law designed to protect the depositors when the banks reopened."

I called everyone into my office. "I've decided. I'm going to sign an executive order and fly down to Cincinnati to announce that we're closing all state-chartered S&Ls until Monday. Over the weekend we will figure out how to proceed."

Everyone flew into action. I needed the executive order ready in an hour. The state plane would fly to Cleveland, pick up Karen Horn, and return to Columbus to get me. In Cincinnati I would make the announcement and sign the executive order. Karen Horn would then reiterate that the Federal Reserve would help expedite the examinations of these institutions in order to get them reopened as quickly as possible.

Having made the decision, I felt good. I was confident that we would make it work. Win or lose, I was doing the right thing. I could almost hear my grandmother telling me that to those who are given much, much is expected. Now I understood. The many opportunities I had been given, my ability to energize a constituency for change, had put me in the governor's office to make a decision that only I could make.

My thoughts were interrupted a half-hour later when my legal team—a pair of sheepish, white-shoe lawyers—came in with Jan Allen. "Governor," she told me, "we have a problem."

"What kind of problem?"

"As they started working on this executive order," said Jan, "these gentlemen concluded you don't have the authority to close the banks."

I looked at the lawyers. "I beg your pardon?"

"Governor," said one of them, "we're just not convinced you have this authority."

"Let me understand this," I said. "Every day this week you told me I had this authority."

They said yes.

"When I was preparing to talk to Chairman Volcker, you told me I had this authority, right? And now you're telling me I don't have the authority?"

That is what they were telling me.

I took a deep breath. "Here's what you're going to do," I told them. "You write that fucking executive order and be prepared to defend it in court this morning because I'm going to issue it."

Fifteen minutes later it was on my desk.

At 8:30 A.M. I signed the order in front of the press in Cincinnati. There's a photo of me standing at the podium under a mural of Atlas holding up the world. All of the S&Ls were closed that morning—except for two. Down along the Ohio River, far from Cincinnati, they defied the order, telling reporters they were going to sue the governor. They kept their doors open.

Until depositors began to line up. Their doors closed by noon that Friday.

On Saturday morning Karen Horn convened a meeting at the Cleveland Federal Reserve and invited the CEOs of Ohio's major banks. I pitched them on a solution suggested by Rodgin Cohen that would involve the creation of a consortium that would bail out the shaky S&Ls.

The atmosphere was grudging at best. The bankers were there because Karen Horn had summoned them and they didn't want to get on her wrong side. *Why should we care?* was their attitude. *Home State was not even a bank— just a savings and loan.*

Karen pressed them hard, stressing that the situation could deteriorate, affecting every financial institution in the state. But they couldn't get over the fear that this could be a black hole that might cost untold millions of dollars. They insisted that only if the state put up $250–300 million would they see what they could do.

I reiterated that there was no way I could sell that exposure to the legislature.

Back at the statehouse, Jan Allen had called in Bill Flaherty as well as Bob McAllister to map out a plan requiring all the S&Ls to secure federal insurance. One controversial provision permitted banks based outside Ohio to acquire weak institutions and recapitalize them. But the key was a fund to cover shortfalls to be financed by unclaimed funds—bank accounts that people had forgotten about. This "bailout fund" eventually amounted to $125 million.

By Sunday morning it was clear Ohio's banks would not provide a resolution. If I did not extend my executive order, the S&Ls were going to reopen on Monday. We summoned the CEOs of the affected S&Ls to Columbus. That evening, ninety executives squeezed into the cabinet room. Ray Sawyer began by describing the unwillingness of the banks to step forward, then turned it over to me.

Announcing the executive action closing the savings and loans in Cincinnati in March 1985

"We face a decision," I told them. "I know that you've been dismayed to have your institutions closed in this way. But I've done it in order to protect your depositors and to restore confidence when you reopen."

There were unhappy murmurs.

"As things stand, you can open at nine o'clock tomorrow," I said. "Or I can extend the executive order until we've passed legislation that will require you to get federal insurance. We have assurances from Paul Volcker that they will help us expedite this process." I paused. "I believe this is the most prudent approach. But I want your views."

It was mostly silent. A couple said they wanted to reopen.

"Look," I said, "if this is what you want, you can open on Monday morning. But you need to be prepared if the runs resume—as is likely. Are you prepared to deal with that?"

At that point most of the CEOs agreed the prudent course of action was to stay closed until they could move under the Federal Home Loan Bank Board and FSLIC. When I asked for a formal vote requesting that I keep them closed, they refused; they did not want to go on the record. "Fine," I said. "We'll let the executive order expire and put a press release out in the morning saying that people can have access to their deposits."

At that point the lobbyist for the State Savings and Loans League stepped up. "Governor," he said, "I don't think we want to take a formal vote, but how about a show of hands?"

I said fine. "How many of you would like us to extend the executive order until we can cover you with legislation and federal insurance?"

As far as I could see every hand went up.

"I'll take this as an indication that we should extend the executive order," I said.

We emerged from the meeting to face a crush of journalists who had gathered to hear what we were going to do. By now the national and international press had joined Ohio's press and TV folks. As they came out of the cabinet room, the S&L execs—who had made it clear that they did not want to open on Monday—expressed outrage to the press that I was going to keep them closed. They clearly didn't want their depositors to know they preferred to stay closed. I knew some of them were operating on the margins and understood they were in trouble.

That night I extended the executive order and called the Speaker to draft emergency legislation. Working with key legislators, Rodgin Cohen, Jan, Ray, and others prepared legislation that would require the state-regulated S&Ls

to secure federal insurance. I stressed that I wanted the legislation passed and on my desk by Monday evening because I was going to Washington to meet with Chairman Volcker and, if possible, Ed Gray.

My father flew with me to Washington. While he played no formal role in the meetings, his presence was crucial. Frank Celeste had always believed in me, and his confidence strengthened me in that unusually demanding situation. While he and I did not trade thoughts, just having him close was reassuring. I suspect I was hoping that he could say to himself: "My son is a damn good governor."

At 10:00 A.M. we were sitting outside the office of Paul Volcker.

"Big time," I said to my father. "Big time," he agreed.

We both laughed, then went in to see the chairman.

I began by walking Volcker through what we had done. He had been getting reports from both Karen Horn and Rodgin Cohen. "Just let me repeat that we will provide as many examiners as we can and as quickly as you have authority to allow it," he said. "The institutions themselves have to make the request, but we have some resources to respond. What about Ed Gray?"

I told him I'd still not been able to get an appointment.

He was clearly surprised. "You've made the request?"

"Not just me," I said, and explained that our congressional delegation had intervened on Ohio's behalf.

"Let me make a suggestion, if I may," said Volcker. "Do you know Bob Strauss?" Strauss was chairman of the Democratic Party at that time, and I had met him briefly on several occasions. "Why don't you give him a call?"

As I was leaving the office, Volcker's assistant stopped me. "The chairman asked me to put a call through to Bob Strauss. Do you want to take it here?"

Soon Strauss was on the phone.

"I think I know why you're calling," he told me.

"You know I've got a problem."

He said, "How can I help?"

I explained the situation with Ed Gray. "He's not returning my calls. The chairman thought that you could be helpful."

"Perhaps I can," he said. "Let me talk to Jim Baker. Call me back at one o'clock and see if I've had any luck."

After a quick lunch, I called Strauss. His secretary told me I had a four o'clock appointment with Ed Gray.

I called my congressional colleagues, Mary Rose Oakar and Chalmers Wylie, to ask them to join me. Both wondered how I had managed to get a meeting with Ed Gray. I assumed Strauss had called Baker, who had given Gray his marching orders. When we met him, Ed Gray was solicitous. "What can I do?" he asked. "Just tell me what I can do to help."

I described the situation. "These S&Ls are going to be required to apply for federal insurance. That means making examiners available for expeditious processing. We need to see that these banks reopen as soon as possible."

"Anything you want," said Gray.

At that point he meant it, having been read the riot act.

When I got out of the meeting at 5:15 P.M., I learned that in Columbus the House had passed the emergency legislation. However, the Senate had adjourned to go to a fundraiser across the street and did not plan to come back into session that night. I was furious and called Paul Gillmor, the president of the Senate. "I understand that you're not going to act on this legislation until tomorrow."

"The thing is, Governor," he told me, "we have this very important matter we're taking care of."

"Your important matter is a fundraiser," I said. "I understand that. However, if you don't reconvene by eight o'clock tonight, I will call a special joint session of the legislature tomorrow morning at 9:00 A.M. And I will say the reason I am doing so is the failure of Senate Republicans to act on emergency legislation that has passed the House. I will put your caucus right in the crosshairs."

"Please, Governor," Paul said, "I think we can reconvene. Let me get the Senate together this evening." By 9:00 P.M. the Senate had approved the House bill.

At midnight, home from Washington, I signed legislation that kept the S&Ls closed.

The legislation included a fund that would invest in troubled S&Ls and take back stock as a means of eventually recovering the state investment. Immediately our focus shifted to the orderly reopening of the sixty institutions. Two weeks later I got a late-night phone call from Jan Allen. I was in bed about to turn the lights out.

"Governor," she told me, "we have a problem."

"A problem?" I asked.

"Thomas Battis," she said. Battis was acting superintendent of Ohio's Savings and Loans Division, a quiet lawyer who had been largely missing in action since March 6. "He's approved the reopening of a closed S&L."

I couldn't believe it. "He did what?"

"This savings and loan had, coincidentally, an application pending with Federal Home Loan Bank Board and had been examined. It received expedited approval by the Feds. So Battis gave them permission to open."

"Doesn't he understand this can unleash unreal expectations?" I asked. "How can he do this without calling our office?"

Jan had no answer for that.

"We need someone who understands the bigger picture," I told her.

It wasn't his decision to allow the S&L to reopen that concerned me. It was his insensitivity to the potential impact this could have on the other fifty-nine.

"Jan," I said, "please tell him that all further decisions must be cleared by our office." She said she would make that clear. "And one more thing," I told her. "Find me a new savings and loans leader."

Jan quickly recommended Bob McAllister, one of the lawyers advising her and Ray. McAllister was a well-respected liberal who was also a tough guy, an ex-marine who would not put up with any shit. I gave him a call, "I need you to take this on. It's going to take you away from your lucrative law practice. But you're going to be a key player at a critical time."

"What do you want me to do?" he said.

"I want you to be our savings and loans czar," I said.

Twenty-four hours later I called a press conference and introduced him. He wore a T-shirt he had made overnight. It read: "SAVINGS AND LOANS CZAR." He would replace Battis. His job was to reopen the institutions in a prompt and orderly manner.

McAllister did exactly that. Over the next several months, he focused on two tasks: first, to get these institutions reopened under tougher standards; second, to put in place meaningful changes in the regulatory process to make sure the same sort of thing did not happen again

McAllister was incredible. He got every S&L—both those that were financially sound and those that needed additional capital—open within six months. Some had to reorganize or raise additional capital. One or two were sold to larger institutions.

The case of Home State called for more drastic action. Consequently, out-of-state banks were permitted to bid for what was left of the company under the watchful eye of the conservator. After an extended examination, Chemical Bank presented an offer, apparently unmindful of a provision in the emergency legislation that gave Ohio banks seventy-two hours to match any out-of-state offer. Which was exactly what Provident Bank did.

Walter Shipley, then chairman of Chemical, pitched a fit. He called and berated me, ignoring the fact that I was home in bed nursing kidney stones.

He did not get my sympathy. Nor did he change the outcome.

Not surprisingly, the Republican DA in Cincinnati began an investigation of the Home State debacle, including my relationship with Marvin Warner. He was particularly interested in whether we had given Marvin a free pass. In the end his investigation found nothing—because there was nothing to find.

When the dust settled, only one depositor lost money—Marvin Warner. His bank's investments with ESM far exceeded the state and federal guidelines defining "prudent management," namely 5 percent of deposits. Warner's son-in-law, it turned out, was a senior officer at ESM. Shortly after ESM's bankruptcy, he died by suicide. Warner himself was convicted of nine counts of fraud-related charges and was one of the few savings and loans officers to serve jail time. Warner described himself as "the biggest victim of all."

I never spoke to Marvin Warner after his early morning phone call on March 6. I knew that folks everywhere—in Cincinnati, in Columbus, in Washington—were just waiting for some sign that I had somehow cut him some slack.

In the midst of the savings and loan crisis, Dennis Heffernan got a call from Gene DiAngelo, a mutual friend who ran a local television station (and an active Republican). DiAngelo wanted to bet Dennis $500 that I would lose the next election, no matter who I was running against. Dennis took the bet.

At that moment in 1985, my stay in the governor's residence looked to some like a short one.

Chapter 11

A Second Term and the Presidency

In the final months of my first term, I had occasion to take on the two undisputed heavyweights of Ohio politics. One was Speaker Vern Riffe, who had ruled the Ohio House with an iron fist for more than a decade. In that case, the choice was mine. The other was a rematch against four-time governor Jim Rhodes. In that case the choice to step into the ring was his. Both battles tested the political insights I had absorbed from my mentors and the skills I had honed over the previous decade and a half.

The challenge from Speaker Riffe occurred in 1986 when he took the extraordinary step of personally sponsoring a piece of legislation that would reform tort law. His bill was of keen interest to personal injury lawyers—to put it mildly. Typically, Democrats opposed efforts to change tort law that made it more difficult for ordinary people to sue corporations. However, Vern, who usually worked hard both to keep his caucus in line and to reach across the aisle for support, was determined to pass legislation that the business community wanted—despite opposition from his own labor stalwarts.

Notably this was the only bill I had seen Vern personally sponsor in the nearly twenty years that I had watched him in action. The message was clear: he *expected* this legislation to be enacted into law.

Vern understood, of course, that the bill would upset some Democratic lawmakers and a few Republicans as well. The issue was not a strictly partisan one and the vote was likely to be very close. Early on I opposed the bill as written because it took away protections for ordinary Ohioans who had been physically or economically injured. I explained my concerns to Vern and urged him to modify the bill.

In response, he let me know that he was confident he had the votes to pass the legislation as it stood.

In other words: we were headed for a showdown.

Our confrontation made my advisors nervous. When I said that I was considering a veto, my deputy chief of staff Jan Allen and my campaign director Jerry Austin urged me to reconsider. If I vetoed the bill, argued Jan, the Speaker would make it impossible to get any of our future agenda through the House. Jerry was more blunt: "You *can't* veto this legislation," he told me. "You'll be burning bridges. It's a serious mistake."

I understood their concerns but was unpersuaded. "I only get hurt by this if my veto gets overridden," I said to Jerry. "If the veto stands, Vern will respect it."

Jerry realized my mind was made up and quickly set about identifying and encouraging legislators who would support the veto. The bill passed the House easily with Vern cracking the whip. Then it squeaked through the Senate despite resistance from several senior Republicans.

When the bill landed on my desk, I vetoed it.

The Speaker easily rounded up the two-thirds margin needed to override the veto in his chamber. The veto override then moved to the Senate, where I knew the real battle would be fought. Vern was calling in favors that he had done for senators who had once served with him in the House. The vote was going to be tight. As the override neared the Senate floor, it became clear that a single vote would either uphold—or upend—my veto. That vote belonged to Oliver Ocasek, who was on vacation with his wife in Florida.

I called Oliver personally to say that I really needed his help. As we talked, it was clear that Oliver didn't want to get in Vern's way; the Speaker knew how to tighten the screws. While he could feel Vern's pressure, he was also resentful of his style. I knew Oliver well and genuinely liked him. He was the single most committed supporter of the YMCA Youth in Government program, which had inspired me almost thirty years earlier. As legislators he and I were the two who could be counted on to speak to the YMCA kids when they came to Columbus. I reminded him of that—and how opposition to this bill was the sort of thing that made young people look up to their elected officials.

Oliver acknowledged that I was right but remained reluctant. I was asking him to come back home and stick his hand in a political meat grinder. "This is important," I told him. "Not only for me but for the state. Oliver, I need you to do the right thing."

"I think it *is* probably the right thing," he admitted.

"Look, Oliver," I said, "I'm going to send the state plane down for you. I need you up here to vote."

Ocasek returned and cast his vote. My veto was upheld.

Early the next day Vern called. "So, *podna,*" he said, "what are we going to do now?"

Vern's term of endearment for his friends—*podna*—was the signal. Our relationship more than survived; it had been strengthened by the heat of battle. Vern respected me for winning, and he knew it did not serve him to hold a grudge.

In 1991 Speaker Riffe would offer an extremely complimentary introduction as I gave my farewell address to a joint session of the legislature. Years later as Vern was finishing his memoir and fighting recently diagnosed cancer, he called to ask if I would write the foreword for his book.

"Really," I said, with a laugh, "you want *me* to write the foreword?"

He chuckled and then there was a long pause. "Dick," he said with an earnest tone that I could not miss, "there's no one I respect more than you in the public arena today, and I'd like you to do this."

I understood how deeply he had come to value our relationship, and I appreciated how, in spite of our occasional differences, that relationship had enabled us to work together effectively on behalf of the people of our state.

Jim Rhodes threw his hat in the ring for an incredible fifth time in 1986. He was seventy-seven, but, even at such an advanced age, his unmatched experience and faithful friends in Republican strongholds across the state helped him to a handy primary victory.

Though I was well ahead in early polls I took nothing for granted. After all, Jack Gilligan had been ahead of Jim Rhodes in 1974. Experience had taught me that while it is not always possible to win an election, it is always possible to lose one.

I challenged Rhodes to a debate—an unusual move because incumbent politicians tend to resist giving opponents the exposure of a debate. In this case, however, we were both well-known, and I wanted to contrast age and vigor without having to talk about it directly.

At first Rhodes refused. He had avoided debates in 1974 and 1978, and he seemed determined to do so again. So we wanted to turn his refusal against him. I think it was Jerry Austin, who had a knack for understanding how to get under an opponent's skin, who said, "How about the state fair as a setting?"

Ohio has a hugely popular state fair—we vie with Texas for highest overall attendance—and throughout my first term we brought great performers to play the fair—the Beach Boys; Willie Nelson; and Peter, Paul, and Mary; to name a few. I loved the fair, unlike Jack Gilligan, who knew he had to make an appearance but gave the impression that it made him uncomfortable. I even moved my office to the fairgrounds and made sure to be present at the fair nearly every day.

We decided to use the fair as a lever to get Rhodes to agree to a debate. With the state fair as a backdrop, we filmed a TV spot in which I challenged Rhodes to a debate. "Come on, Jim. Get into the ring," I taunted, standing in an actual show ring at the fairgrounds.

We figured that might hook him—and it did, though the spot alone wasn't responsible. Failing to gain traction with voters as he had in the past, Rhodes and his team came to the conclusion that the debate would be an opportunity to turn things around.

Throughout the reelection campaign, one of my themes was "Promises Made, Promises Kept." I would often say: "I've delivered on every promise Jim Rhodes made."

This was hardly an exaggeration. Many of the initiatives Rhodes had bally-hooed in office—promoting industry, repairing highways, funding new campus facilities—had become hallmarks of my administration. Rhodes had a habit of promising something each time he visited a community. More often than not, those promises proved empty, usually because of budgetary constraints. I made it a point, whenever possible, to turn *his* promises into *my* realities.

One of the most significant examples of keeping a Rhodes promise involved the Honda assembly plant in Marysville. During his final year in office, Rhodes promised $30 million worth of incentives to persuade Honda to build cars in Ohio. When I took office, the Honda people wanted to know where they stood.

They were right to wonder. I had campaigned against Rhodes's commit-ment, arguing that it was wrong to give money to Honda when we had Ford, General Motors, and Chrysler plants in Ohio that needed our help. After I won, it would have made perfect sense if I had decided to renege on Rhodes's promise. In fact, Jim Rhodes had never budgeted for the Honda incentives, and I faced an enormous deficit. Naturally Honda wanted to know: did Rhodes's promise still stand?

"You tell me," I said when the top Honda USA executives called on me in the governor's office. "What is your commitment to Ohio?" Their leader outlined their plan. They would build the assembly plant in eighteen months and hire two thousand people.

I told them I would keep 80 percent of Rhodes's commitment. Some aspects of it I simply could not afford. But I would deliver on most of the incentives that he had pledged. The Honda team kept their side of the bargain, completing the plant in less than 18 months and hiring 2,200 people.

Mr. Honda—who resembled Jim Rhodes, both high school graduates who had grown into remarkable leaders and who shared a love of golf—came to the dedication of that first assembly plant. I stood with him at the ceremony, head and shoulders taller, but impressed by his energy and enthusiasm in his late seventies. After I left, I was told he took time to shake the hand of every Honda associate that day. He was so pleased with our work together that he hosted an Ohio trade mission during which he brought together fifty of his top suppliers. Mr. Honda introduced me warmly and asked me to describe the investment opportunities that existed for them in Ohio. When I was finished, he pitched them on the advantages of coming to Ohio. He concluded in a stern voice, making it clear that he expected them to follow his example.

During my two terms, Honda would eventually build two assembly plants, a transmission plant, and an engine plant in Ohio. Honda employment grew to more than ten thousand. Those ten thousand jobs, in turn, indirectly attracted more than thirty thousand supplier jobs in Ohio.

The Honda story was the most visible example of a Rhodes promise that Governor Celeste kept. Moreover, it was an important reminder that just because elections can bring a change in political leadership, commitments made on behalf of the people of the state should not be abandoned lightly. My test was: "Does it advance the public interest?" rather than "Does it suit my political purpose?"

My much-anticipated—at least in the press—confrontation with Rhodes finally took place in a Cincinnati television studio. It was plain from the outset that Rhodes was off his game. He was neither as vigorous nor as focused as he had been in the past. I sensed that he was aware that he was well behind in the polls at this point. I could think of no other reason for the strange and desperate allegations he lobbed in my direction.

For example, he suggested that my support of a display from Austria at the Ohio State Fair was evidence of collusion with then Austrian president Kurt Waldheim, who had been accused of being a Nazi war criminal. He connected this with Dagmar and implied my being married to an Austrian was somehow un-American.

I acknowledged that I had led a trade mission to Austria. After all, I noted, we had a number of Austrian-owned companies in Ohio, and we were trade partners.

This was neither the first (nor the last) time that an opponent would go after Dagmar. Occasionally even a close associate would counsel me that Dagmar posed a political liability. I never agreed. Like me, Dagmar was prepared to fight for issues we cared about. She was committed to building a constituency for change that would improve the lives of our fellow citizens. She was brilliant, opinionated, and outspoken. And on important issues, ranging from day care to addiction counseling, mental health reform to domestic violence prevention, women's rights to peacemaking, we were on the same wavelength.

What happened—what often happens in public life—is that when people don't like or agree with an elected official, they go after the spouse. We were no exception. Years later I saw this happen with Hillary Clinton and her health-care campaign. People who wanted to take on the president did not have the gumption to tackle him. So they went after Hillary and "her issue" instead.

As Election Day approached, my victory was even clearer than in 1986. I was the incumbent, had the momentum, and most crucially had concrete first-term accomplishments—not the least of which was the successful resolution of the S&L crisis. The newspapers were endorsing me; the polls were trending toward me. Rhodes was no longer the Ohio colossus he had once been.

I never personally criticized Rhodes during the campaign. Incumbents can only win if they effectively tell the story of what they have accomplished. Sometimes candidates running for reelection forget that as an incumbent you need to hammer home the positive case for yourself. When an incumbent spends time attacking the opponent, voters are inclined to believe that he cannot defend his record.

Jim Rhodes and I were political rivals, but over time a genuine respect had grown between us. He had devoted his life to serving the people of Ohio. And he came to realize that I loved Ohio and its people every bit as much as he did.

Election Day is always a bit surreal. The campaign is over. After you've cast your own vote, there's nothing to do until the polls close and vote counts begin to get reported to campaign headquarters. So, on that November Election Day, confident that I was going to be reelected, I called Carolyn Lukensmeyer and asked if I could come over for lunch.

Back in 1982, when I wanted someone to help shape my staff and cabinet members into a coherent team, her name had kept coming up. "Find her," I remember saying. "She sounds like she has the right skills." Lukensmeyer held a doctorate in organizational behavior and had years of corporate experience. Throughout my first term, she organized and ran our cabinet retreats.

Ray Sawyer was stepping down. Carolyn knew the folks who enjoyed my confidence and had a unique perspective on the prevailing group dynamics from the retreats she had facilitated. "We're going to win," I had told her. "I need to find my new chief of staff. Why don't you prepare a list of candidates?"

At our Election Day lunch, she ran through her short list, describing the pros and cons of each. Carolyn had her usual cup of hot water and lemon in front of her on the kitchen table. When she finished she looked at me, trying to read my reaction.

"There's one name missing from your list," I told her.

Carolyn looked alarmed; she took pride in being thorough. "I don't think so," she told me.

I smiled. "That person is you. You're not on the list. And you should be."

All she did at first was stare—genuinely taken aback by the notion that she might step into the role. I was asking her to cross the line from observer into the heart of the action. It would mark a major move into an unaccustomed role. "Think about it," I asked her.

Several hours later the returns began to come in. I had won with 60 percent of the vote. After thanking our fabulous volunteers in Cleveland, my family and I flew to Columbus, this time on the state plane. There we joined a boisterous headquarters gathering where some of my longtime supporters were proudly wearing the "Jim Rhodes, Pack Your Bags" campaign buttons we had created in 1978. Soon after we arrived, Jim Rhodes called to congratulate me. He said with a chuckle, "Now I can get to bed early."

The next morning, Carolyn agreed to become chief of staff.

The reelection victory meant more than I had anticipated. "Wherever you are, Chester Bowles," I remember thinking, "I want you to be proud of this." In retrospect I realized how often I had heard Chet and Steb share the disappointment of his failed reelection campaign. I thought, too, about my predecessors Jack Gilligan and Mike DiSalle, both principled and dedicated Democratic governors who had failed to win reelection.

My reelection brought fulfillment of an ambition that I did not fully recognize until that moment. Finally, a Democratic governor had tackled tough issues—and been reelected.

Though it was a grand celebration, the second inauguration was more re-laxed than the first. For one thing, I had been through it once. Moreover, the circumstances had changed. No former governor shared the podium with me. And Ohio was in a significantly different place. On the day I was first inaugurated—in bone-chilling cold—ten thousand people were lining up less than twenty miles from the statehouse hoping for a job at a newly constructed JCPenney logistics center. Now, in 1986, Ohio was moving in the right direction. We had put people back to work and had weathered the savings and loan crisis. Ohioans felt an optimism lacking four years earlier.

The reelection was a strong affirmation of what we had accomplished to-gether. It was also a unique opportunity. When you are elected at any level of government, the people are reposing trust in you. That trust is a gift that peo-ple give you, but it comes with strings attached. Expectations—sometimes very high expectations—come with that trust. When I felt the thrill and bur-den of that trust the first time, I was frankly awed by it. As I took the oath of office the second time, I was confident, eager to move forward.

I suspect that when Rev. Otis Moss offered a prayer at my first inaugu-ration, I was asking for strength and guidance. When he graced the second inauguration, I was still asking for strength but probably a little less guidance.

I had a clearer sense about what needed to be done.

My ambitions for my second term were far-reaching. We were in the midst of an energetic economic-development agenda, pursuing an aggressive trade-promotion effort, building out a massive highway-improvement program. And other initiatives were in motion—the most far-reaching involved fundamen-tal reform of our mental health system and creation of a statewide addiction-services framework. I was also an active leader in the Great Lakes Governors Association and the Midwest Governors Association. And I was determined to help champion the Rock and Roll Hall of Fame and Museum in Cleveland.

I suspect that lurking somewhere in my mind was also the possibility of another campaign. In 1988 our nation would be choosing a new president. Ronald Reagan would be term-limited. Did a two-term Democrat from Ohio dare to consider a national campaign?

For the moment my focus was much closer to home, in the week after my inauguration—discussing how to encourage a General Motors investment near Dayton, conferring with several Republican congressmen about key highway projects in their districts, flying to New York to discuss the Rock Hall project with Ahmet Ertegun, the chairman of Atlantic Records (who informed me that, if we agreed to use I. M. Pei as the architect, the Rock Hall would come to Cleveland)—and taking my daughters to a Bexley City Council meeting as a school project.

I find it difficult to convey the breadth and depth of my second term. Days were packed with matters large and small. Take just one day from that period selected at random, February 2, 1987. It began at 8:30 with office time reviewing correspondence, press clippings, and legislative plans; at nine, I had a conference call with Ray Sawyer (in his last days as chief of staff) and Helen Williams (who ran my Cleveland office); at 9:30 I sat in on a briefing on agricultural issues; and an hour later Jan Allen and Dora helped me lay out a block schedule (looking down the road four to six weeks). At noon I had lunch with Ray Miller, a member of the Ohio House who started out as a student intern with me when he was at OSU and I was a state rep. At 1:30 I reviewed our agenda addressing women's issues; at 2:30 I met with Ray Ross, a regional director of the UAW—the issue was how to persuade GM to make the aforementioned investment in Moraine (near Dayton); next were back-to-back meetings with the director of Ohio's EPA and my outgoing and incoming development directors on aspects of that Moraine GM deal. By 4:00 P.M. I was flying to Cleveland. I met with Marty Hughes to discuss labor-related issues. At 6:00 P.M. I attended a reception for *Light of Day,* a movie premiering that evening. After a late dinner with Cleveland friends, I flew back to Columbus.

My Day-Timer notes that I was in bed by 12:30 A.M.

The work of governor involved setting priorities (and keeping the team focused on them); developing strategies to achieve those priorities (and constantly tinkering with those strategies in light of changing political realities); building and nurturing relationships—with political colleagues, with civic leaders, with the press, and especially with concerned citizens—to help reach ambitious goals. Some priorities were very challenging; others more modest. They were all important to me—eager to use the freedom from reelection concerns, on the one hand, and with a new sense of urgency, knowing how quickly four years would pass, on the other.

In the very ambitious category was mental health reform. It was the challenge I had handed to Pam Hyde when I recruited her in 1982 and on which she had been working for the past four years. The need for a system capable of functioning in a sensitive and effective way was something that I had experienced firsthand, educated by Peggy O'Reilly and Dagmar. Ohio's approach had long been inefficient and ineffective. I was determined to do something about it.

This was easier said than done.

Pam had been hard at work during my first term. She was proving to be the right person to tackle the complex challenges involved in reforming the delivery of mental health services. She brought to the job a gift—one that she herself perhaps did not realize she had—for leadership in public management and administration. She was comfortable working with outside advocacy groups and winning their trust. Pam was adept at listening and engaging and keeping them involved in the conversation, the thrust of which was to move from very large state-run institutions to more locally-based forms of service delivery and outreach.

While care at the very large state-run institutions had improved somewhat since the enactment of the income tax, in the decades since they had been built, our understanding of mental illness and how to treat it had improved significantly. We had learned that with proper medication and support, mentally ill people could continue to function in community and family settings. Instead of moving those affected into institutional settings, we needed to serve and support them in the communities where they and their families lived.

This community empowerment was my guiding principle for mental health reform. Some of our first changes were simple one-offs. For example, many homeless people had mental health problems. Because they were homeless, it was difficult to get basic monthly entitlements into their hands. To address this problem, Pam and her colleagues developed a system using post office boxes so that, no matter where someone slept, the check would go to their post office box—a simple, straightforward, community-based innovation.

A particularly sensitive challenge was how to reduce our dependence on large state-run hospitals with the support of the workers who were often trying to do their best under difficult circumstances. Ohio had strong public employee unions—as I knew when I supported the passage of the Public Employee Bargaining Act. However much these dedicated workers recognized the value of community-based outreach and care, they were also concerned about the prospect of losing their jobs. If we closed a large institution, five or six hundred state workers might find themselves out of work.

Thus, the challenge was to change the system in a way that included retraining and redirecting people into positions in community-based group homes or another state facility. In 1987 we were finally able to pass comprehensive mental health reform, redirecting a substantial portion of state funding under Pam Hyde's supervision to the county mental health boards.

This marked a dramatic shift—not just in the funds but especially in responsibility. The care for someone with mental illness stayed with people in the communities. It might involve training for the individual, or a group home, or support for the families. The key was that the individual would be cared for and nurtured in the community.

The success Pam Hyde and her colleagues achieved was based on building a strong, diverse constituency for change.

Interestingly, of all the initiatives undertaken by my administration, our community mental health reform has persisted. It has had real staying power despite being perhaps the easiest to reverse.

Some folks criticized me for having "social workers" in the administration—because we had people in key positions who cared deeply about social problems. But the vision I pursued as governor went back to my thinking, as a young man, about high school teaching and its impact on a community. I had always believed that lasting change must begin at the local level. I still do.

By year six of my administration, Pam Hyde had managed to secure most of the reforms we had targeted. It had not been easy. For six of my eight years as governor, Republicans controlled the Senate and Democrats the House. Getting a major initiative required substantial bipartisan support. That strong

Delivering the State of the State Message in 1984

support on both sides of the aisle, nurtured by Pam and her colleagues, is another reason that this reform has lasted to the present day.

Years later when Bill Richardson was elected governor of New Mexico, I called him to offer one piece of advice.

"What's that?" he said.

"Pam Hyde," I told him.

"Who's Pam Hyde?" he said.

"She lives in New Mexico, and she should be in your cabinet." I explained what she had accomplished Ohio.

Richardson appointed her secretary of the New Mexico Human Services Department, a superagency that oversaw all the human services agencies. Since then, he has told me on several occasions that Pam was, without question, the best person in his administration.

Not a surprise.

Pam Hyde was nominated by Pres. Barack Obama and confirmed by the US Senate in November 2009 as administrator of the Substance Abuse and Mental Health Services Administration (SAMHSA), where she served with distinction.

Again, not a surprise.

I suppose I may have begun to think about running for president when I was a kid and first heard my father tell the story of his civics "lesson" back in Monessen. He knew that he'd never be able to hold the office—but that his son could.

I was that son. I understood.

Though many have assumed that my father was pushing me in that direction from the first, the truth is I only began to give a presidential run serious consideration in 1984 when John Glenn was running for president. I traveled to New Hampshire to knock on doors for him and, though I don't remember exactly where I was sent, I found myself canvasing precincts that were heavily Italian American, families whose forebears had come to the United States to work in the marble quarries. I hadn't realized that there was an Italian American community in New Hampshire.

I'd knock on a door and introduce myself, "I'm Richard Celeste."

"Celeste," people would often reply.

"It's actually Cheleste," I would say, pronouncing the hard C at the beginning of my name as one would in Italian.

That would make folks smile. They were proud of their Italian heritage even though they were two or three generations removed from the old country. They respected the fact that an Italian American was involved in public service. Door-knocking in New Hampshire for John Glenn suggested to me that across the country there would be enclaves like those precincts—where I might get traction if I were running for office nationally. I might have to find them by knocking on doors, but I liked knocking on doors. It would be a place to start.

I began weighing more systematically whether to mount a campaign for president. My reelection campaign had been extraordinarily well run. I had defeated an Ohio legend and garnered national and international attention for the successful resolution of the S&L crisis. Some of my most enthusiastic supporters were eager for what they saw as The Big One. The juggernaut that had just won a second term overwhelmingly was ready to go to Iowa and from there onto a national stage. The Celeste team saw Ohio as the key to any presidential victory.

Ohio is a microcosm of the country, and it remains crucial for any candidate to do well here. I felt that if I could go up against top candidates here and win, I could go up against them nationally and win. The big difference was scale—the intensity of scrutiny by the press corps and the amount of money required for a winning campaign. Unlike today, when a candidate has to raise hundreds of millions to be a serious contender, in the late 1980s it required $75–100 million. Still, that was a daunting number then—at least for me.

Jan and I held a monthly "block scheduling meeting," when we would look down the road and set aside chunks of time for certain priorities. For example, if we were dedicating a long-promised bypass in Jackson or I had been invited to keynote a labor convention, we'd slate it in. During a midsummer meeting I asked Jan to block out a week in Iowa and build me a schedule. It would be a chance to take the temperature of the state and its political activists. Could we put together some house parties? Perhaps some of our people had friends or relatives in Iowa. We could see if one or two Democratic county chairs wanted me to come by. Could I visit a plant and meet with union leaders? Talk to a journalist. Thus, Iowa was penciled into my block schedule.

Jan was not surprised. She seemed excited as if she had been expecting it. She arranged a couple of house parties in Iowa, meeting a handful of Democratic activists and being interviewed by David Yepson, the political writer for the *Des Moines Register*. All in all, the trip had a familiar and positive feel. A few months after Iowa, I was asked by a respected congressman to speak at a Columbus Day event in Chicago. I was invited to address the national United Auto Workers Convention. I was dipping my toe into the water. The water felt good.

I don't recall having a good sense of who else might be running. Gary Hart was on the radar as was Fritz Mondale, our candidate in '84. I asked a staffer to prepare a memo assessing who I might face for the nomination. But I was really focused on whether I should run rather than on potential opponents. I never believed that you should run for office because the field seemed weak. You should run because you have a compelling story to tell.

It is no surprise that those of us who succeed in political life have substantial egos, even if we think of ourselves as humble. You must have an extra dose of self-confidence to survive in the rough-and-tumble of the political arena. People will stroke you whether you deserve it or not. And they will flail you—whether you deserve it or not.

I had faced the equivalent of a national crisis with our savings and loans and come out strong. I'd kept most of the commitments I had made when I ran for office—putting Ohioans back to work and reforming vital human services like mental health. Moreover, unlike many presidential hopefuls, I also had genuine foreign policy experience. I had spent four years as a young diplomat in India and had served as director of the Peace Corps. The global map and global issues were not foreign to me.

I felt that I could be a damn good candidate.

Most people assumed that when Gary Hart left the race it presented an opening for me. I drew a different conclusion. That moment made it clear that my own behavior would make me—and my family—vulnerable during a presidential campaign. I could not take any joy from the Gary Hart episode. It sounded a strong cautionary note for me.

The day of my "Gary Hart question" began like any other.

I met with Jan and Debbie, had a budget meeting, and went back to the residence for lunch with the publisher of the *Akron Beacon Journal*. After lunch I spoke briefly to Speaker Riffe and then did an interview with ABC concerning our mental health legislation. I was feeling good at the time because of the progress on our mental health reforms. In fact, leaders of the Robert Wood Johnson Foundation were due in Columbus the next day to recognize Ohio's reform effort. A press briefing was slated to follow the ABC interview at 2:30 P.M.

The press conference focused on mental health—a positive story. As it ended, a Cleveland *Plain Dealer* reporter named Mary Ann Sharkey asked out of the blue: "Do you have a Gary Hart problem?"

I answered simply: "No."

My response should have been "Frankly, Mary Ann, my personal life is just that—personal." Instead, my answer sounded like a denial in response to the question she was really asking: "Are you a womanizer." Yet, even if I had said that my personal life was not public business, I doubt that it would have made a difference. The *Plain Dealer's* story the next day, under a headline about Celeste's womanizing, quoted one woman who was willing to talk among others.

The truth is that the "Gary Hart question" caught me off guard. Mine was an amateur response to a very well-framed question. My assistant press secretary Debbie Phillips quickly stressed that this was going to be a big story.

As soon as I could, I called Dagmar to describe Sharkey's question and my lame response. Dagmar made it clear that she would stand with me. Our answer was that we were committed to our marriage, end of story. People who knew me well probably had a sense that I wasn't a faithful husband, but I honestly felt that it was not public business. This was between my family and me.

By the time I arrived home, Dagmar was, predictably, hurt and angry. For me it was hard because it was painful for the kids and for her. This especially intimate story was something I couldn't deny. The question became how best to preserve privacy for those involved? How could I preserve a semblance of dignity—for my family, especially for Dagmar? And even for the women involved?

I decided to stick to my schedule. By five that evening I was at a reception hosted by the Chamber of Commerce, followed by dinner with my director of commerce.

The next day in Sandusky, Dagmar and I stood in front of a crush of television cameras and said that whatever had happened in our marriage was between the two of us. It had nothing to do with my ability to govern effectively. We told the press we did not intend to talk further about it. Basically, what I should have said in the first place.

A part of me felt relieved. This was a shoe that had to drop. I had fumbled, then found a place where I felt more or less comfortable. I truly believed that whatever I did in my personal life had nothing to do with my work as governor. But this was also a foretaste of what a presidential campaign would be like.

Several of my advisors thought the question wasn't bad, that it was an inoculation of sorts. The story was out, we had dealt with it, and Dagmar had stood by me. Going forward it would be a footnote in my biography, nothing more. They believed it would not undermine my candidacy or campaign. They were ready to go.

I never got to that point in my thinking.

I did not, however, immediately put the brakes on the nascent presidential effort. That took a while. A number of enthusiastic supporters continued working on my behalf to lay out the timeline for a national campaign.

But as we dug deeper into what it would take to be successful, I had a nagging ambivalence. And I had enough campaigns under my belt to know that either I had to find a way to resolve that hesitation or recognize that I did not have a presidential race in me

Within weeks I reached a decision, spoke about it with Dagmar, and then convened my inner circle. It was September 1987 when we gathered at the residence. "Tomorrow," I told them, "I will announce that I won't be running for president."

In addition to the question of my personal behavior, other considerations gave me pause as well.

During my six years in office, I had faced a series of "scandal" stories. Some were justified. Jim Rogers had let me down badly with his criminal behavior. Problems in the Ohio Bureau of Employment Services had gotten out of hand. In the hardball world of politics, Republican prosecutors—federal as well as local—sought to turn any hint of wrongdoing by a state employee into another "Celeste scandal." Often these stories overshadowed our accomplishments.

One example occurred in 1987 when I removed political appointments from the deputy registrar system. Under the Bureau of Motor Vehicles, politically-connected deputy registrars had been responsible for the distribution of license plates and driver's licenses and collecting the fees. By executive order we eliminated politics, improved the system, and held the line on fees. No one noticed.

Our new business plan is still in place thirty years later—and not long ago the *Washington Post* ranked Ohio first in excellence in the nation for the system we instituted.

Still, I worried that my home state newspapers would not go all out on my behalf—making me vulnerable under the scrutiny of out-of-state observers. I was (and am) a strong believer that you have to "own your base." And I felt uneasy about my support among the Ohio newspapers and, more important, our Democratic voters.

Moreover, my appetite for fundraising had diminished. Asking for money on the scale needed to mount a winning national campaign was daunting. Even though, under the tutelage of Milt Wolf and others, I had learned to do it well, I took no pleasure in contemplating the time, energy, and pleading that raising a presidential war chest would entail.

Finally, a successful national effort would come at the expense of my commitment to governing Ohio. My state was big and highly diverse. I still had work to do to advance the ambitious agenda I had laid out in 1982. I knew in my bones that a presidential campaign would require me to devote every ounce of energy and intellect to articulating a compelling vision, to connecting with folks across our sprawling country, and to building a coalition that would make victory—and real change—possible. Ohio would have to take a backseat.

Years later, when Ted Strickland was considering a run for governor of Ohio he asked me to visit him at his congressional office. "Congressmen seldom win statewide races," I pointed out. I had trounced a popular congressman when I ran for governor. Because he had campaigned over the years in four different media markets, including Cincinnati, Columbus, and Youngstown, he felt he was not the typical member of Congress.

"Here's the thing," I said. "Are you ready to eat that chair?" I pointed across the room.

He looked at me, puzzled. "What do you mean?"

"You have to want it so much," I said, "that you have to want to eat that chair. If you're not ready to eat that chair, don't even think about running."

The "chair" is a way of talking about appetite. You have to be that hungry. You have to be ready to give it everything you have. Or don't enter the race. How hungry are you for the job?

The fact was I was not prepared to eat the chair.

I have come to understand as I have tried to answer the question "Why did you not run for president?" that I have not been completely honest with myself—or others for that matter. I felt as prepared by education, mentoring, and experience as anyone could be. I was also confident I understood and could meet the challenges of the job. In most of the ways that mattered, I felt poised and ready to seek the presidency. My whole life—my education, my business involvement and public service, my range of travel and life experience, my role models, and my faith—all had prepared me for a successful campaign. In my heart, I felt called to serve as president of the United States.

I knew my family and friends expected it of me.

Only now do I realize that, though the thought process I have described above is accurate, it is not the whole truth. In my first race for statewide office, I needed to begin by winning one vote—that of Jack Gilligan, my sitting Democratic governor. Now, contemplating a race for president, I needed to win just one vote at the outset—my own.

And in the end, I could not vote for myself. I felt morally compromised.

In early 1987, when the Gary Hart question was asked of me, I had been involved with a number of women. My infidelities had become a severe burden on my marriage. Dagmar had chosen to accept an unfaithful husband in return for a commitment to our family first. It was an unusual and, in many ways, unhealthy bargain for both of us.

Sitting in our family circle at my father's eightieth birthday party in Key West, we had talked about a presidential race. Many views were expressed. But Dagmar posed the most telling question: "Can you pass the character question?" It was one of many questions raised for my consideration but not resolved that March night in early 1987.

As was often the case, Dagmar was right on target. In my heart of hearts, I believed that I had failed a deeply personal test of character.

Years later I came to describe myself as someone who was more honest in my public life than I was in my private life. That dichotomy, I now see, led me to cast a no vote before the Celeste for president campaign got out of the starting blocks.

Only years later did I feel that my personal life was sufficiently in order to pursue a presidency—just not the one that Frank Celeste had in mind.

In early October 1988, I was in Lakewood, getting ready for an upcoming "Capital for a Day" several weeks off. In the evening I picked up Mom and Dad for our usual dinner at Mahall's Bowling Lanes. While we were eating, my father told us that he had an appointment with a doctor at the Cleveland Clinic. I sensed immediately that something was wrong. Frank Celeste was the sort of person who would do anything to avoid visiting the doctor's office. "Something's bothering me," he said. "I just want to have it checked out."

I was worried but said nothing.

Following tests at the Cleveland Clinic, Dad called me to say that the doctors had diagnosed colon cancer. He would need surgery. Soon.

On the day of his surgery, the family gathered at the clinic. When the operation was over, his doctor came out to tell us that Dad was in the post-op recovery room. My mother and sister went to see him, but, as Ted and I were following, the doctor took us aside. He told us that while he had been able to get the cancer in our father's colon, it had metastasized throughout his abdomen. The doctor thought that he might survive a few months but not long.

Ted and I stood, stunned. Neither of us knew what to say.

"If you were to ask me about course of treatment," said the doctor, "my answer would be nothing aggressive. He should just enjoy the time he has."

We stood there for a long moment trying to process the dire news. It slowly dawned on us that Ted and I would have to tell him. We joined Mom and Pat with Dad in the recovery room and were surprised to find him looking cheerful. He was sitting up in bed relieved that he had come through the surgery. We stayed an hour or so, told him we loved him, and said we would be back in the morning.

That night was one of the worst I have ever experienced as I struggled with the knowledge of the devastating news we would have to share with him. Ted and I went early the next day to talk with him. When he saw his sons walk in, he knew that something was wrong. I think we both winced when we saw how he braced himself for what we were about to say.

"The cancer has spread, Dad," I heard myself say. "There's nothing to be done. You may have a couple of months."

Then Ted: "The doctor says the best thing is to make the most of the time you have."

His face fell. It was like we had hit him with a sledgehammer. He was not expecting a death sentence. Looking at him in that hospital bed, I realized that I had never seen my father discouraged. Not ever. He had been through losing political campaigns and financial setbacks, but he had always been optimistic and upbeat. This was different. The last thing he was prepared to hear was that he was dying.

I watched him retreat into himself.

The Friday before Lakewood's Capital for a Day I got a call saying that Dad had collapsed in the bathroom. They didn't know if he had slipped or fainted. By the time I arrived in Cleveland, he was comatose in intensive care. Doctors kept him alive, hoping for signs of improvement. Machines flushed his kidneys and did his breathing for him as we waited for his body by some miracle to start working again. Technology sustained him for five days. But he never came out of the coma. Finally, after a conversation among the doctors, Mom, and us kids, a nurse turned off the life support. My father died three hours later at 10:40 A.M. on November 9.

Capital for a Day, in the community where my father had been a beloved mayor, was scheduled to start that very afternoon. I had to decide whether to go through with it. In the end we decided that Frank Celeste would want us to proceed.

And so we did—as a celebration of his life! Over and over during the events of the next thirty-six hours I was reminded of the lives he had touched as people came up to offer their sympathy. Somehow, I carried his presence with me as we met in a building that he had dedicated and engaged with community that he loved.

Not long before he died—when he must have sensed that something was wrong—my father took me to the verbal woodshed. "You have been extremely

Presenting the proclamation designating Lakewood as Capital for the Day to Mayor Tony Sinagra, the day after my father passed away

tough on your brother," he said. I had kept Ted at a distance and never let him consider bidding for business with the state, despite the fact that his company might have worked productively with the Department of Natural Resources. "There were just too many pitfalls there," I tried to explain. But my father just shook his head. Dad had favored me in so many ways. He also understood that Ted was quietly frustrated and hurt by the barriers I had erected.

"You have to do something for Ted," he told me. "And I'll tell you what you should do. Make him a trustee of Ohio State University." Without hesitation I said, "You are right—and I will." One of the greatest honors a governor could offer an Ohioan was a seat on the OSU Board.

Not long after this conversation with my father, a major donor began to make noises about wanting to be appointed. I avoided him until I found him waiting for me one night at the airport in Columbus, where we based the state plane. He was waiting to ambush me, armed with a rendering of the $30 million building he intended to build for the university. He said that if he didn't get the appointment that he wasn't sure he would go ahead with the building.

"I'm sorry," I said and told him how much I appreciated his love of the institution. I explained, "I've already made a commitment."

He was not the sort of person who took no for an answer. So he pled his case with Vern Riffe, who then reached out to me. "He talked to me and described what he was prepared to do," said Vern. "I think you should seriously consider it."

"I'm going to tell only *you* this," I said to Vern. "The reason I can't appoint him is because my father asked me to promise him I would appoint Ted. I intend to keep that promise."

"I don't need to hear any more," said Vern. "I agree that's what you should do."

After all, his father, the mayor of New Boston, had been a good friend of my father, the mayor of Lakewood. Vern understood my commitment completely. Several years passed and the man in question gave OSU the money for the building. But he never became an Ohio State trustee.

Among my most committed supporters when I was considering a run for the presidency were my sons Eric and Christopher. As they were coming to grips with my decision not to run, the two took me aside and reminded me that for them it had never been an issue of working simply to get Dick Celeste elected. Our work—an effort in which they had been a key part in recent years—had been to build a constituency for change.

While they accepted my decision not to run, they insisted I had a special obligation to keep young people involved in the political process. This had been an important aspect of our political work from the beginning. They said: "You have a responsibility to find a vehicle to continue to do that even if you aren't a candidate yourself."

We began talking about what such an effort might look like. Eventually we hit on the notion of creating a different kind of political action committee, or PAC. Rather than giving money to political aspirants, we would "contribute" people. We would contribute carefully selected and well-trained young people to work with key campaigns across the country. We called it "Participation 2000."

The core idea grew out of the involvement of youthful volunteers in each of my campaigns. With "Part 2"—as it came to be known—in each election cycle we recruited talented and eager individuals, put them through a campaign "boot camp," then paid them a stipend to work for progressive Democratic candidates. In many of these races—usually down-ticket candidates—the Participation 2000 person was the only full-time staffer on the campaign.

These young staffers often made a difference. Four or five members of congress today benefited from Participation 2000 staffers in their early contests.

There were local government officials and state legislators who were in some measure successful because of our help.

The challenge for Participation 2000—as with any political effort that does not have a sitting officeholder to champion it—was raising operating funds. Our pitch was that for a modest amount of money we could train dozens of people and deploy them in key races around the country. We'd be honing the activism of young people as well as developing the infrastructure necessary to elect change-oriented candidates.

When I left office, I passed the leadership of Participation 2000 to Sen. Bill Bradley and then Ann Richards, who continued to keep it going for a handful of years. Today there are fifty or sixty highly skilled political campaign operatives who got their start with Part 2. As short-lived as it was, Participation 2000 made—and continues to make—a significant impact.

Its core principle—contributing people rather than money—remains highly relevant today. In fact, in an era where Super PACs and dark money have flooded the political arena, I have often wondered how to reignite the spirit of Part 2.

The most high-profile initiatives of my final year in office involved actions I took to commute the sentences of women and men who had been convicted of murder.

In mid-1987 two sociologists from Ohio State came to see me to discuss an in-depth study they had conducted at Ohio's prison for women in Marysville, examining the relationship between abuse and criminal conduct. They had concluded that the vast majority of the more than five hundred women incarcerated there had been abused in their youth and, in some cases, that abuse directly contributed to the crime for which they were imprisoned. This was especially true of the more than one hundred women serving lengthy sentences for murder.

Moved by their presentation and understanding the urgency of the situation, I asked them to work with the prison staff to identify specific cases where battered woman syndrome might account for their violent act and to encourage these women to seek treatment for the abuse and to apply for a commutation of their sentences. Over the next year more than one hundred women participated in the review and follow-up group work addressing the abuse they had experienced. At the time these women were in court, Ohio law precluded them from offering evidence of battered woman syndrome as a defense. I explained that I would consider commuting sentences to three years or time served when the women met several criteria: evidence of actual

abuse (hospital visits, domestic abuse reports, etc.) and successful comple-
tion of the abuse counseling in prison.

Over Thanksgiving weekend in 1990 I read 106 files, most of them brutal
and heart-wrenching. In the end I divided the women into three groups—
twenty-five cases where I felt I could commute with confidence, thirty-two
where I felt more evidence was needed to confirm that they had been abused
before a commutation, and finally, cases that seemed unconvincing. When
I commuted sentences, I required each woman to do at least 250 hours of
community service with battered women.

The files told grim stories. One woman had been sexually abused by her
grandfather since she was eleven. At the age of sixteen she came home from
school to discover that the grandfather had begun to abuse her younger sister as well. That very night she nailed the door of her grandfather's bedroom
closed, poured gasoline on the floor, and burned him to death. Another, a mid-
dle-aged, middle-class woman with two young children, who had been physically abused by her husband for two decades, came home from work to find
her husband beating their nine-year-old son. As she began to drive away with
her son, she saw her husband dangling their three-year-old daughter from the
second-story window threatening to drop the girl if she left. She returned and
was beaten. That night she shot him in the head as he was sleeping. Then another story. And another.

As I was weighing commutations for these women, the Ohio General Assembly passed legislation to allow evidence of battered woman syndrome in
cases in which the accused had killed an alleged abuser. Noteworthy is the
fact that only one of the twenty-five women whose sentences I commuted
returned to prison—for a drug-related crime—in the thirty years since those
commutations. These women defied the usual statistics on recidivism.

As I was finishing my review of the women in Marysville, I received a
request from Ohio's public defender to issue a blanket commutation for the
hundred-plus inmates on death row. I resisted the request for a blanket commutation and instead asked her to identify the ten or fifteen cases first in line
for execution. After reading those case files, I decided to commute the death
sentences of four men and four women (the only women on death row). In
most cases I commuted the sentences to life without parole; in the case of
one women—also severely abused—I commuted her sentence to life (which
allowed the possibility for parole).

My decisions were not based on a belief that these individuals were innocent; most if not all probably were guilty. Rather, I concluded as I read their
files that I was called to exercise mercy on behalf of the people of Ohio. Many

years later I explained to a group of aspiring lawyers my sense that the notion of executive clemency was meant not only to give the executive the authority to act in cases where new facts suggested that a condemned person was innocent but also to permit the executive to offer an expression of the deepest values of the citizens of the state.

As I have observed often in these pages, I look back infrequently—if ever. I have very few regrets. But I do regret that I did not commute the sentences of all death row inmates. The most compelling reason was the racial disparity on death row. Nearly half of those serving death sentences at that time were African American even though only 12 percent of Ohioans were Black. Moreover, out of 88 counties, one—Hamilton County (which included the city of Cincinnati)—accounted for more than 20 percent of the men on death row and three of the four women. Perhaps somewhere in the back of my mind was the thought that I might one day want to run for office again and so I played it safe. My rationale at the time was that a blanket commutation would elicit a backlash that might lead to greater reliance on the death penalty.

But I should have replaced death row with life without parole.

I regret my failure to do so.

Pari Sabety came to my attention through Citizen Action. She joined my administration early in my second term as an economic policy advisor and impressed me immediately. Pari, a Bryn Mawr alum and CPA, was smart and tough, two qualities I valued highly. And she brought high energy and a ready sense of humor to any task.

In early 1988 we had an issue involving the Chrysler plant in Toledo, the factory where the original Jeeps were built. The Toledo mayor had called me urgently saying that Chrysler was threatening to shut the plant if they didn't get $30 million of incentives and relief from environmental regulations. He needed our help.

"I will take a personal interest in this," I said and asked if he had a group of people working on the negotiations. I told him I would send someone who would represent me for those talks.

My representative was Pari Sabety.

Before she headed to Toledo, I took Pari aside and gave her my take on the situation. The mayor is going to do everything he can to make nice to Chrysler, I told her, and we have to help him with the money. As for you, I said, I want you to be tough and kick the shit out of the company on behalf of the state. Ask why we would change our environmental regulations just because one car company wanted a favor? "Here's the deal," I told her. "You can go up to $15 million for job training, but only if they invest in new equipment to keep the plant open. That is the only investment we are going to make. And no easing up on environmental enforcement."

With a grin, Pari said she understood. I think she relished the role of bad cop.

After lengthy and sometimes acrimonious negotiations, an agreement was reached. I was not surprised; I felt that Chrysler was going to have a hard time walking away from their history. I joined Pari in Toledo for the press conference to announce the deal. One of Chrysler's senior vice presidents was there. The mayor was full of praise for Chrysler's investment decision and for the State of Ohio for having assisted with funding.

The Chrysler guy made a statement about the mayor's support and about how much they valued the help from the governor's office. When he sat down beside me, he said, "You are a son of a bitch."

I asked him what he was talking about.

"I thought that you were sending us someone who would be nice to work with," he said. "That woman is the toughest person I've ever met"—describing Pari Sabety.

I said that was true.

"I want to hire her," he said.

"You can't," I told him.

"What do you mean, I can't?"

"She and I are setting up a company together when I leave office in a few months," I told him.

Stepping away from politics was a daunting experience.

I loved being governor. Throughout everything—including the crises, the "scandals," the everyday trials and tribulations—I relished every day on the job. Absolutely. My decision to retire from politics meant not just no longer serving in public office but also leaving behind the intense excitement that came from anticipating the next campaign. I would remain active politically—I'd be closely involved in Participation 2000, for example—but it wouldn't be the same.

No more days like April 2, 1988, to choose another at random: Tennis with friends at 7:00 A.M.; Art View at 9:30 after a quick shower and breakfast; meeting with Senate leadership at 10:30; 11:30, John Meeks and the execs from the Hoover Company; noon, lunch with Lukensmeyer; 1:15, shoot a video for the Columbus Chamber of Commerce; 1:30, welcome Sen. Jose Richa from our sister state in Brazil; 2:00 P.M., remarks at an Ohio Consumers Council gathering;

2:30 (I'm a bit late), a block scheduling meeting; 3:30, John Mahaney, the head honcho of the Ohio Retail Merchants drops by to trade political intelligence; 3:30, Max Guttman; 4:00 P.M., Dick Brennan and Pat Donnelly from Cleveland; 4:30, Warren Tyler with Carolyn. At 5:30, I fly to Cleveland to meet with Bob Horton, CEO of British Petroleum. Our agenda includes fundraising for the Rock Hall, strategies to build a new baseball stadium for the Indians (who are threatening to leave town), what to do about Cleveland schools, and plans for a postgubernatorial visit to London and BP's home office. At 9:00 P.M., we were wheels-up on our way back to Columbus. I was home early at 10:15.

Recounting this day, I am reminded of the biggest perk I missed when I left the governor's office. It was not my desk or the residence, not the security detail or the quick seating at a restaurant. It was the state plane that enabled me to get into every nook and cranny in Ohio—and still be home to sleep in my own bed.

The reality is that as soon as you're not in office, you're history. No plane is waiting for your next trip.

Starting a few months before I was due to leave office, I began thinking systematically about what might be next. Upon reflection, I realized that I had a desire to take a leadership position in a large corporation. It seemed to me that my experience as governor had prepared me for such a role. Therefore, I set up a series of conversations with the top person at each of the nation's five largest executive search firms. These guys each listened carefully as I outlined the range of responsibilities and decision making I had engaged in as governor. Then at the conclusion of each meeting I was politely and firmly discouraged. That was it. The only place where they could imagine a politician in the corporate landscape was in government relations—or lobbying. That was not what I had in mind.

So Pari and I talked about what we might do together. I had a lot of confidence in her, and several people who had supported me politically were willing to invest in our new consulting firm. That said, I did not have a clear idea of what was to come next.

Mostly it was like falling off the edge of the planet.

The phone stops ringing, familiar faces disappear, crowded calendars yield to wide-open spaces. Fortunately, Dora was still with me. But that was it—and very quickly it became clear that the unifying theme of most of my adult life had come to an end.

Was I worried? Not a lot. Partly because I've never been one to worry. And also because I was fairly confident that something would present itself.

Four Ohio governors meet for a discussion about state politics that aired on Ohio's PBS stations. *Left to right:* Gov. George Voinovich, former governors Richard Celeste, James Rhodes, and John Gilligan.

Perhaps some part of me understood that the real challenge that lay ahead had to do with beginning to address my personal life.

The last task as governor is deciding what to do with your papers. What do you keep? What do you send to the Ohio Historical Society? And what do you send to the dump? While I understood the impulse to send everything to the dump, it was not what I was going to do. As a student of history, I felt that I needed to allow access to my archive. So Dora and Jan helped me plow through our massive collection of files and decide what was really personal, what was irrelevant, and what to give to the archive.

A lot of it was correspondence. One letter was from a family in Mobile, Alabama, saying that they had driven through Ohio after spending a vacation in Detroit. With four kids, they had to stop a number of times in our state and had found that the Ohio rest stops were the very best in the United States of America. "We just thought you should know," said the letter.

"Dora," I said, "I think I'll keep this."

Chapter 12

Private Life and Other Unexpected Destinations

The newly formed firm of Celeste and Sabety was an economic development consultancy focused on two areas: The first involved working with communities undergoing transitions because of plant closing, defense downsizing, or other forms of economic trauma. I had seen this frequently in Ohio, and we had a good record of turning things around.

Our second focus was on facilitating international trade and investment, another aspect in which I had been active and successful as governor. While in office I led trade missions to a number of countries in Asia (including India), Africa, and Europe and had brokered significant agreements on behalf of Ohio companies and several large multinationals.

Now with my Celeste and Sabety hat, I went back to folks with whom I had built relationships to see whether we might work together again. I learned that drumming up business in this fashion was hard work. In time, however, we developed a solid client list—from California to Long Island. But it required sustained effort by me and Pari.

I still have folios filled with the business cards of the people and companies I called on. I went literally around the world drumming up business: Moscow, Prague, Hong Kong, and Manila among my early stops. Looking at my calendars from that period, I was logging more miles than a presidential candidate—both inside and outside the country.

A good example of my "prospecting" involved the trip I made to the Soviet Union in 1991—as a follow-up to a conference on defense downsizing that I had hosted as governor the previous year. Though Ohio may not be the first state that people identify with the defense industry, many Ohio firms were suppliers to the major defense contractors and had to bear the burden of any

With a trade mission from Senegal visiting the governor's residence in 1987

spending cuts. Our conference attracted more than 250 businesspeople and featured the Soviet ambassador to the United States.

Word that the governor of Ohio was interested in defense conversion must have made it back to Moscow at a time when Gorbachev was dramatically cutting his defense budget. As a result, I was invited for a workshop there. I arrived in early April 1991 on the day the Supreme Soviet voted to end the constitutional provision that gave exclusive power to the Communist Party. I watched the debate on CNN, marveling at the fact that a camera in the Kremlin about a mile away was sending a signal to Atlanta by satellite, and then back to me in Moscow. While I watched, CNN switched their Moscow coverage to South Africa to show Nelson Mandela walking through the gates of the Robin Island prison, a free man.

The historian in me was in awe at this extraordinary confluence of events— neither of which would have been predicted just a few years earlier.

The following Sunday, my Russian hosts escorted me and my interpreter, Rita Agrachev, to a huge defense research and development facility. It was eerily deserted that weekend. As we entered the executive office, I noticed a red phone that I imagined served for direct calls from the Kremlin. In a large conference room, the top brass had assembled to meet with me.

Sixteen senior R&D engineers were gathered, eager to talk about how they might "commercialize" the until-then largely secret projects they were working on. One after another, each described his particular effort. I recall one project that involved high-resolution satellite cameras capable of detailed soil analysis. Could they capture data from space to guide the tractors of American farmers in order to match fertilizer to specific soil conditions?

After each presentation, I would ask about cost. This question stumped them. They had no idea about the cost involved to produce a specific product. Finally, the last man began with a smile on his face: "I know what my idea costs," making a stab at it.

When it was my turn to respond, I said that, if they were serious about turning their military research into commercial products, they first needed to identify the market for those products. Beyond developing a product, they needed to establish the price they would need in order to recover their costs and make a profit. This was Econ 101—but it was all new to them. If the price is higher than the cost, I observed, you have an incentive to go forward. But if the cost is higher than what the market will support, you have a nonstarter.

This extraordinary exchange went on for almost eight hours, with a brief timeout for food.

Returning to Columbus, I reached out to folks at Battelle Memorial Institute, one of the nation's largest not-for-profit R&D organizations, headquartered there. They have worked for both private companies and government agencies on everything from nuclear technology to the barcode. I suggested that, if they could establish a base in Moscow working with this Russian counterpart, the collaboration might yield significant results. In the end Battelle was not confident how the cost of such an effort might pay off.

That was one of our early business development efforts that did not pay off for the firm.

Another example of work that had its beginnings during my time in office occurred when Pari was asked if we would do a study of the Honda-supplier relationship to address the prevailing view that Honda was only working with Japanese firms. Honda had very demanding supplier requirements in terms of quality, cost, and timely delivery. It was a challenge for domestic parts makers to meet these requirements, but Honda had begun a program to help American companies do so. Honda wanted us to study the impact of this effort to determine if the program was successful and, if so, how to tell that story well.

To provide answers, Pari and I interviewed a number of Ohio-based manufacturers who were either successfully suppling parts to Honda or who were trying but had not yet won Honda's business.

We discovered that Honda's program to help American suppliers meet their high standards had not only enabled many to win business with Honda but also enhanced their performance for US cars manufacturers. For example, a firm making brake pads and selling them to Honda would use the refinements they had learned to improve products and processes for Ford and Chevy as well. Our study helped Honda explain how its presence in Ohio had lifted the competitiveness of the whole supply chain.

Celeste and Sabety's two biggest projects were on opposite coasts. The first was on Long Island where the Grumman Aircraft Engineering Company, the largest employer in the region, was shutting down. In the wake of this news, the Long Island Association, the local business advocacy group, hired C&S to do an analysis of where the prospects of future job growth lay. We interviewed business and labor leaders and heads of higher education and advanced research institutions. Ultimately our report focused on the world-class work at the Brookhaven National Laboratory and capabilities at the nearby universities where we believed the most promising areas for innovation were based. Our detailed report provided insights that guided the strategies the Long Island Association used to attract new investments into their communities.

By far the most significant project that we undertook came as a result of a call from Chris Coburn, who had been a deputy director in the Ohio Department of Development and my informal advisor on science and technology. Chris had taken a position at the aforementioned Battelle. There he spotted a request for proposal from a group of California business leaders—a modest $150,000 project to analyze where California could become most competitive in the next decade. It was funded by fifteen corporations concerned about how defense downsizing might impact them.

Chris and I flew to LA for a preliminary discussion with the two CEO's cochairing the business group. We pitched them on our ability to do the job they had in mind. Battelle had a solid business analytics and development reputation; C&S was strong in research and public policy. After laying out our case, I asked: "Gentlemen, can I be completely honest with you? As governor of Ohio, undertaking a project of this scope and wanting it done right, I would expect to invest at least a million dollars and take a year to get it completed. I believe that you should expect more than a standard boilerplate report. You will need in-depth analysis, specific recommendations, and the action steps required to accomplish those recommendations. Frankly, I believe that, instead of six months and $150,000, you should expect to invest at least $1.5 million and a year to eighteen months."

They were clearly taken aback. But they said that they welcomed my candor.

Fact is, I felt that this project was a long shot for us. A number of big-name consulting firms would be bidding on this RFP. But I also thought their proposals were likely to come across as boilerplate—bits and pieces of previous work with a fancy cover. It comes cheap—and it sits on a shelf somewhere gathering dust.

Going in, Chris and I knew that we didn't have the reputation to match these outfits. If we were going to win this contract, we had to change the rules of the game—just the way I had approached winning an election. We put together our best team, told the Californians what we would do, how long it would take, and how much it would cost (not the offered $150,000 but $1.5 million). We brought in the Boston Consulting Group to work with Battelle on the analytics. And we brought in Tom Suddes, a Columbus-based fundraiser.

Not only would we identify the best opportunities for economic growth, we would provide an action agenda and help them get that agenda moving. And we would help raise the additional funds to do the job right. If they offered us the job for $150,000, we would turn it down. Late that afternoon we were told that we had won the business—and Project California was born.

For the next two years, that work became the central focus of Celeste and Sabety. We began by evaluating the considerable educational and research strengths of the state as well as potential spin-off technologies of California's defense industry. At the same time, Suddes went to each of the corporations that had pledged an initial $10,000, explaining that, to do this project right, they would have to raise their commitment to $100,000. "That's just fifty thousand a year, two years," he would tell them. "It's a tiny bit of your annual budget but huge for the future of California." Fourteen of the fifteen came up with the funds on the spot.

We eventually identified two key opportunities: advanced transportation and alternative energy. In connection with advanced transportation, for instance, we pointed out that Lockheed and others had developed sensors and smart cards that could manage toll systems, reduce gridlock, and improve highway safety. A simple suggestion for how emerging technologies would provide new business opportunities—and enhanced public service—in this area.

In alternative energy we described opportunities presented by solar cells and other emerging fuel sources. California's regulatory agencies could speed innovation through thoughtful rule-making. When we completed our analysis, we provided a report that outlined our examination of seven key industries, suggesting that California could become a global leader in each. And we identified five or six actions that the governor and the state assembly should take to spur this development.

The cochairs of Project California made an appointment with Gov. Pete Wilson so that we could present our findings to him. Over the course of an hour, he asked few questions, and it was not clear that he understood what we were recommending. I was told not to worry by one of the CEOs as we left the meeting: "We'll deliver the governor."

I suggested that we should also meet with the Speaker of the House, which seemed, for them, like saying we should meet with the man in the moon. Since they did not really have a relationship Willie Brown, a plainspoken Democrat, I arranged an appointment. Sitting with the Speaker, we got the opposite of the governor's lukewarm response. Brown grasped the significance of our recommendations enthusiastically. "Look," he told us, "you tell me what I need to do to move this agenda, and I'll move it."

Our CEOs were clearly impressed.

While I was globetrotting for Celeste and Sabety, I was also saying yes to a variety of corporate board work. I did this for a number of reasons, not the least of which was a desire to build some financial security for my family. Also, I think that I was anxious about not having enough to do. As governor I had kept up a demanding pace. In this transition from office, I felt the need to cram things in, to keep busy. I added one board after another: Navistar and HealthSouth to go with the Government-University-Industry Research Roundtable, the Carnegie Corporation of New York, Habitat for Humanity International.

The main responsibility of a corporate board member is to provide thoughtful and independent advice, especially when you see something you believe ill-conceived about to happen. I discovered that corporate boards tended to be populated by men (yes, a few women) who shared considerable cross-board membership. For example, a number of the Navistar board members sat on other boards or belonged to clubs together. Consequently, they seemed reluctant to call out a colleague's bad idea.

But I didn't belong to those clubs. Frankly, I found that political life made me more candid. When someone encouraged you to do something stupid in politics, you knew you would eventually have to defend it. You became comfortable with debate and disagreement.

I learned in my early days as a state legislator the value of posing an "innocent" question. I became convinced that posing a thoughtful or timely question was an essential skill that a leader needed to cultivate. The right question could challenge people's assumptions or get them thinking in a fresh direction.

I found that probing questions were as important for not-for-profit boards as for corporate boards. Just because we were doing something good didn't mean that we were doing it well. We needed to ask, "Why are we proposing to do this? Is it consistent with our mission?"

I often joke that governors are a mile wide and an inch deep—and that our specialization is "data-free research." In fact, governors are constantly learning—about prisons and universities, about early childhood education and services for the elderly or the addicted, about highways and dams, about lotteries and workers' comp insurance. And about the often uneasy relationship between the federal government and the states.

From the standpoint of my family's finances, the transition from the governor's office was a positive one. Positive but not easy. It required considerable time on the road. Usually, I aimed for day trips so that I would be home in the evening. I felt a bit like a pinball. But, whenever I could, I would head up to Kelleys Island. The house there was my refuge—a place to relax and step back from everything. I would work on one of the chores awaiting me or go fishing with my buddy Jake Martin. Sometimes Dagmar would come with me, sometimes one of the children or a friend.

Most of the time, though, I went alone.

Few people believed my repeated assertions that I had left politics for good, especially in the years just after I left office. Some even tried to persuade me to run again. But I had given it careful thought as my second term was coming to its conclusion. In 1990 I put together a list of the pros and cons regarding a political future.

Yes to politics:
- Excellent at it
- Enjoy the people
- Can make a difference
- Unfulfilled ambition

No to politics:
- More to life than politics
- Hard on family (Dagi?)
- Asking people for money

- Step out at the top of your game
- Can think, speak, and write more honestly
- Can learn about myself and life

This list is followed by a series of questions:

- What do I want to be remembered for? By whom?
- Do I want to live in some other place? Is the next stage one of reaching far, or digging deep—or is that a false dichotomy?
- Can I develop a reading list with books that Dagi recommends, plus one from each of the kids?
- Can I learn German and plan to spend at least three months a year in Vienna?

And in smaller print, near the bottom of the page: "What happens to Dora?"

My decision at the end of this exercise was to step away from the life I had embraced—and loved—for two decades, the life of an elected public official. My interest in politics and public service had not diminished. But I would try to feed that interest without the demands of seeking and holding public office. I was proud of what I achieved in the political arena—working with an extraordinary circle of support. Now I wanted to encourage a new generation of leadership and service.

Stepping back into private life would provide a transition deeper and more sweeping than I realized as I penned the note about "learning about myself and life."

December 1992 found Dagmar, the kids, and me in Hilton Head, where we were attending our third Renaissance weekend. Renaissance weekends began modestly with Phil and Linda Lader inviting a small group of friends for a reflective welcome to the New Year as an alternative to the often too-boozy, too-frenzied occasion that it had become. The Laders welcomed an intimate gathering of friends—with children—to share personal thoughts about a series of topics and issues and to welcome in the New Year.

The weekend was a hit, and it grew into a more expansive undertaking. Bill and Hillary had joined early on. And early members were encouraged to invite others they thought would contribute to and benefit from the experience. Bill Clinton began urging us to attend in the late 1980s. I resisted at first; it seemed like an imposition during the Christmas holidays. But to be honest, it was hard to say no to Bill—so we began attending.

We had to haul our carful from Columbus to Hilton Head, and, after initial resistance, our children became enthusiastic participants. If you took a look at the 1991 program, you would see that each of the Celeste children participated on various panels—along with Dagmar and me. That was a defining characteristic of a Renaissance weekend: everyone is expected to participate.

On the last day of 1992 we witnessed a remarkable dialogue on governance between Bill Clinton, the president-elect, and Supreme Court Justice Harry Blackmun. The two discussed the challenges facing the country from two distinctive and thoughtful perspectives. The next day Hillary gave an impromptu talk about her experiences on the campaign trail. She spoke with candor and insight. She was spunky and funny—someone who had spent many years campaigning, had lost none of her enthusiasm or respect for the democratic process, and yet was uniquely able to capture the lows and the highs of a demanding race. Hillary was always very protective of her family, no matter how thrust into the center stage of politics they might have been. That Renaissance Weekend we saw a very different Hillary than did most Americans.

Looking back to my observation of her then, as her husband was about to take office, I am struck by the degree to which the experience of being governor and first lady of Arkansas had not readied them for the pervasive scrutiny to which they were about to be subjected in the nation's capital.

In DC, the Clintons were unprepared for the unrelenting pressure from the press. I know Hillary felt that their family deserved some "zone of privacy." Instead, she found not one square meter of such a zone. Perhaps reporters in Little Rock had cut them some slack. Not in Washington. My hunch is that her hankering for a zone of privacy led her, years later, to use a private email server.

Listening to Hillary speak on New Year's Day in 1993, I said to myself that this woman was as capable as her husband. While she lacked his charm, she certainly matched his brilliance. As someone who had given careful thought to running for president myself, I recognized an individual who had what it takes.

Like all attendees, I was on a panel myself. In a supreme irony the topic was "what I have learned about love." I am sure that whatever I said was platitudinous and vapid. The last thing I was capable of at that point in my life was a frank discussion about love.

But that was changing.

I continued to fill my time with positions on corporate boards. By 1992 I was serving on BP and Navistar boards. Both were well compensated, of course.

But others—like the AFS Advisory Board and the Ohio Rhodes Scholar selection committee—were not. I must have spent at least a third of my time in various board meetings jetting from city to city.

While at Kelleys Island I would take time to reflect on where I was headed. Often, I would jot down goals. When I look at notes written in 1992, I am struck by how deliberate I was about trying to spend time with my kids. Though I had always considered myself to be a caring father, I had not always been present for my children in ways that I was just beginning to understand.

Still, that effort to be present better describes the person I have become today rather than the person I was back in those frenetic days when I was struggling to transition from the urgency of my public life and from the contradictions of my personal life.

For all my travel and activity during the early 1990s, what is clear to me now is that I was struggling to fashion a more genuine connection with my family, something that had been absent during my time in office. Scribbled in the margin of one of my planners during that time I ask: "What are the cost and consequences of being detached?"

While it was clear that something needed to change and while I seemed to feel it deeply, I did not appreciate how much my addictive behavior—and the effort to keep it secret—created distance between me and my family. I knew that something was missing, that parts of me needed to be repaired in some fashion.

It's not easy revisiting those days. As I have repeated in these pages, I consider my ability not to dwell on the past to be one of my strengths. It served me well in public life. But I continued that pattern even after I left office. Those days—like the business cards I gathered and the Day-Timers that record the meetings attended—are tucked away in boxes. Not in my head.

In hindsight, I see my uncertainty and indecision but also the first glimmerings of the direction the next phase of my life would take. I was beginning to ask serious questions about the relationships in my life.

None of it was easy. All of it was necessary.

Between Celeste and Sabety and my corporate board work, I felt financially secure. However, I remained frustrated that I hadn't found the sort of position I had imagined for myself as I was leaving office. I felt my experience as governor had prepared me to run a large business organization and that I would find that work gratifying. But when I left office, I was disappointed that no one in the private sector understood or appreciated my executive experience.

This frustrates me still. As governor I had become adept at drawing a diverse group of people together in order to accomplish substantial and often complex goals. This was public knowledge, but, try as I might after I left office, I could not find the equivalent of that role in the private sector.

My busyness continued unabated.

I traveled to Jakarta in February 1992 for the wedding of my longtime friend Dennis Heffernan. A month later, I was in New York having lunch with Jann Wenner, publisher of *Rolling Stone,* discussing the Rock and Roll Hall of Fame in Cleveland. In April I was in California to make the initial pitch for Project California. On June 23 we won the work. On July 12 I was in New York for the Democratic Convention.

In addition to the consulting and board activity, I was also speaking to groups like the Association of Graduate School Deans, to whom I stressed the importance of integrating the fruits of academic research into the local economy. Fostering a connection between academia and industry had been one of our important successes in Ohio—embodied in Thomas Edison Centers and the Eminent Scholars programs.

In late September I was in Washington to testify as part of a Carnegie Commission study. With some free time before flying back to Ohio, I stopped by an organization called Youth Services America, or YSA. I had just joined its board and wanted to learn more about the organization. Roger Landrum, its president, arranged for two of his team to brief me. One was an impressive young woman named AnnMaura Connelly, his number two at YSA; the other, an enthusiastic—and attractive—young woman was a marketing consultant working with YSA.

Her name was Jacqueline Lundquist.

My memory of that day in the Youth Service America conference room is that Jacqueline tried to make an impression. After the briefing, she walked me to the elevator and mentioned that she knew someone active in Ohio politics. I asked who, and she named a major Republican contributor who had supported every one of my opponents. If this was her notion of how to impress me, I thought, she's a little ditzy.

I was wrong about that, of course. But it took me a while to realize how wrong.

I thanked her for the briefing and got on the elevator. I know it may be hard to believe, given my history with women, but I was not interested. It's more accurate to put it this way: I had *decided* I was not interested. I had finally resolved to extricate myself from the extramarital relationships that had marked my past.

Dagmar had been long aware that ours was not a monogamous relationship. Our unspoken understanding was that whatever I did with other women existed wholly apart from the permanent bond that constituted our marriage. That had been the case for many years.

For years I would say up front to the women with whom I became involved that Dagmar was my wife and nothing would change that. In an unhealthy way (in retrospect), this shared understanding with Dagmar ultimately abetted my infidelity by shielding me from any true intimacy or deeper engagement. I can see now how unfair I was being both to Dagmar and to the other women. If I was not present in the way that I wanted to be with my children, I was even less authentically present to my wife and to my companions.

Thus, ironically, Jacqueline Lundquist appeared in my life just as I began to step back from the extramarital relationships that I had cultivated. She would change my life profoundly, but it took a while to figure that out.

In the meantime, I continued my frenetic travel. Though I have no recollection of it, my calendar reminds me that in early December I was in Geneva drumming up business for Celeste and Sabety. I returned to Washington on business and decided to drop by a hearing on a national service initiative of President-Elect Clinton that was staffed by YSA. I slipped into the crowded room as inconspicuously as possible, but Jacqueline noticed and took the empty seat next to me. As the hearing ended, several people from Ohio came over to say hello. They were active in service projects, and I remembered their names without prompting.

Jacqueline was impressed. "Do you remember everybody's name?" she asked.

"No," I replied with a smile, "but I always remember tall, leggy blondes."

Later she would say that that was the first time she was *sure* I had noticed her.

In 1990 I had noted that one reason to step away from public life was "to learn more about myself and life." The next few years would, whether I realized it or not, be devoted to that effort. My life would change in important ways.

On February 23 my brother, Ted, called to tell me that our mother had been hospitalized. She had had heart problems for years, and she had taken a turn for the worse. I immediately drove to Cleveland to be with her.

We didn't know how long she was going to hang on. It was clear, however, that Mom—at eighty-four—was ready to face her death.

In early March I returned to DC for a YSA board retreat. At this, our third meeting, Jacqueline urged me to come to the board dinner, saying that there was a speaker whom she was sure I would enjoy. I told her that I was sorry but I could not break a prior dinner engagement. Jacqueline then suggested that she could fill me in on the dinner speaker's comments over drinks later that evening. I agreed.

We went to place called the River Club and sat in a corner. We talked for some time, briefly about YSA, and then I described my kids at some length. As we were leaving, the DJ had just put on Frank Sinatra singing "New York, New York." Jacqueline said: "How about one dance before we leave?" I told her that I was not much of a dancer. "Just one dance," she persisted. "Come on. It's not going to kill you."

She took my hand and pulled me onto the dance floor. A few minutes later, as the song ended, I impulsively kissed her on the lips. I think that I was as surprised as she was. As we walked out the door, I said: "I think that we're both in big trouble." When she dropped me off at the hotel, we kissed again.

Neither of us realized at the time where those kisses would lead.

By mid-March my mother was back in the hospital. Her heart was failing, and it was only a matter of time before she left us. Mom had signed a living will with a Do Not Resuscitate order. I knew that she wanted to pass away in peace. However, the young attending physician refused to see it that way. He ordered an IV for her. When I tried to stop him, he argued with me. She does not want that, I told him.

"Well," he told me, "people change their minds. I'm the doctor. I make the decisions."

"No," I told him. "I'm her son. I am bigger than you, and I am not about to let you go into that room to put a needle in my mother's arm."

He gave me a hard look, perhaps thinking about taking a swing at me. He might have if I had not been six inches taller—and the former governor.

"Let's get the admitting physician," he said finally. "She'll agree with me."

Ted was watching this confrontation with a mixture of surprise and discomfort, I think. But we had both watched our father's unexpected death and consequently talked with our mother about what she wanted when it was her time. We were determined that her wishes be respected.

The stalemate ended when the admitting doc arrived. She was older and listened carefully while the younger doctor explained the situation. The two doctors, along with Ted and me, went into the ICU room.

"Mom," I said, "do you recognize me?"

"Of course I recognize you, Dick," she responded.

"Do you recognize the guy next to me?" I asked her.

"That's your brother, Ted," she said. I could hear the impatience in her voice. "Do you know why you're here?"

"I'm dying," she said.

"The doctor here wants to give you some nutrition," I told her.

"Dick," she said, "you know I don't want anything done for me. I don't know why I am still alive. I want to go see my mother. I've had twenty years, and I'm ready to go." Mom's heart had stopped beating when she was sixty-four, but she had been revived—and recovered.

"Why are you not honoring her wishes?" I asked the doctors.

The young doctor began to reply, but the admitting physician intervened, speaking directly to my mother. "Mrs. Celeste," she said, "I have an order that I can write that calls for comfort measures only. If I write this, no IV lines will be put in you nor any other interventions of that sort. We will simply give you a little medicine for pain, but that's it. There is a good chance that you will die before morning. Is that what you want?"

"Of course," said my mother. "Why didn't you say that in the first place?"

The order was written, and the admitting physician walked Ted and me down the corridor. As we thanked her, she put a hand on my arm. "Mr. Celeste," she said, "you should know that the pain medicine we gave her is a very small dose of morphine. A hundred years ago that was the only way to treat heart problems. Even a small dose may have the unintended consequence of keeping your mother alive for a couple of days. I don't know how she will respond, but I want you to be aware of that."

When I returned to the hospital the next morning I found mom alive and eating a hearty breakfast. Clearly, she had some time left, so we arranged for her to be brought to Ted's home in Columbus for hospice care.

When we got her settled in a hospital bed in Ted's sunroom, the hospice nurse took us aside and gave us a booklet about hospice care. "Let me just point out a couple of things in the book," she said. "Sometimes people who are dying will have the experience of being visited by someone who has just passed away. Individuals near death seem to be aware of a friend or acquaintance who has just died."

I had never heard of this phenomenon.

"Even more common is that people near death will wait for some kind of event that brings closure—the presence of a loved one, or the chance to forgive a grievance, or even permission to leave."

My mother stayed with us for several weeks even though her only nourishment each day was a little Ensure and some water. A wonderful hospice nurse came daily. Mom was more relaxed and happy than I had could remember. I had heard stories of how carefree and happy-go-lucky she had been in college. But in the years since, she had become more somber and fretful. In those final weeks she became the cheerful, mischievous person she must have been as a young woman. I remember vividly one day when I came into the sunroom and she was smiling slyly.

"What is it?" I asked.

"I don't know," she demurred.

"Out with it," I said, and laughed myself. "What is so funny?"

"My asshole hurts!" she said as she giggled. "There, I did it. I've wanted to use that word all my life!" What does a loving son say to that?

On another visit she asked me: "What do think I should wear?"

I wondered what she meant. "Wear to what?"

"When I meet my mother and the others," she said.

"For some reason, Mom, I don't think you have to worry about that," I told her. "I suspect that somebody will take of that for you."

I had in mind the comment the hospice nurse had made that individuals are often waiting for something—a person or event—and wondered whether that might be the case for Mom. My father's birthday came and went. Not that. Could she be waiting for my sister, Pat, to arrive from Florida? Ted and I were close by. Perhaps she wanted to see her daughter one last time.

Pat arrived on a Friday from Key West, where she owned an inn. She sat with mom in the sunroom but excused herself to take a phone call with the unexpected news that her father-in-law, Harold Hoffman, had passed away. She composed herself after the shock of the call and returned to Mom's bed-side—but came out of the sunroom thirty seconds later white as a sheet.

"What happened?" I asked, thinking that Mom had passed away. "Is she?"

"No," Pat said, and then hesitated. "As soon as I went in, Mom asked if I knew that Harold had died."

Pat had asked, "How do you know Harold died?"

"He just came to see me," she replied. "He told me, 'Don't worry Peg, it's all right.'"

Pat returned to Florida, and Mom was still with us. Whatever Mom was waiting for, it was not her kids. But a few days later—April 13—Ted called at about 2:00 P.M. and told me to come quickly because Mom was leaving us.

She died minutes after I got to her bedside.

Ted explained to me that my mother's round-robin letter had arrived that morning. When Mom graduated from the College of Wooster, she had orga-nized a round-robin letter with eighteen close girlfriends. They had circulated their letters for more than sixty years. Only eleven "robins" were still alive when the round-robin letter had arrived that morning. My brother had read Mom each of their letters. Even though she had given no sign of recognition in the last couple of days, she had smiled after each letter. She died an hour later.

Mom had indeed been waiting—for one last word from her pals.

After my mother's funeral in Cleveland, I resumed my helter-skelter schedule. I flew to DC with Dagmar, who was eager for some kind of board appointment in the Clinton administration. A day later I returned to Washington, pausing for lunch with Jacqueline, before flying to a Habitat for Humanity board meeting in Africa. My May goals, noted in the margins of my calendar: 1. Habitat Trip, and 2. Decisions.

I cannot say for sure exactly what I had in mind when I wrote down "Decisions." But I know that I was conscious for the first time that my transition from office was about more than simply how I filled my time—what I was *doing*. I had begun to examine *who I was* and who I *wanted to be.*

I returned from Africa, stopping in Washington for dinner with Jacqueline. By this time she had become an increasingly important presence in my life. Then it was on to Ohio and Natalie's graduation from Oberlin. On June 14 John Bissell, the husband of my Indian "sister" Bim suffered a massive stroke. I flew to Hartford to spend time with them. Then back to DC for business. The next day I returned to Columbus.

Late July 1993 I received a call from David Wilhelm, chair of the Democratic National Committee (and a friend from Ohio). He was calling to ask me to assist the Democratic National Committee in promoting the healthcare plan that Hillary was working on.

"Is this your idea, or does this come from Hillary?" I asked.

"We think the Health Care Campaign needs help," he said, "and she would welcome help. She is comfortable with you."

After discussing the matter with Pari, I agreed to consider taking the assignment, and so in early August I met with David and with Hillary. Shortly thereafter, the president called from Air Force One to close the deal. Since I could not join the campaign effort full-time, the DNC contracted with Celeste and Sabety for my work on a flexible half-time basis.

On August 17 my involvement with Hillary's healthcare campaign was announced. The DNC and the Clintons wanted me to become the campaign salesman. I began traveling around the country to speak on behalf of the healthcare campaign to any interested audience. My calendars reflect a guy bouncing from city to city speaking and doing media events while also trying to raise money for the campaign.

I lasted less than six months in this role, and I never felt that I was effective on behalf of the DNC or Hillary. First, it was virtually impossible to penetrate the circle around Hillary—people who were very smart and very devoted to her but who couldn't figure out what I was doing lurking on the edge of the inner circle. Second, Ira Magaziner, who almost single-handedly authored the complex plan, guarded his creation vigorously. When it became clear that key congressional leaders wanted to help Hillary but needed room to modify provisions of the plan, Ira thwarted virtually every move toward compromise.

Finally, devoting only part of my time to the campaign and largely being on the road removed me from any opportunity to effectively advocate for changes in strategy or the plan itself. I knew that I should be in meetings to debate critical strategic or substantive issues. Instead, I was out debating former Ohio congressman Bill Gradison, who had become the leader of the opposition on behalf of the health insurance industry, aided by their highly effective Harry and Louise TV ads.

As I think back to that time, I realize that Jacqueline had also become a distraction. Landing at the airport in Columbus in late August, for example, I met her on the tarmac. She was there with The Beach Boys, with whom she worked, who were about to leave for their next concert. We laughed as I welcomed them back to Ohio, reminding them of how much fun we had had when they had appeared at the Ohio State Fair.

Like me, Jacqueline was married, though she rarely saw her husband. He worked with the Michael Jackson Foundation in Los Angeles while Jacqueline ran the PR business they owned in DC and looked after his mother in the house they shared. I got the sense that she felt a bit neglected or taken for granted. Her marriage of three years wasn't what she had expected. It seemed that, like me, she knew that something needed to change in her life. But at that moment neither of us could have said exactly what that change should be or how to make it happen.

Dora—still with me at Celeste and Sabety—sensed something immediately. She would say with an arched eyebrow: "Jacqueline called from Washington, and she would like you to call her back." Something in Dora's voice made it clear that Jacqueline would not be put off easily.

During this time Jacqueline and I did not talk about where we felt our relationship might be heading. I was still operating on my old "always married" ground rules.

But things were about to become more complicated.

I was in Toronto in mid-October for a Habitat board meeting when I received a call that Dagmar's father had died. She flew to Vienna immediately, and I followed a few hours later.

The funeral, like Vati's sudden death, was very hard on Dagmar. She had had a fraught relationship with her father. But as often—and as intensely—as they had been at odds with one another, she was not ready for how profoundly she would miss him when he died. While he had been sick, she had not had the chance to make her peace with him.

Like my own father, Dagmar's father had been opposed to our marriage, or at least hoped that we would postpone it. Perhaps part of our staying together had had to do with determination not to prove either parent right. Only years later would this notion occur to me.

While in Vienna I received a frantic call from Jacqueline, who had contacted the White House operator in order to track me down. She was in an awful state. Her husband had found out about us, she said, and he was threatening to go public. There was no telling what he would do, she told me. And she was forbidden from seeing me again, even talking to me. She wanted a divorce, but he wouldn't hear of it. In DC, if you had an affair, you got nothing in a divorce.

It was a tearful call. But standing in Dagmar's parents' home, there was little I could say. "I'm very sorry," I had to tell her, "but I am not in a place where I can talk."

From the funeral I flew directly to Chicago for a Navistar board meeting. During my eight-hour flight I had come to the conclusion that I would have to break it off with Jacqueline. When I landed, she called asking what she should do, saying that he was still threatening to go public. I told her not to worry about that. I had dealt with worse. I doubted that comforted her. I knew that she was hoping I would say that everything would be all right.

Instead, I said: "Doing a crossword puzzle will never be the same without you." The call ended on that note.

Up to that point I had not considered the possibility of divorcing Dagmar. I had been clear with Jacqueline about the limits on our relationship. But something was different about Jacqueline. In a remarkably short time, she had found a way to coach me in happiness. After hanging up the phone I was unable to sleep, weighing how much joy the two of us experienced together.

At 4:00 A.M. I decided I could not simply walk away. I reached out to her best friend AnnMaura and explained that I needed to talk to Jacqueline. She arranged for Jacqueline to call me from a pay phone on Connecticut Avenue. Jacqueline said that she thought she was being photographed. I told her to look as if I was giving her bad news.

"I don't know where we are headed," I said, "but I can't walk away."

That made her feel a little better.

The next day AnnMaura relayed another message from me saying that I wanted her to meet me at the Paramount Hotel in New York the following day.

I have no idea how, but Jacqueline made it to the Paramount and called on the house phone.

"Come on up," I told her.

She hesitated, apprehensive about what I was going to say.

"Come on," I insisted.

A few minutes later she entered the room clearly anxious. Just then the phone rang—it was Hillary. It was a tiny room with no proper place to sit. I spent half an hour on the phone while she sat on the edge of the bed staring out the window.

Finally, the call ended.

"I think we should meet here in ten years," I told her. Then, after a long pause, added: "And I think we should ask your mom to watch the kids so we can have some time alone."

I had not promised Jacqueline anything up until that moment.

While our relationship had grown intimate, as was my habit I did not expect that to change the fact that I was married. But I had come to realize that my feelings toward her were different. I understood that, as much as I cared for and respected Dagmar, I no longer felt bound to her by marriage.

Jacqueline went back to Washington the next day and told her husband that she wanted a divorce. She moved out of the house and into an apartment I had rented. Though I did go back to Ohio to spend one more Christmas with Dagmar and my family there, Jacqueline and I lived in that small apartment for the next year or so.

For some time I had been avoiding the question of my marriage to Dagmar, perhaps longer than I realized. But next to the date in mid-January when my portrait as governor was to be unveiled, I had noted: "Talk with Dagmar re separation."

I knew that my life was moving in a new direction, but I also realized it was not simply a matter of divorcing Dagmar. The problems in our marriage were largely of my making. For example, Dagmar and I attended several marriage retreats, but I don't think I ever worked at the process seriously enough to repair our marriage. Dagmar believed that spiritual nurture could heal whatever was missing. But I didn't really give that healing a chance.

Dagmar's faith, her spiritual life, was a key aspect of her identity. When we married, I agreed to raise our children in the Catholic Church. While I did not convert, we went to church as a family—usually St. Malachi's in Cleveland and the Newman Center on the OSU campus in Columbus. Dagmar understood that our marriage needed work. But neither the marriage retreats nor my well-intentioned notes to myself addressed my personal dysfunction.

This hit me like a body blow while I was in Ohio that Christmas holiday. Someone I loved and trusted had sensed my addictive behavior and told me bluntly that I needed to get help. That was my rock bottom.

When you are acting out your addiction, you will do anything to keep feeding it. You tell yourself incredibly inventive lies. You take irrational risks. And it is uncanny how there seems to be a code by which addicts recognize each other. In that moment I knew that she was right.

I immediately began to explore treatment centers for sex addiction. My first choice was Cottonwood in Tucson. I called shortly after my portrait unveiling—sitting alone in the Washington apartment after hours of reflection and perhaps the most authentic prayer of my life.

"How soon can you take me?" I asked.

The person who answered responded: "How soon can you get here?"

I later learned that when someone decides that he or she needs treatment, the last thing you tell them is that they have to wait. In my case, it took about seventy-two hours. I had to tell Hillary. I went to see her to explain that I needed to take several weeks off.

"I want you to understand what I am doing," I told her. She said that she did not need the reasons for my request.

"But I want you to know. I am going into treatment for sex addiction."

Without batting an eye, Hillary said, "Dick, I am supportive of whatever you need to do." She was warm and gracious. I knew I could be completely honest with her—and I knew that her support was heartfelt.

I called my brother and my son Stephen to let them know what I was about to do. They appreciated the call and did not ask a lot of questions; perhaps they understood that this was long overdue. On Sunday, January 27, I arrived at Cottonwood to join a band of fellow addicts on the journey of recovery.

The experience was both isolating and transformative. Usually in life you have familiar faces around to help you through a tough period. This was completely different. You speak to someone at Cottonwood on the phone.

You turn up at the front door. You go through a check-in process. Alone, every step of the way in. And you agree that you will be cut off from all outside communication for the first week of what is usually a three-week process.

At the beginning of my program, I was given the book *Hope and Recovery*, a twelve-step program for sex addicts, the equivalent of *The Big Book* for alcoholics. Most of my time was spent in small groups with other folks who were seeking recovery from all sorts of addictions. There were about forty individuals there during my two-week stay, new folks coming in as others cycled out. Not everyone would stick with it—and some were returning. We were people of all ages and ethnicities and from all parts of the country. We had one thing in common: we were all addicts of some sort bound by a desire to understand how to live a sober life.

We shared thoughts about God or our higher power. We described as honestly as we could our addictive behavior. We discussed how we might forgive ourselves for things that we had done—and how we might make amends to those we had harmed by our behavior. And we learned—and regularly repeated the Serenity Prayer: "God grant me the serenity to accept the things I cannot change, the courage to change the things I can, and the wisdom to know the difference."

The program concluded with a period of family time. Rather than invite either Dagmar or Jacqueline, I invited my six kids. I am sure that was hard for Dagmar. She strongly supported my seeking treatment; she had been trained as an addiction counselor. Whether or not she was in some fashion complicit in my addiction, only I could do something about it.

Three of my children came to Cottonwood—Christopher, Gabriella, and Noelle. In preparation for meeting me, they met with one of the Cottonwood professionals who helped them organize their thoughts. Those sessions were brutal for me. Each child shared his or her frustration, anger, and sadness. My task was to listen and take it in, not attempt to argue or explain. If group work could be humbling, this was heartbreaking. But candor can also be cleansing, and hearts can heal.

As I was preparing to leave Cottonwood, folks who had shared time and group with me asked to write notes in my book. I still have that book and read it—and the notes—from time to time. Most are words of encouragement. But one note stays with me especially. Jenny was not yet twenty-one, attractive but struggling with alcohol and drug addiction. Boy, did she have my number. She was teasing and testing me all the time. In a way it was good to have someone who could smell a phony, someone trying to determine if I was genuinely interested in recovery. Unlike the others, she had no interest in whether I was "a good guy." Her note read: "Be good to females." Jenny had me pegged. I learned that Jenny died on the streets just a few years after Cottonwood.

I have tried, since, to follow her admonition.

I have not gone to a therapist to try to ascertain what might have sparked my addiction. The work at Cottonwood did not depend on plumbing the depths of one's psyche. The goal was to recognize and change the addictive behavior. For some people the work they do in that setting does involve examining the trauma that led to their behavior. Not in my case. I could not blame a trauma or abuse for my behavior.

Still, I clearly had been addicted. I had often resolved to stop. But I didn't. I risked my health and my career. I jeopardized friendships and marriages. Above all, I was dishonest and distant with my family.

But sex addiction is not a disease that responds to a medicine or an elixir. Sobriety—in any addiction—is not a cure. It is a matter of seeing the addiction for what it is and then taking steps to deal with it. Like many, I have found the twelve-step program usually identified with AA very helpful. For several years after I returned from Cottonwood, I went to meetings of Sex Addicts Anonymous (SAA), which were enormously helpful. I still go to meetings from time to time and am grateful to be celebrating my twenty-seventh year of sobriety.

I returned from Tucson to resume my work with Hillary. But after six weeks or so, I met with her to say that I was not being productive for the healthcare campaign. I felt guilty that I wasn't able to have the impact I wanted and she needed. At the same time, I was worried that she wasn't getting the support she needed from either the uncompromising Ira Magaziner or the president's team in the White House.

I suspect that had I made a full-time commitment to the healthcare campaign I could have been more effective. But I still had an obligation to the work of Celeste and Sabety and the many boards, which, frankly, I had put on the back burner for both professional and personal reasons.

It was time to return to Ohio. So, with Jacqueline, I moved back—to Cleveland rather than Columbus. I worked out of a home office in our lovely Bratenahl Place condominium overlooking Lake Erie. After my divorce was granted in 1995, Jacqueline and I were married. In late 1996 Jacqueline was expecting.

What 1997 would bring, however, was beyond my imagination.

Chapter 13

What's the Situation That Prevails?

In 1996 Bill Clinton was reelected. I had campaigned for him and looked forward to what he would achieve in his second term. Shortly after his second inauguration, Jacqueline and I were invited to an event at the White House promoting national service featuring Gen. Colin Powell. Jacqueline was pregnant and decided to forgo the trip from Cleveland. Instead, she urged me to take her best friend, AnnMaura Connolly. AnnMaura was (and still is) a leading national service advocate and huge Clinton fan who had not yet met him personally. As we went through the postevent reception line, I introduced her to President Clinton.

They spoke briefly, and then the president turned to me: "Tell me what you want to do, Dick."

It was not the first time he had posed this question to me. Whenever he encountered one of his fellow governors, he would say, "What do you want to do? Come on, tell me what you want to do?"

I gave him my usual reply that afternoon, "There is nothing I want to do." I had no desire to return to DC. I felt Washington had a way of turning people's heads. While I respected the business of democracy, it was becoming more and more contorted by money and lobbyists. My experience had been that even people in the federal government who genuinely wanted to help tended to have the attitude that they knew better than you. As I have described, when I was governor, both my state and I had been adversely impacted by Washington.

"Come on, Dick," insisted President Clinton. "This is my second term, and I don't have a lot of time. Tell me what you want to do."

I told him that I was grateful for his offer, but I honestly could not think of anything. I figured that settled the matter.

When I arrived back in Cleveland, Jacqueline confronted me. "What do you mean, there's nothing you want to do? That's not true. There *is* one thing you'd love to do."

Apparently AnnMaura had debriefed Jacqueline. "All right then," I said. "What is it that I want to do?"

She smiled at me. "You want to be ambassador to India."

My first impulse was to deny it. But I realized as she said it that I would indeed love to be ambassador to India. But getting the job was another matter; I pointed that out to her. "There already is a US ambassador in India."

She was a step ahead of me. "Actually," she said, "I just read an article about postelection protocol. After every presidential election, even reelection, all ambassadors submit their resignations. Our ambassador to India has already offered his resignation."

Her scenario was improbable but compelling. After mulling it over, I wrote Bill Clinton a letter that began: "I know I have told you several times that there is nothing I want. But there is one thing that I would like to do and that is serve as your Ambassador to India."

I proceeded to outline the reasons that I would be good in that position. I had served in the embassy under Chester Bowles in the 1960s and had stayed in touch with friends and family there. I felt that I had a sense of India's history and knew its people well. As governor I had led the first ever state-level trade mission to India. I believed I could serve him and our country well. After I mailed the letter to the White House, I did my best to forget it. At least I could tell Jacqueline that I had checked that box. The truth is that I doubted anything would come of it.

I was mistaken.

Six weeks later in Chicago after a Navistar Board dinner, I found the message light in my hotel room flashing. "This is the White House operator," said the voice on the messaging service. "The president of the United States would like to talk to you. Please return this call."

Holy shit, I thought. I had missed a call from the president.

I immediately sat down and called the White House. I remembered from my Peace Corps days how famously efficient those operators can be. "The president will get back to you in seven minutes," I was told. Seven minutes later the phone rang. It was Bill Clinton.

"Hey, Dick," he said. "Are you going to be in Washington any time soon?" I told him that, as a matter of fact, I would be there on the coming Wednesday.

He said, "There's something I'd like to discuss with you. I have physical therapy in the morning"—at the time he was doing rehab for his knee—"come by the White House at eleven, and I'll have Betty take care of you."

Two days later Betty Curry, an old friend from my Peace Corps days, led me into the Oval Office, where the president was busy stretching his knee. "Well," he told me, "it's unanimous."

"Unanimous?" I said. I had no idea what he was talking about.

Clinton laughed. "Al thinks it's a good idea. Hillary thinks it's a good idea. And I do to. We want you to be our ambassador to India."

It was an incredible moment.

After a beat or two, Clinton added, "But before I nominate you, I want to ask you a tough question. How do you think Dagmar will react?" Bill knew my family well from our Renaissance weekends together and was aware of how difficult the divorce had been for Dagmar.

"The reason I am asking," he said, "is that my nominees right now are getting chewed up by the Republicans." He had just withdrawn the Lani Guinier nomination. "The last thing I want is to have this nomination come back to haunt you or me. Do you think she might oppose your appointment? How will she react?"

It was a fair question born of hard experience. I told him that I would find out and let him know.

As soon as I got back to the hotel, I called Dagmar. "I just came from a conversation with the president," I said. "He wants to nominate me to be our ambassador to India. I would like to do it with your support. What do you think?"

There was a long silence. I knew that Dagmar regarded the time she spent in India, when we were raising a young family and she was close to Steb and Chet Bowles, as one of the high points of her life. I was asking a lot of her.

Finally, I heard her take a deep breath. "I am heartbroken that I'm not the one who will be going with you," she replied quietly. "But I can't think of anyone I'd rather have represent us in India. No one is better prepared than you." Despite everything that had happened between us, Dagmar was then—and still is—a remarkable spirit and a devoted friend.

When I got off the phone with her, I called the White House to tell Bill the nomination could proceed.

———

If a return to India was unexpected, the same could be said of becoming a father for the seventh time. The idea of having a child with Jacqueline had come up before our wedding, but it did not prove as easy as my earlier children. Jacqueline suffered two miscarriages. However, nine months after a severe November snowstorm had kept most of the city inside for a couple of days, our "snowstorm baby," Sam Celeste, was born.

It is fair to say that my older children, with the exception of Stephen, had a difficult time accepting Jaqueline into their lives. But after Sam was born, the kids softened a bit. It was hard not to be nice to Sam; he was a baby, after all.

It had been rough sailing in terms of our relationship with Dagmar and the kids, especially for Jacqueline, who was saddened by their reluctance to accept her. For my part, I hoped that time would ease their anger and resentment. People's feelings are what they are—neither wrong nor right. When someone is angry with you, you have to try to understand where they are coming from and hope that time will heal the wounds.

Politics is good practice in this regard. In public office you learn quickly that you are always going to make someone unhappy. Trying to please everyone is a fool's errand. As I learned from my father and from Chet, you do what you believe is right—and live with the consequences.

When I decided to divorce Dagmar and marry Jacqueline, I had torn our family apart. But I never stopped loving my children and hoping that one day the wounds I had inflicted would heal. Gabriella began that process for all of us when she invited Jacqueline and me to her graduation from Michigan Law School in December of 1996. For the first time, there and at the dinner that followed, all of my family was together.

As my children have become parents themselves, they seem to have become more patient with me and open to Jacqueline. While aspects of my relationship with Dagmar and our kids are still unresolved, we are growing closer as one extended and bonded family. My older children have a genuine relationship with Sam, who often sees in himself qualities that connect him with them.

Perhaps the best thing about being a grandparent is watching your own children become parents themselves and struggle with the questions of how to parent. It seems to teach them to be more forgiving and more accepting.

More than any other moment in my life, returning to India as ambassador thirty years after I left my work with Chet was like picking up an interrupted conversation. I had been back to India on a number of occasions but not to the embassy. While a number of things about the place had changed—especially thick walls and tight security—it was also intensely familiar.

I felt this the moment I landed. Even as you approach India, various aromas greet you. I think of it as the distinctive scent of India. A mix of cooking scents and wood fires, burning cow dung and gardenia trees, and countless other contributors. Mother India was reaching out to greet me, I thought.

I was met by my deputy, Ashley Wills, and an Indian protocol officer, then driven to the embassy, where the staff—Indian as well as American—was lined up to greet their new ambassador. Among them was a woman named Connie who had been not quite twenty years old when I last worked at the embassy. She had worked with my Indian "sister" Bim then, and here she was now, almost fifty. I gave her a hug to the surprise of most of those gathered there. Ambassadors, whether political or career, seldom arrive at a post with long-standing connections to local employees. Seeing Connie and several other familiar faces reinforced my sense that I had come home.

After being introduced to my country team, I walked into the ambassador's office, which was furnished almost exactly as it had been in the Bowles years. It was almost as if nothing had changed, though of course in the time since Chet Bowles had served as ambassador a great deal had changed. India had grown from a population of four hundred million to one billion. No longer governed by a single dominant party, India was led by a coalition government. And the world, too, was a vastly different place than it was when Svetlana sought a new life in that embassy.

All the same, when I walked into that office, it felt to me that I was returning to a place where I had been headed all along—as if Chet had left assignments for me to pick up in his stead.

I arrived at the post in mid-November 1997. Once the Senate acted on my nomination, the process moved at warp speed. I was confirmed on Friday, sworn in on Monday, and on a plane to India the next day (my sixtieth birthday, as it happened). The reason for this haste was a three-day visit that Secretary Albright had planned for the following week. I wanted to be there for those conversations.

Since I had not yet presented my credentials to the president of India, I received a special dispensation from the government of India to allow me to sit where the ambassador would sit (as long as my deputy, still formally the chargé, was in the room) in the meeting with the prime minister and foreign secretary. The few days between my arrival and Madeleine Albright's visit were chock-full of briefings to bring me up to speed on the issues likely to be discussed, including a Clinton visit that was penciled in for the following February.

As luck would have it, the secretary's visit had to be truncated due to issues involving Bosnia. Instead of three days, she would spend just three hours on the ground in Delhi, meeting at the prime minister's residence. After the preliminaries, the secretary led off with a strong pitch encouraging India to sign the nuclear nonproliferation and test ban treaties. This was a sensitive issue, and Madeline knew it. Prime Minister I. K. Gujral, in response, explained why—despite personally having opposed India's acquisition of nuclear weapons—he was unprepared to do so. He pointed to India's two nuclear-capable neighbors, China and Pakistan, with whom India had fought wars. Secretary Albright reiterated her case, and the discussion continued for fifteen minutes without resolution.

Finally, the prime minister reached past Secretary Albright and patted me on the knee. "Don't worry," he told her reassuringly. "Dick and I will work on this."

A long, surprised silence followed. The secretary of state gave me a look. It said, "Where did that come from?"

Then Gujral raised the subject of a permanent seat on the UN Security Council for India. Madeline listened carefully as he asserted that it was wrong

Secretary of State Madeleine Albright with Prime Minister I. K. Gujral during her brief visit in November 1997

to deny one-fifth of the world's population their rightful place at the table. She acknowledged the strength of the Indian case but pointed to the difficulties inherent in changing the current arrangement. Again, the discussion went back and forth for some time until the prime minister reached past her and again patted me on the knee.

"Don't worry," he told her. "Dick and I will work on this as well."

The conversations continued for about an hour and a half before we moved to his dining table for lunch. Secretary Albright had to depart immediately after lunch, and I joined her in the car to the airport. As I settled in next to her, she said, "What is this 'Dick and I' stuff?"

I explained that when I had been in India with Bowles in the 1960s, I had bought a painting by a talented young artist named Satish Gujral, who had introduced me to his brother—the politician in the family. I. K. and I became friends, and he had stayed with me at the governor's residence when he came to visit his sons, who were in college in the United States. I had not told anyone about this relationship because I did not want to put him in an awkward position by assuming anything.

"This is remarkable," she said. "I don't think there is another place in the world where we have an ambassador who is on a first-name basis with the head of government."

"I don't know how long it's going to last," I told her. "His government seems to be in trouble."

When I got back to the embassy, my DCM—who had witnessed the whole episode—pulled me aside.

"Okay buddy," Wills said. "What the fuck is this 'Dick and I?'"

I presented my credentials eleven days later. I had arrived several weeks after Chester Bowles had presented his credentials in 1963, so I was unprepared for the impressive pomp and ceremony involved. I was placed in a carriage accompanied by a horse guard from the gates of the presidential palace. As I stepped down from the carriage, a military band played the American and Indian national anthems. Jacqueline and three embassy colleagues had preceded me into the huge reception hall. Shortly thereafter the president of India and I entered to a trumpet fanfare. I presented my original appointment letter, signed by President Clinton designating me as his personal emissary, to President Narayanan.

In response, the president of India welcomed me, saying he was optimistic about the future of the relationship between our two nations. The brief formal

Arriving at the presidential palace in India to present my credentials

Presentation of my credentials in India

ceremony was followed by an informal tea for the party of ten. Later that same day—November 28—my friend I. K. Gujral lost his majority in parliament and delivered his letter of resignation to President Narayanan.

So much for my personal relationship with the head of government.

One of my initial challenges to my senior team was to articulate a statement of our mission. They seemed taken aback, saying that they thought it was obvious. We were to represent and promote US interests in India. I

Ambassador Chester Bowles presenting his credentials to the president of India, Dr. Sarvepalli Radhakrishnan, in 1963

Presenting my credentials to the president of India, K. R. Narayanan, on November 28, 1997

suggested that we talk to both our Foreign Service Officers and our local employees for ideas and encouraged my DCM, Ashley Wills, to lead the effort. Within a few weeks we had hammered out a succinct draft and shortly thereafter produced the following:

"Our mission in India is to exercise leadership in advancing the interests of the United States and its citizens. We seek to strengthen mutual understanding and to build a dynamic partnership for the 21st century. We strive to reflect the best of our nation's values and respect the best of India's values in all that we do."

I was proud of the statement and had it printed on small, laminated cards that were given to every employee in the embassy and each of our consulates. In fact, I had the mission statement printed as a poster in my office, and on more than one occasion visitors, especially CEOs, expressed appreciation for that clarity of purpose.

No sooner had we agreed on a mission statement than Ashley informed me, in a cynical tone of voice, that it was time for "the mission pee pee."

"What is the mission pee pee?" I asked.

Ashley responded that it was the mission performance plan, an annual exercise that each post around the world had to submit to Washington. Ashley added that, once dispatched, we would never hear back from the State Department. "I think they flush them down the toilet," he said with a grin on his face.

I wanted to know when it was due and told Ashley I wanted us to take the exercise seriously. "Let's write a plan that we can use to evaluate our own performance—regardless of what Washington thinks," I said, adding, "I'll bet you a dinner that I can get Washington to respond to our submission."

Ashley took the bet with relish.

I set a deadline for the draft MPP two weeks before the April 1 deadline. And when we had completed a strategy for the coming year that we felt was solid, we sent it to the State Department—ten days before the due date.

"Why are you doing this?" Ashley asked.

"You'll see," I responded.

Within ten days we had a response from State with two or three critical comments about our MPP. "So all we get for our trouble are some piss-ant criticisms," was Ashley's response.

But, I pointed out, they had read our plan and taken it seriously; he owed me a dinner.

The fall of the Gujral government meant elections in India and the postponement of President Clinton's visit. The opposition BJP led a coalition to victory in February of 1998. One aspect of their campaign manifesto stirred deep concern in Washington. They pledged that, if elected, they would "exercise the nuclear option."

This language set off alarm bells on the eighth floor of the State Department and at the National Security Council. The Clinton team tasked Bill Richardson, who was headed to India in connection with his responsibilities as secretary of energy, to make the case for why testing a nuclear weapon was a bad idea. Richardson met Foreign Minister Jaswant Singh in a small library at my residence and spelled out the administration's concerns regarding an Indian test. Jaswant Singh, who was to become a dear friend of mine, listened carefully and gave an obliquely worded reply. As we parsed his language, we concluded that testing would not take place in the near future.

Whether he actually meant to give such assurance is an open question. Jaswant was the master of flowery language, which on occasion could obfuscate. In retrospect, I consider his comments to Richardson an example of masterful obfuscation. We chose to hear what we wanted. Certainly, Richardson took away from the meeting the impression that the Vajpayee government was going to take its time on testing and not do anything rash. We concluded that they would not test soon.

Jacqueline and me
(Photo by Dane Har-
baugh)

Shortly thereafter, in late April, I returned to Washington to complete the briefing I had cut short in order to be in Delhi for the Albright visit—first, in Washington and then in Hawaii at the headquarters of our Pacific Command (which included responsibility for India but not Pakistan).

Jacqueline accompanied me to DC and Hawaii. There I was briefed on our strategic interests with respect to India and South Asia. On my second day I was scheduled to speak to the Rotary Club in Honolulu after further briefings. As I was shaving that morning, Jacqueline shouted for me to come watch a breaking news flash. "They're reporting that India conducted a series of nuclear tests," she said.

I said, "Are you kidding?"

I stood with shaving cream on my face watching the report. Despite the apparent assurances of Jaswant Singh, the BJP government had indeed "exercised their nuclear option."

I immediately called Ashley Wills in Delhi. "What the fuck is going on?" I asked.

"You leave," he said in a very weary voice, "and see what happens? The place falls apart."

I was yanked back to Washington immediately—cutting short my remaining briefings in Hawaii—because the Clinton administration was deeply upset with the Indians. Secretary Albright had personally urged the Indian government not to test. Bill Richardson had reiterated that message to the new Indian leadership. Yet they went ahead anyway. It felt as though they were thumbing their noses at the Clinton administration—and especially our nuclear ayatollahs who believed that we could be trusted with nuclear weapons but not anyone else.

Had I been in Delhi I would have been recalled. Instead, since I was in the States, I was put on the shelf while senior leaders at State and the White House examined ways in which we could impose consequences on the Indians. Some sanctions were required by law, of course, but the State Department asked what further steps could be taken to show our dismay. One such step, for example, was to deny visas for any Indian nuclear scientist hoping to visit the United States.

I finally convinced the folks at State that I could better serve our cause back in New Delhi rather than DC. I argued that our embassy was demoralized and that, in the aftermath of the tests, our priority would be finding ways to rebuild trust and reenergize our bilateral relationship.

Only during my hiatus in DC did I learn about a crucial episode involving my predecessor. In the early nineties, we had detected preparations for an Indian nuclear test. Frank Wisner, our ambassador, had conveyed a strong message to the then prime minister of India, V. P. Singh, urging the Indians to forgo any nuclear test, emphasizing that it would be a severe setback to our effort to cement our bilateral relations.

Apparently, the Indian prime minister denied that nuclear test preparations were under way. In response, Wisner shared a series of satellite photos showing clearly that work going on at India's Pokhran test site, then took them back. The planned tests were canceled. No one had told me about this important episode before my hurried departure for India.

As a result of the Wisner exchange, Indian nuclear scientists understood our ability to monitor their test site. Therefore in 1998 they carefully disguised their preparations.

We were completely caught off guard. I believe the nuclear tests felt like such a slap in the face to the Clinton administration because it was as if the Indian government had not been listening to a word that we were saying and were willing to jeopardize, among other things, the first visit by a US president in more than twenty years.

I was frustrated that I had not been filled in on the Wisner episode. I was frankly naive and in no position to properly evaluate the Richardson–Jaswant

Singh exchange. I did not realize how close the Indians had come to testing in the early nineties. Perhaps if I had known about the earlier test preparations, I would have had enough of the Calabrian in me to be suspicious of Jaswant Singh's carefully hedged comments.

Indian leaders were genuinely taken aback by the US reaction. After all, they had been forthright about their intent to test nuclear weapons; it had been part of their election platform. Why should we be surprised when they kept an election promise?

They reiterated a point that Prime Minister Gujral had made to Secretary Albright the previous November. India lived in a dangerous neighborhood. They had fought wars with two nuclear-capable neighbors: the Chinese had nuclear weapons; so did Pakistan. Why should India not be prepared to defend itself?

As it turned out, India's nuclear tests framed much of our work for the next two years. In our mission statement we said that we would "seek to strengthen mutual understanding and build a dynamic partnership." That effort would center on a series of talks between Undersecretary of State Strobe Talbott and Foreign Minister Jaswant Singh. Both were brilliant and articulate representatives of their governments, and neither was inclined to make apologies or flinch during a negotiation. Talbott was a hard-liner when it came to our policy toward India's nuclear program. Singh, a proud patriot with a military background, steadfastly defended India's position.

The meetings between these officials proved to be the most senior and sustained conversations that had ever taken place between our two countries. In a perverse way, the Indians had provoked the sort of serious bilateral dialogue that was long overdue.

I found myself intimately but discreetly involved in the talks. My goal was to make the exchanges as productive as possible. I would try to understand where Prime Minister Vajpayee and his team were coming from and share that with Strobe so that he would be aware of what the Indians hoped to achieve. At the same time, I would encourage Jaswant on what language to use with Strobe—and stressed the importance of identifying ways, however modest, to achieve some forward progress at each meeting. Somehow at the end of each session Strobe and Jaswant contrived to squeeze a positive note into the joint communique.

As a result of these conversations in preparation for his meetings with Strobe, Jaswant and I developed a close relationship. We met, usually over a whiskey or cold beer, at his residence rather than the foreign ministry. Strobe

Talbott's account portrays the talks as a conversation involving essentially the two of them. But in fact a number of us on the ground in India were dealing with the wider repercussions of the testing—and the ongoing negotiations. For example, the tests triggered a set of sanctions under US law that included restricting the transfer of sophisticated technologies to India. This adversely impacted both US high-tech exports and ongoing mutual scientific research projects. Our task was to find a path to roll the sanctions back.

Washington feared that escalating tensions between India and Pakistan might lead to hostilities and the possibility of a nuclear exchange. Indian leaders did not share this concern. Jaswant Singh liked to remind me that "India and Pakistan were born of the same womb." "We understand each other better than you do," he would say, stressing his conviction that neither was out to destroy the other. With respect to nuclear weapons, India had a long-standing policy of "no first use." After the May '98 tests, Prime Minister Vajpayee reaffirmed this pledge.

The most serious confrontation between India and Pakistan during my tenure occurred in the high mountains of Indian-held Kashmir in an area called Kargil. In the early spring of 1999, Pakistani soldiers disguised as civilians crossed the Line of Control and occupied high-altitude posts the Indian Army would abandon each winter. Typically, both sides withdrew from their high-altitude positions because winter conditions were so severe.

In 1999, however, the Pakistanis infiltrated forces across the LOC to occupy positions that overlooked the main supply road to Leh, the capital or Ladakh. When the Indians sent out the usual company of soldiers to reoccupy the posts in the late spring, they were never heard from. They sent out a second detachment, on high alert, and discovered that the first group had been ambushed. The Indian government demanded that Pakistan vacate the posts; Pakistan replied that these were civilians, not soldiers.

India—like us—had intelligence making it clear that this was not the case. We believed that this was mischief on the part of General Musharraf, the army chief of staff at the time. Our military assessment was that India would be unable to dislodge the Pak troops without attacking their supply lines back into Pakistan-held Kashmir. We felt that if the Line of Control was crossed, for example, by Indian bombers going after supply depots in Pakistan territory, the situation could easily lead to wider conflict. Our goal was to prevent that from happening.

I talked to Jaswant Singh almost daily during the Kargil conflict. In part I was conveying messages from President Clinton and Secretary Albright.

But I also added my own thoughts as a longtime friend of India. I stressed to Jaswant that for the first time since Indian independence the United States was recognizing and calling out Pakistani aggression. In the past, US policy had consistently tilted toward Pakistan. In the war between India and Pakistan that led to an independent Bangladesh, President Nixon and Secretary Kissinger had dispatched a US aircraft carrier to the Bay of Bengal to try to intimidate Indira Gandhi. Our knee-jerk response had been to defend Pakistan whether they deserved it or not.

But that was not the case this time. "You jeopardize this breakthrough if you attack across the Line of Control," I emphasized to Jaswant. He understood.

Pakistan's ambassador to India, Ashraf Qazi, a thoughtful diplomat and a personal friend, came to see me at the embassy. He was seeking our help to persuade the Indians to "cease their aggressive actions in Kargil." I pointed out that the Indians had held these posts for some time. Ashraf repeated the claim that civilian "freedom fighters" had occupied the positions.

"Ashraf," I said, "I'm going to let you tell me what your government wants you to tell me. But I know that it is not true, and I am embarrassed for your sake. I'm your friend, so I'm going to be honest with you. We know who trained and equipped those troops, and we know how they are being supplied and directed. Our government cannot accept your plea. I will convey what you have said to my government. But, Ashraf, I will also tell them what I think of it—and I want you to know that."

I think he was relieved. He was going to report back to Islamabad that he had made his case forcefully. However, as far as the American ambassador was concerned, it would not get traction with the US government.

On July 4, Nawaz Sharif, then prime minister of Pakistan, flew to Washington to meet with President Clinton and plead for help in negotiating a face-saving settlement with India. Embassy New Delhi had communicated our objections to Sharif, even meeting with the president. Clinton fully understood our concerns, and he was not happy to have his holiday interrupted. Still, he heard Sharif out, then made it clear that there was nothing he could or would do until Pakistan withdrew its troops.

When the meeting ended, Clinton picked up the phone and called Prime Minister Vajpayee (waking him up) to report what had happened in the Sharif meeting. That call from Clinton to Vajpayee was without precedent in Indo-US relations.

The Indian Army undertook to recapture the Kargil posts without crossing the Line of Control. At a cost of more than seven hundred lives, they succeeded in what the Israelis would call one of the most remarkable military feats in modern history.

Personal relationships are an essential aspect of effective diplomacy. In fact, that underlies the ancient formality that an ambassador is the personal representative of the head of one state to the head of another state, bearing a personal introduction and securing recognition and protection in that role. At its best, this protocol is designed to ensure that an ambassador can convey candidly and confidentially what his or her president wants to communicate to the host government.

This is the strongest justification for political appointees—at least whose qualifications go beyond how much money they raised for the president— namely that they have access to the president directly and not just through the bureaucracy. John Kenneth Galbraith had that sort of relationship with Jack Kennedy. That was his currency as he engaged the often aloof Prime Minister Nehru. The relationship I was perceived to have with Bill Clinton served me well both within the embassy and in my work with Indian leaders.

Some observers view ambassadors as glorified errand boys. That misses the real work of dedicated career and political ambassadors alike. At their best they forge strong relationships with their host country leaders, enabling candid and timely communication. That is what Chester Bowles achieved in his first tour in India in the early 1950s. That is what I endeavored to do during my posting.

Sometimes you are obliged to convey a message on behalf of your government with which you may not agree. I had this experience in early 1999 when an Australian missionary was brutally murdered in Bihar—an act that made headlines throughout the world. The State Department, concerned about the treatment of Christians in India, asked me to convey a demarche to the home minister demanding that India do more to protect its minorities.

I did not agree with the assessment that the government wasn't doing enough to protect Christians, but I had my orders. I did as I was told—my way. When I met with Home Minister Advani, I prefaced my remarks along these lines: "I'm going to convey a message from my government exactly as they have instructed because that is my responsibility. After I do, I would like to share my personal perspectives well."

He said that he understood.

"My government is very concerned that the government of India is not doing everything it can to protect your Christian minority. They are worried that there may be elements who resist taking the necessary steps to protect religious minorities. We want to register our deep concern."

Then I paused. "That is the message I have been instructed to convey. Now let me share my own perspective on this issue. I believe that your government is deeply committed to protecting all of your citizens and that you have the will and the capacity to do so. But as someone who, like you, spent decades in public life, I know that often in the public arena appearances become reality. If there's an appearance that the Indian government is tolerating violence against Christians, that negative message can become a reality with which your government will have to contend. Yes, the Indian constitution protects all religions. But it seems to me the challenge is to find ways to communicate your government's efforts convincingly to the rest of the world."

"Mr. Ambassador," he replied, "I am dismayed that your government would think that either I or my government would in any way permit, much less encourage, violence against our Christian brothers or sisters. We strongly support the secular nature of our country. We have Christians in our government itself, and I reject the premise of your country's concern."

After a moment he continued. "But I do appreciate your thought about the importance of appearances. I believe your concern is one that we should take seriously. I appreciate your sharing it with me frankly."

I felt that I had done my job. I had presented the demarche as instructed. I had also communicated my perspective on a volatile issue. My ability to do both were expressions of my role as ambassador.

My father had reminded me frequently that appearances could become reality. You had to take both into account. The images we project and the language we use become part of reality. When I failed to frame my early tax increase properly, the "90 percent tax increase" became a reality in the minds of most Ohioans. LK Advani knew that I had been a successful politician, and he recognized our shared experience in electoral politics.

He would have loved Frank Celeste.

My mentor Chester Bowles felt that the Roosevelt House, designed and built as part of Edward Durrell Stone's vision for the embassy compound, was too ostentatious. For me, arriving with Jacqueline and Sam, the residence became an asset for personal diplomacy. We invited hundreds of Indians from all walks of life to events that ranged from small dinners for twenty-two (the capacity of our dining room table) to large receptions and dinners taking advantage of the vast patio and garden stretching for half a cricket pitch behind the house. At the back of the property was a guest house where visitors could stay and relax on their own.

Jacqueline quickly built an ever-expanding circle of friends. Some were young women her age who had children in preschool with Sam. Others were ambassadors' spouses and pals who joined in weekly water aerobics in our pool. And frequently we hosted fashion shows that not only featured up-and-coming Indian designers but also raised money for Indian charities from the Cancer Society to an AIDS awareness initiative.

I remember one occasion in particular. An American friend contacted me on behalf of the WPO (basically folks who had aged out of the YPO—a leadership organization of young CEOs and civic leaders). He said that a group of five hundred were going to be in New Delhi, and he hoped that we might host them for a dinner (the organization would cover the cost). We said of course. And our visitors were overwhelmed to be treated to a music and dance program (on a temporary stage) featuring Bollywood choreographer Shiamak Davar and his company, followed by a sit-down dinner under moonlight and surrounded by candlelit ice sculptures. By morning all evidence of the party was gone, the magic of remarkably skilled Indian workers.

While I traveled to every state in India to meet with the chief minister and get a sense of the particular issues there, our home became a crossroads for political, diplomatic, artistic, and civic leaders—sometimes visitors from the United States but more often Indian friends and colleagues.

My most significant and memorable accomplishment as ambassador was ensuring that President Clinton visited India. I was keeping a promise I had made to the First Lady.

During the summer of 1997 Jacqueline and I joined friends at the Habitat for Humanity Jimmy Carter Work Project in Kentucky. One day Hillary Clinton joined us to work on a "woman's build" house. At lunch I sought her out to thank her for endorsing my nomination as ambassador. Hillary leaned in toward Jacqueline and me, grabbing my arm for emphasis. "Dick, you must promise me one thing. You have to make sure Bill visits India. Chelsea and I had a fabulous time when we went." And then she tugged us over to where President Carter was standing. "President Carter," she said, "you were the last president to visit India twenty years ago. Don't you think Dick has to get Bill out there for a visit?" Carter enthusiastically agreed. Typical Hillary, focused on making things happen.

But India's nuclear tests blew the presidential visit off track. And there were many frustrated folks in Washington who argued that it would be "wrong to reward India's misbehavior with a presidential visit."

So as President Clinton's final year in office approached I had to find a way to make the visit happen. I knew that the president himself would have to insist on it.

Back in the 1960s Chester Bowles had arranged a back channel to President Kennedy that did not go through the State Department. My sense is that he may have overused that channel. I had my own not-yet-used channel. By late fall 1999 it was time to do so.

I wrote a personal letter to President Clinton explaining that he needed to decide promptly on whether he intended to visit India. If he wanted to come, he should do so in early 2000. "The visit has to happen in a small window of time that closes before March because next year you will be perceived as a lame duck and if you come later in the year here in India it will be too hot . . . for it to be successful, you need to make a decision to visit India as soon as possible so that we can plan for it."

After putting my letter in an envelope marked "Personal and Eyes Only for the President," I put that envelope into a second envelope addressed not to the president but to Betty Curry, his executive assistant. Betty and I had become friends during my Peace Corps days when she was working in Sam

The Clinton team during his visit to India in 2000. *Left to right:* John Podesta, Sandy Berger, Madeleine Albright, President Clinton, me, Bill Daley, and Strobe Talbott.

A few words with President Clinton as he departs India after a highly productive four-day visit

Brown's office. I added a short note: "Betty, would you please put this at the top of the President's inbox?"

I was confident that Betty would make sure that the president saw my letter.

Sure enough, within a couple of weeks the presidential visit was on. No more discussion of tying it to the Talbott-Singh talks. No strings attached. I was never told what triggered the green light for the visit. But I have a pretty good idea.

President Clinton's visit was a remarkable success. It was notable for several reasons. It was the first such visit in twenty-two years. He spent five days in India and only three hours in Pakistan (where he addressed the Pakistani public on national TV in an unexpectedly forthright fashion). And he bonded with India's leaders and people at a deep level.

The visit was diverse and productive in many ways. But for me the high point came on Clinton's second day when he addressed a gathering of Indian parliamentarians in the Central Hall of Parliament. I sat on a folding chair between Madeleine Albright and Jaswant Singh. We faced a small platform positioned directly under the compelling portrait of Gandhi on his famous Salt March. Prime Minister Vajpayee entered with Clinton alongside. A moment later Vajpayee introduced formally the "president of our natural ally, the United States."

As President Clinton spoke eloquently of his hopes for the relationship between the United States and India and the bonds we shared, tears rolled down my cheeks. I thought of Chet Bowles's bold vision for that relationship dismissed by cynical policy makers in the mid-1960s. I thought of the mission statement we had crafted just two years ago—"to build a dynamic partnership for the twenty-first century." Chet, you planted the seed.

Now I have the unexpected privilege of being here to help make it happen.

If you ask Jacqueline what our time was like, she is likely to say: "It was a thousand days of awesome."

As if a replay of years before—when Eric (then Christopher and Gabriella) were in diapers and Steb and Chet would host celebrities (because Steb loved it), we had our share of distinguished visitors spend time with us at Roosevelt House. It began almost as soon as Jacqueline arrived with Sam in diapers. First came Sen. Chuck Robb (D-Virginia), who had spoken at her UVA graduation. He was followed shortly by Donna Shalala, secretary of Health and Human Services, who was a longtime friend and whose mother, a prominent Republican, had endorsed me in my first race for state representative.

One day I received a call at the embassy. The caller asked whether I could organize a dinner for Richard Gere, a frequent visitor to India, who wanted to meet a group of business leaders to solicit their help to raise HIV and AIDS awareness. As it turned out, I had a conflict on the date he had in mind and expressed regret that I couldn't help.

That evening I recounted the call to Jacqueline. "What did you tell him?" she asked. I explained that I had expressed my regret because I was going to be in Bombay. "But *I'm* here!" she exclaimed. "*I* can host the dinner."

I knew I couldn't head her off. So I arranged for my deputy to cohost to make it an official dinner.

I called Gere's person back and said that my wife and my deputy would host the dinner. We invited a group of respected Indian business leaders and one or two Bollywood stars. Gere had taken up the mantel of Elizabeth Taylor, an early and effective advocate raising awareness regarding HIV and AIDS.

That evening I called from Bombay where I had ducked out of a large gathering. "How's it going?" I asked Jacqueline.

"It's going great," she told me. "We're having the best time."

"Really? Can you put Richard on the phone?" Gere thanked me for the arrangements and said he wanted to say hello when I got back to Delhi the next day. Richard Gere persuaded a number of Bollywood stars, business leaders—and an ambassador's wife—to become deeply involved in promoting AIDS awareness in India.

Arlo Guthrie was another of our visitors. I first met Arlo when I invited the Weavers reunion tour to the Ohio State Fair in the mid-1980s. He took the place of his father Woody in the band—along with Pete Seeger, Ronnie Gilbert, and Fred Hellerman. Arlo sent me an email saying that he and his son Abe were traveling from Ireland to Australia and had a few days in between. Could they stay with us in Delhi? I said, sure. Next thing I knew, Arlo said, hey, it really is a week. Is that okay? I responded, of course, but he would be obliged to sing for half an hour for a group of friends one night while he was with us. He said, sure.

On the Saturday of Arlo's visit we were hanging around the pool at Roosevelt House while an army of workers was preparing for the evening concert, dinner, and dance. Tables and chairs, dance floor, lights for all the trees, and a sound system. Arlo turned to me and said, "I don't think I can do half an hour tonight."

"Hey," I said, "Just do twenty minutes if that works for you. The folks who are coming just want to hear you sing."

"No, no, Dick. 'Alice's Restaurant' is going to take half an hour. I'm going to need more time," he said. I laughed and said that he should play as long as he and Abe wanted.

It was a beautiful Delhi evening with a star-filled sky. After his first song or two, Arlo looked up to the sky. "Woody, look at me!" he called out with a big grin. "I'm singing on government property!"

The audience—half Indian and half American—roared with laughter and applause. After a rollicking version of "Alice's Restaurant," we adjourned for dinner and eventually dancing to a DJ. But what stood out for me that evening was listening to the number of our team—military attachés, DEA staff, marine guards—who came up to Arlo to tell him that "Alice's Restaurant"—an antiwar, druggie anthem—had gotten them through their tours in Vietnam. Who knew?

In the Bowles era, Roosevelt House had been used only rarely for a musical or dance evening. For us, the house was full of life with more than 250 house guests and countless events—receptions, fashion shows, dinners, performances. From Michael Bloomberg to Jay Peterman, from Bianca Jagger to Roberta McCain, mother of the senator—we wanted everyone to come to know and love India as much as we did. And nearly a thousand guests endured a withering sun to greet President Clinton in our back yard during his visit.

A fundamental Indian belief is that "the guest is god." Hospitality is a way to welcome god into our presence. So the well-trodden welcome mat at Roosevelt House was both a reflection of our nation's values—and respect for India's values as well.

We would bring that spirit with us to Colorado College when we arrived in 2002.

An ambassador not only serves as the personal representative of the president, she or he is also called upon from time to time to explain what is happening in the United States to host country audiences. In most cases, that task came naturally—recounting American history, describing the American economy, explaining current events. But sometimes it could be challenging.

The Monica Lewinsky affair was one example. Most Indians and virtually all of the diplomatic corps did not understand why this was a public issue. From their perspective, it was purely a personal matter and certainly not justification for impeachment. Given my own personal conduct issues, I found myself avoiding public comment on the proceedings.

Another challenging moment occurred when the election results in 2000 came down to hanging chads and a recount in Florida. My diplomatic colleagues assumed that since I had been involved in politics myself, I should be able to explain what was happening. I, of course, had no idea.

The one observation that I could make with confidence was that, whatever the outcome, the American people would respect it. There would be no upheaval. The American political system would endure.

And it did.

Like ambassadors around the world, I submitted my resignation letter to be on the desk of the incoming president, whoever that might be. Soon after George W. Bush was declared the winner, I received a call from Colin Powell, who had been nominated as secretary of state. He asked me to stay on for a few months to avoid a long vacancy between my departure and a successor's arrival. I agreed to do so.

Within a few weeks I found myself preparing to accompany Jaswant Singh on a visit to Washington to meet the new Bush team. The Indian ambassador and I were part of a very carefully orchestrated program—accompanying Singh to meetings with Secretary Powell and National Security Advisor Condoleezza Rice, with the prospect that the president would drop by when we were gathered in the cabinet room.

I knew Rice. She had been Christopher's thesis advisor at Stanford. After exchanging pleasantries, she and Jaswant started to work their way through a list of topics of mutual interest. Before long, President Bush emerged from the Oval Office. He was introduced to Jaswant Singh and, after shaking hands with him, continued around the table greeting everyone with genuine enthusiasm.

As he got to me, last in the circle, he asked with a grin, "Do I call you Governor or Ambassador, Dick?"

"I don't know," I responded. "Should I call you Governor or President?"

"I guess it's Ambassador then," he said as his grin widened.

Then he turned to Jaswant and asked unexpectedly, "Have you ever seen the Rose Garden?" Jaswant said no, and the president took him by the elbow and steered him through the door to the Oval Office. This was totally off script. I signaled my counterpart, Lalit Mansingh, India's ambassador to the United States, and we followed into the Oval Office—which was vacant. As Condoleezza Rice joined us, we spotted the president and the foreign minister standing side by side in the garden.

At that moment, the two turned and returned to the Oval Office. As they came in, the president said to Jaswant: "Do you have a few minutes?" Without hesitation Jaswant said, of course.

The five of us sat down. The president and the foreign minister were side by side and flanked by their respective ambassadors, with Condoleezza Rice at the far end.

The first words out of the president's mouth were "Look at Condi. She's nervous because she knows I don't have any talking points with me."

She nodded in agreement, and her look said, please don't do this.

"You know," began Bush, "I believe that our relationship is vitally important. I say that for three reasons."

"In the first place," he said, "India is a model of democracy in a world facing a challenge from Chinese-style leadership. We have a tremendous stake in the success of the Indian model. We share a devotion to democracy and the rule of law."

"Second," he continued, "I admired the decision to liberalize the economy in 1991 and to begin to compete in the global marketplace. Your move toward less regulation and a more market-oriented economy is something I respect."

Where did this come from, I wondered. I had no idea that Bush had thought about any of this. My mind flashed back to Chet Bowles briefing Richard Nixon in 1967.

President Bush continued. "If you can unleash the skills and energy and work ethic of your people, it will not only benefit India but it will help people around the world."

"Finally," he said, "The Indian community in the United States is large and influential. I can speak from my experience as governor of Texas. Indian Americans in Texas are successful professionals and entrepreneurs. And, by the way, many supported me in my elections. When you consider the significance of India's democratic model, its economic liberalization, and the positive Indian presence here, there are compelling reasons to strengthen our partnership."

I was thinking to myself I could not have written a better set of talking points. Condoleezza Rice looked both surprised and relieved.

"I appreciate your words, Mr. President," said Jaswant. "There is only one true superpower in the world today, and that brings great responsibility. We want the United States to succeed."

"There is great responsibility," Bush responded, "and also a lot of envy. People do not really understand that. Take this issue of missile defense. India faces neighbors who pose a nuclear threat. We face nuclear adversaries, too. I believe that an effective missile defense system would enhance the security of both of our nations."

"Mr. President," said Jaswant, "just before I left on this trip, I circulated a paper to my government suggesting that we should explore the development of a missile defense system. We would welcome discussions on this subject."

As we departed, I was busy recalibrating my opinion of George W. Bush. He was clearly a whole lot smarter than I had given him credit for. Like Ronald Reagan he was often underestimated—to his considerable advantage.

My brief service in the Bush administration meant that I reported to a new secretary of state. Colin Powell had shared his guiding principles when he addressed assembled State Department employees on assuming his duties. The highlights of his talk were circulated widely. Two comments caught my eye.

Years of military service had taught him, he told us, that the field is always right. When there is a difference of opinion between the field and headquarters, it is wise to assume that the field knows best.

He also said that, when confronting an important decision, "Don't send me a smooth stone when a sharp rock will do." He didn't want the bureaucracy to massage a tough issue until everyone agreed. He wanted to be exposed to the sharp edges of the decision.

Both struck me as sound rules of leadership. I took them to heart.

Not long after reading his remarks—just as I was to leave for Bombay to celebrate the first official visit by a US Navy warship with the senior Indian military brass—the State Department issued a press statement on a matter relating to India's defense posture that was contrary to what we in the embassy had been advocating. No heads-up from Washington. No chance for an appeal. And the timing couldn't have been worse.

I fumed all the way to Bombay, did my best to dance around the issue with upset Indian defense officials, and fumed all of my way back to Delhi. The idea that the State Department would issue a sensitive statement like that without consulting the embassy was unacceptable. They might overrule us, of course, but not to alert us and give us a chance to discuss timing was just wrong.

Back at the embassy I fired off an "eyes only" message to Secretary Powell expressing my frustration. I said that this action violated his cardinal rule, that the field is always right. I briefly explained what had happened, making particular note of the awkward position the timing had created for me. At a minimum, I told him, I thought that his rule required that the field be consulted.

Twenty-four hours later, Secretary Powell called on the secure line. I excused myself from a small dinner to take the call. Since he already had my resignation letter, it occurred to me that he might be calling to say that it had been accepted.

"I'm calling in response to your message," he began. "You are right," he said, not wasting any words. "We screwed up. Let me ask one question, though. Would you have disagreed with the position we came to?"

I told him that we could live with the position as it was announced. "But," I emphasized, "we should have been consulted not only on the substance but also on the timing of any announcement."

He said that he agreed and would pursue the matter. Two days later I received a call from the deputy secretary of state for South Asia, a smart and likable career officer. "I'm calling from the doghouse."

"What's that?" I asked, not sure what he was talking about.

He continued, "We were wrong to issue that statement without consulting the embassy, and I respect the fact that you called it to the attention of the secretary. He called it to my attention, and you can rest assured that it won't happen again."

It was not about who was president or secretary of state. It was about how best to "exercise leadership in advancing the interest of the United States."

———

As the end of my tour drew near, I began a round of farewell calls. Some involved my diplomatic colleagues. For example, the Russian ambassador hosted a small luncheon that featured generous amounts of caviar and vodka. Jacqueline was surprised that I was still on my feet after all of his toasts. By contrast, I spent a quiet hour or so with Jaswant Singh, enjoying his whiskey and sharing recollections. I knew that we would do our best to stay in touch.

I also visited each consulate, where I looked for a venue to give a farewell speech. My favorite was in Calcutta, where I was invited to address a joint meeting of the state assembly, led by a homegrown Communist Party. In my remarks, I observed how much Calcutta made me think of my hometown, Cleveland. Both were industrial cities with a prosperous past and a challenging future. I talked about the great art and literature of which Bengalis are so proud—noting the world-class art museum and orchestra in Cleveland.

When I concluded, I offered to take questions.

Indian politicians are notorious for turning a question into a speech. As the first questioner dragged on, the leader of the upper house leaned over to me and asked, "Are you really from Cleveland." I told him I was. "My brother lives in Cleveland," he said.

"Really?" I said. "Where?"

"Medina, actually," he said. I asked what he did for a living. "He's a mortgage broker" was the response. "I visit him every year. I love Cleveland."

I then answered the question that had been posed at such length, and, when I finished, another fellow stood and began another five-minute exercise. As I listened, the leader of the lower house leaned over to me. "Cleveland, Ohio. Really?" I told him it was true—born and raised. "I have a brother in Cleveland," he said. I thought he might be kidding and asked where his brother lived and what he did. "He's a dentist in South Euclid," was the reply. "He's been there for thirty-two years. My family visits him every year."

Here I was, sitting between two Indian Communists, leaders of their respective chambers in the West Bengal State Assembly—and both had brothers in Cleveland and loved my hometown. Can the world get any smaller?

In spite of India's nuclear test and our harsh response, I believe that the relationship between our two nations was stronger than ever as I prepared to leave. During the Y2K fright at the end of the millennium, Indian software engineers had proven their worth in the United States and beyond, and our economic ties were growing. The candor that marked the sustained dialogue between Strobe Talbott and Jaswant Singh raised the bar in terms of the seriousness with which we took each other. The notion of a strategic partnership began to take shape. And Bill Clinton's extraordinary visit and the warmth reciprocated by Atal Bihari Vajpayee made manifest what Vajpayee termed "natural allies."

The Edward Durrell Stone–designed embassy in Delhi was inspired by traditional Indian architecture. Its chief feature is a beautiful pond in an atrium open to the sky, meant to capture cool breezes. Back in the 1960s, before the threat of terrorist attacks, more than a thousand visitors a week came to enjoy what we then affectionately referred to as "the duck pond."

That inviting architectural feature gave birth to an embassy tradition. Senior diplomats—including the ambassador—were expected to "walk the pond" on their final day in the building. Thus, one fine day in April 2001, Jacqueline, Sam, and I stood at the far end of the atrium—opposite the door through which Svetlana had entered thirty-four years earlier—and stepped into the eighteen inches of water. Only as we began to make our way to the opposite end did I realize that the bottom was very slippery from accumulated dust and grime.

Surrounded by hundreds of embassy employees cheering and snapping shots (this was, fortunately, before smartphones and social media), I failed to notice an underwater conduit feeding the lights on one of the small islands in the pond. I tripped. Down I went, taking Sam with me. Jacqueline laughed. Sam wiped his face. Cheers turned to a roar. I had not only walked the pond, I had "dived" it. And for the rest of our ceremonial farewell, I was soaked.

At least my tears went unnoticed.

During my final days in the governor's residence, as I was preparing for my transition out of public life, my sons Eric and Christopher said that they wanted to talk with me. They had some advice, they told me. We sat together on the steps into the living room, and they made their case for my next career move: "We think that you ought to become a college president."

This notion came out of nowhere—why did they think such a thing?

"Because you would be very good at it," was their response. "You have spent a lot of time on college campuses. You love engaging with young people. And you know how to make a place better."

I just listened.

"And you would love it," Christopher added.

As good career advice as it was and as serious as they were in offering it, I told them that it did not seem like the right time in my life to pursue such a position.

A decade later, in my final months in India, a major headhunting firm contacted me to ask whether I was willing to be considered for the presidency of a large public university in Ohio. Recalling my sons' advice, I said that I would be willing to take a look.

Jacqueline and I agreed that a college presidency could be rewarding and fun—a chance to run a complex enterprise, where both my business and political experience would be helpful. Most of all, I would be engaging with young people, which I had loved ever since my first campaign for state representative.

As we began to pack our belongings, we talked at length about where we would like to live when we returned. Since we weren't clear about what I would be doing, we could at least decide where we would like to be. Jacqueline was no more enthusiastic about Cleveland than I was about Washington, DC, so we spread out a map and began circling interesting alternatives: the Bay Area; Austin, where I had been invited to interview for a position at the LBJ School of Public Affairs; Annapolis; Denver; and the Front Range. For the time being, after debriefing in DC, we returned to Cleveland. We bought a house—necessary to accommodate a growing family and everything in two shipping containers bursting with what we had accumulated in our time in India.

Austin did not pan out. Nor did the public university in Ohio. But my phone had began to ring. Would I consider the University of Vermont? UMass? And so on. Usually, Jacqueline would object to the location before the conversation got serious. Then the president of Case Western Reserve announced he was stepping down. The firm Isaacson Miller was handling the CWRU search. Arnie Miller was a friend who had handled White House personnel when I was Peace Corps director.

I called Arnie to explain my interest, and he introduced me to his partner, John Isaacson, who was handling that search. When John called, he was pleasant but reserved. "John," I said, "the chairman of the trustees at Case Western is a good friend. Do you mind if I express my interest to him?"

"Certainly not, Dick. Go ahead," he responded.

Several weeks later I was having lunch with Charlie Bolton, whose grandmother was a famous Ohio political figure, Frances Payne Bolton, the first woman elected to Congress from our state. She served for fourteen terms after succeeding her husband, who had died in office. Charlie had been appointed to the Ohio Senate in 1973, and I had helped guide him a bit in his early days there.

I described my interest to Charlie: my father had earned his law degree there; both my mother and my sister had master's degrees in social work from

Case Western; I had taken a summer course there and been a visiting fellow. More important, I thought I was well prepared to lead the university. I knew that one university ambition was to generate more federal research funding. I had spent nearly a decade on the Government-University-Industry Research Roundtable at the National Academy of Sciences. I knew the senior decision-makers at each of the major federal funding agencies.

I also knew the city of Cleveland well and understood the civic, business, and political dynamics. I could strengthen the ties between the university and the community that would generate economic growth in the region—work that Celeste and Sabety was skilled at—and increase the constituency of private support for the institution.

As I talked, Bolton grew more attentive. When I concluded, he acknowledged that he had not been familiar with much of the experience that I described. He expressed excitement about my candidacy and said that he wanted to convene "a rump group" of the search committee to sit down with me.

After that lunch in October, I did not hear anything until John Isaacson called me just after the New Year. "Dick, I think you are going to be a finalist for the Case Western job," he said. "And I think that if they wanted to move quickly, they could choose you now and not go wrong."

I said that was fantastic; I remained seriously interested in the job.

"But here's my take on it," John continued. "I think you will be a finalist. But, in the end, they won't choose you." I asked him why he thought so. "When they get down to the short list," he explained, "I believe they will worry about their ability to keep you. They'll imagine that a couple of years after they appoint you, you'll be running for the Senate or for governor again. I just don't think that they have the confidence as an organization to expect to keep you. From our standpoint you are an outstanding candidate. You will certainly be on our short list. But our read is that you will not get the nod, and my question for you is whether you want to go through a public process when the likely conclusion is that you get passed over."

He waited for me to process this. It was good advice but disappointing. "Look," he told me, "I know you'll want some time to think about this."

He paused, and I thanked him for his candor. I knew a number of the Case Western trustees, and several had expressed frustration with the board's inability to make tough decisions. "John," I said, "I think you're right. Take my name off the list." I paused. "Now what?"

His immediate response was "Colorado College."

I asked him to tell me more.

"It's in Colorado."

"Don't be a smart-ass," I said with a chuckle. "Tell me something I don't know."

"Here's how to think about Colorado College," Isaacson told me. "Take Oberlin, put it at the foot of Pikes Peak, and give it a funky curriculum called the Block Plan where students take one course at a time."

I was intrigued. I had always been enthusiastic about the liberal arts—and Denver had been in one of the circles that Jacqueline and I had drawn sitting at the dining room table in New Delhi. "Let me ask you this question, John. Why do you think the final decision would be different from Case Western?"

"I believe they are looking for a nontraditional candidate," he said. "That's my feeling, anyway. But we'll have to see."

Thereafter the quest for a college presidency began in earnest. I flew to Denver for an airport interview with a subset of the search committee, as other candidates did the same. I liked the people I met—trustees, faculty, staff, and a student—and felt energized by our exchange. They posed interesting and probing questions.

After that first stage concluded, Van Skilling, chair of the search committee, called me. He wanted to pose a critical question—was I still interested in the position? "Did you learn enough in our exchange to want to continue?" I told him that I had found the session engaging and, yes, I was willing to move forward. At that point, Van said that he wanted to make sure that, if the committee chose me as a finalist and, more important, chose me for the job, I would say yes. Therefore, he suggested that they arrange a visit for Jacqueline and me—under the radar—so that we could see the campus and the town. The last thing he wanted was for me to say yes only to be overruled by my wife.

We stayed at the beautiful Garden of the Gods Club and took a stealth tour of the campus guided by a lively staffer who had been sworn to secrecy. She had young children of her own and spoke enthusiastically about the schools, the cost of living, and how family-friendly the campus and town were. I think that Jacqueline was as struck by the natural beauty and livability of Colorado Springs as I was. When we got back to Cleveland, I called Van to say that Jacqueline was on board, should I be chosen.

As I prepared for the final round of interviews—first with the search committee, then faculty and staff, and finally students—I outlined the challenges I anticipated at the college:

1. Nurturing and enhancing the Block Plan. How?
2. Strengthening the reputation of the place to attract top students and top faculty. What is their story? Where is it told?
3. Cultivating a diverse but coherent community.
4. Ensuring the necessary resources for people—a performing arts center and what else?
5. Improving town-gown relations. Who can help with a road map?

My final meeting with the full search committee was as exhilarating as the airport session. My meeting with the faculty—more than a hundred individuals all looking to take the measure of this academic outsider—proved to be both challenging and reassuring. Frankly, I enjoyed the spirited exchange. Early the next morning I met with twenty-four student leaders whose questions were sharp and probing. I found one of the students, Menelek Lumumba, especially impressive, and our brief conversation convinced me that I would truly enjoy engaging with Menelek and his fellow students.

A potential hurdle, I was aware, was the recent publication of Dagmar's book, which, for all its honesty—perhaps *because* of its honesty—cast me in an unfavorable light. As difficult as it was for me to read, Dagmar's book about her life and our lives together was written in the wholly authentic manner I expected of her. She had always encouraged women to tell their personal stories in their own voices. Her book was distinctively her story.

How did I respond? I found it hard to read, to see her pain and hurt. Occasionally I wanted to correct the record. But as I have said more than once, I do not dwell in the past. I know I cannot change it; I only hope to learn from it.

On the one hand, I am proud of my public service. Proud, too, of what Dagmar and I accomplished together as part of it. I am especially proud of the children we gave life to and nurtured. On the other hand, I am not proud of my behavior as a spouse. I respect the example that Dagmar sets for us all and know that her spiritual journey continues. I was grateful that she could come and visit us when I was serving in India—and, to anticipate a bit, would come to spend time on campus with us at Colorado College.

Before the search committee recommended my appointment to the board of trustees for a vote, Van Skilling and Bill Ward, then chairman of the board, asked me to sit with them. They were aware of what Dagmar had written. As a consequence, they wanted to know one thing: was I confident that I was capable of serving as president with dignity and integrity? It may have been difficult for them to pose this question. But I welcomed it. Their question spoke to their commitment to the highest standards for Colorado College and to their high expectations for me.

I answered, as I could not have a decade earlier, "Yes, I am confident."

I arrived in New Delhi in 1997 not expecting that the government would fall on the day that I presented my credentials. I arrived in Colorado Springs just after the Fourth of July 2002 not expecting that my first months on campus would require sorting out a political tempest.

The Political Science Department was sponsoring a two-day symposium on September 12–13 with the theme "September 11, One Year Later." The keynote speaker was Hannan Ashwari, a distinguished Palestinian leader with a PhD from the University of Virginia. When her participation was announced, it aroused a firestorm of opposition, largely from the Jewish community in Colorado and among our alumni. Almost before I was settled into my office, I was barraged with calls demanding that the college disinvite Ashwari.

As a devoted believer in academic freedom and the importance of free speech on a college campus, I made it clear that I would defend her invitation and right to be heard. But I knew that simply staking out that position would not be sufficient. I did not want to alienate an important constituency in our community and among our students and alumni.

So I began a series of meetings with Jewish leaders to explain the event's background. No, this was not how we would memorialize September 11. We had a service planned for that day to do so. No, she was not invited to present a justification for the terrorist attack. Finally, I suggested to Lief Carter, the professor in charge of organizing the symposium, that we invite the government of Israel to send a speaker to make sure we had a balanced forum.

As preparations proceeded, the event continued to provoke strong feelings on both sides. A demonstration was announced against Ashwari's appearance. A counterdemonstration was announced in support of her. The campus quad would even feature a "free speech zone" that some students promoted. Professors and staff worried about the potential for clashes. I told Lief Carter that the answer was port-a-potties. He was taken aback.

"What are you talking about?" he asked.

"Lief, if you have ever been involved in a serious demonstration, you know that one of the most neglected arrangements is a convenient place to pee. Put port-a-potties on the quad, and you will have the demonstrators standing side by side to use them," I explained.

Finally, with the port-a-potties installed on the Armstrong Quad and the

Israelis sending a well-known political scientist, Gideon Doron, to participate (and correct any Ashwari misrepresentation), some of the tension had
eased. Then Lief Carter came to my office to ask: "The Colorado Springs police want access to our roofs for their sniper team. What should we do?"

That traffic light that Chet Bowles had counseled me to develop immediately flashed bright red. I suspect that the May 4, 1970, shooting at Kent State
may have been at the back of my mind as the signal flashed red.

"Lief, there is no way we are going to let armed police officers on this campus on the twelfth. In fact, I don't want police uniforms anywhere in sight.
Our campus security can handle this. Tell the police that if they want to give
us a number to call should we have some unexpected need, that would be
fine. No cops, no weapons. Got it?"

"Yes," he said, with a look of relief.

My favorite memory of the symposium itself occurred on the first evening,
when Jacqueline and I hosted a reception and dinner for all of the participants.
We had a no smoking rule in the house. Both of our keynoters, Ashwari and
Doron, were chain-smokers. So for two hours they sat side by side on our verandah eating dinner and enjoying their cigarettes. A day later, Doron began
his talk by acknowledging his Palestinian counterpart, saying that, after their
extended conversation on the verandah of the president's home, he believed,
given a week or ten days, the two of them could settle the issues dividing their
people. I sensed that he was only half-joking.

Shortly after I arrived, I convened an off-site retreat for my ten-member
senior staff to begin the process of updating the strategic plan that had been
guiding the college during my predecessor's final years. For our first exercise
I posted five college mission statements and asked folks to pick from a list of
ten liberal arts colleges which each belonged to. Less than half identified the
CC mission statement with Colorado College. Clearly, we needed to come up
with something more distinctive.

It took months, more than one faculty debate, and the wordsmithing of
one of the college's distinguished poets, but eventually we were able to produce a laminated card that read: "At Colorado College our goal is to provide
the finest liberal arts education in the country. Drawing on the adventure-
some spirit of the Rocky Mountain West, we challenge students, one course
at a time, to develop those habits of intellect and imagination that will prepare them for learning and leadership throughout their lives."

Unmistakably CC.

We spent that first year in a series of conversations across the campus aimed at shaping a fresh strategic plan for the college. As that process got under way, I decided to introduce myself—and learn more about the academic core of the enterprise—by going door to door, so to speak. Or perhaps it was more like visiting Peace Corps volunteers in the field. I made it a point to visit each academic department in their office. I wanted to get to know our faculty members and their work. I would ask a series of questions: What are you most proud of in your department? What is the biggest challenge? How do you attract your majors? What do you tell parents about the value of your major?

When I asked that last question during my meeting with members of the Philosophy Department, Dr. Jonathan Lee said: "I tell them that the voice of Daffy Duck is one of our philosophy grads."

I also asked them what would happen if every teacher was a coach. I had in mind what would happen if academics recruited students with the same energy that coaches recruited players. Suppose the Philosophy or History Departments sponsored an essay contest with a modest cash prize, say $500, and invited students at the nation's top one hundred high schools to submit entries. I had been impressed not only by how hard coaches work to recruit athletes but also by how they continue to encourage those players to succeed. Of course, the pressure on a coach's time was less than the pressure of the Block Plan on a professor's time. And faculty members were articulate in describing the difference.

Our strategic plan, called Vision 2010, set some very clear goals. To enhance academic rigor, for example. That required us to increase our tenured faculty positions and reduce our dependence on part-time visitors, something that was important to both students and faculty. Another was to reinforce our sense of place. Many of our classes took advantage of fieldwork throughout our region and around the globe. To take it further, we initiated a State of the Rockies program that supported student and faculty research on all aspects of our five-state region.

We aspired to increase our selectivity and our diversity in admissions simultaneously. We set specific goals—to move the application pool from 3,400 to 4,200 and to increase our students of color from 12 percent to 26 percent, and international students from 1 percent to 7 percent. We blew past our applications goal in just a couple of years, so we raised it to 4,500 and then 4,800. Last year the college received more than 10,000 applications, and today the student body is 27 percent students of color and 9 percent international.

Setting goals, especially what I think of as "stretch goals," matters.

We identified three major capital needs—a new performing arts center, a renovated health and fitness facility and a reenvisioned library. All three are now complete, including the next-generation library, completed under my successor, that is carbon-neutral.

We set a goal to raise $300 million to support Vision 2020. The most successful previous campaign generated $93 million. In the end we generated more than $200 million, contending with the 2008 downturn during the heart of our effort. In fact, the downturn was a real test of our priorities.

Colorado College, like many small liberal arts colleges, depends on its endowment to generate about one-third of its operating budget each year. In 2008 the trustees made it clear that we were going to face a significantly reduced endowment payout. We needed to cut several million dollars. The dean, Susan Ashley, came to see me. She wanted to know whether we should put a hold on recruiting for faculty positions that we had advertised. I said no. The success of the Block Plan requires small classes taught by talented and devoted faculty. That had to be our first priority.

A month or so later Ken Ralph, our athletic director, came to my office. "Dick, we have done a very careful review of all of our programs, and I believe we are going to have to drop football, women's water polo, and softball."

Bear in mind that the first football game west of the Mississippi had been played on the Colorado College field. But we were (and still are) the only Division III school in our time zone. This meant nearly every away game required one or more airplane flights. Our college was spending nearly a million dollars a year on team travel alone, much more than Amherst or Middlebury or any other college like ours. And so, with the support of our trustees, we eliminated our 110-year-old football program.

As I said, in politics you learn that you can't make everybody happy. But it is really hard when you make *everybody* unhappy.

I made one person especially unhappy—a tenured faculty member who was a bully and a slacker. During my first year, the then dean forwarded an email to me from a professor who felt unsafe near this fellow. The dean described a series of complaints about this man's behavior. My response was a one-line email: "Isn't he a candidate for the broom." It didn't make sense to me that he was still around.

Two years and two faculty reviews later, this man refused an assignment he had accepted as part of a probationary plan. I terminated him. He claimed I was denying his academic freedom and sued the college for $12 million. He insisted on going to court. After a two-week trial, the jury found in favor of the college on every issue. To those who say you can't fire a tenured faculty member, I say nonsense. If they are not doing their job, they have to be swept out of the institution.

But the tenure process can be painful in many ways. At one point, the Faculty Executive Committee and the dean declined to recommend tenure for two young women teaching in the sciences. Some of the concerns behind the recommendation were legitimate. But I felt that both women showed considerable promise in departments where talented women faculty were hard to attract and retain. So I recommended that they receive tenure, and the board supported my recommendation. Recently, half a decade after the controversy, a college publication featured the work of those professors.

A small liberal arts college is like a small town. Being president is like being mayor. You know everyone, and everyone knows you—or thinks they do. Gossip is the local currency. Rumors abound. My favorite was gossip that Jacqueline had a $90,000 clothing allowance from the college. I suspect that this was because she dressed so well (always in outfits bought at TJ Maxx or Ross on sale). Not true, of course, but juicy enough to circulate.

In some respects, Paul Volcker's caution about banks was also true for colleges. I would put it this way: no matter how good things look from the outside, when you get inside, it is less tidy. Some issues have festered for years. Some grudges have been on slow boil for decades. Some numbers have been manipulated for a generation.

But I found my political experience relevant. A college president needs to nurture a set of constituencies—the trustees, the faculty, the staff, the students, the town. Each is important in its own way. And I enjoyed working with them. A college president needs to articulate the mission and vision and keep everyone focused.

In an institution where most people tend to confine themselves to their own world—their discipline, their major, their team, their special interest—building a sense of shared effort requires daily attention. And a college president needs to make decisions. Ending a major sport, overruling a dean, terminating a tenured faculty member—each is a tough decision. But not as tough as raising taxes or commuting a death sentence.

I believe a nontraditional candidate can do a fine job of leading a college or university, just as a noncareer ambassador can do a fine job. But it requires a willingness to listen and learn. And to know when to move on.

I was about to start my ninth year at Colorado College when Eric, my firstborn, called. "I am just calling to warn you, Dad," he said.

"Warn me? About what?" I was at a loss.

"You are sailing into uncharted waters."

"What uncharted waters?" I asked.

"You have never held a job for more than eight years," he said with a chuckle.

Eric was right. On July 1, 2011, I stepped down from a position that I loved virtually every day—after nine years.

Truth be told, I really had entered uncharted waters when I left the governor's office more than two decades earlier.

Epilogue

For my seventieth birthday, while I was still at Colorado College, Jacqueline gathered my family for a celebration—and I mean a celebration!

We had a big party at Stewart House, our campus home, and were joined by friends from the college, the community, and far beyond. Food and drink were abundant. I was able to introduce my children and grandchildren to faculty members and neighbors they had only heard about. Music and dancing highlighted the evening.

Yes, we enjoyed some Frank Sinatra.

The next morning our family caravanned out to a rugged seventy-acre parcel of land we had purchased a couple of years earlier. We drove for an hour and a half west to Hartsel and then south toward Guffey. The property sits at nine-thousand feet at the end of a dirt county road butting up against the Pike National Forest.

We call it Celestial Spirits Ranch (a bit of an exaggeration). From it you can see a vast stretch of the Rockies and the Continental Divide.

Jacqueline's birthday present, a 400-square-foot haul-in cabin, waited to greet us that beautiful sunny morning. No water. No power. Just a propane grill to cook food or warm coffee. And plenty of pine trees to provide privacy for those who needed to relieve themselves.

My kids had arranged their own surprise for me. They quickly went to work assembling it. It was a mash pole, which they erected with some difficulty in the rocky soil. Then they proceeded to attach to it, with loving care and one or two debates, a series of arrows pointing in several directions. When it was completed, they invited me down to the work site.

There I read:

- Lakewood, Ohio, 1425 miles
- New Haven, Connecticut, 1959 miles
- Oxford, England, 4699 miles
- Monessen, Pennsylvania, 1149 miles
- New Delhi, India, 7755 miles
- Columbus, Ohio, 1310 miles
- Washington, DC, 1706 miles
- Colorado Springs, Colorado, 65 miles

That moment took my breath away.

Whenever I have the time, I drive out to the Celestial Spirits Ranch and walk down to the mash pole. I am reminded of the immensity of God's creation that surrounds us. And of a sign that sat on President Carter's desk: "Lord, how great is thy sea and how small is my boat."

I have been blessed with wonderful opportunities to learn and to serve. Many were completely unexpected. I never dreamed that I would serve as an ambassador's personal assistant, let alone ambassador. I never dreamed that I would be asked to serve as director of the Peace Corps. Yes, I did dream of running for office, and I did aspire to do what neither of my role models—Chester Bowles and Jack Gilligan—had been able to do, namely win reelection. Perhaps I even dreamed of being president.

But I certainly had not dreamed of becoming president of Colorado College and holding that job for an unprecedented (for me) nine years.

Not infrequently someone will ask me, "What should I call you—Governor, Ambassador, President?" Sometimes it is meant as flattery; sometimes, it is a genuine desire to be correct and respectful. According to protocol, Governor takes precedent. But for me the answer is simply "Just call me Dick."

My father's favorite greeting was "What is the situation that prevails?" I have no idea where it came from, but anyone close to Frank heard that expression often.

If I were to describe my "situation" to him today, it would go something like this:

I have come to a deep appreciation of the role of the Holy Spirit as a presence, a gift, in my life. I have become aware of how richly blessed I have been by my family, my friends, my mentors, and so many people who have placed their confidence in me over the years. I realize that I have not shared with my family the many ways in which, early in my life and at critical moments over the years, prayer has served as a source of comfort and equilibrium.

While I have mentioned my children in these pages, I have not begun to describe their remarkable and quite distinctive qualities. Or how much they have been the source of insight and hope for me. Each day I offer a prayer of gratitude for their presence in my life—and wonder at how they and their families are managing the challenges of daily life. I look for ways to spend more time with them and with my grandchildren, and now great-grandchildren.

Living in Colorado has brought me closer to nature. On a bicycle trail in Colorado Springs or hiking the fence line at the ranch, I am in awe of the beauty and grace of our natural world. I find myself breathing more deeply and appreciating the fresh air. In that breath and in that air I feel the Spirit. And feel deep gratitude. What a blessing it is to be as healthy as I am at a time when more and more of my friends, some much younger, are dying.

When I was twelve or thirteen, my mother encouraged me to design small posters with wise quotations I found in popular magazines. My favorite reminded me: "He who never made a mistake, never made a discovery." And that insight helped me often in the years since.

As I have labored on this book, I have spent much of my time recalling the past. And I find myself becoming more reflective. I believe today that, while my nana's advice to keep my cards close to my chest may have been useful in the political rough-and-tumble, my inclination to secret places and shrouded relationships led to deeply flawed behavior. I would have been better guided by my alma mater's "Lux et Veritas."

If I were to design new posters for my wall today, one would declare, "Every day is a gift," and the other would ask, "How much is enough?"

My hope in describing my life and work is that I may inspire a younger generation to embrace public service as a career or as an avocation. Recent events have underscored the reality that we cannot take our democracy for granted. Years ago on the two-hundredth anniversary of the Declaration of Independence I wrote a brief essay arguing that "politics is not a spectator sport." These days I welcome the chance to discuss life choices and dreams with my grandchildren, with recent Colorado College alums, and with others along the way. On occasion we find ourselves strategizing how to make change happen, through political action or community engagement.

In the heart of it all has taken on new meaning for me. Not a place, but moments in time.

If I were to describe to my father the situation that has prevailed during the past twenty years of my life, I would say it has been a series of unexpected next acts. Each act has been informed and enriched by what has come before.

Left to right: Stephen Celeste, Natalie Celeste, Christopher Celeste, Eleanor Celeste, Maxwell Sparr, Gabriella Celeste, Eric Celeste, Noelle Celeste, and Sam Celeste, October 2021 (Christine Saragolos Photography)

And each has brought a generous measure of fulfillment. Especially the decades since I left elected office have brought me an understanding that I am not defined by what I am doing—by positions or titles, or by power or influence.

Instead, I am defined by who I am being. A husband being faithful. A father being present. A friend being thoughtful. A citizen being engaged. An individual wondering what the future might bring.

Index